SICILIAN VESPERS AND OTHER WRITINGS

Other books by Michael Davidson

THE WORLD, THE FLESH AND MYSELF
SOME BOYS

Other books by Edmund Marlowe

ALEXANDER'S CHOICE

SICILIAN VESPERS

AND OTHER WRITINGS

by Michael Davidson

Edited with notes and a brief biography by

EDMUND MARLOWE

ARCADIAN DREAMS
London

First published by Arcadian Dreams 2021

ISBN 978-1-914571-00-8

Contents

Editor's note

Most of this book has been a very long time in the planning. When Michael Davidson, a journalist who had retired to his beloved Italy to write, took up abode in Favignana in January 1966, it was inevitable that his thoughts would soon turn to the island he described at the outset as "magically lovely." He began writing about it in 1968, as soon as he had finished *Some Boys*, and has said he had thought of it as *My Sicilian Vespers* even before then. It was intended purely as a travel book. Though he had much to say in it about all the members of the local family he more or less joined, he did not let on in it that he had become close to them through having a passionate love affair with their fifteen-year-old son, or that this was the main key to his happiness in Favignana, presumably because the controversial character of the affair would have impeded the book's marketing as travel. Seven months later, he delivered half of it to the unknown publishers, but towards the end of 1969, they changed management and the focus of their interests, and dropped it. It is not clear whether all the chapters had been written by then, but in any case, he rewrote some of them in 1972.

In February 1975, Quartet Books in London commissioned him to write a sequel to his autobiography *The World, The Flesh and Myself*, which had ended in 1958. Though this was spoken of as a new book, he understandably planned to include in it much or all of *Sicilian Vespers*. Adaptation of the text was inevitable since the new book had a quite different focus and was expected to be like *The World*, a candid account of his life, including his love-life with boys. He thus began to redraft it to be open about his love affair with the Favignanese boy, as well as to fill in the missing years 1958-66. Unfortunately, neither of these tasks had progressed far before he had a bad fall in July, which led to his hospitalisation and eventually his death.

His great friend Colin Spencer, whom he had made his literary executor, was determined that in due course he would finish "the book" himself, but other tasks intervened, time slipped away and he never quite did. Just after Davidson's death, he also conceived the idea of another book for Davidson's correspondence, realising that this included some of his best writing, and made a considerable effort to gather it together from Davidson's friends. To this, the correspondence section of this volume owes its existence.

In 2019, Colin handed over to me Davidson's old suitcase containing book drafts and correspondence with the task of editing them and bringing them to publication, which I enthusiastically accepted as an admirer for forty years of his writing. It was only after I had read everything carefully that I realised two books, not one, were involved. Had Davidson brought them together by finishing at least a first draft of the sequel to *The World,* I would of course have followed suit. As it was, the sequel was hopelessly far from complete, while the original travel book, *Sicilian Vespers,* though a confusing miscellany of overlapping chapters in need of much editing, was capable of standing on its own. I therefore decided to keep them separate, and to publish only those parts of the sequel that are not a repetition of the earlier book.

The only section of this volume that is a new idea, and mine, is the short life of Davidson I have provided. *The World* is a candid and beautifully-written account of his life, and is richly supplemented by his stories in *Some Boys.* Nevertheless, I thought it worthwhile to include my own brief account, partly for the benefit of those who may choose to read this book before Davidson's others and partly to fill in the last seventeen years of his life,[1] which are particularly relevant here because they are when *Sicilian Vespers* and most of the correspondence was written. There is besides some interesting additional information on his earlier life, which I have gathered from unpublished sources.

In the years following the publication of *The World,* many people wrote to Davidson expressing admiration and wanting to know him better. In accordance with the manners of the time, they all initially addressed him as "Mr. Davidson", but, as one might expect where such a warm and unpretentious personality was concerned, they were soon calling him "Michael" (with perhaps

---

[1] *The World, The Flesh and Myself* ends in 1958. The only chapter of *Some Boys* set later than that is "Catania", set in 1959.

an intermediate "My dear Davidson" if they were his age). I like to believe I would have been one of them had I been older, but unfortunately I was too young to have read his books by the time he died. I say this to explain that it is not out of coldness towards my subject that I have felt bound to refer to him as "Davidson" in my biographical sketch and editorial notes, but from a feeling that it would be pretentious to do otherwise without having had the personal introduction I sadly missed.

Some of the personal names in *Sicilian Vespers* and the sequel were changed, often with different versions in different manuscripts, and most of these changes have been retained. By contrast, the names in the biography, correspondence and reminiscences are all, with one Sicilian exception, real to the best of my knowledge.

As already explained, *Sicilian Vespers* has necessarily been heavily edited. Such being the case, it made no sense not to extend the editing to spelling and punctuation. Many words were missing, due both to typing errors and to the pages of some manuscripts being badly frayed. These I have filled in without comment where all that was needed were an easily-guessed few words, but in the one instance where I had to resort to wilder invention to retain sense, I have put my words in square brackets with a footnote.

With respect to the correspondence and reminiscences, I have amended a few spellings and uses of punctuation that looked to me like unintentional mistakes and are disruptive, but I have otherwise preferred not to "correct" what may be the idiosyncrasies of the writers.

So that the footnotes can be reserved for fuller information, translations of single words and short phrases in French, German, Greek and Italian follow them in [] brackets. {} brackets are used to distinguish the occasional use of square brackets by Davidson and his correspondents from my editorial insertions. All the footnotes are mine except those marked "[Author's footnote]", which are to be found only in *Sicilian Vespers*.

Letter headings, whether printed or not, are included except for two where Davidson also wrote a different address in his own hand.[2]

My greatest thanks are owed to Colin Spencer, as Davidson's literary executor, for his faith and kindness in entrusting me with his papers and the task of editing and publishing them. I would also like to thank my wife, who has patiently supported me in every way, and my friends Stephen Nicholson, who introduced me to Colin and checked my transcripts but sadly died before the work was finished, Dr. Maximus Pascal, who brought to bear all the benefits of his experience producing fine academic books at Cambridge, John Hamilton for some very thoughtful proof-reading, and Benjamin, who helped transcribe some letters that were hard to read as well as giving valuable advice.

Edmund Marlowe

---

[2] These were letters xi-xii, written on paper with the same heading as letter xiii, qv.

I. A BRIEF LIFE OF MICHAEL DAVIDSON

by Edmund Marlowe

As the author of a superb autobiography, The World, The Flesh and Myself, *admired for its candour, Michael Davidson is in much less need of a biography than most. That book and his later memoir,* Some Boys, *each chapter of which combines first-rate travel-writing with the story of one of his liaisons with boys, should always be the first port of call for anyone seeking knowledge and understanding of this extraordinary character. To them can now be added the present volume, which gives a vivid picture of his life in Sicily in the sixties, together with correspondence and reminiscences which shed further light on him and offer other perspectives.*

This essay is therefore strictly limited in its aims to giving a succinct summary of what Davidson more eloquently described himself, continuing the account given down to 1958 in The World *to the time of his death, and offering the occasional insight offered by the still unpublished documents I have had access to.*

Michael Childers Davidson was born on 24th February 1897 at 101 Warwick Road, Paddington. His father, Walter Burn Murdoch Davidson, a timber merchant, was an alcoholic wastrel whose failings obliged the family to move from London to Guernsey when Davidson was one. He died in 1910 after eight years as a paralysed invalid, barely known to his then thirteen-year-old son. His upbringing was thus in the hands of his mother Clare Mostyn Davidson, née Childers. In his memoirs, she comes across a saintly figure, kind and devoted to her children, but much too genteel to risk upsetting with intimations of sexual heresy.

Much of the first three chapters of *The World* is devoted to sketches of his various uncles, aunts and remoter antecedents, partly it seems out of fascination with the genetic origins of his own personality. The dour Davidsons of supposed Scottish origin intermarried with the alcoholic Freelings to produce his father, from whom he inherited a fondness for wine, which led to too much drinking (in the view of many) throughout his adult life, but not in his case to alcoholism, because it was limited to evenings. In contrast, his maternal kin, the Childers, were colourful with flashes of brilliance. Both Childers and Freeling were vaguely aristocratic families, and Davidson's upbringing was largely what one would expect of a hard-up branch of an upper-class Edwardian family.

He was the youngest of three children. He disliked his brother Eardley, known from his profession as "the doctor", who was described by their nephew as "a monument to pomposity on Primrose Hill" and was clearly a radically different character. On the other hand, he adored his warm-hearted sister Nancy, a communist turned Catholic, who was also a writer under the name Anne Freeling.

Unlike most boys of his class and time, Davidson was not sent to prep school, but soon after the family moved to Bitterne in Hampshire, when he was still eleven, he was sent to Lancing College, a boarding-school in Sussex. Academically, he found it uninspiring, but it was there, aged nearly fifteen, that he first fell in love – with a boy of thirteen named Ernest Millard. Such feelings for younger boys were then commonplace in boarding-schools, but he was conscious that they were more than a passing phase for himself. Whether they ever translated into sexual action was something that varied very much according to particular time and place; he was unlucky in that Lancing was "pious", as it was often called, and his feelings had to be repressed.

As he was to open his autobiography with the arresting sentence "This is the life-history of a lover of boys", which has often elicited admiration for its daring frankness, it would be absurd not to give this aspect of his life the prominence he gave it and wanted it to be known for.

It should be explained at once that he was not in any remotely accurate sense a "paedophile", a lover of pre-pubescent children, though that is doubtless how the gutter press would now choose to describe him. Rather he was what is now known in psychiatric jargon as a "hebephile", though that word is also unsatisfactory, missing the masculinity that was an essential characteristic of the youth he loved. He was attracted to boys of twelve to eighteen (at a stretch), with fifteen cropping up most frequently as the age of those he had liaisons with. In imagining this today, it should, however, be borne in mind that adolescent boys in his day, and especially in the poorer countries where most of his later liaisons took place, were a couple of years less physically developed than now. The best word to describe him is "pederast", though he himself was wary of it because it was oddly then sometimes defined as one who commits sodomy, which held no appeal for him.

England then was one of the worst countries to be homosexual. All sexual acts between males were criminal and widely regarded as depraved. Though men of the ruling class often retained from their boarding-school days some understanding of the distinct character of pederasty, it was generally regarded as rather worse than sex between men because it was believed to corrupt boys into lasting homosexuality, a recipe for an unhappy life. However, terrible as the prejudice and legal danger they faced was for men like Davidson, he had no inkling in his lifetime of the witch-hunt and intense social hatred which was to begin soon after his death and which would have made his literary success impossible; the dogma that sexually mature boys were mentally as well as legally incapable of meaningful consent and that they were inevitably traumatised by sex with adults was yet to be born.

Though he left school a reluctant virgin, he was too intellectually honest to be in denial of his sexual nature, nor did he try to repress it. At once he started befriending local boys and longing for sex with them. The next year, 1914, he finally had his first sexual experience with a pub boot-boy of fourteen in Chichester, where he was training after signing up to serve in the war. Thus freed of his sexual reticence at seventeen, the search for the ideal boy was to be central to the rest of his life, with money and career taking second place.

Commissioned into the Oxfordshire Light Infantry, Davidson was not sent abroad until 1916, but he was in time to serve at the Somme and was wounded at Paschendaele. Reading between the lines of *The World* suggests he was a braver soldier than he admitted to himself, and, prompted by an agreeable vision of what life as an officer in peacetime would be like, he opted for a commission in the regular army. Recuperating in London and in subsequent leaves there, he plunged into a double life of heavy drinking at night with high-society friends ignorant of his sexual heresy, while frequenting swimming-baths to look at boys and, increasingly, to bed them. In less than two years, he spent his small inheritance and realised his real unsuitability for army life. Suddenly determined to go abroad and see something different, he seized an opportunity to board a ship bound for Durban in December 1919.

He ended up spending about two years in South Africa. An exceptionally happy time as apprentice-assistant to a farmer in the uplands of Zululand ended when the farmer's wife found pornography in his drawer. Then he fell in love with a Welsh boy of sixteen named Theron Hughes and made his first attempt to live with a boy, while using his future inheritance from his mother to try pig-farming in southern Natal. His high hopes ended in failure and disillusionment, the final blow coming when a neighbour snooping around his financially-failing farm spied him in a compromising position with Theron, causing an already strained relationship to end in bitter recrimination, fortunately the only time in his life this happened to him. Finally, a stint as lackey to a brash businesswoman in Johannesburg determined him to return to England.

Back in London in 1922, he had his first tiny brush with the law when a policeman escorted him away from the males' bathing area in the Serpentine for loitering there rather than bathing, leaving him so shaken that he took himself off to his sympathetic sister in Norfolk and unburdened his soul to her. Here he got his first job as a journalist, becoming sub-editor of the Eastern Daily Press in Norwich, and joined her intoxicating social circle, which soon led to an introduction to the extremely precocious sixteen-year-old poet, Wystan Auden. An intense friendship, passionate on Davidson's part, but chaste in thought and deed, ensued for two years, despite being forbidden by Auden's school and mother.

In 1924, Davidson suddenly threw his new life and security to the winds and moved to London to be sub-editor of a short-lived weekly and assistant in an associated literary agency. He rented a room in Gower Street, his first home to which he was free to bring back boys without fear of being snooped on, and found it easy to pick them up. Meanwhile, he became friends with a number of much older homosexual literary figures. Of these, the one he was easily drawn to the most was Christopher Sclater Millard, "the most *important* person I've ever met". He had only three years to bask in this new friendship before Millard's untimely death, but he ever after wrote of him with the greatest reverence, and in the meantime Millard introduced him to a new social circle centred in Bloomsbury around the antiquarian bookseller Boris de Chroustchoff and his wife Phyl. With these new friends, many of them brilliant in diverse ways, who met in a pub called The Plough, he not only could reveal his true heretical self, but was almost bound to do so: "nobody seemed to be shocked or disgusted by anybody's unorthodox appetites; one was required to be amusing, or at least not a bore, and morally and mentally *honest.* The social offences were dullness and sham."

During this period, Davidson was not only flitting from boy to boy, but from job to job. In about 1926, he worked as a proof-reader and literary assistant to the editors of periodicals produced by Sun Engraving. The following winter he spent several weeks living in the hills of Provence, whence he wrote some of his most entertaining letters to the de Chroustchoffs. He even contemplated buying a ruin to live in there. Towards the end of 1927, he moved to Oxford to work for the Clarendon Press and stayed there until the following October. He then suddenly threw the job up to go off to Berlin, on the urging of the tormented artist Felicia Browne, whom he had befriended as a co-lodger in Gower Street.

Following his rescuing Browne in Berlin from a suicide attempt for the second time, they were briefly engaged, though she accepted his love of boys and knew their union was not to be consummated. There are indications, however, that despite an unchanging preference for boys of around fifteen, Davidson was more sexually flexible in his youth than his memoirs allow. A letter from Oxford and reminiscences from his employer at Sun Engraving, both to be found in this volume, suggest he was not impervious to the attractions of girls. When he was eighteen, he had an affair with a Malay prince of twenty-one, albeit an unusually boyish-looking one, and eighteen-year-old boyfriends are mentioned in his early correspondence, but never later. His letters from Berlin also show him much more promiscuous than one gathers from his memoirs, carrying on with a multitude of boys at once.

Once he settled in, Davidson found Berlin intellectually vibrant, sexually liberal and enormously exciting. He had always had some feeling for languages: he was proficient in French and had learned basic Zulu in Natal. His German was soon better than these, the learning process no doubt sped up by the quest for boys. Of these, one stood out as the first of the four in his life with whom he had a sustained and passionate love affair, a half-Latvian of nearly fifteen called Walfried Reile-Reiljon, so beautiful that he was chosen for the cover of the Socialist Labour Youth's magazine. Together, they cycled and swam by day and drank by night, often in Berlin's famous homosexual bars. Walfried was both giving and possessive: warily, he allowed threesomes with Willi, his own little Ganymede, but was intensely jealous if Davidson showed interest in other boys. This did not stop Davidson from carrying on with them without Walfried's knowledge. "Exactly five boys, including W., have determined to come to England with me; it is very difficult," he reported to the de Chroustchoffs after only a month in Berlin.

Davidson tried supporting himself through teaching English, but evidently struggled to survive, and in March 1929 he took a comfortable job for eighteen months as a proof-reader at the International Labour Office in Geneva, which he found boring and bourgeois. His eagerness to be back in Berlin with Walfried did not stop him from having an affair with François, the boy whose death in a climbing accident was to be the subject of the earliest-set chapter of *Some Boys*, or with the usual multitude of other boys. In July, he was over-spending through indulging a new constant companion, Victor Tullio Lapertose, a fourteen-year-old Italian butcher's boy "with the perfectest face & figure", whom he planned to take to England. In January, however, following a high-spirited winter holiday in Berlin and the Kalkberge with Walfried, he was back to his plan to take the latter to England once he had given up Geneva. By May, his pennilessness ruled this out and he was planning instead to enjoy Arab boys and kif in Tunis.

In the event, it was to Berlin that he returned. His German was by now good enough for him to earn money for several years as a translator of leftist books and articles. Davidson's sympathies and his greatest friends had consistently been leftist since he left school. His sister had been a communist and he had helped out with the workers' cause during the General Strike of 1926. His political instincts were romantic and libertarian. He and Walfried were, for example, strongly drawn towards the German nudist movement. However, as the National Socialist threat grew, he lay aside his distaste for stern organisation, discipline and ruthlessness and joined the Communist Party of Germany, as the only people who were doing anything about the Nazi menace. He became the London *Daily Herald*'s correspondent in Germany, and, understanding the danger National Socialism posed to the world beyond Germany, he tried in vain to interest the *New Statesman* with an article describing it as seen close-up.

By the time Hitler came to power in January 1933, Davidson had a good job as translator with a publishing firm, and was enjoying the warm friendship into which his love affair with Walfried had evolved, so he stayed on to witness with horror the transformation that Berlin now underwent. He continued to meet fellow members of the now outlawed communist party, and, very dangerously, to post articles to the *Daily Worker* in London. In March, he had a narrow escape when arrested by Brownshirts during a raid on a bar.

Davidson's ongoing affair with a new boy, Kurt, soon brought more serious trouble with his frequent stays in his flat, especially after a bicycle he gave him attracted the jealousy of the Hitler Youth who frequented the neighbourhood. When Kurt's newly-Nazi step-father arrived one July evening brandishing threats, he knew he must flee. By the time he boarded a train out of Germany the next day, with nothing but the clothes he was wearing, police and S.A. were already posted outside his abode, awaiting in vain his return.

In London, Davidson reported to the London District of the Communist Party of Great Britain, and was assigned work translating from German, on which he lived, and helping exiled German communists. He also wrote more articles for the *Daily Worker*, and joined the group who founded the *Left Review* and the Writers' and Artists' International, formed to bring together against fascism the leftist intellectuals of Europe: he served on the executive committee of its British section.

As early as August, all this brought him to the attention of M.I.5, who got Scotland Yard to watch him and, from January 1934, intercepted his post. M.I.5 would continue to watch him as a suspected subversive until his retirement from public life in 1957. He suspected this was happening, but never knew for sure. The truth emerges from M.I.5 files preserved in the National Archives, which provide an interesting alternative to his memoirs for information on the next quarter-century of his life.

He was now "Age 36, height 5′ 10 ½″, eyes grey, hair brown, complexion pale, thin face, small chin, large acquiline nose, clean shaven, very slim build, wears horn rimmed spectacles with gold side pieces," a spook reported. Besides noting the communist activities that were their real interest, M.I.5 soon learned that he was "a moral degenerate" and a suspected "sodomite". They were well aware that his homosexual liaisons were with boys, not other men, but this did not apparently make them any more or less interesting to the authorities. Though they could presumably have used them to make trouble for him had they wished, there is no indication they ever considered doing so.

Besides surveillance and a little hassle with border formalities, the only recorded actions they took against him were two. In May 1934, M.I.5 got him removed on essentially spurious official grounds from the Regular Army Reserve of Officers, to which he had belonged since resigning his commission in 1919, the real reason being that "in the event of mobilization he might be dangerous from the point of view of morale and discipline." In June 1943, which was, after all, in the middle of the war, they advised that "Davidson's appointment to the B.B.C. would be most undesirable. [...] he has a long association with communists in this country and in Europe, and he is an unsavoury person who would not seem capable of holding down a responsible post."

On 29th June 1935, at St. Pancras Registry Office, Davidson married Kathe Hedwig Bodey, a young German refugee, at the request of a communist friend who knew he "wasn't by nature a 'marrying man' ", so that she could get a British passport and legal residence. He underwent this farce out of hatred of Nazism rather than his nearly extinguished enthusiasm for communism. They said goodbye after a brief party in a pub, but M.I.5 were confused, noting the marriage might have been "one of convenience", but "Davidson's moral perversion may have caused the separation."

"Mrs. Davidson" disappears from M.I.5's records after 1942, when she was living in the East End with German refugees, and "her loyalty to this country was questioned owing to the fact that she had given two different and untruthful accounts to the Police regarding her relations with her husband." Her husband could no longer remember her name when he wrote his memoirs, but thought she had divorced him in the late forties.

Neither Davidson nor anyone else seems to have mistaken his early enthusiasm for serious revolutionary zeal. M.I.5 had described him in 1934 as "an intellectual, ineffective, but enthusiastic in a milk and watery way." Despite all the help "Comrade Davidson" had given it, the Communist Party itself issued a warning to leading members of sub-districts in London not to trust him, notwithstanding his professing to be an ardent communist, according to an M.I.5 report of September 1935. However, the latter's informants in the Metropolitan Police were often remarkably inept in drawing the right conclusions. In 1943, they thought that in view of this warning against him "even at the time of his greatest communist activity; that he had every opportunity, while in Germany, of becoming inculcated with pro-nazi views; and that he married a German woman, it might be argued that he has never been a true supporter of communism, but rather a nazi sympathiser."

Boys remained a much more serious pursuit. Besides the incident by the Serpentine, he had been once shown the door at a fashionable bar he frequented after his dalliance with two 15-year-old page-boys there aroused the jealousy of a third, but now he ran into the most serious trouble of his life. His search for boys drove him beyond the bounds of caution, leading to him becoming "known". He and one of his boys were followed back to his lodgings by a detective, who arrested him. Knowing the police had managed to extract a statement from the boy, he prepared for the worst and, a week later, on 25th November 1936, pleaded guilty to importuning for immoral purposes at North London Police Court, where he was sentenced to four months in prison with nominal hard labour and sent to Wormwood Scrubs.

He remained always entirely unconvinced by the rationale of protecting boys' innocence that was supposed to justify the cruelty he now suffered, later drawing unfavourable comparisons between the dire social effects of the "prohibition and insulation against knowledge" inflicted on English boys and the sexual freedom of Italian boys. He was more impressed by the designed inhumanity and cruelty of life in prison, and its uselessness as a form of punishment except for the unintended effect of making its victims more humane through suffering.

Following his release on 5th March 1937, the communists no longer wanted him for translation work, so he got work proof-reading for printers, while taking a flat in Kilburn. He entertained boys there, but felt haunted. He was wise to feel so, as he was still involved in anti-fascist demonstrations and was still being observed, it being noted that he was "giving French and German lessons to youths ranging from 12 to 16 years of age." A warning from a menacing plod in Piccadilly that he was being watched finally determined him to seek a new life in a more benevolent land, somewhere promising adventure, warmth and erotic enchantment. Like others before him, he settled on Morocco as an obvious choice and went there in January 1938, hoping to support himself as a writer or translator, and with a small allowance from his mother on which to subsist in the meantime. This time he was not to set foot in England for more than three years or to see again his mother, who died just before his return.

Not long after his arrival in Morocco, he went to Rabat, where he met the second boy with whom he had a long-lasting love affair, a Berber of fourteen named Mustapha. After an idyllic stay together in Beni Mellal, they brought Mustapha's mother and sisters to live with them in a house in Salé, which was essentially the "native" quarter of Rabat. There Davidson went indeed thoroughly native, revelling in the archaic charms and customs of the land and writing a book about them between bouts of smoking *kif*. The war only intruded on this bliss when his allowance could no longer be sent, obliging him to earn his and his Moroccan family's living by teaching English to French colonial high society. He had to take a lodging in Rabat proper in May 1940, in order to be closer to his pupils, and was thus a witness to the anguish of the local French over the fall of their homeland.

In July, growing rumours that the Britons remaining in Morocco were about to be interned forced him with extreme reluctance to leave for the international enclave of Tangier. According to a "rather rambling note" later received by the British Consulate General in Rabat on behalf of M.I.5 from "a local resident", he "made out a will in which he left all his property goods and money – whatever that might have been – to the boy Mustapha", before miserably parting from him in Rabat railway station. "I thanked heaven for Islam; which permits even a 16-year-old to accept with fatalism the crassest quirks of fortune", he recalled.

Cosmopolitan, tolerant and well-known for the sexual availability of boys, though depressingly commercial, Tangier was bound to fascinate Davidson, who also found the local expatriate characters congenial, but after a few months he still hankered after Mustapha and managed to get the sponsorship of the *Daily Express* for a rather crackpot scheme to smuggle himself across Spanish Morocco and back into French Morocco to spy on German activities there. Thoroughly disguised as a mendicant pilgrim and accompanied by a guide he had to take on due to his Arabic not being fluent, he got as far as the Spanish border town of Ksar el-kebir, but there he was abandoned by the guide and arrested when he went to the market for food. After six weeks half-starved in prison in Tetuan, the Spanish suddenly released him in July 1941 into the hands of the British in Gibraltar, who shipped him to Glasgow. There he was interrogated by intelligence officers who reported that he was "extremely affable and plausible".

Back in London, Davidson wrote about his Moroccan adventures for the *Daily Express,* which led to a job on its Foreign Desk, while the War Office, the Admiralty and the BBC also took an interest in employing him, but repeatedly dropped him at the last moment at the behest of "some hidden hand, called, perhaps, 'security'." As was always to be the case, he could not tell whether the problem was his communist past or his homosexual offence. The latter was soon compounded.

As usual, Davidson had been having brief liaisons with boys and courting yet more, when a dirty trick by the police led to his most serious "row" apart from his imprisonment of 1936-7. A friendly chat in Highgate Fields with a handsome boy of 15 led to an assignation to go swimming together a week later, but when Davidson turned up for it, he was met by two detectives who had looked up his record and arrested him for "insulting behaviour", the pretence being that he had annoyed three boys by "accosting" them. Turning up at court without a solicitor two days later, he was persuaded by one of the apparently kind detectives to plead guilty so that he would only get a small fine, only for the detective to pre-empt this by describing his previous conviction to the magistrate. The result was eight days pointlessly remanded in Brixton prison for a report, before receiving his fine on 29 February 1942.

Mortified, he resigned from the *Express*. He was too demoralised to find another job by feelings of vulnerability and of there being a "hidden force" that was denying him useful employment. He made no bones about ever having a capacity to save money or handle it wisely, so by 1943 he had spent what little money was left over from his inheritance and was so penurious that at one point he was driven to what he, with typical honesty, called the theft of a brooch, but might more fairly be called selling something that was only doubtfully his.

As usual, Davidson's lack of interest in money was outmatched by his enthusiasm for boys, and one of these drew him out of his dejection. He was so infatuated with a boy from a remote West Country town he met holidaying that he got himself a job as sub-editor with a local newspaper and was even taken as a lodger into his boy's home. After six months, the infatuation wore thin on both sides and the town's parochial affairs palled until he "felt the call of larger events" and got a job with Reuters in London in 1944. There he got what he considered seriously valuable training as a journalist and did so well that after a year he was promoted to Chief Night Sub-editor, but he found he lacked the ambition to endure the extra pressure for more than six months and asked for his own demotion.

His two years at Reuters coincided with a friendship with an Irish delinquent of 14 to 16. Paddy, as was his name, was not inclined to sexual intimacy, which Davidson of course respected, but their friendship was affectionate and sufficiently close that after the boy wrote asking him to visit him at an "approved school" to which he had been consigned, Davidson could not resist. Arriving at the local train station, he was met by detectives, who warned him they had his record, but could not do more against him. It was enough, however, finally to convince him that since he could not change his character to stay out of prison in England, he must change his domicile. He got himself a job as a "stringer" for *The Observer* in Morocco, where he arrived in February 1947. He barely set foot in England during the next five years, and thereafter was only ever to live there intermittently.

In Rabat, he refound Mustapha, but well-advanced into manhood, and by then Davidson had already found a new boyfriend, 14-year-old Sidi Salah. As with Mustapha, he joined in the boy's family life, even saving his little brother from death after a botched circumcision, while he learned the skills of a foreign correspondent reporting on the adroit manoeuvres for independence of the Moroccans led by their attractive Sultan. A stay in Marrakech enabled him to see one of the Chleuh erotic boy-dances that were still semi-secretly performed, while another in Tangier not only enabled him to re-immerse himself in its distinctive charms, but led to a fortuitous meeting. Somerset Maugham's nephew Robin, also a writer and a lover of male youth, sought him out in Dean's famous den. The friendship immediately forged, though sometimes trying, was to be important for the rest of his life.

In December, he and a few friends impulsively set out on a dangerously ill-equipped expedition to Timbuctoo in a single-engined biplane, travelling a circuitous route via the coast of West Africa. Timbuctoo then merited well its reputation in the popular imagination as the most distant outpost, and his journey was to furnish him with the material for some of his finest travel-writing, both then for *The Observer*, and later, for a chapter of *Some Boys*.

Soon after returning to Tangier, *The Observer* took him on as one of their correspondents, which he was to remain in various countries for the next four years, initially sending him to Israel to cover the war with the Arabs that had just broken out. There he was enthralled by the looks and spirit of the new generation of boys born in Israel, and enjoyed getting to know some of the many foreign correspondents there, including Arthur Koestler, another new friend.

Next, Davidson spent six months in recently-independent India and Pakistan, reporting ironically on the politics and the war between the two. He was mostly in Old Delhi, where he was attended by a self-appointed 17-year-old, whom he later discovered had been married and had two babies.

In April 1949, he moved on to Rangoon for two months. On arrival, he was thoroughly searched by customs, which he attributed to suspicion following the expulsion of the last two British journalists for allegedly instigating rebellion. In reality, it was arranged by the British security services, who were still keeping an eye on him on account of his suspected communism and had been warned of his coming by the Burmese embassy in New Delhi. Otherwise, his reception was mixed. He was cordially received by the British ambassador and became close friends with his Political Secretary, while his Oriental Secretary reported to the security services that he "struck him as being quite definitely Communist and he made biting references to the 'fascist' Daily Mail who were trying to re-introduce British imperialism into Burma." Despite this, most reports to the security chaps, who had the support of the local police in keeping him under observation, "laid stress on his 'drunkenness and degeneracy' rather than his Communist associations."

Davidson loved Burma and south-east Asia in general, which he described as "the last repository of simple human happiness." His happiness in Rangoon was increased by a touching love affair with Maung Tay Ba, an affectionate local boy of 14, whom he moved into his room in the Pegu Club without anyone seeming to raise an eyebrow. Their parting at the Rangoon River pier, where he was taking a flying boat for his next assignment, left them both weeping helplessly in public. This boy had apparently not come to the attention of the security services who were told "that he was particularly attached to Chinese youths in Rangoon", leading them to observe that he "doubtless will enjoy his stay in Singapore," which was his next destination.

He did indeed enjoy Singapore, which he was in and out of for the next three years, and partly for the expected reason. Initially, however, he was only there for a week, and a year of busy travelling around the Far East ensued in which he reported on the fall of Canton to the communists and the British fight against communist insurgency in Malaya (where his reports on grossly inadequate provisioning helped put things right), besides multiple stays in Hong Kong and visits to Macau, Taiwan, Vietnam, Java and Bali. Of them all, the latter was the place he waxed most lyrically about as "the world's last island of innocence", but in most of them he got to know many of the colourful characters coping with the local turmoil and made interesting friends amongst the others writing about it, besides enjoying an endless succession of liaisons with easily-found local boys.

In July 1950, just after the Korean War broke out, he was sent to Korea to cover it. He loathed the experience for the exceptional brutality he witnessed, but stayed until he discovered he could actually cover it much better from Tokyo by collating all the newest sources of news. Reports on him by British intelligence over these years continued to worry over his articles doubting ordinary Koreans could be anti-communist, or suggesting that "the average Vietnamese knows nothing about communism; for years he has been a passionate Nationalist, with Ho Chi Minh as his hero" Rather, however, than being the biased lefty they feared, he was simply a shrewd observer doing honour to the name of his newspaper, as was well recognised by the various editors given access to his reports.

Apart from reporting and enjoying the company of some brilliant fellow correspondents, Davidson's time in Tokyo was mostly taken up by the third of his four great love affairs with boys. Fifteen-year-old Eikichi "Eibo" Suzuki was hardly special for either looks or intelligence, but he was passionately loving, sweet and gentle, and for four or so months they lived in bliss together in hotels and then in their own home with the full approval of Eibo's mother and the easy acceptance of the other Japanese around them. The physical affair was short-lived compared to Davidson's other great ones, being heart-breakingly broken off, like that with Maung Tay Ba and so many others, when his job moved him to another country. Nevertheless, Davidson was to write of Eibo ten years later, that "of all the boys I've loved, he, more than any, was the 'divine friend, much desired' - the perfect one", while the letters from Eibo in this volume are testament to the boy's lasting love.

After several months stationed in Singapore and Malaya again, Davidson took four or so months' unpaid leave to go yachting with Robin Maugham in the Mediterranean, visiting the aged writer and boy-lover Norman Douglas in Capri and frolicking with boys in Ischia and Sicily. Then, on his own initiative, he went off for the last two months of 1951 to report on the troubles in the Suez Canal Zone, which had flared into near-war, though he seems to have spent as much time on muddled attempts to access it as anything else.

Summoned back to London by *The Observer* at Christmas, he was then given the sack without explanation. He suspected it was on account of his sexual reputation, aware that he had, for example, gone "a bit far" in "almost flauntingly" taking his beautiful sixteen-year-old Indian boyfriend, Somo, into some stodgy bastions of British colonialism in Singapore. M.I.5, by contrast, noted that he was sacked by *The Observer* because "he ran into debt." The more likely truth recalled by a fellow *Observer* journalist was that it was because "he did so little". He worked to live, not vice versa. This must have become particularly apparent recently.

The Observer was, however, generous, and paid him to resume his job in Malaya until the following July. His final months there coincided with the dictatorial rule of a new High Commissioner, Sir Gerald Templer. Though Davidson admired him as much as he despised him, they inevitably clashed badly. His sympathies were always with the aspirations of the "natives" versus their colonial masters. His endless liaisons with local boys brought him into much closer contact with native life than most British, his realism as well as his sense of justice told him that their aspirations should be met, and his sympathetic nature always drew him to the downtrodden, whoever they were. Writing, for example, about the former grandees of wartime Japan whom he met when they were impoverished and subject to constant humiliation, he admitted some of them may have deserved it, but commented: "I never think of deserts when I see sorrow."

With a £500 severance payment, Davidson next took a cottage in Corfu for three months and found a boy to look after him in it, while he started writing a lively book about Malaya, but he ran into writer's block when he moved back to England. Nearly a whole year passed there for which Davidson mysteriously had nothing to relate in his memoirs besides, towards its end, helping out the men charged in the Montagu of Beaulieu homosexual scandal. Maugham then took him on another holiday to Ischia, where he ended up staying on for a few months in his own little house in the fishing village of Forio, which already attracted a sprinkling of foreign writers and artists.

From this time until near his end, Italy emerges as the country where he usually wanted to be and mostly was, though there were also to be many more stays in England. The struggle to support himself financially was henceforth to be incessant and he seems to have found it easier during his sojourns in his homeland, though no sooner was he ever there than he started pining for Italy and seeking the means to return there.

It is not hard to explain. He preferred warm climates and warm people, and especially warm and willing boys. Italy had for many centuries built such a reputation for the latter that it had long become the favourite refuge of pederastic exiles from the much more repressive countries of the north, and especially those of a creative temperament. Helped by relative poverty and easy-going attitudes, she was essentially a throw-back to much older times and values when boys being enthusiastic for sex with males did not mean they were gay. Teenagers still had real lives of their own, most of them working when they could, and the virginity of girls until marriage was still highly valued and protected, the corollary to which was indulgence of the freedom of boys to play as they wished with each other.

Davidson had apparently introduced himself to Italy in the summer of 1948, when he spent a week in Rome waiting for a flight on to Israel, and had discovered a bathing establishment on the Tiber that operated discreetly as a freelance boy brothel. Three years later, he had already introduced himself to Forio and its happily less commercial boy attractions, and, on his way to Corfu, he introduced himself to Naples, perhaps then the European metropolis most renowned amongst tourists looking for sex with boys.

During his long stay in Forio in late 1953, Davidson discovered a truly pederastic culture, with an old and enduring tradition of pubescent boys expecting to be sought out by men, and he happily availed himself of the abundant opportunities for short encounters whilst also having his first longer-lasting relationship with an Italian boy and writing a little novel for which he never quite managed to find a publisher.

Then he moved on to Rome, where he stayed for ten whole months, supporting himself precariously by "stringing" for British newspapers. There he lived a strange life of poverty, punctured by the occasional splendour of an aristocratic or diplomatic party, or the mediaeval pageant of a canonisation. Though often hungry, he found the small change needed for priapic encounters with boys in the undergrowth on the banks of the Tiber or the dark of the city's cinemas, to which droves of Roman adolescents resorted (but *not* to watch films). He was happy enough despite finding the boy scene heartlessly commercial.

Chance then suddenly diverted him to a more purposeful life in Cyprus for three years. He was asked to show a visiting rich Greek Cypriot around Rome, and this led to an invitation to join in the founding of the *Times of Cyprus*, as its deputy editor. The point was to have an English-language newspaper that was willing to be critical of the British colonial government there at a time when tensions were mounting over British rejection of the Greek Cypriots' aspirations for union with Greece. He arrived there in October 1954, five months before the EOKA guerrilla organisation began its armed struggle to achieve this, and the British responded by sending a new governor, Field-Marshal Harding, who sought to defeat it through harsh repression, including torture and the perversion of justice.

As one would expect, Davidson was perfectly attuned to understanding and sympathising with Cypriot aspirations, despite his horror over EOKA's own atrocities. He was, moreover, outraged by Harding's measures, and he realised they were bound to alienate the population further and thus to be counterproductive. By exposing the truth to the British public, he and his newspaper ultimately played a useful role in getting the British government to be more reasonable, but to Harding criticism of his policy was simply incomprehensible.

In 1956 the colonial government's security liaison officer suspected him of having apprised the *Daily Worker* of one of its official's embarrassing manipulations, and had him investigated by its Security Liaison Office. This led to the last additions to M.I.5's files on him, though the last report already available to them, from "a reliable and well-placed source" in 1953, forewarned them that "he lacked the discipline necessary as a communist." Their new investigation soon concluded that he was indeed unlikely to be the *Daily Worker*'s source, explaining that "he is the sort of man to whom a good deal of mud sticks, partly no doubt on account of his unsavoury moral reputation and the type of people with whom he associates."

Davidson finally infuriated Harding beyond remedy by publishing, as acting editor, an article exposing in meticulous detail the mendacity of a White Paper by the colonial government attempting to refute allegations of torture. Soon, he was warned that the police were looking for charges to bring against him. He knew these could not be charges under the notorious Emergency Regulations, and also that his "private life had for long been immaculate." Nevertheless, he was sufficiently frightened that the police might secure his "previous" from Scotland Yard, and then use it in combination with hiring some young Turks to bring false accusations, that he decided he must leave promptly, and he boarded a ship for Italy in August 1957.

His statement as to his private life in Cyprus sits just a little oddly with his mention of a boy, aged 15 to 18, who lived with him through most of his time there and insisted afterwards that once he was married he would have him to live with him and his wife.

Davidson next went to the island of Procida in the Bay of Naples, and wrote a book about Cyprus, which he realised himself was "too hot with recent anger" to be publishable. From there, he moved for several months to Naples itself.

In May 1958, he obtained his last job as a journalist, a well-paid one reporting as a stringer in Aden for several newspapers. This ended abruptly after ten weeks when the Immigration Police told him he must leave. He was baffled, as he had for once supported government policy, and he felt sure nothing could be known about what went on in private between him and his handsome young Somali bearer. Neither he nor his employers could get the Governor to explain or change his decision, and the Colonial Secretary was unwilling to interfere. An editor had the matter about to be raised in Parliament, but was warned that reasons would be given that were personal. Davidson backed down, afraid his old sexual offence was going to be raised, but soon regretted it greatly when he became convinced that the personal reason was nothing more than his exposure of Harding's tyranny in Cyprus. Harding had promised revenge, but such a justification would have been easy to contest.

Effectively now retired at sixty-one, nine months in London followed, which were chiefly notable for his meeting and becoming fast friends with Colin Spencer, a talented young writer and artist, who, aside from his last love, was to be the greatest friend of his old age.

For at least the middle half of 1959, he was back in southern Italy, mostly Sicily. This was the time he went to Catania as later described in a chapter of that name in *Some Boys*. As may be gathered from it, observing boys and their sexual antics and, when possible, joining in, was his main preoccupation during this period and was to remain so until he refound love six years later.

There are no grounds for doubting the following self-appraisal or that it applied to his sexual conduct as much as anything else: "Looking back, I've enjoyed it all; sometimes it's been disagreeable, but never uninteresting. I don't think I've done much harm; I don't believe anybody's been unhappier for knowing me, and perhaps some have been even a little happier. If that be true, I couldn't wish for a better epitaph." So far as one can tell, he never harmed a boy, or would for a second have risked doing so, with the important and self-acknowledged exception that due to the exigencies of his job, he disappeared suddenly from the lives of some boys who had become emotionally or materially dependent on him. It is hard not to feel sorry for Maung Tay Ba, for example, and to escape the feeling that he had been badly let down. Still, it may well be that he and the others preferred to have had what they had than nothing. All that is known of what boys thought about him in retrospect suggests enduring gratitude for the warmth and care he brought into their lives.

Even in the ephemeral sexual encounters in Italy which are all that is known of his sex life in the first half of his sixties, there is nothing to cast doubt on his saying that the boy's pleasure was the focus of his own. There are, however, some darker sides to what happened or did not happen that give cause for questioning how happy his own life really was. These are likely some of what he had in mind when he said in his self-appraisal, "my unhappinesses were inherent in my nature."

First, there were the implications of his own description of his pursuit of boys in his late twenties: "the unceasing search for the 'divine friend, much desired', which, as every paederast must know, imposes a hunger for fresh experiences that's sated only when the 'right' person has been found." By this much later stage of life, "while I had always sought to signpost my path with a sequence of small loves rather than dot it with heartless pick-ups (though it would be dishonest not to confess to plenty of those too), I now found myself moving away from promiscuity and aiming at passionate attachments lasting as long as circumstances or the transient bloom of adolescence allowed." But how often was this attainable? What has already been quoted of his feelings for Eibo suggests it had been very rarely and perhaps only once. And what about the many periods, ignored in his memoirs (which are naturally about what happened rather than what did not), but more apparent from his correspondence, when he could find either only very superficial contacts with boys, or none at all? The testimony of his friends is that such periods often left him utterly miserable and disillusioned with his fate.

Secondly, there were the consequences of the largely illegal status of pederasty, even in Italy. Though both the law and social attitudes were remarkably benign by British standards, they were still corrosive. Sex between a man and a boy under fourteen was illegal, as was sex with boys of fourteen or fifteen, the age group to which Davidson was most drawn, unless the boy was "already a morally corrupt person" (obviously hard to prove). The main consequence of this was that the tendency for pederastic encounters in Italy to have a corrosive commercial edge lent itself to blackmail. Davidson colourfully recounted one instance of this in his chapter on Naples in *Some Boys*, but the reminiscence published here of his friend Colin Spencer makes it clear that the problem was recurrent. He sums up a letter Davidson sent him from Messina on 17 September 1959 as "Same old trouble that recurs. After about 4 months M has to leave because boys start blackmail." That this was an unhappy problem for boy-lovers in general may be gathered as well from the memoirs of the French writer Roger Peyrefitte, who also frequented southern Italy in that era and with the same motive.

There was also a third danger to himself that Davidson recognized. In Catania for instance:

> I found myself on the brink of becoming obsessed; and obsession of any kind means atrophy of mind and spirit. There are, I dare say womanizers - "mulierasts", to borrow Robert Ross's famous coinage - given over to the exclusive pursuit of fornication; but the boy-lover, perhaps because of the impermanence of his amours as well as of the social hindrances in the way of his having any amours at all, is specially prone to the malady of obsession - paederasty becomes paedomania and, as the alcoholic's mind is dominated by his need of liquor, so the paedomaniac is driven by his compulsive craving for pubescent novelty round an endless circle of prowling in the wake of his sexual curiosity - without love, without emotion, without joy, without satiety, and to the exclusion of every other interest.

He had gone to Catania aware of a spiritual need to avoid this, and on this occasion, he forced himself to leave accordingly.

At any rate, what Davidson yearned for was to elude him for years to come, and, towards the end of 1959, he reluctantly returned to England for what turned out to be nearly two years, for at least the last nine months of which he lived in a little cottage near High Wycombe. In October 1960 he had a reunion with his old friend Boris de Chroustchoff, whom he had not seen for three decades and was now living in Oxfordshire with a second wife and a daughter; henceforth, they were to remain close. By this time, he had half written his memoir, *The World, The Flesh and Myself*, and was waiting exasperatedly for a publisher to make up its mind about it, so that he could return to Italy.

Finally, the following June, the book was sold to Arthur Barker, and with the advance given him, he was off. The next month he was working enthusiastically at it in Taranto, and already had an "SB-presumptive"[3]. A week later, he had two of

---

[3] "SB" or"s.b.", with a verbal form "s.b.ing" (doing something with "s.b."s) is a code word that recurs so often in Davidson's correspondence as to be of importance, but precisely what it stands for is mysterious. The "b." clearly stands for "boy", as it emerges from letter xii that the feminine equivalent

thirteen and fourteen who were no longer presumptive, and before long he had a "team", but he still compared the local boy scene unfavourably with Sicily's. Thereafter, it was downhill: struggling penuriously to survive and freezing in the coldest winter in memory, he became thoroughly disenchanted with Taranto and its people, but, with local debts, could not afford to leave.

The book, including heavy cuts his publisher insisted on, was finally finished in February 1962, and a bank loan to tide him over until its delayed publication enabled him to move to Calabria in May, and then on to Sicily, where he remained for a year (excepting two brief trips to Morocco, on a humanitarian mission for Amnesty International, and Geneva). He was living in Palermo when his book came out in October.

The reactions of those who knew him to his memoirs were mostly positive, but interestingly mixed. Predictably, his sympathetic sister loved it and "on her instruction half the Prelates of Ireland are buying it," while his stuffy brother complained that he would be "ashamed" to show it to any of his friends. De Chroustchoff initially disliked it, being embarrassed by the effusive description of himself and "shocked" by the strong opening sentence, besides complaining it was unsuitable for his daughter, to which Davidson replied, "Did you really suppose all this time that I've been writing something for 16-year-old schoolgirls?" De Chroustchoff soon warmed to it for its honesty, which was indeed the general reaction, especially amongst his

---

is an "s.g.". The same letter dispels any notion that the "s." might stand for "sexy", "sweet", "special", "superb" or anything similar to them, as in it Davidson refers to an "s.b." who is "very ugly". A theory that "s." might stand for "small" sits very awkwardly with the known age range for which it was used, which, like the age range that attracted Davidson, was never less than twelve, centred on fifteen and stretched to eighteen, but in one notable exception went well beyond that: in a letter of 2 December 1960, Davidson asked Boris de Chroustchoff "Did I ever tell you about the present Sultan of Johore who was for a time a special friend when we were both SBs?" When they remet in 1949, "I went along with in my mind the delicate SB image of a bronze faun". When they were lovers, in 1915, Davidson was 18 and the future Sultan was 21. A possible solution is that "s." stood for something like "suitably-aged", as that definition at least fits all the known usages.

journalistic friends. Arthur Koestler named it in *The Observer* as one of the three best books of the year, describing it as the "two-fold story of a courageous and lovable person's struggle to come to terms with his Grecian heresy and of a brilliant journalist's fight against colonial jingoism".

Over the coming years, numerous readers were to write to him expressing their admiration and a few became his friends. Often, they were moved by his expressing their own sexual feelings, but one early and grand exception was the purely heterosexual eminent literary critic, John Davenport, an amusing and extraordinarily decent man who had been a close friend of Norman Douglas. Davenport wrote to admire *The World* the month after its publication, already intending a review which he got *The Observer* to publish, and which opened, "Candour and forthrightness are rarely found in autobiographies. Mr. Davidson is the happy exception: he neither glories in nor grieves over himself and his objectivity is a delight." A lively correspondence ensued and in a month they were close friends without having met, Davenport's letters thereafter being signed off "Love, JD." Soon they were befriending each others' friends and family.

The income from his book was disappointing, however, and Davidson was still struggling to support himself, partly dependent on small handouts from his sister and friends, so in August 1963 he returned to England for another two years. He missed Italy, but enjoyed visiting his sister in Ireland twice and seeing his friends, principally now Spencer, Davenport, Maugham and de Chroustchoff. For more than the last year of this time, he lived on a boat moored in Sussex and lent to him by Maugham in recognition of considerable literary help over the years. Maugham then deprived him of it rather suddenly and shabbily, obliging him to move in temporarily with Davenport, but after a fortnight felt guilty enough about it that he gave him £200 as what Davidson called "conscience money." With this, Davidson was off back to Sicily like a shot, arriving in Trapani, a new destination for him, on 14 November 1965. Sadly, he was never again to see Davenport, who died seven months later, aged only 58.

He found he liked the people of Trapani more than other Sicilians, and a fortnight later he heard that the paperback rights to *The World* had been sold for a £300 advance against royalties, securing him a much longer stay there. He had always been drawn to islands, so on the 18th of December, as a day trip with his new boy Ignazio, he crossed the eighteen kilometres to the island of Favignana on the hydrofoil, the only public transport there in those days before tourism began to spoil it. "Very alluring" was his comment in a diary on the mountainous little island with some four thousand inhabitants. Ignazio, though "sweet", was untrustworthy and had to be dropped a week later, but he already had another "sweet boy", Salvatore. On the 28th, he scribbled, "[Salvatore]'s *ruining* me. Favignana?" On an unrecorded day in January, he returned there on his own and with all his baggage, so evidently hoping to stay, though not in the one dingy little hotel that Favignana then had.

So, what was the immediate and strong allure of Favignana? *Sicilian Vespers* answers that to an extent. Unfortunately, he left conflicting accounts of exactly what happened. His diary allows one to determine some of the truth, but it stops on 2nd January. It looks, however, as though, among the group of boys who had been on the jetty when he arrived on his first visit, he had beheld a "Greco-Saracen" boy of stunning and movingly melancholic beauty who had touched his heart. He was thus following his instinct in coming back, and it was to be the luckiest decision of his life.

It nearly went wrong, as he could not find a room for rent. In despair, he stopped on his way back to the port to ask the unsmiling woman in the tobacconist. No sooner had she suggested her husband's little warehouse than the Greco-Saracen appeared, "beautiful, grave and shy," to buy petrol for his father, the butcher next-door. The woman sent the boy to fetch her husband, and once an agreement over the warehouse had been made, the boy bargained for Davidson's necessities, fetched a handcart for them, loaded it, and then rearranged everything for him in his new home.

Thus did Davidson meet Luigi, who had just turned fifteen, and was to be, almost at once, the greatest love of his life. When the usually taciturn boy returned to his mother that evening, it was with uncharacteristic excitement over the unexpected gift of a thousand-lire note. The next morning, on his way to school, he returned with his own touching gift and an invitation to eat with his family. Davidson did not record whether they had made love that first day, but it looks so, since, in his first letter to de Chroustchoff from Favignana, "ecstatically content ... on a magically lovely island", he wrote, "Next Sunday I am lunching with my boy-friend, his father & mother and six brothers & sisters: rather an alarming prospect."

It turned out that there were really only two sisters and one brother, and no need for alarm. The family all received him with simple friendliness. At first, real conversation had to be conducted through Luigi, who alone could interpret between his family's Sicilian dialect and Davidson's more official Italian, but evidently they liked him, as they invited him back. "At lunch with the family one day after I'd been on the island a week, I felt suddenly so dazed with happiness that I blurted out: 'why are you so kind to me? Why are you all so good?' " Luigi's father answered: "You love our son, so we love you." Davidson had been welcomed by the mothers of Eibo and his Moroccan loves, but he seems never to have experienced such a father before. "I wonder what Papà really thinks or suspects – or cares?" he commented in his next letter to de Chroustchoff, after giving him an enraptured description of Luigi and their love-making. Within a few months, all formality with "his" family gone, "Michele" was lunching with them every day instead of every Sunday, and they moved him from the warehouse to his own little house outside town.

All this could hardly be more different from Davidson's commercial interactions with boys in Italian cities. He was intensely aware of what an extraordinary stroke of good luck it was to find such a boy, and when he himself was so old – sixty-nine his second month there: "it's extraordinary that I should find one at all – let alone this superbly beautiful creature whose face & figure almost make me swoon when I see him naked, & whose nature is sweet & simple & frank." That on top of this the boy's family, "whose members became dearer to me than anybody I've known since childhood," should be so welcoming overwhelmed him. Years later, he had to explain how unusual his circumstances were to Tim Brierly, a new and naïve correspondent who had heard about his love-life on Favignana and was tempted to move there himself:

> there's no "trade" here, in the special sense of that term: anything anybody does is known to the entire population within an hour of its happening. When we meet I'll tell you the story of my good fortune when first I came here - which is why I stayed here - & met Luigi & his father at one & the same moment - but if in these last four years I'd so much as raised an eyebrow at anybody else the whole thing would have been ruined & I'd have been removed from the island. The place is too *small.* My experience has been quite exceptional simply because I had an astonishing piece of sheer luck.

His happiness with Luigi was such that nothing could tempt him away from Favignana and he stayed there without interruption for more than two years. This was facilitated by Oliver Layton, an American publisher who wanted "books that *emphasize* the sexual side of boy-love" and wrote to him in August 1966, urging him to write a sexually explicit book for them, and sending him a copy of Dukahz's *The Asbestos Diary* as evidence that such had become practicable. Early in 1967, they gave him an advance of $1000, and by the end of the year he had half-finished *Some Boys,* which he described as "a work of literary pornography" about his boy-loves in different parts of the world. Despite this, he was already running out of money, and in March 1968 he finally had to leave, tears streaming and unable to speak for grief as his family bid him farewell.

Back in London and desperate to return to what he now regarded as home, he worked hard and finished *Some Boys* in July. Oliver Layton hardly got exactly what they had asked for, as the book had no graphic sexual content, but it was certainly devoted to boy-love and was, besides, beautifully-written and evocative travel-writing. With the new payment, he bought fashionable London clothes as gifts for his family and returned to them. Luigi and his brother met his train in Trapani, and he was blissfully happy, but unfortunately he still only had enough money to stay for five weeks.

There followed another eight months in England, during which he began the book that has only finally seen publication with the present volume, and which was his new hope of being able to afford to live in Favignana again. "Now I'm getting down at last in earnest to my Sicily book," he wrote in September. On the 18th of the following April he announced excitedly to de

Chroustchoff, "next week I'm going *home.* ... [I've] delivered half my Sicily book & now am going to finish the other half. They're providing some dough, well below starvation level. But who cares about starvation, when it's at HOME?" Sadly, this turned out to be his last letter to de Chroustchoff, who died a month later.

The next four and a half years were roughly equally divided between Favignana and England, his stays in both usually lasting at least half a year. His love for Luigi was undiminished, but presumably no longer had sexual expression. Besides having attained manhood, Luigi must at some point in this period have left Favignana for the career in the police which he was pursuing in Padua by 1974 (when he got engaged to a girl there). In November 1970, after explaining to a friend that 99 ½ % of pederastic relationships are necessarily ephemeral, Davidson said, rather enigmatically, "The remaining *half* %, after the above 99½ %, is represented by such rare beings as my Luigi, or by the sum of the circumstances of my friendship with Luigi." Confirming that their love was no longer physical, he said in an interview with *The Examiner* in 1973:

> I have a boy in Europe... he's 22 now, but I knew him first when he was fourteen; well, I think I can say, I know I can say, that with one exception, since I knew him 8 years ago I haven't so much as looked at another boy. Although we're separated by distance I'm in love with him and shall continue in love with him until I'm dead. Physically, he's too old for me, but he absolutely absorbs me emotionally now.

Davidson finally left Favignana in December 1973, due to severe flooding, and moved to Malta, where Tim Brierly had a flat to lend him. There was no talk in his later correspondence of going back there, so presumably he did not mind: Luigi had long left and Favignana was rapidly becoming spoiled by tourism, hordes of visitors coming in with a new car-ferry, vulgarising the way of life and eroding old customs. His primitive living conditions there had also been harder to endure once he was well into his seventies.

He did not like Malta much, and found the boys "standoffish." He was, however, to have one last amorous liaison. In March 1974, Brierly lent him another flat he had in his old haunt of

Tangier. In a prospectus he wrote the next year of a book he was intending to write, he mentioned a "pederastic interlude" in Tangier with a fifteen-year-old which would illustrate perfectly his point that there are many boys with desperate longings for tenderness and emotional and material security, as well as sex, whose needs can only be fully met by pederasts. The boy, whose name was Hassan, was presumably the Arab boy of whom snapshots survive showing him and an aged Davidson locked joyfully in kisses and embraces.

In the summer, he went to London and stayed there until January, when Colin Spencer had him live in his holiday home in the little Maltese island of Gozo, which he found "enchanting", friendlier and quite different to Malta itself. One of its charms was "an extremely agreeable & decorative Personal Assistant" of fifteen who bicycled out to him every day the two kilometres from his home in the capital, Victoria. The assistance, officially at least, may have had something to do with a sequel to *The World*, which he was commissioned to write in February. The publishers who had given him an advance for *Sicilian Vespers* had lost interest in it in 1969, when they had a change in management, but Davidson made plans to adapt its content to the new book.

In June, he fell and fractured his vertebrae, and for a month was looked after by nuns in the Dominican clinic there. A few kind British friends were keeping a caring eye on him in Spencer's absences, one of whom, a retired composer called Alfred Arnold, brought him to recuperate in his old farmhouse. There he stayed until September, when his fractures reasserted themselves and necessitated hospitalisation again.

This time, he went into the public hospital, Craig's, in Victoria, where one ailment led to another and he died of pneumonia two months later, on 19th November 1975, aged seventy-eight. Though he was never a believer, his friends in Gozo arranged a Catholic funeral as best suited to his tastes, and he was buried in the Catholic cemetery of St. Mary's in Xewkija, Gozo on the 21st. Everything he owned, which no one can have expected to amount to much, was bequeathed to Luigi.

II. SICILIAN VESPERS

Sicilian Vespers *survives in a multitude of differently-phrased drafts, none complete and some very short. Though Davidson had thought of writing a book about Sicily even before he discovered Favignana, the earliest evidence of his having written anything for it is from 9th September 1968, ten days after his return from Favignana to London, when he wrote to his friend Boris de Chroustchoff, "Now I'm getting down at last in earnest to my Sicily book, which has been hanging fire for so long." The next 18th April, he wrote to him from Favignana, "I've been slaving these last weeks, & have delivered half my Sicily book & now am going to finish the other half on the spot." On the 10th September of that year, he told Tim Brierly, "in the middle of my Island book (which I know, & other people know, is excellent of its kind) the publishers which commissioned it changed managing directors & the new man is interested only in Sporting Books!!!" Presumably he then stopped writing it, though whether he had by then written a first draft of all he intended is unknown. At any rate, most of what survives is either stated to have been written in 1969 or can be dated to that year from other internal evidence. The only exception was a redrafting of what is presented here as its five chapters, which was done in 1972. Presumably he was still hoping to get it published as a travel book, since as late as September 1974, he said in an interview "It's not of special interest to boy-lovers, though perhaps glimpses may be caught between the lines: it's a portrait, I suppose, of the tiny Sicilian island on which I lived these last eight years."*

As explained in the Editor's Note, he had to change his plans in February 1975, when he was commissioned to write a sequel to his autobiography, The World, *and the barely-begun redrafting of* Sicilian Vespers *as part of that has been ignored in what follows, to avoid producing something that is neither fish nor fowl.*

1. The Island

I like white dusty narrow lanes that wind between low walls of loose piled boulders and are speckled with cowpats and sheep's crap. I like a countryside where the donkey is still ridden, harnessed to the trap, or – often side by side with a cow – yoked to the wooden plough. I like chattering family homes whose women, when dinner's done with, quietly knit or fuss happily over a table-load of pins and paper-patterns. I like a piazza where children playing are more important than motors hooting. I live at the remote dead-end of just such a lane, two miles from such a piazza and a village of such homes, beneath a great yellow bluff of limestone that rises like an island from the pastures to drop three hundred feet sheer to the sea.

I even like living in my one-roomed stone shack, without lighting, heat or sanitation – who needs a bog when, armed with a handy little mattock, he can dig his own latrine wherever the whim of the morning may take him over a hundred hectares of rocky wilderness?

The ravens' double croak is the sound that haunts this stony solitude, though it's a winter cry rather than a spring one; it's full of the melancholy threat of a cold northwester and leaden sea – and full, too, of that strange note of sadness which one can always catch behind the brightest of Sicilian happiness. Along with a colony of falcons, the ravens roost and breed among the high rocks above my home: in pairs they sweep over the fields at two or three hundred feet, poised to drop for the kill; last year one of these violent birds let fall a headless rat bang on my *terrazzo* as I was drinking coffee, headless and oozing crimson vitals; yet there's something endearing as well as ogrish in the double "qua-qua" as the huge spread of dark pinion wings flaps relentlessly above. In pairs they hunt: T. H. White wrote that the raven mates for life – certainly here they always fly two together, as much a mated team as two fishermen working from their jointly owned boat.

At this season clouds of flashing goldfinches dance in the fig trees, now well in leaf again after the bare bones of winter; and infant lizards hardly bigger than tadpoles are magically appearing on the warm stone walls – tiny bloodless copies of their flamboyant elders. It's early yet for the wild caper to bloom, but late in May the girls will be here stripping the buds for pickling – buds still hard and rounded like nuts – while the long clustered tendrils already in flower will be showering from the rocks, as if struck by Moses's rod, in a torrent of strange delicate blossoms like mauve-and-white hummingbirds.

At this season, the first storks should any day now come flying over the house from Africa, as they do each year, set for summer quarters in Vienna or Munich: a purposeful, isosceles arrowhead of solemnly dipping wings: necks intently reaching forward like compass-needles. Soon the quail will be here, speckled and squat-rumped, diving into the corn or rank grass; already the first turtledoves have arrived, darting about in their airy, nervous flight. Each April the migrants, going north, make a brief stay on the staging-post of our three small islands; and each August or September they stop again on their way back. But there are fewer each year: the accursed *caccia*, the official shooting season in Spring and Autumn, is remorselessly paring down the migrant numbers, especially the shy, whirring quail. But these intrepid huntsmen who, wearing fancy dress, swarm over the island during the *caccia*, pay for a licence for the right to do so and also, coming from all over Sicily proper and even the Italian mainland, compose a sizeable block of votes – and licence money and votes aren't things that Italian politicians fly in the face of. They are really figures of fun – or would be if they weren't ferociously massacring small frightened birds – those bandoliered braves, dangling with fringed waistcoats and game-bags and cowboy effects, stumping over the island with valiantly levelled guns or standing frozen at a pit-edge, waiting for an infant rabbit to come out and offer battle; swaggering about the piazza like big-game hunters, filling the bars and the village hotel with their tales of valorous encounters with a few small birds and vaunting the evidence of that valour – the pathetic bunches of freckled quail and downy grey dove that dangle head down from their ample girths. Each migration, northward and southward, at either end of the summer, brings them over to our island by the boatload: although mostly, thank God, they're pretty bad shots, the magnitude of their combined blasting is enough, given time, to annihilate our Mediterranean migrants. Oh well, these gallant *cacciatori* pay cash for their licences, and spend cash in the hotels and bars, so who cares if these useless birds, as the papers report, are each year becoming fewer - or if, as happened to me a few seasons ago, some eager but uncertain fellow blows a load of lead into one's front door? And yet, one has to suppose, once home again in some Palermitan suburb or even Roman palazzo and out of their Red Indian rig, these boastful men assume their natural character of gentle, perhaps even henpecked, ordinariness.

A stone stairway leads to the garden from the platform of solid rock on which the house is built. Another flight, into what was once a small quarry, takes me to the pulley-and-bucket *pozzo* which provides "bitter" water - "sweet" water I bring from afar in a fifteen-litre flagon. The entire tufa foundation of this island, at or below sea-level, is honeycombed with underground streams and cisterns; but most of this water, seeped from the sea through the porous tufa, is brackish - the few sweet-water wells must be fed by some effluent from the mountain. But most of our fresh water is brought from Sicily in Navy tankers.

The garden - a couple of hectares of fruit more wild than cultivated - drops towards the edge of the sea within converging loose-piled stone walls whose apex encloses a great evergreen umbrella of carob; the black pods in late August make splendid fodder for Tommaso's pigs. The house and rear walls of the garden are founded on a wide arc of outcrop limestone, like a tier of an arena, in one angle of which, hewn out of a mass of rock, is the arched portal of a Punic tomb, opening vaguely toward the East: a tomb built for two persons, the experts say (though the cavern surely could hold a family) and early Phoenician, probably rather than late Carthaginian; the doorway must be about four feet high, and the neatly excavated cavity some seven feet square and the same in height. Today it gives shelter to a couple of Tommaso's pigs which are grazing here: I can't remember whether there was a Punic prejudice against the flesh of swine?

Close by, at the foot of a ten-foot face of rock so overhung one could sleep under it untouched by a cloudburst, there are a series of man-made niches, ledges, and miniature caves - scooped, I suppose, by prehistoric tenants here: funereal cavities, perhaps, for infant corpses or the storage of burned bones. I like to ponder on these tenancies of long ago: to think of these people, not much different surely, in their feelings and needs and enjoyments and fears, from me or Gigi's family, who since perhaps palaeolithic times had been hunting and later cultivating this patch of ground where I now live and am happy. Under this projecting rock, too, ringed by a grove of fig and tall, plumed canes like pampas (used here for thatching), stands a huge Sicilian stone oven, elegantly XIIIth century in style, in which, when the whole family come to me for a hilarious day's outing, Damianina and the girls and the in-laws bake bread and *pasta al forno* and the local kind of *pizza*.

It's a lush wilderness of a garden, sliding seawards from under a ten-foot ridge of overhanging rock from whose face small caves and man-made niches have been scooped - scooped, I suppose, by pre-historic tenants here: funebrial cavities, perhaps for infant corpses or the storage of burned bones. The western arm of the garden (we look due north across the sea) follows the length of a Roman road, gauged and chipped out of the raw rock in the Roman way of road-making and grooved with parallel wheel-ruts six inches or so deep. This road led from an old stone-quarry to the creek below my garden where the small lateen-rigged boats from Sicily still load the unique cellular blocks of tufa called *cantuni*: stone quarried on this island since Roman times and still in demand for building on the Sicilian "mainland". Tommaso, showing me another complex of quarrying and tunnelling deep into a cliffside, said: "That was worked in Saracen days", as if this were but the other day - a mere eight hundred years ago! Westwards from my garden, half a kilometre away, there's a field where one may kick about like tennis-balls the rounded bosses of Roman amphorae - and Carthaginian too, for here was a military camp that often changed hands during the Punic wars and served as a base for the current siege of Lilybaeum (today, and since Sicilian times, called Marsala).

A little further round the shore, past the tiny haven of San Nicòla and the modern cemetery, I know of a couple of troughs cut out of the rock from which human bonefragments may be scooped up by the handful - antique burials that haven't yet been archaeologically categorized or dated. This curious reliquary (perhaps by now adulterated, like the shrine of Santa Rosaria outside Palermo with the bones of goats), is the private property of a farmer, a friend of mine whose son goes to school with our Duzzo; he allows me to visit the cave in which he fattens cattle – incised on a wall is a Phoenician text; I don't think it's yet been deciphered. In another cave there's an inscription in Byzantine Greek, and another Latin. I know of no Arabic graffiti: the Arabs, at the end of their lordship in Sicily a thousand years ago, left few imprints on the social surface of our island – beyond their contributions to the techniques of the tunny fishery and to the vocabulary and practice of irrigation and these Arab influences are very much alive today. Living here, for the most part in solitude, one feels very close to the beginnings of history.

More recent – almost brashly modern – are the Spanish and Latin inscriptions and Hispanic coats-of-arms which embellish a number of secretive caves that one comes upon shyly concealed within the walls of sunken gardens and ancient quarries: caves furnished with beds, shelves, larders and fireplaces hewn out of the rook and providing, in the XVIth and XVIIth centuries, homes for island settlers dodging the Barbary marauders from the African ports of Tunis and Algiers. So cosy and lived-in are they, I find myself waiting for the sound of Spanish voices. This was the time when Sicily, with her islands, was under the crass and leaden thumb of Spain (that through her history she has been, one after another, under some foreign thumb explains not only the Mafia but also this inkling of wistful defeatism which one discerns in the Sicilian physiognomy).

Just now the figs, which magically seem to form without a flower, are swelling: but the vines, untended for decades, are hopelessly barren. The garden is chiefly overrun by that South American cactus which, in the XVIth century, was brought by the Spanish to both banks of the Inland Sea. The French call it the Fig of Barbary, the Italians the Fig of India and the Arabs the Nazarene Fig, since it was Christians who seeded it in African soil; while the English, knowing it isn't a fig at all, compromise with the name Prickly Pear, knowing it isn't a pear. Clumps of tall cane, feathery-flowered like pampas, bow gravely with the breeze, and soon the dark green of the pomegranate will be dotted with its delicate crimson flower (a saucer-shaped blossom which, fallen to the ground in the high drought of August, will be eagerly used, if it chances to catch a few drops from a watering can, as a drinking bowl by the parched lizards that can smell moisture from afar - could Beatrix Potter herself better that?). Nobody in England would allow this place the name of garden - it's two or three acres of jungle in which rabbits thrive and a pair of Tommaso's hogs rootle and grunt around. Yet it's sparkling with butterflies, Red Admirals and Purple Emperors and clouds of the familiar Cabbage White, and with a multitude of birds - last year an oriole, glittering with gold on black, swooped over my shoulder; and only yesterday a hoopoe, skewbald and plumed like a lord mayor, was pecking about for an hour under the carob tree. To the children when they come out for the day, nine-year old Duzzo and his friend Peppe and twelve-year Caterina, its rocks and hiding places and bouldered walls and caverns of evergreen foliage are paradise.

From the stone bench on my miniscule *terrazzo*, I look across the garden and sea to a small dark island like a drowsing leviathan less than three miles to the north, whose 300-odd inhabitants live from fishing and the growing of a good white *vino di campagna*. Westward, beyond the flat roofs of the *paese* (in this context, the "village")[4] and the bay, the humpety profile of our own bare brown mountain like a huge corrugated dam against the sky, unrolls for two and a half miles along the girth of the island, topping a thousand feet at the highest of its five monticles. In at the birth, so to speak, of the antique world, our mountain naturally conforms to the antique convention that mountain ranges, when possible, should be seen to have five peaks or humps - should be, that is, "pentadactylos", five-fingered, and so equipped to protect all within its shadow from what malignancies constantly threaten. How many times does the name "Pentadactylos" appear on the maps of Greece and the islands, of Corfu and Cyprus? And here, just across the Strait on

---

[4] The word "paese" is used for a village or township smaller than a "città" - for any human habitat that's not quite a town. It can also be used for an entire country - "the 'paese' of England" - or for one's birthplace - "Rome is my 'paese'". It does not mean "countryside". On Egusa, the village is always known as the "paese". [Author's footnote]

the Italian mainland, there's the Latinized Pentedattilo, a branch of Aspromonte in southern Calabria, which Edward Lear set out to paint in 1847.... All round the Mediterranean, wherever Greek or Arab went, and one may assume Phoenician too, the figure or number 5, or any symbol of it representing the open hand held defensively in front of the eye, has always been, and still is, a powerful prophylactic against the Evil Eye and similar troubles – as witness the doorknockers in the shape of a hand which are almost universal in Morocco and frequent in southern Spain and on Italian islands like Ischia and this present island – here the front doors of houses even quite recently built bear this important safeguard in brass or cast-iron. So our bare brown mountain is a perfect pentadactylos – and so, if I come to glance at it, is that little island straight ahead: if you count correctly, you can generally make any skyline in those parts come to five.

And to the right, a little north of east and twelve miles away above the shore of Sicily and the port of Trapani – Drepanon to the ancients – there soars the fabulous hyperbola of Eryx. As I see that uncanny height from here, and as sailors of all times coming up through our islands from points west saw it, Eryx presents, when she wants, a spellbinding profile which, though it must have many imitations, must strike any eye and mind with a mystery, an aura and a glamour that make it unique among all mountains. The Rock of Gibraltar, the Alpine horizon above Milan or Turin, Fujiyama from Tokyo bay, the Great Karakoram seen from Srinagar, even Etna's white pinnacle, fifty miles away from Quattr'occhi on the island of Lipari, leaping skyward from the heights of all Sicily – admire what mountain mass you will, the cliché evoked will surely congratulate Nature: "Nature at her most awe-inspiring", "the glory or the majesty or the romance of Nature", "the noblest of Nature's works" – something of the sort. But Eryx, a sight of her instantly tells one, owes nothing to Nature: in all her changing aspects, she is essentially unnatural, supernatural, numinous – the mystery of her protean forms and ever-changeful moods must, if not divine, at least be magical. That this has been the human reaction right down the ages to the aura and immanence of this mountain is witnessed by its recognition from the earliest classical times, and even before and after them, as a seat of divinity – as the home of goddesses.

A long slow slope rises as straight as a climbing jet-aircraft to a height of two and a half thousand feet – to that tremendous consummation of a sheer plummeting drop from the point where Venus had her most famous shrine in the whole Roman world, and before her Aphrodite in the Greek, and before her Astarte and the Punic Tanit; and where the Madonna today reigns nominally, although she dwells comfortably below sea level in the village of Custonaci, only returning in festive procession every two or three years to her historic, and almost prehistoric, citadel.

Mystery, the produce of the endless mutations of her guise and stance and temperament, is Eryx's most obvious attribute – to me the mountain seems feminine, although it is named after a son of Venus and half-brother of Aeneas, because of her equivalence with the queen of females and because the Italian name for Eryx, *Erice*, has a conventionally feminine form: the mystery of her phantasmal appearances and transfigurations and obscurations; her apparent withdrawals and advances from the Sicilian strand, her swift dissolution into a myopic blur and equally sudden resumption of startling sharp focus – all this the ancients noted with awe and devotion, and all this one notes still today, and quite marvellously from my *terrazzo*. Depending on the light, the texture and content of the atmosphere – and these depend chiefly on the direction of the wind at different seasons – Eryx approaches or recedes, looms darkly in the foreground or shrouds herself in a veil of opalescent haze through which her outlines can be faintly discerned; lifts her head above a foam-bath of white cloud or soars as if air-borne over skirts of pale mist. Sometimes, when a slight bright scirocco is blowing from the south-east – or, better still, the soft breeze of a perfect summer *tramontana* from due north – she stands close at hand, almost, one would say, within hailing distance, and displaying the exact photographic detail of a Canaletto, or else the more romantic values of a Guardi – let the wind change a point or two, and she will vanish from the skyline, leaving no trace. At times, when the atmosphere's right, she's the sovereign of a whole range of Sicilian hills – yet an hour later she may seem a solitary island, standing out of the sea in absolute isolation, as if the rest of Sicily had fallen to the bottom around her. The "floating cliffs" of the

Aeolian islands north of Milazzo can be hallucinatory enough, seeming to draw close to each other or drift apart like the floating gardens of Kashmir; but Erice too is seldom still, never appearing the same in substance or temper, eternally moody - now sharing in the Sicilian melancholy, now gay as the colours the sun splashes her with; for ever a deity of whims, for ever enigmatic and yet ineffable and rather weird. No wonder the ancients, native Emylians or travellers from Tyre or Crete or Carthage or Athens or the Tiber, seeing her mysterious profile as I see it from this stone bench, instantly divined her divinity. No wonder, coming up in their beaked ships from the west, the earliest navigators of this inland sea - Phoenicians, Greeks, Carthaginians, Romans - were intoxicated by her mutations and the versatile perfection of her profile, and perceived in her the source of fecundity and sexual delight and the promise of an imminent resurgence of life and its pleasures after the long denials of incarceration afloat. No wonder, safely ashore at Drepanon, these seamen were eager to make the long steep haul to the cliff edge at the summit where the priestesses of Venus Ericina (as she was known in Roman days) were ready to welcome them with, so to speak, open legs. The holy whores of Venus Ericina were renowned throughout the Roman world - a temple to the Eryx goddess in the capital itself was garrisoned with some of them. M. I. Finley, in his *Ancient Sicily*[5] writes: "Diodorus says that when Roman officials visit Eryx 'they put aside the gravity of office and enter into play and intercourse with slaves amidst great gaiety'." No wonder Eryx's supernatural masquerade has fascinated men for fifty centuries or more; it has fascinated me for these last six or seven years. I find myself constantly gazing over towards that fabulous mountain across twelve miles of sea, and find there sometimes comfort, sometimes perhaps an omen. I do it thoughtlessly, as some people finger an amulet or rosary or dash off a cautionary sign of the Cross, or give a circumspect twirl to a thaumaturgical finger-ring.

It is this amazing continuity of this female identity, steadfast in the human mind since first it bore the notion of the mothering

---

[5] Chatto & Windus, 1968 [Author's footnote]

of the gods, that more than anything seems to affirm the immense antiquity of this island - one feels that memory here reaches back to the birth of life, each stone and shrub and rocky profile being pregnant with experience as old as the fossil-shells tens of millions of years old which stud the tufa rock like rivets in a ship. Cybele, Rhea, Astarte, Aphrodite, Venus, Mary - the eternal matriarch under any name. And to these, here in and around Sicily, must be added Demeter/Ceres and with her of course the child Persephone. It was, of course, on the central plateau of Sicily, in the neighbourhood of Enna, that Demeter, the goddess of corn, taught men how to cultivate and harvest it. It was surely inevitable that when the ritual exactitudes pertaining to the various goddesses gradually became loosened down the centuries, these goddesses should bit by bit become confused together, or at any rate interchangeable; this was particularly likely in the region around Eryx where Demeter/Ceres and Aphrodite/Venus occupied thrones of equal and often competitive power. On our island, one of the major festivals of the year, held on the last Sunday of August, is that of the *Madonna Campagnola* - the "Rustic Madonna": her effigy carries a sheaf of corn: she has become for the day Ceres or Demeter, and the infant held in the crook of her left shoulder is obviously Persephone.[6] Now, the feast of Our Lady of Custonaci - the successor on Eryx as we have noted, to the classical goddesses - falls on this same day: one may take it that both Madonnas, our own and she of Custonaci, on the last Sunday of August, stand in for Demeter, recalling the fusion in the popular mind of this goddess with the Aphrodite/Venus of Eryx.

---

[6] Writing at the beginning of this century (*Sicily*, Methuen 1905), Douglas Sladen said: "The people at Enna could only be converted to Christianity by the identification of Ceres with the Virgin Mary. More than one antique statue of Ceres pursuing the girl-child still exists at Castrogiovanni (Enna) as the Virgin carrying the Child Jesus." The conventional Christian posture of Mother and Child obviously descends uninterruptedly from the equally conventional pagan posture: I remember an amphora of the Vth century BC in the Lipari Museum, depicting, I think, Aphrodite with the infant Eros held on her left forearm which is exactly the prototype of almost any Virgin-with-the-infant-Jesus from the Renaissance onwards. [Author's footnote]

When Damianina, or anybody else on our island, exclaims "Madre! Madre mia!" in astonishment, or exasperation, or alarm, she is not calling for the intervention of her own mother, or of the Mother of God, or even of the mother of the Love-god; although she doesn't know it herself, she is ten to one apostrophizing the Great Mother, the Phrygian Cybele, Magna Mater of the Romans, the primaeval Earth Goddess, fount and womb of all things. How puny the ordinary Christian memory seems, going back barely a couple of thousand years - an infant's span, compared with the hindsight of our island.

So often, in Sicily and her islands - and even here in my garden - some piece of antique myth and credence explains itself; suddenly these fantasies unravel themselves as simply as a piece of knitting. Last year, through the hottest, stillest weeks of the summer, when even early in the morning the hot silence still seems ominous, a man who had rented a cottage about half a kilometre away used to bicycle past my garden to fetch milk from a farm; and as he rode he whistled - a formless irrelevant whistling like the novice notes of a boy who has just cut himself a reed-pipe. Now, over this sea and in the breathless days which a Sicilian July and August bring, the atmosphere is so diaphanous and subtle that the speed and provenance of sound often appear to break the laws of physics - fishermen chat casually to each other across a mile of water separating their boats; one can hear the engines of a steamship passing twenty miles away beyond the northern horizon; the voices of my neighbours a thousand yards off are like echoes coming from an opposite direction. And often this subtilized air, lively and susceptible as vocal chords, throws sound around as children waft balloons - one can hardly guess where it is or whence it comes. And so it was with this man's whistling: I knew where he was, away to my left - yet often the sound seemed to come from the rocks to my right, beyond the Roman road; or else from behind the thicket in the very garden, among the figs or the cactus or from under the dark canopy of the carob. No wonder the ancients found the player of such elusive pipings: how inevitable was the discovery of Pan.

At this time, they're cutting the hay for summer feed, against three months or more of burned brown pasture. In the *paese* small boys in the piazza are scrambling for fledgling sparrows which, making a first adventurous flutter from their drainpipe nests, tumble down; some little boys throw them up again into the air to see them fly, but others hobble them on the end of a string, as other boys bobble crickets, and hope they'll make pets of them before they die. The meaning of cruelty can't be taught; it comes with the experience of cruelty. Our youngest, nine-year-old Duzzo, used to believe his puppy enjoyed being held by his hind paws and pushed along like a wheelbarrow; he used to think it was a kindness to take a chick-linnet from the nest and try to force bread down its throat. Now he's discovered that creatures have their rights. There's a story that a XIXth century ambassador (British of course) sounded the Pope about a society for the prevention of cruelty to animals. His Holiness replied that Christians owed nothing to animals, which didn't possess souls. Well, this is Italy, where every cat is born to be chased and every lizard made for stoning. And in the *paese* too, just now, everybody's eating with delight the first fresh young baby-green broad-beans, always a signpost to the *stagione*, the "season" of long summer just ahead.

In this month the *tonnara* is reconstructed off the island's northern coast, as it has been year after year in April since the Arabs brought it twelve or fourteen hundred years ago – or, probably, since the days of Carthage, a thousand years before that: the "tunnery" we might anglicize the word: the vast complex of note, like under-water catacombs, through which the huge tunny fish are channelled to their capture and death between mid-May and mid-June as unsuspecting they swim in herds from the depths of the western Mediterranean to spawn under the warming spring sun in the shallows about these islands and the shore of Sicily. Year by year, century after century, they forge ahead along the surface of the sea, prancing like dolphins – to be trapped, hundreds of them, and killed at the very threshold of love and procreation.

To the island and islanders, till a couple of years ago, the annual tunny-fishing season (or "campaign" as it's known locally) marked, so to say, the economic New Year. The tunny fishery and the cannery which it fed provided the fuel that drove the island's economy – four or five hundred people were fully employed in the factory, a hundred or so fishermen enjoyed two months affluence, relatively, after ten lean months of contest against diminishing shoals and prohibitive storms. The shops, the craftsmen's benches, the markets, all became enlivened by the extra flow of money whose source annually was the *tonnara*; the fishery and its ancillaries formed the economic heart of the island, and the April start of the preparations for the fresh season seemed to set off a new annual cycle of conception, gestation and parturition – it began the yearly process of economic renewal. A closure of the cannery, and the marketing of the tunny-catch "abroad", that is in Palermo and Trapani or even the Italian mainland, must mean about four hundred wage earners out of work and the equivalent of some two thousand pounds sterling *a week* "taken out of the economy", as financial editors say. And that is what happened in 1968, and has been happening since. But more of that, and more about the *mattanza,* the massacre of the tunny – that gruesome, appalling, yet perversely fascinating spectacle of gladiatorial battle when the sea itself becomes diluted with blood.

2. The Arrival

In November 1965 I was back in Sicily after two years away. For fifteen years I had at intervals been moving from place to place southwestwards from Apulia down through Calabria to Sicily - seeking, I suppose, some ideal spot where, settling there, contentment would come. On Sicily, because I need the sea and enjoy mountains only at their foot, I had lived in a dozen places round the north and east coasts from Palermo to Noto south of Siracusa, including all the Lipari islands, one after another. This time, I asked myself: why not the west coast? What about Trapani, which we have never seen? So I took the train which, after the famous *mafioso* towns of Partinico, Alcamo and Castellammare, settles down for the long pull up through the gathering mountains, and half way to the top for a flashing glimpse of Segesta, most immaculate of Doric shrines, still after twenty-five centuries alone and aloof in the privacy of these empty, violent heights. The train climbs heavily, puffing - those days steam still took over from Alcamo junction to the coast - and then, running easily over the neck between Monte Grande and the high black brow of Eryx, begins to slip downwards towards the western sea. And suddenly approaching the dead-end of Trapani, one sees the islands. Standing offshore on the left they seem, as Sicilian islands do, to be floating free, black and eremetical against the sinking round red sun, the largest with its long, five-humped crest, that known as Homer's "Goat Islands", lying southwards towards the Marsala point; a bit to the north the small, low-lying hulk of its nearest neighbour, Levanzo; and between the two, another ten miles out to sea, the second largest, with a population of 1200 named, today, Marettimo, "on the horizon all highest up towards the West" - old Samuel Butler's rendering of Odysseus's words to King Alcinous about his own island of Ithaca.[7] It's Butler's thesis in his *Authoress of the Odyssey*[8] (a

[7] *Odyssey*, Bk IX, v.25 [Author's footnote]

[8] First published 1897; reissued 1967 in Phoenix Books by University of Chicago Press. [Author's footnote]

woman of Trapani, he amusingly and persuasively argues) that almost the whole voyage was a circumnavigation of Sicily and that Ithaca must be recognized from internal and topographical evidence as an amalgam of Trapani and this outer island of Marettimo.

Trapani, though an interesting harbour, gives most visitors an unmerited impression of an offhand and rather shabby town. "Not a place to pause in", wrote Peter Quennell in *Spring in Italy*[9] rather too hastily - tourists who do bother to pause, discover a very individual little city, full of hidden beauties and charms and unusual delights of history, architecture and legend. But all through my time there, my thoughts and eyes were on the island. Any island is to my aptitude for unsociability a lure; the largest of them with the beautiful name of Favignana, was soon tugging as compellingly as a siren's song. A few days after Christmas, therefore, I crossed over in the *aliscafo* - that odious marine vehicle on stilts which the English unimaginatively call a hydrofoil, while the Italians label it charmingly, though unwarrantably, a "winged hull".

These waters, often sapphire blue, more often grey, which incessantly batter or suckle, ferocious or idly tender, at the feet of three small and sparsely inhabited islands in a patch of the Mediterranean where few strangers pass or give a second glance, have, in their obscure way, played an extraordinary part in Europe's history. It was in these waters, within sight of my own *terrazzo*, that the Punic fleet was finally smashed by Rome in 241 BC and Europe thus secured from African colonization. It was past here that a British squadron, including, I think, the then HMS Lowestoft, sailed in 1718 to beat the Spanish off Cape Passaro, the southernmost tip of Sicily. It was in the lee of this very island that Napoleon's fleet sheltered (our islands still today often provide shelter to ships driven beneath our cliffs by winter gales) on the way to Egypt; and within view of it Nelson's ships must have gone down to Syracuse for water and "over 40,000 gallons of Sicilian wine"[10] before sailing on to the Nile. And it

---

[9] Weidenfeld & Nicolson, 1952. [Author's footnote]

[10] D. Mack Smith, *History of Sicily*, Chatto & Windus, 1968. [Author's footnote]

was the sight of these islands on the horizon that told Garibaldi's "thousand" they were nearing Marsala, where their landing in 1860 brought an end to the Bourbon kingdom of the Two Sicilies and secured for Cavour and the Savoy king in Turin a united Italian realm. This is how one of Garibaldi's enthusiasts saw these islands - Giuseppe Abba, whose age at the time was 22:

> A lovely view of little islands; may seem just risen from the sea. There is green of all shades, there is a dazzling cliff, and everything enshrined in an atmosphere of blue. The islands have a silvery fringe at their feet.... The King of Naples keeps his political prisoners....

It was on our island of Favignana ("Goat Island") that the Bourbon kings kept their political prisoners; and it was on this same island, and on most of the other little islands strung around Italy's coast that Mussolini kept his political prisoners; and here on Favignana today we have some 150 convicts, murderers and the like, doing anything from thirty years to the rest of their days, housed in the antique fortress known for two centuries among old lags as *la fossa*, The Pit - or, if you like, The Grave. Having plenty of small islands handy makes gaoling easier.

It was early May when young Abba (whose diary of the Thousand has been published in English) saw the islands; and so "green of all shades" their flanks can well have been - after the April rains and before, by June, nearly all vegetation has been scorched to straw. He was lucky, too, with his light - he must have had the sun just at the right station in the sky, and the right kind of wind, to catch the "dazzle" of the cliffs, the "atmosphere of blue" and the "silvery fringe" - though this last he overreckoned, for long silvery beaches of the Calabrian kind are, on our islands, the exception rather than the rule - generally the shore is a black barrier of jagged tufa. One may often, given the right climatic moment, see the islands quite as Abba saw them: lively with leaping colour and brilliant with the light caught between the blues of sky and sea; yet a veer of the wind or an hour's advance in the day can change their aspect as instantly as the electrician at the switches in the wings can change the character of the stage. That "green of all shades" is more often a monotone; a lichenous sage or matt olive which, as the last rains are left behind and the daily hammering of the sun gathers power, quickly turns to a tawny grey, the colour, perhaps, of a lion, and the mountain becomes what in my mind's eye is always the "bare brown mountain". It is, then, I think, at its most beautiful: the mountain then seems to me to reveal all the strength and ruthlessness and yet too the sadness and pathos of Sicily - like a growling caged lion.

The green of spring is delicate and fresh and welcome, - like cool water when one's thirsty; but it mustn't last too long - too much green can become sickly. Norman Douglas laments somewhere the "salad green" of England; and Wilde talks almost identically of the "wearisome green of England - I only like green in art". Coming up by train from the toe of Italy to the hip, I'm always given a turn of queasiness by the abrupt change in the colourscape, somewhere between Naples and Rome, when the dear dry drabness of the south changes to verdure too flourishing for emotional comfort; and I find the lush green tumult of Tuscany, abruptly replacing the harsh summer glitter of Sicily and my island - so close to the beginnings of things - almost nauseatingly upstart. In the South, the solitary solemn cypress, or a small funerary avenue of them, utters a restraining note of grave and venerable serenity to the dry torrents of tawny violence that surround them; but the lavish groves and copses and even plantations of them in the North have the effect of too many emeralds on an overdressed woman. When one lives in the South one comes to love the harsh yellow aridity of the land, as one loves the tough, cynical and candid simplicity of the people. When my eyes have to soak up the sugar-sweet vegetable greenery of a Northern landscape, I feel it's something of an emotional fig leaf drawn over the stark nakedness of rock and clay, like Christmas decorations; and I think of the unglamourised veracity of the bare brown mountain.

The island wasn't looking its best the first time I came. It was near January, when wind from any quarter can cut you in half with cold. A flat slate sky lay close over the long ridge of the mountain; the heaving sea was smoke-coloured and fitfully broken by curls of white - even a light wind blows the tops off the waters that run between these islands. It was the sort of weather that makes one feel, as one so often feels in the southern

Mediterranean, in winter, twelve hundred miles north of it.

And yet, when I looked around me from the narrow stone-flagged jetty, I knew I had come to stay. Something told me that here happiness was being held out for the taking. I knew at once that this was an island to fall in love with, though I could see little lovable - a big bare mountain above a small grey jumpy bay; a couple of rusty trawlers alongside, and another of small trading craft discharging gas cylinders and crates of wine; and behind me, the drab flat roofs of a village crouching low against the sea. Here was no picture-postcard scenery, nothing for a travel-brochure to gush about. This was just an immense, lonely, lump of geology, without accessories.

The mountain just then, because of the winter rains which would continue on and off into April, had a patina of greenish shadow, as if its limestone slopes had been thickly sprayed with dried herbs. Across the bay, at the mountain's foot, there ran like a dado the long low frontage of the century-old canning factory; a charming curious sweep of one-storey gables and arches and portcullises, with four tall Victorian chimneys, like a mid-nineteenth century engraving.

This was no tourists' island: it was a workaday island, almost functional, without frills, sentimental or dramatic, spectacular or romantic. Here was the *paese* where the people lived, some 4000 of them all told; there, beyond, were the fields and pastures and stone-quarries where they worked; here was the *porto* where the small trading schooners berthed and in an angle of the bay the little fishing harbour crowded with high-prowed coloured boats. Even the fortress that dizzily crowns Santa Caterina, the mountains' highest crest, overlooking the African sea, had always had a purpose: first a Saracen stronghold and watch-tower; then, from Norman times, an inaccessible castle a thousand feet up where the seigneur and his people could wait till an enemy siege tired, then, under the other emperor, Charles V, a fort and crow's nest from which warning of Barbary corsairs was given; in later years its dungeons held King "Bomba"'s intellectual captives - men like Poerio and Nicotera - after the worsted revolution of 1848; and until recently it was used by the Navy as a "semaphore". Today, supplanted I suppose by things like radar, it's an empty antique.

Wandering through the *paese*, sitting enchanted in the spacious *piazza*, paved and tree-encircled and grown up around the eighteenth-century church, I was thinking: nothing here that can be called a "tourist attraction"; nothing here a tourist agent could be tempted to "develop" - no flashy ribbon beaches, no spectacular "views" or obvious sites for a discothèque or dance-hall or "lido" apart from the one small modest one already in existence which any English "resort" would turn up its nose at. Years later I saw a *Sunday Times* headline in its "travel section": "HOW LONG CAN A RIVIERA STAY SECRET? - Europe still has a Riviera waiting to be discovered - the coast of southern Turkey".... Poor Turkey, I thought then - but that January of 1966 my regrets weren't needed: here's no kind of Riviera, God be thanked, not even a secret one.... Alas, later on I found that a "developer" can fabricate his own "riviera".... "So it goes" - to borrow Kurt Vonnegut's laconic comment on death and destruction.

Nobody with a taste for human squalour should quit a new place without visiting a wine-shop; so I filled the wait for the *aliscafo* that would take me back to Sicily in 'Masino's, as I later learned it was. For ten years or more I've been a frequenter of these dingy, dirty, dismal places from one end of the Two Sicilies to the other, from the Adriatic to the Ionian and the Tyrrhenian; chiefly because it's one of the whimsicalities of Italian custom that in this wine-growing country one can't drink wine anywhere else. I suppose the reason is that, Italians being an abstemious people, nobody respectable drinks wine apart from meals and therefore a place where wine is drunk is frequented only by the unrespectable.

Roman writers in the last days of the Republic - Cicero, Virgil, Horace - described the wine-shops of Rome with words like dirty, greasy, smoky, grimy; today's wine-shops, which one may suppose are little different from their antique forbears, merit exactly the same adjectives; it seems odd, but it does look as though it were a point of honour among publicans to keep one's tavern dirtier than the next. A Fulbright scholar might well choose the history and ethos of the South Italian wine-shop as the matter of his thesis: it's a subject going right back to antiquity, but he'd need a hardy liver. The wine-shop has little in common with the French working-man's *bistro*, or with the four-ale bar of the British pub (and nothing whatever to do with the saloon bar!); its real business is the retailing of wine to respectable people who bring their bottles to be filled for the family table; there's a slight disreputability of the secondary side of the trade – the sozzling of wine by men who enjoy sozzling. I'm used to these dingy planes, often reached down cellar steps, always offering the stranger a cavernous and ungenial welcome; and I always go into the one I don't know with some shyness – it's rather like walking into a club in St. James's one's not a member of. There are always, even in sober Sicily, a few old soaks sitting fustily around, who seem to glare resentfully at intruders; and generally there's one of those inquiring men whose innocent sociability is so maddeningly well-meant, wanting to know how many children you've got, what rent you pay, how old you are, what you're doing here, and if you haven't brought your wife, *why not*?

But here at Masino's nobody gave me a look; just the quickest inquiring glance from the few fishermen sitting around or arguing at the bar – enough to note that here was a foreigner and no business of theirs what he was about. Now, almost anywhere in Sicily, a foreigner's presence in places where foreigners don't usually go, instantly draws curiosity – if not, of people on the make, than surely of the simply curious. "Are your teeth your own?" they'll sympathetically ask. But on Favignana no: heaven knows when last a foreigner, apart from occasional sailors, had sat down in Masino's; and I know that during the next three years no others did. This was my first lesson in the land's absolute respect for persons: for everybody's right to be what he is and mind his own business. Nowhere, ever, have I seen less agitation about other people's singularities or less meddling in other people's concerns. Nowhere is a person's title to his own individuality more honoured.

Masino's, I must say, fond as I later became of it, seemed that first day more unsavoury than most of its kind: it hadn't even the architectural merits of many Sicilian boozers – the shapeliness of the vaulted ceiling, the cunning of the antique walls, the craftsman's beauty of those huge oval casks of brass-hooped oak built into a wall like regal sarcophagi (at Masino's the casks are piled in pyramids outside the w.c.). Looking round, I thought I'd got into a proper thieves' kitchen: the place seemed to hold more malignity and blight than a mere pub deserved (I ask myself why, now that I know it so well) – it was like a scene, perhaps, from Mayhew's London; or one of those vagabonds' dens in Mark Twain's *Prince and the Pauper*. Even Masino's own semi-squint, which in fact added humour to his benevolent face, seemed disquieting. In one murky corner of the inner room, some shadowy men were crouched over an enormous caldron which stood on the floor, eating bits of the stewed squid it contained with their fingers – silently, ritually, as if taking part in same frightful cannibal solemnity. The faces of these few fishermen – which, once familiar, became the picture of kindly innocence – appeared that day to leer and threaten; the musty stink of stale wine and smoke mixed with the smell of men who lived by handling fish, acquired an unimaginably sinister origin.

Altogether I felt I'd landed in a very odd place. And suddenly I discovered it was even odder: a bizarre kind of comedy was being played almost each minute between the street-door and the bar in the outer room, as more and more fishermen, mostly from middle-age up to near-decrepitude, kept coming in. These men, most wearing whiskers and wedding rings, many sixty and seventy years old, all rugged with masculinity, were jovially exchanging greetings by chucking each other, not under the chin, but under the testicles; or by diving a hand from the rear in between a friend's buttocks and affectionately tickling his arse. A popular joke was to tiptoe up behind some unsuspecting old fellow standing at the bar and give him a hilarious feel under the bum; this was sure of a good laugh all round. One bluff-looking mariner I remarked returning from the *gabinetto* behind the barrels with his penis still dangling out of his trousers, as if he'd absent-mindedly forgotten to return it – this brought chuckles form the old gentlemen sitting around. I began to wonder whether I'd arrived in one of those "buggers' clubs" about which some British people were so upset during the debates over the "consenting adults" bill; yet it seemed unlikely that so tiny an island would possess a club of this sort of magnitude – a considerable number of the island's fathers and grandfathers were there at the moment. There wasn't, of course, a bugger among them: all this equivocal jocularity was simply a genial old custom with origins buried I never discovered where. Fond fathers, however, are often in the habit of playfully and proudly grabbing their infant sons by the genitals.

Suddenly my attention was drawn away from this matter by a singular figure which, for a second, I thought was dancing, in the middle of the outer room – I was sitting almost in the doorway between the two, and so could watch both sides. Though long accustomed to the deformities of the Italian South, I felt that the creature I now saw was about the most inauspicious and disturbing I'd come across; but nobody else in the cantina paid any attention to him. Plainly, for one thing, this extraordinary presence was taken for granted; for another, every man there was too much engrossed by the vehemence of his own arguments to think of anything else. Yet none was more vehement than this mute clown: his lust for declamation was unending. But it was a soundless decimation: an eloquence that issued silently from passionately miming lips, grimacing skull-like features and hollow eyes that looked through us all at some unseen and unhearing audience; while his arms sawed and swung, beckoned and poked and probed in the air and his whole body, tiny and wispish like an emaciated child's, writhed and twisted with a kind of frenzied urgency. But this unhappy creature's deaf-and-dumbness, unlike that of his four or five fellow-mutes on the island, was part of a larger palsy which kept his scarecrow frame in a constant turmoil of motion and his mouth in a torrent of unspoken speech and untutored rhetoric. He appeared to be perpetually enacting a theatrical role of scarcely bearable drama; flinging his arms in the tortured gestures of one passion or another, twisting his horrific gargoyled face into grimaces of fearful threat or the agony of despair, and declaiming an unceasing flow of soundless eloquence. It was like a tumultuous scene in a film drama, with the sound turned off. These eerie contortions continued, I later saw, without interruption wherever he might be – walking through the piazza, sitting outside the stone cabin he lived in on the edge of the *paese*, resting from the summer sun beneath a mulberry tree. Winter and summer he wore a long, torn overcoat, which hung in tattered folds down to his ankles, and he looked as if he never had enough to eat. Yet he always had money for cigarettes and for several glasses of wine (which didn't seem to make him more or less mad); and he seemed fascinated by the complicated contortions of his own personality, engrossed in the kaleidoscopic animations of his eternally private mind. And who knows: these passionate gestures without shape and these outpourings of wordless and soundless utterance - mayn't they be the frenzied struggle for release of a shackled and gagged genius? But what can an analphabetical deaf-mute St. Vitus do with his sepultured masterpieces?

Within two or three weeks I was on amiable drinking terms with all these fishermen, and others besides, for Masino's - the nearest of the four wineshops to the *porto* - was more like a fishermen's club than a public house; and Masino himself was soon to become a friend. Before long, too, the tiny deaf-mute hobgoblin, when he saw me across the street, would pass the time of day in a fantastic charade of nods, mouthings and bodily gyrations, with all his limbs flying.

3. The Family

I feel no affection for Signor Alcamese and his wife, but a lot of gratitude. She's a wooden-faced woman who, it's said, hasn't smiled at a customer during her forty years behind their counter, selling anything from bottled gas to knitting needles and petrol and from brassieres to postage-stamps and tobacco. He's a self-important seventy-year-old, so pot-bellied that he leans backwards while walking, to keep his balance. Half a century ago he came from Sicily to open his business on Favignana; he now owns more house-property in the *paese* than anybody else and is a town councillor (Christian Democrat, of course, though I've never seen him at Mass except on municipal occasions). He was one of the first on the island to buy a car, when a few years ago cars became "status symbols" - he uses it to drive the two hundred metres between his shop and his home. He loves only money and his piddling little position within the commune - every village has its Signor Alcamese, often, like himself, a "foreigner".

I didn't like Signor Alcamese from the start; not even at our first meeting in the shop, when he raised his eyes ecstatically to the ceiling and sighed: "I have a passion for flowers". And yet I owe to him, really, all my happiness of these years. He it was who provided me with my first house - just when, a week after my first visit, I was giving up the search as hopeless. And it was in his shop, by one of those extraordinary fortuities which by a minute's margin can switch one's life in the most unexpected ways, that I got to know Gigi and his father Tommaso and thence became a permanent member of their family.

The "house" which Signor Alcamese allowed me to rent from him was a warehouse or store which he'd jerry-built behind the *porto*; it cost me no more than three pounds a month, but a Sicilian would have paid two. At the first rain the concrete floor was awash in two inches, and some of my books were soaked: when I informed Signor Alcamese, he said I was of course mistaken - the roof he'd built couldn't leak, he told me sternly. When this had happened four more times and I'd taken four more complaints to the shop, all within the first month, and all made light of, I put my keys on the counter beneath the Signora's hard-grained features, and said I was leaving next day. Both were deeply affronted, and neither has since acknowledged any "Good Day" from me. I moved to my little house in the country which Tommaso, Gigi's father, had found for me, and almost at once Signor Alcamese rebuilt the roof of that "house" - and the next tenant had to pay four pounds a month.

Despairing of finding a room, on my second visit to Goat Island, I dared to ask this unsmiling woman in the tobacconist's on my way down to the port. "Well," she said ungently, "there's the *magazzino*" (store). As she spoke, a tall, pallid, long-faced boy came in, beautiful, grave and shy. He's come for petrol for his father's *motoretta;* at that date Alcamese was the island's only purveyor of petrol.

"Gigi", she told the boy, "go and call my husband. Say there's an English wants the *magazzino*". While the boy was away, fetching my landlord-to-be, a man came in wearing a long white apron dappled with blood - Don Pino's, a butcher's shop, was next door: an enormous man - enormous in height, sinew and presence, but lean as a mule. He and the signora exchanged a couple of Sicilian sentences, and the man threw me a quick glance of curiosity and as quickly, with the good manners of the island, turned away. Obviously he'd asked about the boy's whereabouts, and been told about the foreigner; and then I saw that thirty years ago he'd have been the boy's double: this was clearly the father.

Thus it was through the unlovable Alcamese that, so very soon, I became inducted into a family whose members became dearer to me than anybody I've known since childhood; a family which, during the next few years, was to show me as I'd never been shown before, how absolutely good, simple human beings can be.

Gigi, that day, did the bargaining, while I bought household necessities - wire camp-bed, mattress, blankets, gas-ring, table and the rest; he fetched a handcart and loaded everything on to it; at my new house he carried the things in and decided where they were to stand. Ha was startled when I gave him a thousand-lire note (surely twelve shillings wasn't overtipping for nearly half a day's work?) He was just fifteen then, and a schoolboy still.

His mother, Damianina, told me long after that he'd run into the house that day unusually for him, excited - a taciturn, uncommunicative person. He'd burst the door open, calling: "*M-ma, m-ma*! The English gave me this! That one (*idro*) gave me a thousand!" - and he held out the note. "I'll keep it for you," she said, and put it under the second of a row of best coffee-cups at the far end of the dresser, which was where she kept his money: each of the children had a special cache.

Gigi, helping this foreigner, hadn't looked for payment - a cigarette perhaps, or a 100-lire piece, not more. Where else in Italy - where in England for that matter - would a fifteen-year-old have brought such a windfall as this straight to his mother? But the island is like that: the local boys don't look upon each foreign visitor as a victim to cadge from; here are ten square miles of Italy where the curse of tourism hasn't yet started to corrupt.

Next morning he came, before going to school, my first visitor; and offhandedly took an object out of his pocket and put it in my hand. "For you", he said sharply. "You needn't have it if you don't want it." It was a sea-horse, a hippocampus, perfectly preserved and undamaged - he'd caught it among the rock-pools beyond the piazza one summer as a child. Since then, my *cavallino di mare* has hung over my pillow where some people hang a crucifix or a pin-up or a diploma of honour. He had come to invite me to eat with the family.

On the seashore north of the piazza, where Gigi took me the next Sunday morning before the time came for dinner at his house, which was to be my ceremonial introduction to the family, we found Nicòla, a school friend, absorbedly shooting at small crabs among the rock-pools with a bow and arrow made from two spokes from an old umbrella. This weapon is commonly fabricated by the small boys of the island and used for fishing and crabbing (some South American Indians too fish with bow and arrow), and also for hunting lizards along the stone walls which enclose the *campagna* fields (though happily, to my mind, the lizards are generally too quick for the hunters). This is a pleasant example of how primitive inventiveness in different continents can devise similar answers to the same problem. Years ago at Crotone, in Calabria, I watched boys catching crabs by thrusting long reeds, which the creatures clawed, into crannies among the rocks - exactly as, thirty years earlier, I'd watched Moorish boys near Rabat in Morocco luring scorpions out of their holes by pushing down long grass-stalks. Some boys at Crotone - more advanced, I suppose, technologically - used for crab catching a cunning sort of slipknot at the end of a rod. I shall always remember that day: my first with the family. It was one of those rarely windless winter days, with a hot sun after a stormy night. The great motherly flank of the mountain was sage-green under the broadside of morning light. It was Sunday morning, with no school and no work. The shops were busy till midday and, its being Sunday, the butchers were selling all the meat they had (on Monday butchers are shut). The fishermen, storm-bound last night, were already wearing their Sunday suits and on their way to Masino's for the usual dominical drink. There was a vaguely festive feeling abroad, brought about by a concurrence of fine weather and a general day off.

But Gigi's father, Tommaso, was working that morning, as every Sunday morning. Each weekday he worked at the *stabilimento*, the tunnyfish cannery across the harbour, where he was a foreman; every Saturday evening and Sunday morning, and on any morning of *festa* too, he did the heavy work in Don Pino's butchery; Don Pino was past eighty, and Papà was a butcher by trade. Most evenings, too, after work at the *stabilimento*, there are jobs to do at the *macello*, the abattoir which is a stone shed belonging to Don Pino; Papà is the slaughterman called by any of the island's four butchers who has beasts to kill. Yet I don't think these jobs together bring in weekly more than L12 to L15, for a family of six people - a family, however, always beautifully dressed, always well-fed, always being given toys and sweets and ices; who live in a pleasant four-roomed house in the pleasantest corner of the piazza and have TV, a washing-machine, a motor-scooter and the *motoretta*. Papà would work through the night too, if that could make his family happier.

There's wasn't any ceremony about that first meal. There's little ceremony about anything on our island: an attempt at over-politeness, any effusion of feelings above the level of ordinariness becomes embarrassing and people don't quite know how to react. Affection is so strong here, it can afford to be taciturn.

Gigi led the way in, calling "*Mma, mma*" – the Sicilian equivalent of "Mum", and Damianina came away from the stove, wiping her hands on her apron. "Io sono la mamma", the words which, said by any Sicilian mother, make her at that moment the most important person in the world, the symbol of all maternity, the heiress of the Great Mother. Then came simple greetings from the others: Maria, the eldest daughter; eight-year-old Caterina, a lively and passionate miniature of her sister; and "our Duzzo", then three and a half , sweet-mannered and yet impish as one of Serapotta's artful *putti* which, in certain Palermo churches, take the mickey out of saints and angels, blond and blue-eyed, – "our German". They didn't gape at the *straniero*, the foreign oddity, or stand awkwardly, tongue-tied; they simply went on with what they'd been doing.

Then Duzzo, who'd been looking through the glass panes of the street door, suddenly shouted excitedly *'u papà, 'u papà* ("the father") the family cry went up, *viene papà, viene papà* (pap's coming), and Damianina ran to the stove to drop the spaghetti into the boiling pot (it was Sunday; therefore, *past'asciutta* – "dry pasta", spaghetti with tomato sauce). By now Duzzo's tiny legs were carrying him like the flashing spokes of a wheel to meet Papà, and, looking out, we could see Tommaso across the length of the piazza with his patrician head tilted high and the long bloodstained butcher's apron looped over one arm.

At the beginning there were conversational impediments. Bad Italian spoken with a British accent and bad Italian with a Sicilian don't always reach the right answer. Papà's Italian is almost wholly Sicilian: my conversations with him, if Gigi's not there to interpret, are largely guess-work. Now and then he'll make a show out of spelling out the headlines in the local newspaper. "Blood of the Madonna!" he grumbles, "I need spectacles – can't read no more!" Sweet Damianina can't read or write her own name. "No, Michele", she told me sadly, "I don't know how to read." Gigi and Caterina, school-taught, speak Italian and read and write worse. Even my written Italian was better than Gigi's:

he'd bring his exercises to me for spelling and elementary grammar! State education on the island is only about a generation old: not many people of Papà's age are literate.

But now there's school for all from the age of six (Duzzo proudly started in the autumn of 1968), with the obligatory tribulation of exams and holiday cramming and the emotional strains over promotion or relegation. But little is learned, because few have much inclination for learning and there's little in the curriculum to arouse one; and before a boy of 15 has learned to speak Italian properly he's made to waste two or three hours a week "learning" French, of which he acquires not one usable phrase by the time his schooldays are over. That small boys on Goat Island shall "learn" French is, however, laid down by the Ministry in Rome – I suppose in order that the Christian-Democrat government may show the world on paper how liberal and progressive Italian education is, even in the remotest outposts, where the young are "taught" French, but leave school unable to write Italian or count without their fingers.

So at first our talk, and our comprehension of it, weren't fluent: Damianina was constantly throwing asides at Maria or Gigi: "What is the Christian saying", "What is it the Christian wants?" – for at that stage I was still in the unintimate category of *cristiano.* At first, while I was still in the Alcamese store-room, Damianina insisted on sending me something cooked every day – Gigi or Maria brought it: a covered can of *pasta in brodo* or the like, or some grilled fish; but soon after, when my terrible English prickliness was crumbling before the compelling kindness of this sweet family, I began to eat my daily meal at their house. I soon had my regular place: my back to the piazza door and Gigi on my right; Papà opposite, with Duzzo next to him, and the women to the left, among the saucepans. By watching and occasionally asking, Damianina discovered my likes and preferences; soon I was one of the family and no longer just a *cristiano.*

Tommaso would sometimes put me right on points of behaviour. From him I learned it's ill-bred to refuse a cup of coffee from a bare acquaintance whom one distantly salutes on entering a bar. "No, no", you protest, "so kind of you, but I don't *want* another coffee, I've just *drunk* a coffee and I *couldn't* drink another, I swear it!" All to no purpose. *Mi offendo,* says the acquaintance, "I'll be offended": and he holds his palms up to the front to show how offended he'll be. By that time the coffee will have been ordered, and there's nothing to do but drink it. Or, if you firmly hold out and get away before the coffee's ordered, you'll be told, next time you're in that bar, and order a coffee because you want one, that it's already been paid for "by Signor so-and-so". So now you owe him a coffee. The tyranny of *mi offendo* can be trying: the nervous expectancy each time one enters a bar of either giving offence or drinking an unwanted coffee, and the nervous strain of trying to remember to get in first with the proffer of a coffee.

I also learned from Papà that it can be bad manners to say "thank you". Norman Douglas has noted in *Old Calabria* that the word *grazie*, thank you, except from the "most cultured", isn't heard south of Naples. This is not quite true, of course; you do say "thank you" for some service which has plainly incommoded the doer of it – to a person you've halted in the street to ask for information, or to one who's come out of his way to bring a message to your house. But one doesn't say "thank you" in the ordinary course of daily affairs – to a shopkeeper when he gives one the change, to the man who brings a fresh *bombola* of liquid gas for the cooker. Nor does one say "thank you", as we northerners do, to the "no" which refuses a second helping or an offered cigarette. Papà didn't like my formal English gratitude – my automatic thank you every time he poured me a glass of wine, each time Mamma handed me a plate of pasta or Caterina sprinkled cheese over it.

"You mustn't say *grazie, grazie,* like that", he reproached me one dinner-time. "It's not said – *no si dice cosi.* When you thank me for filling your glass, you're acknowledging that you feel you're under an obligation to me; and that means that you think I filled your glass in order to put you under an obligation to me, and so I'm offended by your *grazie.* I fill your glass because I see you need some wine, just as you would do for me". After that I did my best; yet "thank you" is a habit remarkably difficult to break.

But there's another sort of "thank you" which one looks for after giving a present. One wants, in exchange for one's gift, to be told what a good and kind person one is. Otherwise, half the fun of making a gift is missed and one's vanity is offended. Vanity this may be; but I confess I'm disappointed when, full of smug delight over the pleasure I think I'm bestowing, my gift is received in dead silence and a nod like a signed quittance. The children are never disappointing: their enjoyment of something new is the thanks one wants; Gigi, thought naturally reticent, is always calmly and sweetly appreciative of anything given him. But the response of the grown-ups, until one gets used to it, does often seem a let-down - because it's negative; one's gift is taken and put on one side like a pail of pig-food. Perhaps here again the matter of "obligation" comes in: a show of warmth might indicate a sense of indebtedness. But one learns that, in fact, their appreciation is profound and always remembered. Norman Douglas, in the same book, attributed this apparent callousness towards donors to the Greek convention exemplified by Achilles's ingratitude when his mother and the god Hephaestus went to a lot of trouble to provide him with a suit of magic armour. The Greeks, Douglas said (and the Calabrians about whom he was writing), regard a thing given "as a thing found, a *hermaion*, a happy hit in the lottery of life; the giver is the blind instrument of fortune". In Sicily, too, there's some truth in this - certainly anything found is legitimately the finder's, as the Arabs of North Africa consider it left purposely by Allah: our children once found a pair of spectacles somebody had dropped; they were solemnly presented to *la Nonna*, grandma, whose eyes they didn't suit at all; but nobody thought about the unfortunate who had dropped them. There's no truth, however - certainly none on this island - in a further judgement Douglas delivers on the Calabrian estimation of a gift: "what it would fetch if bartered or sold, or, if to be kept, how far its possession may raise the recipient in the eyes of other men." Truly, a gift of some value is enjoyed the more if it's praised for its worth "if bartered or sold". Gifts aren't in any circumstances bartered or sold; anything received, even a cheap toy, is an addition to the family chattels and, though "belonging" to the person it was given to, becomes also an increment to the total 'personality' of a family utterly united and indivisible. A bicycle, say, given to Gigi, is "his", but any member of the family may use it and it becomes an integral furnishing of the joint home. A toy for Duzzo, once it's grown out of, is conserved in the house, perhaps as an ornament, until one day there's a grandchild to play with it. There's a sanctity in family property, an almost mystical worth unconcerned with intrinsic value, which rules out any thought of "barter or sale".

From Tommaso I learned also that here, as further east in Magna Graecia, there's a blind spot for the comic side of things, a deadly earnestness in the face of absurdity. I'd had a first lesson in this nearly ten years earlier at Taranto, on the Ionian coast of Apulia, during the festivities in honour of Saints Cosmo and Damian, whose renown is prestigious in southern Italy, especially on its eastern side, and whose thaumaturgical powers have made them patrons of the medical profession. An exciting happening in these elaborate celebrations is the launching into the air above the Little Sea of a number of enormous paper balloons, onion-shaped and almost as big as space capsules: open-mouthed at the base so that, held briefly over a pile of burning straw, they fill with hot air and are borne splendidly over the water into which, from their zenith of two or three hundred feet, they rather seedily descended. The first balloon to go up was blazoned with portraits of the two saints in their colours of red and green (which all the small boys of the town also donned that day) and the words VIVA I MEDICI MARTIRI – "Hurrah for the martyred doctors". The second bore a picture of the Madonna and the words viva MARIA SANTISSIMA: and the third, the arms of the city of Taranto and 'VIVA L'AUTORITA LOCALE – "Hurrah for the local authorities", the mayor and councillors, the chief of police and the carabineers, the admiral, the archbishop and the canons.... I thought this so hilariously funny – the Establishment, the architects of the whole *festa,* sending up a balloon in their own praise – that I described what I'd seen to a local acquaintance in the wine-shop, expecting at least a chuckle. "Oh yes", he commented with unsmiling gravity, "you see our local *autorità* are held in great respect". He was, of course, a Christian Democrat.

Tommaso hugely enjoyed a joke of the teasing sort, heavily making fun of Damianina or some of the children and requiring a lot of elbow-jabbing and some enormous theatrical winks; but his apprehension of what's in the north called humour isn't quick. One dinner-time, waiting for the pasta, Damianina gave me the hunk of parmesan and the grater. As I set to work I thought of another Taranto story, and told it to amuse Papà. "There was a *cantina* where I was such a regular customer that I sometimes helped the *padrone* by filling the wine-bottles from the casks or by grating the cheese for the pasta. The first time I did the cheese, everybody in the place began shouting at me, *fischiare, fischiare*!, "whistle! whistle!"- a local witticism saying that so long as the person with the cheese kept whistling he couldn't nibble bits of it on the sly. While I was chuckling at my own tale, Papà looked at me almost severely. "Oh, no", he said flatly, "you mustn't believe that. Nobody would *really* want you to whistle." The Sicilian sense of humour isn't readily susceptible to the mildly ludicrous.

4. The Butter

When Damianina bit an inch off my butter as she was bringing it round to me in its Milan-labeled wrapping (butter's a "foreign" substance, not native Sicilian), I must have looked surprised, as I felt. I sat staring at the row of big, matronly toothmarks, perfectly excavated like a dentist's impressions, before melting the butter onto the spaghetti. I knew she was looking at me; I knew exactly, and now could feel fixed on me, that sweet gaze of solicitude which disarmed her vigorous face whenever she thought one of the family wasn't happy. Then she left off dishing out the pasta for the others and came round, ladle in hand and big dark eyes strained with concern, to my end of the table opposite Tommaso. "*Che hai, Michele? Cosa c'è?*" she asked, her sharp Attic features intent and puzzled: "What's up? What is it?" Poor love, she must have thought there was something wrong with the butter.

This happened about a week after I'd moved over to the island – I was already having my midday meal with the family. I had just become "Michele" to Damianina as well as to Tommaso and the children. For the first few days her remarks to me had been allusive, in the third person – I'd been a *cristianu*, the Christian – "Has the Christian had cheese on his pasta?" Damianina would ask obliquely; or, "Would the Christian like some more wine?"

The euphemization of "person" into *cristianu*, and in the plural – *tanti cristiani*, "so many people, such a crowd" – is colloquial all over Sicily: a survival, the theory goes, of the Arab incursions and occupation of the ninth and tenth centuries when, perhaps, the invading non-Christian became equated with a non-person. And yet, once the slaughter was over, such of it as there was, the native Nazarenes of Sicily got along well enough with their new Moslem rulers; so much so, Gibbon records, that in one year alone 25,000 Sicilian boys were circumcised on the same day as the caliph's son (as a kind of "christening present", presumably). Historians of the period, above all the great Michele Amari, vouch for the high content of benevolence and good sense that made Saracen rule far more disagreeable to the subject Christians. My own notion is that the "moral" note in *cristianu* was acquired, not during the Saracen dominion, but in the later, and far more dreadful, centuries of the "Turkish" corsairs from North Africa (only a hundred miles off this island's southern coast), whose savagery when they came slave-raiding on these shores must certainly have made them look, if that was how non-Christians behaved, like non-persons. Today, of course, the vernacular *cristianu* has lost any religious reference: its meaning is nearer "one of us."

So for a while I was *u cristianu* - at least judged as a person: until, received into the family, I became Michele; and from then on so remained to everybody on the island - rarely Signor Michele and only once or twice, in very formal and rather elderly company, Don Michele.

Damianina's bite off the butter was important. Its comical unexpectedness jolted me into seeing that what to me was startling was to her a matter of course - it showed how mean the little snobberies of our "superior" Northern upbringing can be. Why shouldn't Damianina bite into my butter? How, really, could I justify this prim faddishness about another person mouth? What about kissing? What, really, when one stops to think about it, can be more repellent than the British habit of exchanging osculatory mouthings, humid, odorous and unhealthy, on almost any pretext of kinship or gossipy intimacy? How many British spirits have been warped from infancy by a surfeit of smacks from the frothy lips of aunts and other well-meaning fusspots? As for sexual kissing, this is so disgustingly on public display in buses, tea-shops, supermarkets and even South Kensington drawing rooms, that those aunts who dribble over the faces of their family young don't know where to put their tongues. Italians, however, at least outside the matrimonial bed, are lukewarm kissers; children mostly rebel against adult lips at about three years old, and thereafter at all ages the embrace falls into disuse except for a few quick pecks at departure or on return. These occasions for minor family drama, however, can sometimes require a deal of kissing: a pair of *sposi*, for example, being seen off from the jetty for their honeymoon, have to kiss everyone connected with the two families present round the gangway - if there are forty well-wishers, bride and bride-groom must each dab at eighty cheeks, a total between them of 160 kisses, plus the extra ones needed while being clung to by mothers and favourite sisters. Surely this mass misuse of the mouth is a coarser indelicacy than merely biting what's just been bitten? One doesn't mind drinking communally from a loving-cup – why than be squeamish over somebody's licked spoon? For a decade I had been here and there in the Two Sicilies, in Apulia, Calabria, Sicily, flattering myself how easily I fitted in, how creditably I adjusted my English allergies to the cruder manners of southern Italy. But all the time there'd been the presumptuous whisper: "Well, *I* don't spit fish bones on the table, *I* don't talk with my mouth full, *I* don't eat with my mouth open ...." All the time I knew *I* was "superior"....

But now, here I was part of a family, one of a small island community: their conventions had to be mine, their "right" way of doing a thing made my way wrong; the manners I'd been brought up to were no longer in context – it was the wont of this family and island that was now *right* and therefore "superior" to my foreign ways. I had come in from the outside and had to conform to what I found. My finicky northernisms had to be chucked out. "Cannibalism", remarked Samuel Butler, "is moral in a cannibal country".

Damianina has large handsome teeth which she uses involuntarily to supplement her hands: not only, as all needlewomen do, for nipping off a thread or securing pins, but also wherever teeth come handier than knife or scissors; and especially in the kitchen where they can do the job of an extra set of fingers. She will hold steady with her teeth a hunk of meat while she trims pieces for the stewpot; she strips garlic or beans with them; or, after taking a *torta* from the oven (a *torta* is a kind of custard encased in sugar-icing), she will nibble level a ragged edge of icing, employing her teeth as a sort of sculptor's chisel. She needs this extra pair of hands as she's always working against the clock. With twenty years of family management behind her and a cornucopia of inherited domestic lore, Damianina is up to every time-saving dodge; and yet, what with the unending needs of her family – washing, mending, shopping, cooking – and frequent calls from neighbours to administer injections, unravel inexpert knitting, advise on baby ailments, resolve some young wife's cooking dilemma (everyone in the piazza comes to Damianina), her mornings pass with such a rush that almost before she can exclaim *Madre mia!*, Papà is coming back to dinner and it's time to "put" the pasta. So much has nibbling become a habit, or sampling whatever she's busy over at the stove, that Damianina pops into her mouth a bit of anything edible within reach as involuntarily as her fingers find thimble or broom or salt-crystals or whatever's needed in the instant. Tearing open a steaming fresh loaf, she'll take a bite before breaking it up for the family: scraping out the seeds from a slice of water-melon, she'll nip off with her teeth any corner that looks like dropping before offering the slice to a guest.

Papà, aged 45 in 1966, was named, because his grandfather was too, Tommaso – thus Gigi[11] is Luigi because Tommaso's father was Luigi: that's how it goes: an eldest son takes his paternal grandfather's name; the second son his maternal. Papà makes a great show of ruling his home with a hand of steel, and blusters a lot when his children wink across the table or throw him smiles of affectionate derision. *Sono io chi commanda a casa mia!*, he shouts – "It's I who give the orders in my own house" – but quietly, hardly perceived, it's *la Mamma*, Damianina who makes the family decisions. She was forty then; her home had been on the Gulf of Taranto, at the extreme south-east of Italy where he had met her and married her while serving with the Navy; now, for twenty years, she's lived in the extreme south-west: Sicilian is her language and she's guided by Sicilian lore – though her Apulian provenance comes out now and then in an appetite for mussels or horseplay and crude jokes – they adore each other and cheerfully squabble in a bantering way; she skillfully, and happily, combines wifely submissiveness with the capacity to get her own way every time in the running of the household and children.

Damianina serves out family meals as if she's doing a sum in her head. Her sharp, classical face becomes peaked with concentration: she knows to a mouthful how much, and how compounded, each will eat – in those moments the sole purpose of her being is to supply these needs. As she ladles each plate full,

---

[11] A diminutive.

or apportions pieces of meat or fish with her fingers, she murmurs a name abstractedly, almost secretly, as if the tally she's keeping is for herself alone. "Tommaso", she enumerates: this plate is brimful, and with it a special basin of extra tomato gravy, and also a spare plate for cooling off (as some English drink scalding tea from the saucer); "Gigi" she whispers (the males, of course, are served first) – a plate half full and, if it's *pasta a fagioli*, then beans only, without the pasta; "Duzzo" – a little pasta with no tomato on a specially small plate (the only blonde in the family – "tedesco nostro", Papà calls him, "Our German") – Duzzo was three and a half in January 1966: Duzzo is short for Alduzzo, and Aldo short for Cataldo, the name of Damianina's father); and finally Caterina, aged seven – not much pasta but plenty of tomatoes. Then Damianina's features relax: the sum has come out right. Maria, the eldest, probably hasn't been in the count: a girl of inner turmoils, interleaved with patches of rage and radiant gaiety, then a moody, capricious creature of seventeen, was probably in the kitchen, darkly brooding, cooking something for herself – a few spaghetti, perhaps, if the others were eating a minestra. Damianina understands, and lets her have her way. At meals, as in most things, they all have their way: some days Mamma will cook two or three different dishes because of her children's likes or dislikes. There's nothing in this house of "eat-up-your-rice-pudding-and-like-it"; this is a family of individuals, of *persons*, just as the island's population is one of individuals each with a right to his (but not her) individuality. Almost the first rule of life here seems to be: respect other people as *persons*, no matter how freakish they may appear. People's habits, like their deformities, are their own business: people aren't made alike, and a man's entitled to his oddities.

The intruder from the pernickety north can't be censured for his sense of shock on first encountering Sicilian eating habits; he's to blame when he fails to get over the shock. Our ways at table on the island – less polished even than on the Sicilian "mainland" – are medieval or surely Roman, like much else of our daily life. We eat with our fingers, tearing our meat as, no doubt, Henry VIII of England did – as those old Norman buccaneers who in the XIth century came down to rule southern Italy, and Sicily too, certainly did; and as did the guests of Socrates as well as those of Trimalchio. We pick flakes off our fish like people eating sponge cake; or when we have small fish like sardines or *violi*, fried or griddled to a crisp tautness, we nibble at them as if playing the mouth organ; and Papà keeps up a quick fire of spitting the tiny bones on the table. We have napkins, as diners in Imperial Rome had napkins; but ours, washed once or twice a week, are common to the family, chucked from one to the other and smeared with everyone's tomato drips. What we don't want on our plates we put on the table-cloth: bones, fish-scales, bits of gristle. Damianina and the girls of course use their hands for dishing out solids: boiled meat or chicken steeped in tomato gravy; fish from stewpot or pan; chickory, artichokes or egg-plant. Now and then she wipes them on her apron – especially to mark the point of transition from, say, boiled octopus to the creamy cakes bought for somebody's *festa*. We don't often wash our hands.

It was in elegant Florence that English viewers first saw the newfangled fork towards the end of the XVIth century. Fynes Morison, about 1600, found forks in Florence "because they touch no meat with the hands"; and in 1611 Thomas Coryate wrote: "I observed a custom not used in any other country .... the Italians do always use a little fork. ... The Italian cannot endure to have his dish touched with fingers, seeing all men's fingers are not alike clean." (It could be argued that the absence of the fork, except for spaghetti, on our XXth century tables is a legacy from two hundred years of Saracen example. But surely not: if ours were Arab manners, then eating habits would be exquisite here and our tables more refined than in Europe; where are meals more delicately served and gracefully eaten, using only the fingers, than in a Moorish household? More likely, our ways of getting food from kitchen to table, and from plate to throat, are exactly those of the European Middle Ages; and the eating habits of the middle ages hadn't then changed much, one may guess, from those of Imperial Rome.

A Florentine named Giovanni della Casa published some rules of polite behaviour in 1558:

> .... When you are eating, do not masticate noisily or crouch gluttonously over the food without raising your face, as if you were blowing a trumpet. Don't hiccup.... Don't scratch yourself or at least do it

> only 'reservedly'.... Don't bend over the glass of wine or plate where someone else is going to eat or drink, in order to take a sniff, and don't offer your neighbor something which you've already bitten.... On rising from table, don't stick your toothpick in your mouth, which makes you look like a bird carrying a twig to its nest. ... If you speak, don't go so close as to be breathing in his face. ... Don't nudge people with your elbow, saying "Isn't it true?" ...[12]

Giovanni's "don't" four hundred years ago, can today be seen and heard round any table on this island; our family would stare blankly without understanding, at anybody who told them their manners were scarcely civilized – the manners that to them and their forebears have always been second nature. It is indeed strange to find surviving on a Sicilian island little social tricks four centuries after they were deplored as solecisms in Florence! That nudge with the elbow – what conversation is without it? What assertion made into one's ear isn't followed by *Non e Vero*? – "isn't it true?" And yet – who wouldn't put up with some small affront to his fastidiousness in exchange for a selflessness and chivalry, a generosity of spirit and absolute loyalty of a quality today unknown in the dehumanized and perverted civilization of the urbanized north? If civilization means the illumination, refinement and ennobling of the human sensibility, then often the undercivilized is he who possesses the highest virtues of civilization.

It's difficult, of course, to defy one's own upbringing – to accept things one's been schooled from childhood to repel. At first, after I'd been received into the family, I allowed feelings of repugnance, irritation, impatience, to be seen, when I should have hidden them. Fortunately though, my displays of exasperation and edginess were regarded not as criticism of my family's behaviour but as symptoms, in myself, of foreign dottiness. If I flinched from a plate handed me containing a pig's liver and fish nestling side by side, if I winced when Damianina, her mouth dripping with tomato gravy, took a swig from the family wine-bottle on the table, if, off guard, my glance showed repugnance over Tommaso's spitting fishbones over the table-cloth – I could see, when anything like this happened, a looked of puzzled

---

[12] Quoted in *Daily Life in Florence in the Times of the Medici* by J. Lucas-Dubreton. [Author's footnote]

concern came over their faces. "Che hai, Michele?" Damianina would solicitously ask, always sweetly watching our needs and whims, "cosa c'e?" It didn't cross their minds that any of their habits could be the matter.

If I was to survive in their view as a reasonable person, I had to re-learn my own habits. It couldn't occur to the family that their way of life, which had always from all time been the proper way of life and therefore couldn't be anything other than proper, might seem, to somebody from another world, improper. Luckily for me, secure in the inherited *rightness* of their manners, they at first considered me rather feeble-minded. "Don't give Michele that dirty fork, he doesn't like it", Damianina would say to one of her daughters, throwing me a pitying look. The bizarre antics in the piazza of some tourists are more often ridiculed as "foreign" (even though Milanese or Roman) silliness than condemned as the boorishness it so often is - "tourists" of all nations tend to think that their fare buys also the right to behave as they never would at home. (Our summer holiday-makers, until two or three years ago, were mostly north Italians or day-trippers from Trapani and Palermo).

One of the first tourists to perceive that people among whom they "tour" may consider some of their conduct as ludicrous, was old Patrick Brydone, an 18th-century British tripper round Sicily of more than usual sensitivity, traces of which can be found in the writing of his descendant, Bertrand Russell. Like many after him, Brydone wrote a travel book after six weeks or so in Sicily - one so good that exaggerations can be forgiven; it was compiled from letters he wrote in 1770 to one William Beckford (not the author of *Vathek),* in one of which he observed: "It is with some degree of caution, we should ridicule the customes of other nations. A Sicilian, perhaps, will laugh with as much justice at many of our customes." Brydone's words might well be written into every travel-agent's brochures, in these days of mass trespass on other people's privacy.

A little more than a century later, near the end of the 19th century, another sagacious English tourist was wandering through the Italian South, though he got no nearer Sicily than Reggio di Calabria whence he "saw the evening fall on cloud-wreathed Etna". George Gissing, like many solitary and melancholic men who cling tenaciously to their rights to seclusion and eccentricity, had an invincible respect for other men's incongruities and an understanding that, cantankerous as he might be himself, they had an equal right to be cantankerous too. No traveller was readier to take other human beings as he found them; in this his tolerance was Sicilian. Yet even he, eighty years ago, reproached himself for the touristic arrogance that kept rising through the surface of his mild affability.

> "... I asked pardon for all my foolish irritation, my impertinent fault-finding," he wrote in his endearing and beautifully observant *By the Ionian Sea*. "Why had I come hither, if it was not that I loved land and people?" ... A wandering stranger has no right to nurse national superiorities, to indulge in contemptuous impatience. It is the touch of tourist vulgarity."

Yes, the touch of tourist vulgarity; it takes a long time to cleanse oneself of it. Even now, after six years of happiness, six years of acceptance, six of loving in return, I catch myself in spasms of irritation, impatience, disdain – towards people who for more than six years have shown me only *goodness*. This snobbish "civilized" finicality is ingrained like soot in a chimney-sweep's skin: it needs a lot of washing out. The many details of life here which to us from the North seem ugly, uncouth, even repellant, are in fact the marks of a spirit so simple, generous and *happy* that we sophisticated scoffers ought instead to be silenced by a huge humility.

5. I Famigliari

The strada Vittorio Emmanuele, which runs downhill from the piazza to the harbour, with the open-air fish-market at the bottom of it, is our High or Main Street; in it the housewives do their shopping and the card-players meet in three of the seven coffee-bars. Like the piazza, it's flagged with slabs of rock and its arches and balconied facades have an air of modest Bourbon elegance. Here, between Catalano the tobacconist and Gioacchino's bar where the public telephone is, Tommaso has his butcher's shop. Double doors open on to a cupboard-like alcove off the street which recalls a shop in a Moorish *souk*. This little box of a shop has been a butchery for at least a hundred years; before Tommaso took it over it belonged to Don Pino who in Mussolini's heyday was the fascist *capo* of the island – what Don Pino said went: splendid in boots and blackshirt, he was then surrogate here of the Duce himself, dictator absolutely over the island life. Today, Don Pino is a sweet-natured gentleman of eighty, who daily propels himself by bicycle across the piazza to sit in Tommaso's shop or outside it, quietly watching the passing days from where he had lovingly sliced fillets of veal for sixty years. It's hard to believe that this kindly old man, of whom we're all greatly fond, was, not so far back, strutting about the piazza, eliciting as the personification of fascist power either fear or subservience – yet Tommaso and men of his generation, boys at the time, well remember the awe that Don Pino's presence imposed.

But nowadays it's Tommaso who dominates the street. Just as I first saw him seven years ago, an eagle of a man with his enormous frame all bone and sinew and his long cadaverous face and horny nose, blood-stained apron caught up over one arm, standing outside his shop between customers, shouting drolleries uphill and down to Napolitano the grocer or Pedro the cabinet-maker whose workshop is opposite, or roaring jovial indecencies to old hunchbacked Marianna the greengrocer – that's how he was then and that's what he is today: a great blustering boy with the poise and profile of a Roman emperor and the smile of an angel - a man enormous in height and presence, but lean as a mule and artless as a child. He was, and still is, tremendously handsome in the heroic style - this must have been how Perseus or Ajax looked; always I've thought of him since that first sight as one of those roaring Achaean kings and generals, quaffing and quarrelling before Troy (but Papà is no roisterer, save for very rare outbursts, and his quarrels are all bark and no bite - or else as a swaggering Norman baron in the Hauteville brothers' conquering train. John Julius Norwich[13] quotes Anna Comnena as saying of Robert Guiscard:

> Now Homer says of Achilles that when he shouted his voice gave the impression of a multitude in uproar, but this man's cry is said to have put thousands to flight ... This Robert the Norman ... in temper tyrannical, in mind most cunning, brave in action.... His stature was so lofty that he surpassed even the tallest and in frame he was so well-built where nature required breadth and was neatly and gracefully formed where less width was necessary....

This Byzantine princess might have had Papà for her model, so exactly does this inscription fit. But the voice thundering across the piazza or roaring over the dinner-table is one his family love and revere and often indulgently giggle over; the tyrannical temper, always on the simmer and often erupting, will as instantly dissolve into an endearing gentleness and that sweetest of smiles which is a family gift; and the cunning is the shrewdness and instinctive common sense of an inborn individualism.

When I first met Gigi I saw at once this man as he had been thirty years before: the same long, sombre, big-boned good looks, the same dominant height and easy strength, the same dazzling smile suddenly illuminating the dark passion of the face - and the same Sicilian sadness, hovering, like a wry dimple, at the corners of the mouth. But here, in place of the latent violence that always threatened in Tommaso's tightly drawn features - all jaw, cheekbones and long bony nose -- was only an ineffable gentleness - an intrinsic generosity of spirit was written all over that tall, sallow, long-faced boy, with his expression of diffident gravity.

---

[13] *The Normans in the South*, Longmans, 1967. [Author's footnote]

When, some ten years ago, I lived on the island of Lipari off north-eastern Sicily , I could go and look at five thousand years of history, from the present day backwards, spelt out in the characters of human handiwork on ten or so feet of earth and rubble. All I had to do was to climb up the path to the castello, once the acropolis, and gaze at Professor Barnabò Brea's excavations which dramatically exhibit, in layer after layer of subsoil, one above the other, the marks of human habitation through some half-dozen or more cultures since about 3000 BC. But in the faces of the old Liparotes, or in their language or customs, one couldn't see anything of their history; for in fact, they haven't long been Liparotes – their forbears were imported by Charles V from Calabria and Campania to re-populate the Aeolian islands after they'd been stripped of inhabitants in the sixteenth century by "Redbeard" – Kheireddin and his Barbary pirates.

But on this island it's the other way about. Here there's no excavation to speak of: archaeology has barely scraped over a bit of topsoil, although rock and grotto, mountain and lowland, are rich in evidence of antique man, from the Neolithic onward, and even backward. Geologically the story must be simple: the walls of our houses are studded with fossilized scallop shells embodied in the locally quarried stone; and from these and the myriad petrified particles which compose the island's platform, a scholar can tell how old we are and when we became detached from the Sicilian "mainland".

But here history is written in the people's faces. Most of our families of today first settled in the seventeenth and eighteenth centuries, after the Genovese Pallavicini, who had bought the islands and lordship over them from the crown, developed the fishing and salting of tunny into an important export industry; but many of the people are descended from those earlier inhabitants whose sojourns here, and in western Sicily – though often transient, punctuate the past through millennia. Norman Douglas, writing in 1915 of Taranto, once a Spartan settlement, declares he was unable to detect Greek profiles or a trace of Greek phrases.[14] On this island, however, idly watching the folk walk-

[14] Secker, 1915; Peregrine Books, 1962 (with an introduction by John Davenport). [Author's footnote]

ing by in the piazza, you can spot in no time the features and eyes and hair and skin of any of the races or nations which in 5000 years have come and gone, and left their imprint on the island. Favignana, certainly, hasn't had a continuous population for such a span – often the island has been tenantless; but Sicily has – a stream of population constantly fed by new tributaries – and the people here are Sicilians. In our family alone I can see, in different moments, the lineaments and complexions of Spaniard, Roman, Arab, Greek and even Norse through Norman-Phoenician too, or Elymian from Erice and Segesta, if I knew just what features to look for (but the Punic type, if there was one, must be fairly common still in the Trapani of today, and up on Eryx). The long, sallow faces of Tommaso and Gigi, both sombre with the immense Sicilian melancholy that underlies even the most halcyon of days; both apt, from darkest dejection, to be abruptly transfigured by that smile which surely nowhere outside Sicily can be so illuminating – those two faces, depending on tilt of head or angle of view or on the light and mood of the moment, may reveal the features and traits of any or all of the races from which they were bred. Papà's fierce swarthy face would be perfectly framed in the hood of a Moorish *djellaba*, yet a Spanish cloak or a Roman toga could equally well become him. But above all, as I've mentioned above, his splendidly patrician profile and the commanding thump of his hand on the table and the blend of joviality and rage in his thunderous conversational roar, bring to mind those Achaean kings and generals bellowing with Menelaus and Agamemnon. And often, when I look at Gigi's gentle olive-sad face, so young and sensitive and handsome and yet somehow suffering as if with some age-old recollection, I think of those Moorish youths who twelve hundred years ago overran Andalusia and of the Spanish girls they bred from. As for Norse – our Duzzo – "tedesco nostro" – is yellow-haired and blue-eyed, an examplary Nordic – surely a throwback to those Norman-French who vanquished Saracen Sicily in the same decade as William the Conqueror was overcoming England.

Damianina and her daughters come straight from a Greek vase: those sharp birdlike profiles one sees so often on coin or ceramic or sculpture, with that classic unbending line from brow to nose-tip and a backward drawn hair-do. There's many a Demeter and Athena for whom Damianina could have sat; and recently, seeing photographs of a sculpture in the Metropolitan Museum, New York, I thought for a second this grave beauty fondling a pair of doves was really our Maria. Damianina, especially, is the purest classical; the Greek strain in her heredity must have been blended less with other stock than that of the Sicilian-bred - especially western Sicilian, so abundantly infused with North African blood, and then with Spanish; Damianina's Apulian homeland at the eastern shore of Magna Graecia, peopled by Spartans twenty-seven hundred years ago, has had shorter conquests and fewer invaders.

Maria, beautiful and sultry as a dark peony, was at that time seventeen and in love with love and the wonderland of matrimony - the *nom de guerre* of masculinity. The ivory pallor of her face clouded and lightened like a thundery sky with the moods and passions that changed as often and as quickly as her appetite - that radiant smile, like her father's and Gigi's, could crumple in a breath into a sullen pout and those huge starry eyes could suddenly be scowling. She was a tall, strapping girl, wide-hipped and big-breasted, and was famed too in the *paese* for her competence in the arts of domesticity - just the sort of wife any young gamomaniac would see himself nicely bedded down with. That's just what Virgilio, a Neapolitan and one of the prison warders here, was. He proposed at their second meeting that he should ask Tommaso's consent and she agreed. Suddenly our Maria was madly in love, not only with love but with the first man who chanced to offer her love - and he rather plain and portly for his twenty-one years. That's how it goes often in Sicily: a girl accepts the first offer of marriage, and from that moment is infatuated, though she'd hardly noticed the man before the proposal. First come, first served: romance haloes the fact of betrothal, not the betrothed - after the engagement ceremonies every brand-new bride-to-be parades proudly through the piazza every Sunday morning with her hand on her affianced's arm, and with *la Mamma* in train, the message being "I've got my man".

But before the betrothal festivities, poor Maria and the whole family endured three weeks of frayed tempers and nerves: Tommaso, for three weeks refused his consent - mainly, we privately thought, to emphasize his mastery - *Sono io chi commanda a casa mia*! Of course Damianina and Maria got their way in the end, as from the beginning they knew they could. And the official betrothal was quickly arranged; volatile courtship had to be jelled into an indissoluble compact. Thereafter - once rings had been formally exchanged in the presence of all the relations sitting round the walls on hard chairs, and once the family had recovered from two days of almost continuous dancing - thereafter no occasion was lost for emphasizing how absolutely Virgilio had become part of the family. The children referred to him as their *cognato*, brother-in-law ("Duzzo, pass your brother-in-law an orange", Damianina would say at dinner); for himself, from now on, Tommaso was his *succero*, his father-in-law, and he addressed both parents as Papà and Mamma; he was encouraged to use the house and all its contents as his own. He wasn't for an instant allowed to forget that he was irrevocably agglutinated into the family structure. The early espousal of virgins is still, in remoter Sicily, a fundamental of the social canon; and an engagement to marry, once authorized, is sewn up almost as tightly as the marriage itself.

Girls are often affianced very young, one reason for long-lasting engagements; for another reason, poor Maria's time of waiting was to be as long as Jacob's. By law, at that time, young men in the Armed Forces, the prison service included, might not marry until their twenty-eighth birthday - Virgilio was than twenty-one. Seven years is a long time, which is just what Virgilio thought; as time went on, his impatience brought quarrels with Maria and often tears to Damianina as he goaded and badgered her to take his part. I believe Damianina would, allowed her way, have left the decision to her daughter (and, after all, the Pill was known even on our island); but she was stifled by the overpowering presence of Tommaso, rigidly conservative, in the background. Of course, officially, he knew nothing of Virgilio's opportunities; but suspicions were fed by all kinds of hearsay information and he would come to me, or even to little Duzzo, and whisper: "What has *he* been saying? Has he been annoying la Mamma?" or "Have *they* been alone up in the attic?" The idea that his daughter, whom he adored perhaps more than the other children (and he adored them all), might have been led astray, was agony to him!

"*Sangue della Madonna*!" he would roar across the table at me, making the coffee cups rattle with his fist, "Blood of the Madonna! - never, NEVER shall it happen till she has THAT on her left hand!" - and he'd stab with his right forefinger at his own thick wedding-ring.

Virginity, that particularity of maidenhead which is of real importance only when lost, is worshipped like a sort of totem all round the Mediterranean littoral - in Morocco the wedding guests wait expectantly during consummation to see the blood-stained towel which is held up to show that all is satisfactorily over. In Sicily, a father or brother, ordinarily amiable, will unhesitatingly kill in order to prevent or avenge such an affront to the family "honour" as the seduction of a family virgin. Has this mystical devotion to the principle of virginity, a fetish-like worship of maiden untouchability, which has nothing to do with morality, some connection with the notion of blood-sacrifice? Or is it a ritual safeguarding of the hearth, the home, the family, as personified by the goddess Vesta, or the Greek Hestia - yet, rather, wasn't Vesta invented to provide divine patronage over something infinitely older than herself?

But the old attitudes and credulities are passing, the good ones often more quickly than the bad, fretted away by the insidiously "civilizing" action of television, "tourism" and the daily car-ferry - that modem Moloch of the Mediterranean. Leaving aside the old Sicilian practice of betrothal-by-rape (as practiced by car-ferry passengers?) - now, since a spirited girl's defiance at Alcamo a few years ago, on its way out too - I would guess that in the last decade or less the conjugal gun in Sicily and even on this island, has been jumped by *fidanzati* much more often than one knows about. Nowadays, engaged couples, unlike their parents, can read the newspapers which give lots of space to the Pill and Vatican pronouncements on its iniquitous effectiveness (on a largely pagan island like ours, not very many people heed the Vatican or go to confession).

An explosive "Blood of the Madonna" is a usual expression of Tommaso's astonishment or displeasure - it's a common expletive, indeed all over the South, from here to Bari or Brindisi. Often, when his feelings are a bit stronger, he'll come out with

"Pig of a Madonna" or even "Whore of a Madonna" - not blasphemies these, but commonplace oaths in the classic tradition of taking it out on the gods when things go badly: you made your votive bargain with your chosen god, and if he or she lets you down, rounded on them with abuse. Tommaso was roundly anticlerical, but a great respecter of the saints (the modern name of the gods), among whom, of course, was the Madonna in her various guises. He and his brother Salvatore had inherited from their father the courtesy office of manhandlers to the saints when, in effigy, these issue from the mother church on the evenings of their festival for their annual perambulation of the *paese*. The brothers, in their best suits, wheel the saint out of the church, aboard the gilded chariot used for the calendared processions, and push it through the streets of the *paese*, preceded by monsignore and the populace carrying candles, and followed by the village brass band. Tommaso appears in this role, like a King's Champion, half a dozen times a year - only when it's some specialist Saint's day, such as the October feast of the Madonna of the Rosary, does he surrender the honour to the people whose patron it is, in this case the fishermen and watermen - or the Rustic Madonna in August, when the chief farmers take over. To justify this collusion with the Church by one whom only a baptism or marriage in the family could get inside a church, Tommaso will say: "I serve the Saints, *not* the priests" (for saint read god); and the *bistecca* courtesies, exchanged when Monsignore looks in for his Sunday *bistecca*, do nothing to hide Tommaso's hearty dislike for the priesthood.

Papà is a puritan really: he becomes furious, muttering curses under his breath, at even the mildest sexual flaunting in public - an engaged couple, say, cuddling in the living room or holding hands instead of eating up their pasta; and, of course, he will never condone copulation (between young people) before their lawful union by that same despised priest. And I remember his head-shaking disapproval when, just before my first *carnevale* on the island, seven years ago, he said to me sadly, "I don't like it, I don't like it" - while we were sitting in the piazza watching the crowds of children showing off their carnival fancy dress. "Why not?" I asked. "It looks innocent enough ...." "You'll see, you'll see", he muttered sternly. Later I did see what he meant - a very jolly, and by northern standards quite outrageous "permissiveness" in the choice and execution of "fancy-dress", and in the realism of an uproarious fertility rite.

Tommaso is prudish about sexual things when, to him, they appear solemn; yet when they seem comic he can be an uproarious bawd. At dinner sometimes, in a rollicking mood, with the children around the table and perhaps his mother (*la nonna*) visiting from across the piazza, he'll suddenly start slyly giggling over the pink flesh of water-melon – putting two crescent slices together he plants his knife upright between them and grins triumphantly around the table. Or, a buxom matron calling, a friend of Damianina's, he'll bring her a glass of wine amid, from her, a ripple of deprecatory titter, and fondle her fat thighs and breasts, saying, "Oh, what lovely tits!" to the delight of all the family, with Damianina jocularly bridling. The word *cazzo*, commonly used all over the south as a pejorative, is one of Papà's favourites – so and so's a *cazzo*, he exclaims impatiently of a man he thinks a rogue or a clot; or, of some project that's gone wrong – *è un cazzo* – it's a muck-up. *Cazzo* all over Italy, is precise slang for the English "prick" or "cock". Coming home in jovial humour, he will greet little Duzzo with a teasing tickle round the scrotum – the bantering gesture with which most grandfathers and the like greet small boys here until, at about the age of six, the lads begin to rebel.

To the northerner, this kind of paternal influence must seem bizarre: how does it shape, or misshape, the growing mind of a child like Duzzo?

The answer is Duzzo. He is now nearly eleven: year by year, almost day by day, since he was three and a half, among his family, with his friends, in school and out, at home and in his father's shop, in piazza, farmyard and empty countryside, I've been his companion, and have seen him grow as near-flawless as any child short of the angelic can get. So I know him pretty well: Duzzo is a boisterously normal boy of that ragamuffin age – and yet, engrafted by upbringing upon innate intelligence and charm, he had the unboyish virtues of obedience, unselfishness, willingness and such improbabilities, as well as the natural Sicilian manners (which do not include table manners) – all were as unselfconscious as a smudge on the nose. How can that be possible, you ask, with such an upbringer as Tommaso? But you've only seen one side of Papà: the roaring, blustering, bombastical side, which really, like an aspirant gangster's dark glasses concealing eyes of a gazelle-like timidity, is a facade of bravado, behind which lies the exact opposite. His family, and Duzzo too, know what's behind and quietly wink at each other at the height at each storm. Papà, in fact, is everything one's first feeling about him belies: gentle, generous, tender-hearted, infinitely loving to his family – notwithstanding that roar of "I give the orders in my own house", he foregoes for himself the tiniest luxury so as to afford some to the children. Take off those fierce dark glasses – you'll find nothing but sweetness and that deep Sicilian tragedy in the huge lambent black eyes.

Duzzo, it should be said, in these paragraphs is something of a generalization. Family relationships on this island, leaving room for individualities and temperamental differences, run generally along similar lines: an endearingly unembarrassed rapport allies fathers and sons; they speak the same idiom and no wedge of self-consciousness separates them; they are, and feel themselves, absolute equals, and yet paradoxically this sense of equality doesn't at all conflict with the absolute deference which every Sicilian son pays his father. There is, on the island, no "generation gap": at Uccio's bar, or Gioacchino's, striplings just in their teens enjoy complete social parity with grave elders of the parish and discuss with them on equal terms Italy's chances for the World Cup or which card might better have been played in the last hand dealt.

When Duzzo was nearly five, Tommaso gave him a lamb, a female which he named Ninuzza and brought up on the bottle. Becoming too big for Damianina's house, Ninuzza was brought to my garden where she learned to graze; in due course, with the precocity of lambs, she grew ripe for mating and was put to run with a flock which morning and evening passed my house – the ten-year-old shepherd was told to let us know what happened. And here's the point of this story: each afternoon Duzzo, now something over five years old, came out to the garden and waited for the flock to pass: "Has Ninuzza been covered yet?" he'd call up to the boy, almost as soon as the tinkling of the ewe's bells came up the lane like a bubbling brook, "has the ram mounted her yet?" - asking with the assurance and experience of an old hand at sheep-breeding. And there is the point: Duzzo's sexual learning, his awareness of the "facts of life", like that of most Sicilian boys (and girls too) had grown with the growth of his own frame without his even noticing it; he hadn't been taught, he hadn't even "picked it up"; the rudiments of it had come to him, and elaborations were still coming, as naturally, almost unwittingly as the earliest elements of speech came to him. As for Papà's dirty jokes - what could be saner than the habituation of children to the truth that the largely ridiculous mechanics of reproduction and the mystique that generally surrounds them, can be highly comic and are better giggled at than sniggered at as a matter for guilty or furtive brooding? At present, to Duzzo, sex is a segment of daily life, only slightly more mysterious and magnetic than other amusing things; in a couple of years, no doubt, he'll become as randy as most Sicilian boys and will soon, in summer be joining the wanking parties that one happens upon anywhere in the rocks. But, again like most Sicilian boys, he will grow into a fairly simple sexual life and avoid the frustrating kinks. Sicily's fantastic history of subjection, vassalage, disappointment and a sort of shoulder-shrugging despair, the harvest of twenty centuries of multiform exploitation, has left a trail of neurosis and eccentricities - yet sexuality, for the most part, seems to pursue an ordinary straightforward course. Although most South Italians and Sicilians are ready to have a go at anything pleasurable and profitable, one comes across few, outside the large cities, true deviants from the sexual norm; on this island, where we have perhaps one thousand adult males, I know of just six who are constitutionally heretical.

6. Carnevale

We have three carnival days, which work up to their orgiastic climax on the night of Shrove Tuesday, the whole celebration, unknown to the celebrants, being a sexual sacrament; yet I doubt if, throughout the revels, there's a single bout of coition unblessed by the Church. We're a chaste island, on the whole.

I remember so well that Sunday of February 1966; it was one of the crystalline afternoons of gentle breeze from the north and warm blue-gilt sky, the blessed *tramontana* which comes like an act of charity between the winter gales. We were sitting, Papà and I after a big dinner, outside Uccio's socially elegant barber's shop which, facing the piazza, stands between Ciccio's coffee-bar and the Hunter's and Angler's Club (where Papà often plays cards or dozes on a Sunday afternoon - and where, in season, the braves of the chase gather, rigged out with guns, bandoliers, fringed Redskin jackets and tassell game-bags: apeing tiger-hunters, they stalk tiny birds; most however, luckily, are luckless shots).

This first day of *carnevale*, the children's day, was already in full swing. The paved expanse of our noble piazza was glowing with choreographic and chromatic merry-go-round of a multitude of children - the entrancing children of all sizes who, brilliant as peacocks in a medley of fancy-dress, strutted to and fro, back and forth, round and round, charmingly showing themselves off, archly or noisily according to sex and age, engagingly self-important. The piazza was the children's: in those days a donkey-cart or two might be standing drowsily beneath the trees, but the motor was still an intruder.

"What a delicious *festa* this is, Tommaso!" I exclaimed. "How delightful they are, and how they're enjoying themselves! What a little it takes to give so much simple pleasure!" I remember feeling so sentimentally benign that I was full of exclamation marks.

"Yes," he answered drily, "they're pretty, the *bambini*" - his two youngest, Duzzo and Caterina, were in the throng, carrying beribboned shepherds' crooks; "but you wait - wait till tomorrow and you'll see: it'll be *better*." He spoke the word *better*, I thought, with some intent of malediction.

(Next year, 1967, Duzzo, by then four and a half, was put into a ballerina's get-up, handed down by a larger female cousin. He was delighted at first, and went out into the piazza hopping like a cock-sparrow. In five minutes he was home, howling with indignation: *Non sonno femmine, io*, he roared, "I'm no female!")

Already on Saturday there'd been outbreaks of carnival excitement: small boys had given themselves burnt-cork whiskers and funny hats, and were already clubbing passers-by with plastic coshes (the commercial successor to the blown-up sausage-skin); while at Masino's wine-shop there'd been more drinking than usual and more touching-up of old cronies' bums and similar genial indelicacies. Even Gigi, two months past fifteen and by nature grave and taciturn, talked briefly, without doing so, of buying himself a funny hat.

"Do the bigger boys, and the grown-ups," I asked Papà, "join in too and dress up, or is it only the children?"

"Just you wait, you'll see," he said. "Wait till tomorrow – wait till *day-after-tomorrow*. I don't like it." I didn't know then, what a puritan Tommaso is.

The piazza has an air of mob-caps and spinning-wheels, having grown up around the mother-church which, with its great emerald cupola, was auspicated in 1766 after eighty years of building. It's a nobly spacious square for a township of some four thousand inhabitants, infants included (very few islanders live outside the *paese*) – a football field would nicely fit into it. The houses, two-storeyed except for a handful of upstart moderns, flat-roofed for the laundry lines and bright-eyed with balconies, have round-arched gateways leading into courtyards and stone stairways and, like the flagstones that pave the piazza, seem to throw off a soft honey-coloured light even when the sky is grey; the faded lemon-yellow of the church's fabric is pink-tinted in patches as if the stucco had been dusted with a rosy lichen; the tall, spare façade elegantly baroque yet parsimoniously ungarnished, follows the familiar "head-and-shoulders" style with the fenestrated belfry and its three bells set centrally like a neck upon the shoulders of the west face, and is strictly undecorated except for the marquis's coronet and shield above the great door: one supposes that the Marchese Pallavicini, who bought the island and all rights over it and who built the church, was willing to provide his tunny fishermen with the essential framework, and no more, for the salvation of their souls without spending money on mere mundane ornamentation.

Here and there round the periphery of the piazza, leaning obligingly over the pavements and projecting circles of deep green shade in which chairs and tables are often set, are groups of carefully barbered *ficus* – that useful and compliant Asian evergreen, of the mulberry family, which has deservedly become the municipal tree of southern Italy, so benignly and with such trim felicity does it create pools and canals of cooling shadow against the harshness of the sun. One has only to think of towns like Reggio di Calabria, Taranto in Apulia, or Noto in south-east Sicily, to remember how perfectly these alien trees with their clipped flat crowns of ivy-green opacity, do their work, slaves in a foreign land.

The church, instead of centrally presiding over the piazza like an altar or throne, is pushed nearly into a corner, producing an agreeable asymmetry; this was done by order of the Spanish governors when the church was planned late in the XVIIth century – had it been conventionally placed in the centre it would have blocked the view of the sea from the castle that then stood at the highest point in the *paese* where today stands the prison, whence watch was kept for "Turkish" corsairs.

The piazza contains the island's only cinema and its only pharmacy and three of its coffee-bars and the principal barber's, Uccio's, outside which Tommaso and I were now sitting; but chiefly it is a place of *homes*. People, families, inhabit it and stroll up and down it, gossiping, and crowd into it for festivities or for displays of public indignation as when, in 1968, the tunny fish cannery was closed by its "foreign" proprietor from Genoa and a third of the island's wage-earners were put out of work. But this afternoon, under the shining February sky, it was the children's piazza They swarmed and strutted in a kaleidoscope of colour and masquerade – yet even the fancy dress was restricted by tradition to an historical choice: apart from ballet-skirts and shepherds' crooks, the costumes all represented four or five periods of fairly recent subjection: ladies of Old Spain with fans and black lace walked with hidalgos and bullfighters; there were powdered perukes and beauty-patches of the Bourbon court of Naples, and Barbary pirates and the Saracens of an earlier incursion – as well as small boys in red tarbooshes recalling the long intimacy between western Sicily and Tunisia – there can be few families in Marsala, Trapani, or this very island which hadn't some member settled in Tunisia as fisherman, shop-keeper or farmer until independence was won from the French. (In the bars of Trapani one still encounters nostalgic old men who greet each other with French pleasantries like: "Comment ça va, jeune homme de bonne famille?") A couple of knights in cardboard armour, but no evocation of those paladins immortalized on the painted carts of Palermo and in the Sicilian marionette theatres as well as by Ariosto and others; nor did I see uniforms among the Bourbon lords and ladies; nor any Garibaldi or Bixio or other hero of the Piedmontese invasion of Sicily of 1860 – and certainly there were no reminders of the House of Savoy. Most of these costumes, elaborate, stitched by mothers and elder sisters, were so lavish that there's hardly anything for fantasy to add; yet such is the power of a child's imagination that a number of small boys, with no more to aid it than a smudge of burned cork and a wooden sword, felt themselves as totally and authentically transformed as any in the costliest disguise.

Tommaso was right: *carnevale* began properly on the Monday. By mid-morning, in the side-streets around the piazza, one was already being slightly alarmed by small troops of bizarre vagabonds, enigmatic and epicene: cloisters of whimpering youths unrecognisable even to their own mothers, shrouded from head to heel in female or vaguely monkish attire, their faces amorphous and featureless beneath stocking masks (their sisters' nylons?); moving in a shuffling half-jogtrot that was not walk or run or dance but a kind of glide, an uncanny and oddly mincing gait, with broomsticks or even complete brooms in their hands; and uttering a continuous chorus of shrill yet muted squeaking, "gibbering like bats that squeak and flutter" – and though these creatures were lively adolescents of flesh and blood and no phantom ghosts of slain Suitors, yet one felt, confronted by their grotesque anonymity and the strange sexlessness of their cryptic forms, and with this extraordinary shrilling, like a nestful of mice, in one's ears, a faint shiver of the unearthly. If these hadn't come from another world, they couldn't be far off. Now and then, weaving through the village, a group of these twittering hobgoblins would hem in some man who caught their attention - a schoolmaster, perhaps, they wanted to take the mickey out of (*prender in giro*) - and hold him to ransom till he'd paid up the price of a few cigarettes. And then they'd be off again, shuffling and squeaking and wielding their broomsticks, about their weird business.

None of these boys, nor their grandmothers either, could explain this curious charade: it's always been like this at *carnevale*, they'd say. Yet the solution seems obvious - until one looks further back in time - when it's seen how the boys' ritual fits into the vividly explicit pattern of the Dionysian fertility mysteries which carnival on the island turned out to be. The ankle-length skirts and enveloping headdress, the grotesquely womanish gait, the shrill feminine gibberish (intelligible speech could betray a boy's identity and also destroy the illusion of demonic weirdness), the canonical carrying of that essence of housewifeliness, the broomstick - all these, surely, accentuate aspects of the female sex; and since the business of the festival (it soon becomes clear), the whole point of it, is fecundity and the reproductive energies of male and female, especially the female, this burlesque transvestism of boys roughly in their mid-teens becomes part of the general female impersonation indulged in for a couple of days by a large proportion of the male population over the age of twelve.

But, behind this interpretation, isn't there an even more obvious one, realizing that *carnevale* here is a survival of the Dionysia or Bacchanalia and that I believe these boys' extraordinary masquerade is the still-living twentieth-century perpetuation of the myth of the maenads, the bacchae or bacchantes, those demented women who with old Silenus and the satyrs were Dionysos' and later Bacchus' indefatigable attendants, and who were essential to the Orphic and the Eleusian mysteries. These boys personify the female, the insane, the aggressive; when they crowd dottily round a victim, menacing him with their squeals and broomsticks, they are symbolically tearing him to pieces as the maenads tore Orpheus. And is it far-fetched to guess that their stockinette veil, which must, in effect though not in material, be traditional, may descend from the "web" of that other Penelope whom a pre- or non-Homeric legend makes a maenad and one of the putative mothers of Pan? Robert Graves, in his *Greek Myths*, suggests that Penelope's "web" may have been tattooing or painting in stripes, quotes Plutarch's statement that tattooing occurred among maenads, and says a vase in the British Museum shows a maenad "whose legs and arms are tattooed with a webbed pattern". Is it too much to suppose that the crude webbing pattern may have become rationalized down the millennia into the splendid opacity of nylon netting, which provides the absolute facelessness required by modern carnival.

I believe that on this tiny island off western Sicily - insular indeed, until so recently, in a life of the past, unperplexed by the notions and motions of modernity - one of man's oldest and most powerful fantasies persists and is re-enacted each year, although the last vestigiary memory of what the actors are up to vanished aeons ago. As far as I know, similar maenads have not been found elsewhere and nobody has yet identified our own maenads; no other interested visitor has been on Favignana at Carnival time.

On that Monday evening, in Masino's wine shop by the harbour, a trio of the older maenads jovially appeared and rousing one or two simpering octogenarians to their feet, stood holding them in a warm embrace while performing (despite a temporarily feminized nature) a lively mimicry of copulation. And as Monday was succeeded by Tuesday, it became hourly more evident that copulation, or more especially the product of copulation, was the topic of the *festa* - like the dionysiac rites and those of Demeter and Kore, *carnevale*'s real theme was fertility, generation, reproduction, proliferacy - the earth's fertility symbolized in human fecundation and pregnancy: The streets and piazza became full of young men dressed up in "drag": some in their grandmothers' gowns, others in their sisters' "hot pants", some grimacing through absurd masks, some wearing make-up and wigs - but all with stuffed-out bellies billowing in a parody of pregnancy and with hugely generous bosoms, to which many clutched a life-size plastic doll; one I saw with two dolls, one at each breast, plus a paunch manifestly in the family way. There were newly-weds, both boys, in full bridal garb; or, as a variation, "going-away" couples carrying suitcases and plainly hurrying to the first night. Comic sandwich-men wandered about, displaying satirical improprieties or familiar joke-insults like "*Anche tu sei ...*" followed by the *cornuto* sign – closed fist with fore-and little fingers extended in two "horns" ("You too are a cuckold"). Later, the throng of mamma-impersonators was joined by other young men, in a variety of male fancy-dress, who pranced through the crowds with large-sized simulant penises obtruded from their trouser-fly – toy truncheons of plastic or some sort of "rubber goods" (in the old days it would have been sausage-skin). Thus the male element in the life force was acknowledged, but emphasis everywhere was on the female – the harvesting of the crop was being celebrated rather than the sowing of it; the female was being given the credit for fecundity, as if the male merely turned on the switch.

At the antique Greek fertility festivals (Dionysia) the sexual buffoonery seems to have been principally phallic; could the preoccupation here with pregnancy and motherhood have originated in the femaleness of Sicily's classical deities of fertility – Demeter and Persephone (Kore)? Anyway, the power of tradition in these parts is perhaps demonstrated by the unanimous readiness of the young men of this island, normally randy and normally masculine, to mime the female role instead of seizing this chance of publicly brandishing, even symbolically, what they've got.

It's possible too, I dare say, that the close association of Demeter with Sicily (it was near Enna, the "navel" of the island, according to Cicero, Ovid, Diodorus and others, that Hades snatched Persephone from her mother) rather than Dionysus himself, explains the absence of the vine from our local dionysia. No honour is paid to wine (except, by the fishermen, in Masino's bar) and the only foliage singled out by tradition for display is the laurel or bay (*alloro*) – which, significantly perhaps, is classically a favourite of the maenads. It should be said that Sicilians generally and our islanders in particular aren't drinkers: a lot of fishermen might be called professional soakers, and most men now and then have a gregarious booze-up of *bicchierini* "little glasses"; but everyday habit limits wine to a little for dinner and supper and nothing in between. In Apulia, by contrast, a lot more, and more often, is swallowed, and the number of real drunks is noticeable. One may wonder if this difference is the result of Saracen, officially teetotal, influence in Sicily and especially western Sicily - and of Greek in south-east Italy.

Greek comedy originated "in the often obscene seasonal revelry forming part of the Dionysiac fertility cult ...".[15] The Rural Dionysia, Hooker says, included "processions in which model phalli were carried and carnivals with contests between groups of revellers in disguise, whose competitive and indecent buffoonery may have been a source of Greek comedy; in the fourth century, tragedies, comedies ... were performed." The performance of comedy is a component of our *carnevale*: a lorry parked in the piazza is the stage, and a trio of the island's stock comics, stevedores from the *porto*, keep the people laughing till midnight with slapstick clowning and juicy adlibbing in broadest Sicilian, accompanied by the cooking and eating of a great many spaghetti and the passing round of a two-litre *bottiglione*.

At that *carnevale* (= "Goodbye Meat") seven years ago, it was noticeable that Monsignore and his curate, young Father Scoldi, kept to their quarters behind the church during the last two days before Ash Wednesday, and were hardly seen in the piazza the whole time - but in the last five years, and especially since the *traghetto*, that indiscriminator of myth and ancestral dogma, began its daily "roll-on, roll-off" voyage of mischief, *carnevale* has been becoming each season less meaty, less fruity, less authentically the posterity of the Eleusinian mysteries; today's carnival could hardly offend Monsignore and is reduced chiefly to a general bashing among the young with inflated plastic bludgeons. Our local *carnevale*, unique, I believe, for its vivid perpetuation of observances elsewhere lost in remotest antiquity, is being ousted with the island speech and so much else that keeps the islanders insular, by the monotonic norms of television, *turismo*, and the standard commonplaces of the Ministry of Education.

---

[15] G.T.W. Hooker, Lecturer in Classics, Univ. of Birmingham, writing in *Penguin Companion to Literature*, vol.4. [Author's footnote]

7. The Piazza

The first time I saw the piazza, at the end of 1965, four motor-cars were parked under the mulberry trees; I saw an enormous leisurely expanse of spacious paving, at once grandiose and comfortable, where children were running and playing, and dogs sunning themselves. Today, in August, there are nearer four-hundred cars; they stand, axle to axle in two ranks, all the way round beneath the unboastful two-storied stone houses, balconied and arched – and a child crossing has to dodge and side-step and the air screams with their klaxons.

Similarly, in 1965 there weren't more than a dozen scooters and motorcycles among the island's population of four and half thousand. Don Pino, the only citizen given the honorific of "Don" by everyone – from the mayor, Dr. Baffi, to our own little Duzzo – can remember the time when a sensation was created by the arrival of one single pedal-bicycle: brought across the water by some enterprising modernist for riding instead of a donkey between his garden and the *paese.* That was a long time ago; Don Pino, who stills cuts up meat in his butchery for about ten hours a day, is over eighty.

The day isn't far off, I'm afraid, when there'll again be only one bicycle on the island; even during my three years I've seen the number of them diminishing like a rare species of game that's dying out; Nowadays any schoolboy rising fourteen is badgering his father to buy him a Vespa or Lambretta on hire-purchase. Don Pino's own bicycle will last as long as he does. He lives off the north end of the piazza, his shop is at the south; and he rides with splendid dignity over the intervening expanse of paving-stones, holding a crutch in one hand and jerking himself along by giving his pedals the see-saw motion of the balance of a watch.

But in the last two years the bigger shopkeepers and bar-owners have been buying cars – they couldn't see a man like Alcamese owning one while they had none; social vanity has become as tiresome among the thirty or forty "rich" (or would-be rich) on Goat Island as it is in London or New York – these people must have their car even if they use it only to drive five hundred yards down to the porto. But they're content with a sensible little *topolino* or at most a Fiat 1200. The huge vulgar vehicles – the Lancias and Alfa Romeos and the Common Market grandees like the Opels come in the summer with the alien holiday intruders from Turin or Rome or Milan, laden with aqualungs and fancy beach-pants; often I've stood on our solitary jetty watching the offloading of these juggernauts – far too long to be comfortable in our narrow streets, far too powerful for our blind country lanes, far too fast for the welfare of the children playing in the piazza – and hoping that one of them will tumble into the water.

For three years Tommaso has been telling me what splendid plans are being laid for the economic welfare of the island: the oil-refinery, or some such industrial plant, which is to be raised above the eastern coast; the huge hotel that's to bring tourists by the hundred; the *traghetto,* the car-ferry which will allow people to bring their cars at a quarter of the present cost and ten times the present rate; the modern petrol-pump which will bring down the cost of fuel....

The industrial plant, the one project of real human value because it would offer jobs and even careers for boys leaving school, who at present, after ten years of schooling, are launched into a certainty of unemployment, unless they're heirs to a boat or a business – the industrial plant hasn't got beyond the dream stage. The hotel, I'm thankful to believe, will never be built because Goat Island has none of the "amenities" required by mass tourism. But late in 1968 the *traghetto* arrived.... And they're digging a hole near the ports for the petrol-pump.

The first fatal motoring accident the island had ever known occurred in 1967. From now on we may look forward to many more.

And yet, notwithstanding the increasing mechanical incursions into the island's basically archaic preferences (the motor-cars sit rather incongruously on our conservatism – we feel the donkey is the *natural* mode of transport, whatever the advantages of the car); and notwithstanding the multiplication of television aerials popping up over the flat roofs round the piazza (which produce an illusion of entertainment as often as its reality, for frequently what appears tremblingly on the screen can best be identified by listening hard to the sound-track - Milan is a long way from Goat Island) - in spite of this oncoming of modernity, the island's outlook and individualism are those of a century back; and that means six or ten centuries back, those of the Middle Ages, or even twenty centuries back, into the times of the transition from B.C. to A.D. So many of our modes and customs, agronomical, architectural, domestic, are medieval or Roman; besides Saracen or Byzantine, as well as antique Greek; and if, shutting one's mind to the motors, one watches the human traffic of the piazza, one sees almost nothing that wasn't the rule at the turn of this century or earlier. The children here still bowl hoops, as Victorian children did; small boys still play that satisfying game called in early twentieth century Britain "tipcat", in which a wedge of wood is tapped into the air with a stick and then smitten with a wham as it falls; schoolgirls wear big bows in the hair which grows down their backs like Alice's; ring-a-ring-a-roses I've seen danced in a side-street by some infants, to the point of "all fall down", dialect words sung to the tune, or nearly, as we knew in England (can any folkloristical professor explain this remarkable coincidence in two such disparate cultures?) - and when Gigi's aunt Caterina's last-born child was baptised, it was clad in *long clothes,* an infantile fashion which surely went out in England before the turn of the century. Household refuse is still thrown out of every front door or window, and swept up by a boy with a brush made of dwarf-palm and a donkey and cart. The cries of the fishermen peddling their catch through the streets won't have changed these thousand years (since no new kinds of fish have been invented) - phrase and melody, for each species sold, have been handed down like heirlooms. Beside this poetry, the calls of the haberdashery hawkers have the nasality of cheapjacks. The ambulant vendor of home-made frying pans still bangs his wares together like cymbals as he passes through the piazza. The chemist's shop, the only one on the island, is still a centre of gossip for men of importance with time on their hands - men like the retired Marshal of Carbineers, the Postman between deliveries, the Exactor of taxes, the Mayor, and so on; when you call to ask the *dottoressa* for some medicament, conversation stops so that the company may hear what's wrong with you.

Clothes, it's true, have leaped several decades forward in the last five or six years. The young men, though they still have their hair out, now dress with delightful elegance and vie with each other to appear in the latest modes (the excellent mass-tailoring firms of north Italy sell the latest fashions even in small towns like Trapani): but Gigi is the only boy of Goat Island who has ever possessed a genuine Carnaby Street suit, 1968 model. The girls' dresses are pretty and in the fashion (got from the women's magazines) but always demure; and nearly always made by the girls and their mothers. Only one mini-skirt has been seen, worn by "La Colonnella", so-called from the elegance and swagger of her carriage as she saunters alluring across the piazza: La Colonnella is a very beautiful girl of sixteen who, as Damianina puts it, is a *donna perduta*, a "lost woman": she lost her virginity two years ago and the young men since have all been after her – but not as suitors for her hand. Clothes and motors apart, there's scarcely a thing in the piazza that looks later than 1900: unless one counts the poster that advertises the latest film to arrive. The cinema, the island's only place of entertainment besides the five coffee-bars (where the men can play cards and the boys games like billiards and hand-operated "football"), opens three or four evenings a week, entrance about two shillings; most films are stories of cowboys, gangsters or mythical heroes, with occasionally a vaguely biblical saga. Once I came upon Monsignore, the Archpriest, examining with timorous interest a poster advertising that evening's show: "The Prodigal Son: a Story of Youth and Love."

This is a village life. The excitements and crises which keep the matrons chattering outside each others' doorways or screaming across the piazza from balcony to balcony are domestic: betrothals, illnesses, food, what was bought yesterday in Trapani, and how much: today's prices of fish, and money – or perhaps this list should start the other way round: where nearly every family's margin money wobbles unceasingly though cheerfully between the red and the black, money and its manipulation is of fascinating interest and always a favourite subject of talk. Nobody, except people like Alcamese, enjoys money for its own sake: everybody's concern, or every woman's, is to make too little money do the work of more than enough. And, thanks to housewifely genius and the wonderfully accomodating Italian credit system, most succeed. I don't suppose anyone on the island would stay solvent if every *cambiale* (promissory note - an indispensable component of the monetary system, almost counting as legal currency), hire-purchase contract and other form of loan and credit were suddenly called in. Until that happens, however, all who want can have TV, sewing-machine, motorcycle, washing-machine, and so on; and there always seems to be money for an attractive length of material for dressmaking, or some bargain addition to the girls' dowries, or an ornate new candelabrum for the family bedroom (which is also the *salone).* Money, and the daily domestic events, are the absorbing matters of gossip and re-gossip; there's little malice, and almost no scandal - nothing scandalous happens. One morning the piazza was for a few minutes in uproar because a woman, screaming abuse and promises of vengeance, pursued another woman (in flight) who, she declared, was trying to seduce away her husband. But this row soon died down, and nothing more was heard of it. Most quarrels between matrons arose from allegations of violence or toy-filching or unfairness against each others' children: imprecations fulminate across the piazza briefly and then all is peace again.

It takes a happening of some magnitude to outdo in interest these little daily topics; but nothing much does happen. Dramatic crimes aren't committed. The island's last murder, still something almost nostalgically recalled, occurred eighteen years ago when a cuckolded husband put nine bullets into his wife caught in the act. Nothing has since equalled this. When I moved into the country house he'd found me, Tommaso reassured me (knowing that all foreigners sought the Mafia round every corner): "There's no Mafia on Goat Island", he said. "Nobody will disturb you - you can leave your door open!" And, to be sure, throughout my three years here, I've only heard of two offences grave enough to give the carbineers some sleuthing, a couple of silly sacrilegious thefts: an unhappy youth, in the boredom of unemployment, took a little Madonna from the Mother-Church;

and some day-tripper louts from Trapani broke open the rural shrine of the Madonnina and stole some votive ornaments. But such things are merely momentary interruptions in the hourly manufacture of fresh links, tiny but vastly important, in the unending chain of family and communal life.

Death, of course, is an event that can overshadow most else. Not death in itself – that's an everyday happening, which comes anyway to everyone (four or five funeral processions cross the piazza in every week of the year, the bell tolling three melancholy strokes at a time). A death of one's own, obviously, for a while charges the whole family being with emotion and drama to the exclusion of all else. But other people's deaths too, can be surrounded by such glamour or melodrama that they generate a vast amount of public sentiment and emotional satisfaction, as moving sometimes as a *festa;* though generally one hardly turns one's head to look at the mourners.

The tragic accident in which a foolhardy young motorcyclist died, riding too fast along a blind and narrow road, had everything needed for a great effusion of public feeling and an extra-dramatic display of mourning by the stricken family. So glamorous a death hadn't come to the island in memory. The victim's youth, little more than twenty; the pathos of his death occurring just as he'd come for a few days at home from the "continent" where he was working; the esteem in which the family was generally held; the tears of the surviving brother who was so popular a young man, and capable a stone-mason: these factors in combination offered a rare occasion for a luxury of vicarious suffering and collective condolence. By the time the funeral was to start next day, the anguish of the family had reached heroic proportions and could be heard by the crowd mainly of women, waiting below in the piazza. This crowd had gathered less in homage to the dead boy when he was borne out in his coffin on the shoulders of his young friends, than to savour and relish every shriek or sigh of sorrow emitted by the female members of the bereaved family who had all, profoundly veiled in black, come out as far as the street in order to display their grief as loudly and dramatically as they knew how – while the cortège moved across to the church, headed by Monsignore and followed by the male mourners, most weeping and all with jacket collars turned up as if against a cold wind. In front of all went a long crawling file of men and boys carrying splendid funerary flowers built up on wooden frames and swathed with black and gold sashes identifying the donors – "Football Club of Goat Island", "Hunters and Anglers Club of Goat Island", and so on; as well as the names of numerous private families. Sicilians are among those ancient peoples for whom the appurtenances of death are more important than the thing itself which, if it's coming to a man, will come; such feminine rituals as shrieks of lamentation, near hysterics, the tearing of hair, are by way of being a kind of prophylaxis against unnamed influences both for the dead and for his surviving kin. I haven't been able to explain the turning up of coat collars, which is often a formality of our funerals. Men I've asked either reply: "No, no – that's never done"; or say that it's always been the thing to do at funerals. Could it indeed have an origin in the noting of Death's breathing coldly down one's neck? For a longer time than usual the females of this family wore deepest mourning, even the girls going veiled and in black from head to toe; and once a week they made a solemn and self-conscious pilgrimage to the cemetery. It's neither untrue nor unkind to say that had this young man died a quiet and undramatic death, the funeral would have been no different from any other, and the mourning no more intense; but the drama of the death glorified it, and the island's mass emotion rose on the wings of glamour to such a height that the family had to live up to it. The same kind of thing happens, say in Palermo, after a Mafia murder.

The loss by death of a member of a family always acts as a tremendous reinforcement of the rest in that stronghold of a united spirit which the Sicilian family is. And, socially, it gives the bereaved family a certain prestige, an aura of heroism – one can't say social distinction because almost any family at any time is in some degree of bereavement. It's the custom, when death occurs, to stick on street-door or window a small strip inscribed "For my husband", "For my mother-law" or whomever it may be: sometimes handwritten, sometimes bought at the stationers. In Sicily this modest statement is deemed enough; in Apulia, I remember, one was more explicit about one's sense of loss: the shops kept a wide range of black stickers with gold or purple lettering from which one chose the one closest to one's feelings: "For my wife", "For my dear wife", "For my beloved wife", "For my adored wife".

Emotions, one's own or other people's, and especially the extremes of anguish and joy, largely occupy in a community like ours the place of "art" in others more sophisticated. Displays of emotion, again one's own or others', are the powerful stuff of melodrama or of self-dramatisation; they're the books which few are capable of reading, the theatre which doesn't exist: they feed the human hunger for human dramatics. The Sicilian towns for centuries have had the puppet *teatrini,* where the analphabetic could be emotionally entranced by the epic stories of Orlando and the paladins; even today one can occasionally come across in Palermo an ambulant story-teller narrating these same tales, or rather chanting them in a dolorous Saracen strain, and illustrating each episode with a big coloured poster which he changes for another as a lecturer his lantern-slides. But on Goat Island there are no such diversions; it's the young who go to the cinema a couple of times a week; and though in a number of houses now the television flickers it's watched often with more curiosity than comprehension. Thus the most is made of other people's emotions, when one's short of them oneself. For many people, a drama a day keeps boredom away.

The crowd in the piazza on the day of that funeral, emotionally gorging on the dramatic lamentations of the dead youth's womenfolk, was an example of this. Another came, so sad for all our family, when a woman called in to tell Damianina that Gigi on his scooter had been hurt in a collision and taken to the doctor. She went tearing through the streets, choked with the sobbing of fear; I tore after her, and we found that Gigi was little the worse – a few cuts and bruises; and we went home again. This came at the end of a week of strain for Damianina: a week of difficulty with Papà who was opposing Maria's engagement to a young Neapolitan *guardia di finanza* stationed here – a "soldier" of the Customs Corps, the men with yellow facings on their green uniforms. For this week our sweet Damianina had been overwrought and nervy: Gigi's accident was the last straw. Suddenly, back in her home from the public clinic, she went into hysterics. I was outside in the piazza, waiting for Gigi to return bandaged and plastered – a neighbour with a car was bringing him – when the unutterable pain of this wailing and shrieking rose like a sudden terror. One or two women were with her already, Maria and Aunt Caterina and a couple of friends – but within seconds of the first shriek, women came running from all directions to pile into Damianina's front room – there was of course no knocking, nobody bothered with formalities, they pushed in and crowded round, anxious lest they miss a single note of this dramatic eruption of suffering. I went in and shouted: "Can't you leave her alone? Can't you let her breathe? Get out, can't you!" They didn't notice I was there. I went outside again; and then Papà came, called from work. I said: "Tommaso – all these women – she needs air, and quiet, and a chance to calm down. Can't you throw them out – there must be thirty women crammed into your house." He shrugged his shoulders: *"Sono femmine"*, he said, "they're women."

It was Gigi himself, who, when he arrived, limping and a bit shocked, calmed his mother; and then the women came out again: they'd drunk all there was of poor Damianina's personal drama. I think Damianina herself expected and enjoyed her audience. Private emotion won't do; it's got to be shared, exalted into a kind of collectivist involvement. The home-coming of Luciano after his two years of military service beautifully showed how private feeling is transfigured into public spectacle. This happened early on a day of summer while the sun was high but not yet fierce and the sky's gentle pastel tones hadn't turned to the white heat of mid-morning. Luciano was coming, it was known, by the first *aliscafo,* about half-past seven; there was no traffic yet in the piazza – it was as clear as a stage. His mother was a neighbour of ours; her door faced right down the piazza to the corner round which her son must turn walking up from the *porto.* The young man's grandmother and sisters and friends had gone down to the jetty; but the mother stood at her doorway, alone. Everybody had woken up to an awareness that there was drama today; all the balconies looking down on the piazza were empty, little clusters of people stood on the pavements outside the doorways. The mother, an untidy woman with her hair in pins and wearing an apron, stood waiting, showing a bit of fret: her hands were fiddling with her apron. And then he turned the corner; and she became the protagonist awaiting her entrance. The young man came slowly sauntering into the piazza, a debonair hero, chatting gaily with his sisters, an arm charmingly round his grandmother, old friends surrounding him like an escort. His mother didn't budge, nor make a sign: she stood now erect and attentive, her cue. Then, as the boy and his party neared the centre of the empty piazza, her moment came. The skimpiness of her frame and the ungainliness of her form seemed suddenly bewitched into stateliness: she stepped magnificently out into the piazza all by herself and strode across to meet her son – appearing to all who watched, just what she felt herself to be, a heroine. Her slightly waddling, short-legged gait suddenly acquired grace: what ought to have been slightly ridiculous turned to dignity. Half way across the piazza Luciano halted; and the people with him, even the grandmother, directed by instinct, stepped back a yard or two. The mother flung out her arms and stood waiting, for a moment the symbol of all motherhood; the embrace was magnificent.

And yet there was nothing false in all this. Luciano's mother wasn't play-acting as she strode over the flagstones like the head girl going up for her prize: she was that morning's heroine, and knew it. It was her day. The heroic role, or the martyr's, is necessary now and then to people on our island; like hysterics, like the jollity of a *festa,* it acts as safety-valve for the super-charged yet fundamentally melancholy Sicilian temperament: a temperament as volatile and perfervid and somehow inwardly agonized as Sicily's violent climate and geology. Our own sweet Damianina, who can see no purpose in life beyond love and work for her family and kindnesses for her neighbours, whose each day is an unbroken sequence of happy self-sacrifice (even asleep she has one ear alert for any whimper of need), is a great hand at melodramatics: whether Duzzo breaks the vase that holds the artificial flowers or one of Papà's jovian roars provokes a brief tiff, she finds comfort in heroical self-martyrdom: the house fills or whispers with her shrill lamenting and muttered orisons to St. Joseph or the universal mother: "Madre mia! Madre mia!" she protests; and the family takes it all as a matter of course.

Naturally, the endless stream of tiny family and communal happenings that's been flowing, one may say, since the Phoenicians were here, is pretty often overshadowed by some occurrence such as *carnevale* or the feast of San Giuseppe - Joseph - which on Goat Island towers above all others in public esteem and celebration; or like one of those frequent winter storms that cut the island off from the world for a day or two at a time; or that brutal disaster of the capitalistic closure - a lockout for reasons of profit - of the vital tunny-fish cannery, which put a great many wage-earners out of work at the end of 1968, including our Papà; or that other disaster, more natural or supernatural - the month of earthquakes which brought tragedy to western Sicily early in the same year and a great deal of terror to our island as well.

Or even such a bizarre incident as Signor Mangiapane's hundredth birthday. I came into the piazza that morning, about eleven o'clock, and was perplexed to find the island's brass band standing about with their instruments - but only about half their number, and they not wearing their smart blue-and-gold uniforms. The band normally turns out only about five times a year, on festivals of sufficient municipal moment to justify the outforkings of the fee. But this was no *festa*; and here was a quorum of the band, including the big drum with its forelegs, the little deaf-mute water-carrier, obviously with a job on hand. A number of the musicians are friends of mine: Peppino the newsagent with his clarionet; Carlo the electrician who plays a trombone; the flautist son of the blacksmith; Emilio from the bank who beats the bass drum which is mounted on the back of the deaf-mute; and a schoolmate of Gigi's who fits himself into an enormous tuba.

I asked Peppino: "What's up? Why the *musica?*" He grinned in his gentle, self-deprecating way: "For Signor Mangiapane - he 'makes' a hundred years today." I had never heard of Signor Mangiapane; nor, for a long time, had many others; for some decades the old gentleman had led a withdrawn life. But a hundredth birthday was plainly a notable event - don't centenarians in England receive telegrams from the monarch? So here, on Goat Island, was the band. Just before eleven-thirty Dr. Baffi, the Mayor, came bustling into the square, with that air of beaming condescension which mayors assume with their chains (or, in Italy, their tricolour sashes inherited from Napoleonic times). Immediately other notables joined the Mayor; most of them had been sitting, as they did every day in periods of leisure, under the mulberry tree outside the *Circolo di Caccia e Pesca*, to which most men of consequence belong even if they don't shoot or fish; the club's chief asset is a cluster of handsome green basket-chairs on which only members may sit. The retired Marshal of Carbineers stood one pace behind the regnant Marshal of Carbineers; who had placed himself half a pace behind the Mayor; the Marshal of the Customs Corps and a Brigadier of Prison Guardians; the *veterinario*, a gentle man with a sweet smile and yet a passion for card-playing (the animals on our island are pretty healthy); the exactor, an aggressive polemicist in the coffee-bars where he spends more time than in his municipal tax office; Monsignore, slowly pacing, with his vaguely quizzical hover of a smile and usual air of slight bemusement when outside the mother-church to which for forty years he's been single-mindedly wed; the Cavaliere, a whimsical character who likes to play a diversity of roles – war-veteran, aristocrat, sportsman, poet, financial pundit – and always dressed appropriately to the role he's chosen for the time being; Ciccio, the agent for the *aliscafi* and universal middleman in any deal he can manoeuvre himself into *(è furbo idro,* Tommaso told me, "he's sharp, that one"); Catalano, the most revered of the barbers, who'd even shut his shop for ten minutes. A patriarchal absentee was Don Pino, but only death could get him out of his butcher's shop while there was work to do; at about eighty-five, he didn't think much of hundredth birthdays.

Towards midday the Mayor gave a sign; the band struck up one of its three or four marches; the notabilities, followed by a few citizens of lesser quality,[16] moved behind the Mayor to the upper part of the *paese* and clustered round him in the piazzetta where Signor Mangiapane lived. By ten to twelve the municipal serenade was over. At noon precisely Signor Mangiapane died.

---

[16] In the eyes that is of a few of the notabilities. There is, in truth, no "class" on Goat Island, no consciousness of it. Stendhal wrote somewhere that an Italian with a miniscule income speaks to a millionaire "as simply as he would to an equal". And so it is here: there's no class distinction – save only that invented for themselves by a few pompous well-to-do (mainly Christian Democrat councillors). [Author's footnote]

The news ran round the piazza while every household was bent over the midday pasta. "What a fortunate death!" said some. "With the music of our band in his ears, and the words of goodwill of our Mayor!" But political opponents of the Mayor blamed that official; it was enough to kill any centenarian, they said, to have a Christian Democrat making speeches outside his window. Everybody expected a specially grand funeral next day; but the Mayor, I suppose, felt he'd done his part, and Signor Mangiapane's exequies were meagre.

But there was a postscript to this story, which amplified its curiosity, but left it even more tantalisingly orbiting through the unexplained. Casually, while she was washing up the dinner things, Damianina remarked: "Poor old Mangiapane, after all this time! Of course, it's only fifty years he's been a *signore,* before that he was a *signorina.*" But Damianina knew no more; that was the fact, and more than state it she couldn't: for the first half of his life Signor Mangiapane had been a "Miss"; at fifty he suddenly changed to a "Mister". Life, perhaps, was like that. Alas, one will never know more about this switch, apparently both spontaneous and sedate, from Signorina to Signore long before these days of surgical and judicial certification. There are, of course, people still living here who knew the ex-Signorina Mangiapane - Don Pino, for example, and our children's *Nonna,* Tommaso's mother, both well over eighty; but they don't remember the transition being a matter for remark. Here, what people are or do is taken as a matter of fate, like the shape of their faces, and the concern of themselves and nobody else.

8. The Bottle

During my first January and February on the island, the coldest and windiest months of the year, while I was still living in the *paese* as tenant of Alcamese's *magazzino,* I used to spend a couple of hours every evening at Masino's. Sometimes Gigi would come in for a *gazzoso* or a hardboiled egg out of the big glass jar; or I'd sit alone sipping at my litre of "white" – when that was finished I'd be in a communicative mood, sometimes, and start swopping half-glasses with some acquaintances; and so became on good terms with quite a lot of the fishermen.

One evening, when I arrived, Domenico, the eleven-year old potboy with a peaky mouse's face, was looking out for me from the doorstep. "Come on – they're waiting for you, Francescone and his brothers," he said. "They've found a bottle." His pale little eyes, shy and sly, peeped up at me hopefully; 'Menico need tips: his daily wage for working all his after-school hours is the equal of about tenpence a day.

In the inner room, where the stewed octopus diffuses its odious vapours from its huge earthenware cauldron, and where, for the sake of the fug, I sat those winter evenings, I found "the Romans" sitting round a small table and well into their fourth or fifth litre; they were three brothers and a cousin – Francescone ("Big Frank") was the oldest and captain of the family boat. The bottle had been found about midday; it was now six; and what with the excitement of talking about the finding of the bottle and the excitement of speculating over the message which was in the bottle and the tantalising possibilities it might reveal; and what with the excitement of the wine that the celebration of these earlier excitements required – by the time I arrived the Romans' excitement was high.

I've called them, in my mind, "the Romans", from the moment of my first seeing them: here in Masino's wine shop, I saw them at once as Romans because of their splendid profiles: those imperially imperious noses and those magnificently senatorial jaws. All four appeared much of an age, forty or fifty or between: thick wiry hair freckled with grey; skins crinkled and crosshatched like old mailbags yet glowing about cheekbones and nostrils with the lilac bloom of two or three decades of robust wine-drinking ("I'm a two-litre man", Francescone liked to declare - and two litres of rough Sicilian is a lot). And not only their profiles; the proud tilt, and a touch of arrogance, of their classic heads; their trace of carriage and the lean, powerful vitality of their brawny frames; these are men, I felt, born to the purple. Sir Osbert Sitwell, writing of "King Bomba", that particularly detestable Bourbon, the second Ferdinand of the Two Sicilies, who died in well-merited agony a year before the extinction of his kingdom in 1860, said: "His was a face altogether impossible to get on to a coin or postage-stamp and failure in this test should surely disqualify any prince from reigning."[17] The faces of these Romans of Goat Island would do honour to the noblest coin and postage-stamp minted or printed, and they could worthily stand in for any of the better looking emperors. Their features are Roman - and why not their blood? Rome, republican and imperial, dominated these parts - and therefore, too, my island for 700 years; in the very waters I'm looking across now, the Roman fleet destroyed Punic power two and a half centuries before Christ, and there was Roman rule still in Sicily five or six hundred years later. Surely there must have been Roman garrisons and settlements, even on this tiny outpost of the empire? While Sicily is richer than Greece herself in enduring evidences of the labour and imagination of the antique Greeks, the Romans have left of themselves almost nothing visible - some restoration of earlier theatres and a great imperial villa, not much more. But in the small human habits of daily life, one's meeting Rome all the time - the hard wooden bedsteads one often sleeps on; the "Isolato" B or F, or whatever the letter may be, which one adds to one's postal address in Messina, identifying the "block" in which one's flat is - exactly as, in Augustan Rome, the big tenement buildings divided into cheap apartments and "isolated"

---

[17] Giovanni Nicotera, a leading liberal imprisoned on Goat Island in 1857 was advised by the governor of the Santa Caterina fortress to beg the king for his liberty, and to address his letter "To his sacred royal majesty Ferdinand II King of the Two Sicilies"; instead, Nicotera wrote: "To the ferocious brute Ferdinand II, not yet satiated with the torture of humanity." [Author's footnote]

within a rectangle of streets were called "insulae".... And here on our island we've got two reminders of Rome: the deep wheel-tracks furrowed into the old rock-road along the coast, and that solitary field strewn with the ghostly shards of amphorae and tiles – ghostly because nowhere else on the island is there trace of Roman building or brickwork. Surely, then, I argue to myself, my "Romans" at Masino's may be descended from ancient settlers come down from Lazio? Why not?

The Romans, on working days, which means most days, wear the uniform of the fishermen: a small tight beret – almost a skull-cap – of a type worn only by fishermen, and blue dungarees buttoned up close at the throat, like the jacket Stalin used to be photographed in.

The message, in English, was written on paper headed P. & O. – Orient Line; there was no ship's name. The date was Christmas night 1965; the ship, at the moment the bottle was thrown overboard, was about three hours' steaming west of Gibraltar. The writers were New Zealanders: they gave two names and two addresses, and asked anyone who picked the bottle up to write to them. I visualised two sandy-haired Scots, full of Christmas beer: young stewards perhaps, or apprentices. Messages in bottles can't help being romantic; this one, in a nicely sentimental manner, once again confronted me with the inveterate puzzle of what we call coincidence and what the ancients thought of as fate: the mystery of the hazards that can indifferently switch one's little private life into disaster or delight ("Oh darling, d'you realise? If I hadn't turned that corner just when I did, and you hadn't been gazing into that shop window, we'd never have met!"). So here was the mystery again: what brought these New Zealanders' predestinated bottle, after sixty-five days of harassment by wind and current over a crow's flight of 1200 miles in an ocean of two million square miles, right under the Romans' gunwale and so to the drinking table of the only person within miles of its landfall who could read the message it carried? The prevailing winds – or more likely gales – at this time of year were the maestrale from the north-west and the scirocco from its dead opposite, the south-east, which seemed often to take over from each other as if working in shifts – the northwester blowing mercilessly for three days and then abruptly turning round and blowing back again the way it had come for another three. This bottle, surely, should have been buffeted back and forth until finally shattered on some rocky shore. Yet it had made its way across the western Mediterranean, and on to my table at Masino's, as unerringly as the tunny's navigational senses bring it to its mating grounds between the very islands. But what power guided it? These were the questions I was asking myself: how were these things ordained, and why?

But these weren't the questions the Romans were asking. To them, this message in a foreign language, which had tantalisingly lain under their eyes since midday, could only mean some degree of fortune: a millionaire yachstman, perhaps, aground on some African reef; an American heiress kidnapped by some modern sort of corsair - either, obviously, would be offering a reward. By the time I came, the Romans had become convinced of the urgency of the message the bottle had brought: nobody who valued the utility of a serviceable bottle and who begrudged the expenditure of pointless effort would be fool enough to write a letter, cork it up in a sound bottle, and throw it into the sea unless there was a good reason for doing so. Although Sicilians enjoy fun and often do useless things for serious reasons, they can't see the point of doing useless things just for fun. It was therefore in all seriousness - but, as the afternoon wore on, with a growing flush of confidence - that the Romans waited for me to tell them what reward was being offered in the foreign letter in return for what service or work. If the message had been written in Italian the Romans themselves couldn't have read it: on this island most parents over forty have to get their children to write and read for them. Schooling is barely a generation old.

A Sicilian is popularly supposed, by people unfamiliar with Sicilians, to be a person of ungovernable passions who flies to violence whenever things fail to go the way he wants: a smiling charmer with a knife up his sleeve and dynamite in his breast. This is the romantic view held by people who obtain a gothic thrill out of the notion of the Mafia. Real life Sicilians, however (and especially the gentle, conciliatory people of our island), keep a firm hold on their emotions, particularly when they feel mortified by events or duped by their own hopes. Certainly

Sicilians can, at the smallest prompting, go into transports of anger or despair or grief (outbursts of enjoyment, lacking drama, are publicly more restrained) and as quickly out of them again; but these are generally formal, even ritualistic, expressions of passion, required by certain social circumstances. A man would, however, sooner drop dead than show by his face or manner that he's been made a sucker of. Sicilians have a splendid, private pride and the stiff upper lip is its symbol: if you find you've been worsted in some matter, you shrug it off in public by making the what-do-I-care gesture of flinging the right wrist over your right ear like salt over the shoulder.

And so, when the Romans learned that the bottle had brought no more than Christmas wishes, two months late, from two young New Zealanders who'd probably forgotten all about the bottle next day, they flung their disappointment over their right ears and swallowed their broken hopes with another litre of wine; and immediately discovered fresh hopes in the remains of the old. Sicily herself is too old to nurture hope; the beauty of her violent stony mountains is the beauty of a pile of bones; the great grey heights of despair that her landscape seems, are like a huge dried heap of dead hydrangea heads. And yet the Sicilian, in spite of the dimple of melancholy that seems to curb even his loudest laughter, is an unflagging short-time optimist; he knows in the belly of his being, though he's never thought about it, that in the long run all is gall and wormwood; but he knows too that tomorrow, or the day after, he will win the pools or the *lotto*, the "numbers". So the Romans were now persuaded that the bottle still held promise.

The New Zealanders had asked the finder of the battle to write to them, hadn't they? They gave their addresses in New Zealand, didn't they? They want to know what happened to their bottle, don't they? All right Michele, said Francescone to me, you shall write to them. Write to them from us; tell them who we are and where we found their bottle. Tell them what a hard life we fishermen of Goat Island have, how little we make, how the Government doesn't think of us. They sent us their good wishes, these odd New Zealanders - we must send them ours. And who knows what they might send back in return? Write tomorrow, Michele - and if tomorrow morning you come to us in the market, there'll be a kilo of fish for you *senza pagare,* without paying.

I wrote to both New Zealanders, one in Wellington, the other in Auckland; I even, in the name of the Romans but without their knowledge, urged the New Zealanders to come and stay with us should they come to Sicily. The airmail postage cost me the price of about three and a half litres of wine. That evening I took an Italian translation of what I'd written to the Romans and assured them the New Zealanders would answer by return of post. I didn't go to the fish market; but we feasted on red mullet next day – Damianina told me that Francescone had brought her a kilo, saying it was a present for me. Promises are always kept on Goat Island.

For months afterwards I was haunted by these sandy-haired phantoms from New Zealand (even their faces took shape in my mind's eye – one snub and freckled, the other sharp-nosed and looking as if he came from Glasgow); each time I met the Romans they told me: "There you are – no letter has come, you see"; and week by week the note of disillusion and umbrage in their voices seemed louder: "They won't write now, you'll see – I knew they wouldn't all the time." But I promised that if they had patience, the answer would come in time. I told them: "New Zealanders are a sort of English – and the English always answer letters." But I was wrong; and gradually as the year advanced a slight triumph sounded in their announcements that no letter had come: "I told you so," they seemed to say. I never felt thereafter that I enjoyed the Romans' unqualified confidence.

Another sad consequence of the finding of the bottle was my discovery that the Romans weren't Roman after all – a Saracen ancestry was more likely. Through writing the letters I learned for the first time their family name – first names are usual on Goat Island at any social level below that of Mayor and Marshal of Carbineers, just as conversation, except that of the most formal kind, is conducted in the familiar second-person singular (for the conventional northerner it's at first uncomfortably solecistic to address a stranger as *tu*). I had to look again at those splendid aquiline profiles and agree that, instead of Roman, they were more likely Saracen – and true semitic Arab rather than North African Berber. Their *cognome* is one of those curious Arab-Italian hybrids that occur in Sicily – like Mongibello, a "folk" name for

Etna, oddly composed of Italian and Arabic words for "mountain" run together and forming "Mount Mountain"; or the appalling double howler of Gibilterra, which is the Italian name for Gibraltar[18]. The first half of the Romans' name is the Arabic for harbour and the second the Italian for war; in English, therefore, their patronymic would be Naval Base. But in my mind they'll be forever Romans; and those tiresome New Zealanders stay sandy-headed and speaking a vague Scottish.

Masino's stands in a commanding position at the corner of the grand-sounding Piazza Municipio, which is little more than a forecourt to the Town Hall, and the grand-sounding Strada Vittorio Emmanuele, a stumpy slope of shops which connects the proper piazza with the harbour. Masino thus catches any drinking trade that may pass to and from the *porto;* it's the natural resort of the fishermen and anybody whose business is maritime. The fish market, too, is roughly on Masino's doorstep: two or three trestle tables on which, when the boats have been out before dawn, the catch is displayed with the catchers standing behind; and which, as the sun swings over, move with the morning to the shady side of the street. In the fishing harbours of Apulia - Taranto and Molfetta for example - an incoming trawler's catch is auctioned then and there on the quayside almost before the boat has been properly made fast: the wholesalers close in, bid, buy and despatch the fish to the inland markets leaving the locals to pay high prices for what's left over. There's none of that on Goat Island. We have no middlemen: our crews either themselves sell what they've caught from the trestle tables outside Masino's, or themselves carry the boxes through the streets, crying in sweet musical phrases the kinds they've got; and housewives from their balconies lower their baskets with the money and haul up their buy (vendor and customer will call each other by their first names and probably be connected in some degree of cousinhood).

---

[18] *Gibil* being the Arabic for "Mount" and *terra* (earth) an Italian botch-up of the Moorish name Tarik. At least the English Gibraltar keeps somewhere near, in meaning and structure, the Moorish Gibiltarik. [Author's footnote]

Also just outside Masino's, in the precise centre of the municipal *piazzettina,* there's a wonderful example of the monumental art of the 1890s: a bronze counterpart in civilian clothes of those grandiosely funny statues of the first two Piedmontese kings of united Italy which one sees in almost any town - bellicose and bewhiskered turkey-cocks in plumes and baggy Victorian trousers. This frock-coated and bearded figure, as excellent a likeness as any daguerreotype and an exemplary specimen of the period's prim zeal, is about eight feet high and stands on another eight feet of stone plinth; the back of the head is about on a level with the mayoral windows - if not, indeed, a little higher. A comfortable circlet of watch-chain rests on a rich stomach and each button of the weskit has been modelled to look quite real. The left hand, sculpted within the trousers pocket, is obviously counting the small change; but is held at decency's distance from the noticeable bulge of what an English tailor calls, or used to call, "dressing by the left". The face gazes out over the heads of anybody in front with an air of unapproachable benevolence and an expression of ruthless stupidity. Every line of the statue pays tribute to its model's total satisfaction with himself. The model had reason to be satisfied: he was then the lord of Sicilian tunny fishing, a magnate of the Marsala wine industry, a shining bigwig, and, in the last decades of the nineteenth century, the squire of Goat Island, all of which he owned: he granted the inhabitants a living, and they thanked him for being rich. The thanks are engraved on the side of the pedestal which faces the municipality, and are thus expressed (here literally translated:

The Workers,
As a Spontaneous Offering,
The Municipality
With Official Concurrence,
Have Raised this Monument
to the Benefactor
of
GOAT ISLAND
in order to demonstrate
that there cannot be discord
between Capital and Labour,
between Riches and Want,

Where there preside
Justice, Compassion, Love

That benefactor, though he lives on here in the worst bronze taste, was removed nearly a century ago; the fortunes of his firm have declined and his name survives on Goat Island only as a trade mark. Today another "foreigner" owns the *tonnara* which has a thousand years of history, and the canning factory; and on his marketing of the tunny-fishery products the well-being of Goat Island's people chiefly depends. The present population of the island won't thank this Genovese millionaire for benefactions as their fathers thanked his predecessor a century ago; in 1968 this man upon whom so many families depend suddenly closed the cannery and so took away the livelihood of about one-third of the island's wage-earners, a deprivation which has been felt in every corner of our financially fragile community. This piece of feudal brutality by an absentee capitalist could mean the murder of an island. But capitalistic extinction is legal in Italy, and doesn't interest the "autorità".

An old-fashioned barometer hangs in the doorway between Masino's two taprooms; everybody who comes in taps it before getting a drink or finding a seat. He doesn't do this because he expects to learn anything from the barometer; he wants to see whether his own forecast, which he knows to be right one, happens to be backed by it. I used to ask some fisherman, usually 'Bastiano, almost every evening about what weather was ahead; I don't think I ever had a wrong answer. It's as if, after a lifetime of reading the wind and the sky and a hundred lifetimes of their forefathers' doing so, they share a language with the elements as the birds and fish do.

But as good a barometer as any is the way the wine's selling at Masino's. In fine weather, when the boats come easily in during the morning after a good night's work since three or four a.m., the wine flows through the afternoon and early evening (if you're a fisherman here, you're in bed by around nine); but when the maestrale's raging from the northwest and a "wicked" sea keeps all boats at their moorings, sometimes for two or three days on end, the men sit about glumly at Masino's and the

Romans look like children who've been kept indoors because it's raining and can't find their toys.

Quite nine out of ten of the regular customers are fishermen. Masino's, really, is more of a fishermen's club than a public *cantina;* they come to talk, and do business, and get away from the shrill feminine turmoil of their homes. They talk about fish, money and children or grandchildren: I don't know, and I don't suppose they do, which is more important to them - fish or children: for fish are their life and children the aim of their life; money, the vital consequence of the fish and the vital support of the children, horribly seems to assume an importance greater than either. Here, in the evening following a night's work, after they've sold their catch, mended their nets and gear, and made ready the boat for going out again, they meet for the share-out. Round each table there'll be a boat's crew: the Romans round one, 'Bastiano and his nephews and Tommaso round another, and so on; at each a boat-owner and his crew - brothers, nephews, cousins and sometimes, like Tommaso, a working partner from outside the family. Fishing is a hereditary calling, and the family boat is handed down from father to son; a born fisherman wouldn't know what to do away from the boat and the sea. So men who have fishing in their blood but have inherited no boat join up with a captain who needs crew - like Tommaso and Nino who "work" for 'Bastiano. They share in the labour and in the takings; in the frustration of a gale and a fishless sea and in the prosperity of a good catch. 'Bastiano, the owner of the boat and its skipper, is first among equals - he takes a higher percentage than his mates, since he must bear the cost of repairs and replacements. So now, in the evening, each boat crew sits round a table with a litre bottle in the middle and glasses all round - and, if there's a boy, perhaps a fizzy lemonade (boys generally join their father's boat at about thirteen of fourteen). Then the captain empties his pockets on to the table of notes and coins and starts dealing the money round like cards - a pile of each denomination in front of every man, according to the share due to each: round the circle the captain deals, 100-lire pieces in turn all round the table, so that one could think some gambling game was going on. This is the way the pay-out is done, and always has been done; few of our fishermen could do a sum on paper.

It's a simple, friendly way, and it allows justice to be seen to be done. It will die out, of course; though I can't see why it must: what more satisfying and convivial method of dividing up the day's earnings could be devised? But no: it won't be allowed much longer: the State and up-to-dateness will require returns to be made, forms to be filled up, receipts to be signed, and bureaucratic pettifoggers to oversee all this, while "deductions" are made from these pitiful earnings from the sea. Mothers of families complain that fish costs more than they can pay; yet often the fishermen take home to feed their families something between fifteen shillings and a pound a day. They say there are fewer fish in the sea, that the cost of gear is for ever rising, that the Government doesn't give a damn for them. No doubt these things have always been said; but I believe they are all true. There *are* fewer fish off many of the coasts of Sicily, because of the impudent operations of the dynamiting fish-pirates (though none dare work off Goat Island shores). Now and then the newspapers report arrests by the maritime police; but the poaching blatantly goes on. Several years ago I was bathing in a small and deserted cove within view of Cape Passero, the southernmost tip of Sicily, and near the site of ancient Greek Helorus, which I reached by following, foothold after foothold, a path gauged out of the rock by an infinitude of human feet – when I was jumped out of my happily quiescent skin by a huge bang and a rearing water-spout a couple of hundred yards along the coast. Two men were on the rocks high over the scene of the explosion; one of them, when the commotion had calmed, climbed down and waded into the sea with a net and a basket; and scooped up the stunned corpses. But it isn't the corpses they scoop up that matter: it's the annihilation of life and incipient life for acres around. Occasionally, as I've said, arrests are made; a year or two ago, I've forgotten when, two foreign tourists underwater-diving were killed by one of these piratical bombs. The men who did it were identified, tried and sentenced – to a short time in prison. Meanwhile the fishermen have fewer fish every year to catch, and the people to eat.

Almost a century ago a Palermo magistrate, pronouncing judgement in a case which turned on the communal character of fisherfolk, said:[19]

> The people of the sea are a kind of tribe, who regard the people of the land as an aberrant tribe, whom they fear, with whom they don't like being in contact, and whom they shun as much as they can. The fishermen contract their marriages among themselves....

A few years later George Gissing was writing, of Taranto in Apulia: "Today the fisherfolk form a colony apart; they speak a dialect which retains many Greek words unknown to the rest of the population." Not only, he could have added, a colony apart, but one almost hostile to non-fishermen; I've seen small fisher-boys in Taranto throw stones for a lark at old men because they were silly old landsmen; and once, outside Mussolini's grandiose post office in New Taranto, I was hit in the face by a squashy old peach thrown by boys from a passing fishmonger's van. Gissing was misinformed, I think, about the Greek words "unknown to the rest" – not used by the rest, would be more like it. But the speech of Taranto, like any other in the South, is an amalgam of many: the fishermen there don't say "buon' giorno" – "b'on gior'" they shout to each other (none shouts conversationally louder than an Apulian): which is "bon jour" with a provincial accent. Provençal perhaps? Norman? "Merda" is a popular expletive there – one rarely hears it in Sicily; while a pure Arabism, totally absent from Sicily, is "mafeesh" instead of "non c'è" – "there isn't any". There's a Tarantine word for cheese which I've heard nowhere else in the Two Sicilies and whose origin is unmistakable: "ches" or" chesa", pronounced "kez". Would the German "Käse" have been in use among the thirteenth century soldiers of the Hohenstaufen?

The fishermen of Goat Island, too, have certain vagaries of pronunciation peculiar to themselves, as well as their special vocabulary of fishing and the sea. One day 'Bastiano was telling me sadly that he had no children, and I noticed he said it in a way I'd not before heard: "Yo non gio figghi", for which the Italian is; "Io non ho figli". ("ho" having no aspirate). 'Bastiano departed from ordinary dialect in his rendering of "ho" – "gio", he said, spoken like the English "Joe".

I wonder if any classical author has noticed how rigidly closed-shop the hereditary fishing community was, not only in

[19] *Giornale di Sicilia*, 10 April 1877 {Author's footnote]

the trade-union sense, but also in the social. For I take it that the fierce particularism which one finds among the fisherfolk right round the coast of Magna Graecia, from Ischia to the Adriatic, and the undisguised dislike they have for any outsider, must go back to an ancient cause; unless, something like the antique Phoenician trading posts, the first Greek fishing settlements were maintained in the face of native hostility?

Recently I read a book about a coastal trip round Sicily in an English yacht. In one passage the author describes how in the harbour of Trapani he watches a local boatman at his oars. "He rows standing up, the way they all do here in Sicily." As it happens, Trapani and our islands form the one corner of Sicily where rowers do *not* stand up; their usual position here is seated and facing aft, just as one rows on the Serpentine in London. My own suspicion is that this custom came about through Muslim influence – that is, North African; my recollection is that Moroccan boatmen usually row sitting down. But elsewhere in Sicily, and all round the coasts of southern Italy and Greece too, boatmen row standing up and pressing forward on the sweeps like figures in an antique fresco: oars crossed, left hand operating the starboard, right the port; exactly, in fact, as boatmen work in the Rangoon and Bangkok rivers, in Singapore harbour and the roads of Hong Kong. I've often wondered, since the Mediterranean shores are said to have been peopled through migrations from the East, whether this gracious mode of rowing wasn't brought to Europe thousands of years ago from the waters of South-East Asia. But not to Trapani.

On this matter of rowing, there's a puzzle which in southern Italy, from Naples to Crotone and Taranto, from Reggio to Palermo, I've for years been wanting to unravel: Why do the watermen of these coasts prefer to row their boats stern first? There seems to me to exist here something of a philosophical conflict – an instance of truth divided against itself. For millennia the theorists of boat-design have been shaping their crafts to move bows first – that, they'd say, is what bows are for; through the same immensities of time, the practitioners of boat-propulsion have been contradicting the designers by rowing astern with their stern high in the water behind their backs. Presumably both are perfectly right: the boat-builders can prove beyond doubt that their design is correct; the boatmen know from experience and tradition that their practice is the proper one. What is the reason for this apparent discord between the two halves of truth? It's no good asking the boatmen.

9. La Tonnara

Greek galleys putting out for battle from Samos, Salamis or Syracuse must have looked like this: the same long, low black hulls; the rows of oarsmen hauling on their great sweeps – ours today, like those of antiquity, thickened near the grip for counterpoise; the stumpy mast canted forward and a square-sail hoist for a following breeze – here in Favignana the scirocco or south-easter to carry the black barges out, a north-wester called maestrale to bring them back to harbour when the battle's won. And battle it is, the tunny-fishing as it's done here and has been done, almost without change, since Saracen times – perhaps even Phoenician: dangerous and gruelling for the hundred odd men whose hereditary skill it is, and always deadly, on a good day when wind and current are right, for two or three hundred gigantic fish, nearly half a ton some of them.

"È la Guerra," Francescone had told me at Masino's, "è la guerra fra noi e i pesci" – "it's war, between us and the fish." *Battle* is the notion intrinsic to this fearsome and magnificent struggle; and down the ages the word seems to have come naturally to the *tonnaroti*, the men who fight it. Henry Festing Jones, friend and biographer of Samuel Butler, described more than seventy years ago watching, at some Sicilian "tunnery", boats, nets and men being blessed by a bishop at the start of the season. Festing Jones, unfailingly British, asked one of the men: "Do you think it is quite sportsmanlike to pray that many tunnies may be killed?" Yes," said the man, "it is right to pray to win the battle – and we battle the tunnies, so we may pray."[20]

It's a terrible, yet superb, war for the hour or so it lasts; splendid and horrible, thrilling and gruesome, spellbinding and sickening. The spectacle of it is incomparably exciting and, in a hellishly dramaturgical way, beautiful; afterwards, mind deafened by such a splendid discord between horror, awe and glamour, one thanks one's stars for the chance to watch – but one never wants to watch again.

---

[20] *Diversions in Sicily,* p. 317. (Alston Rivers, 1909) [Author's footnote].

Sex is the undoing of the tunny-fish; it's that inescapable biologic compulsion which brings swarms of this titanic mackerel, after thousands of miles of travel through two oceans, every year to the same waters between our islands and on almost exactly the same day of the month - only to find, instead of fulfilment in reproduction, a frenzied death in the bloody turmoil of a mass suicide. For they kill themselves and each other, these enormous fish: gasping for freedom of movement and flaying and lashing with their scimitars of tail and fin; while the sea turns crimson and the frantic crush of fish becomes ever more constricted as the narrowing net in which they are trapped inch by inch is drawn tighter by a hundred chanting sailors.... One wonders why the tunny hasn't learned better after so many hundreds or perhaps thousands of years of pursuing the same pattern of disaster. Every spring, as they have for millenaries of springs, great schools of ocean-going tunny set off for the breeding from the Atlantic depths into the Mediterranean and head for the same shallows that their forbears headed for just west of Sicily. Here they arrive about the middle of May: shallows no deeper than a hundred feet and warming up quickly enough at that season for the spawn to hatch and the fry to thrive.

Instinct sets the tunny's course; but a fair wind can help him on and an adverse current impede him. A strong maestrale from the north-west brings him leaping down the channel between the northern point of our island and the south-western corner of Levanzo; if a northwester is blowing really hard, the tunny rides the waves like a dolphin or an Australian surf rider - and this wind rejoices the owner of the *tonnara*: it blows the fish right into the corridors of the trap.

Once Mediterranean man comprehended the inflexible mating habits of the tunny, and the clockwork accuracy of its timing, he started thinking out a way of ambushing the fish; and the system he worked out a thousand years ago or two thousand or even, perhaps, three, is the same as that used today. Materials and methods have here and their improved (the final net which contains the slaughter is today made of nylon), but the principle of the trap is unchanged. Probably the Arabs of North Africa brought their system to Sicily in the ninth century. Citing the Moslem writer Ibn Hauqal, Denis Mack Smith says "... perhaps an altogether new and elaborate technique of tunny fishing was now adopted".[21] And in every Sicilian *tonnara*, an Arabic title is given to the chief of the fishermen manning it, the man upon whose judgement, knowledge and power of decision the whole operation depends; he is the *Raïs* – the word for sea-captain which can be heard along any North African waterfront today. One may surmise that the idea of the present day *tonnara*, before it passed to the Moors who brought it to Sicily, was a Punic one; until fairly recently there was a *tonnara* operating near the island of Djerba off the Carthaginian shore of Tunisia – and in Favignana, within sight of my present house, on the shore near San Nicòla, a tiny harbour used by both Romans and Phoenicians, there are workings in the rocks which surely can only have been made for the cutting up and washing of tunny just caught; it includes a tunnel bored through the rock in exactly the manner of the Punic tomb in a corner of my garden. San Nicòla is an obvious creek from which to have operated the relatively uncomplicated system of nets which one imagines must have been laid in those early times, when skilled men were perhaps fewer and materials more primitive; and from San Nicòla today one looks out, to left and right of Levanzo, at the two *tonnare* that here are fished each year – that at the mouth of Favignana bay and the other off Formica rock, "Ant rock", away north-east towards Sicily itself.

The principle of the *tonnara* (which we might as well translate "tunnery") is simple and ingenious. The fish, intent on reaching their spawning grounds and forging onward in schools of between fifty and five hundred, are deflected from their unvarying course by baffle-nets into a submarine corridor along which they swim to a huge trough-shaped net of immense strength, deep fifteen or more fathoms but with no outlet. From the surrounding barges, this net is steadily and inexorably drawn up, raising the fish to a slowly-contracting surface and crushing them into an ever dwindling volume of water. It's like siphoning out, drip by drip, a crowded gold fish bowl.

The blue-fin tunny, the variety which comes mating in these waters, is a giant of the mackerel tribe (*scombridae*) with retract-

[21] *A History of Sicily*, Chatto & Windus, 1968, vol. I, p. 8 [Author's footnote].

able dorsal fin, presumably for speed, and – alone, it seems, among fish – a thermo-regulating mechanism in its system of blood vessels that keeps the body temperature above that of the water it's swimming in: one wonders why it's been equipped with this oddly unique device – the tunny isn't the only ocean-going fish that voyages through changing climes. The blue-fin that visits these islands reaches often a length from tip to tip of ten or twelve feet, and may scale four or five hundred kilograms – going on for half a ton; five or six hundred pounds is a common weight. He's a very strong swimmer; and running with the waves before the wind he's like a torpedo. It takes a powerful net to contain him – or two or three hundred of him.

Journalists and romantic writers call the last and fatal compartment of the whole "tunnery" system – the section of net in which the water turns red with blood – the *camera della morte*, the Chamber of Death; but to the fishermen themselves it's simply the *coppo*, the bowl or basin: this is an enormous colander, an acre or even two, in area, of netting as heavy as the thickest carpet and close meshed as chainmail. This net sags to the bottom from the surrounding phalange of black lighters to which its edges are lashed. There's only one opening in this net: that from the corridor of guide-nets which brings the flotillas of tunny to their end. This *coppo*, for strength and endurance, is nowadays made of nylon; for centuries it was woven of hemp and earlier still of esparto or palm fibre.

The tunnery spreads over two or three miles of netting, with baffle-nets led far to north and south and the long channelling corridor divided into three "chambers" which end in the *coppo*; the chambers have connecting "doors" that are raised or lowered to control the volume of fish entering. All this netting is made of wide-meshed hemp annually renewed – the *tonnaroti* start working on them on the harbour foreshore about mid-April, a month before fishing begins. Once the tunnery is set, your eye can track the nets' position by following the lines of floats which hold them to the surface; fifteen fathoms down they're secured to the sea-bed by huge antique iron anchors of the old "Admiralty" type, cast a good century ago. At the end of each season these rusty great anchors, two or three hundred of them, are winched aboard the lighters and brought to the beach where they're laid out in rows to await another year, making the foreshore look like a wide field sown with dragons' teeth. Each anchor needs half a dozen men to carry it ashore. They're heaved aboard the lighters by ancient wooden capstans which a team of men turn by straining on the cross spars and chanting like the pigtailed tars at Trafalgar.

Each April, half way through, ordinary fishing comes to a stop; the few family boats that still go out are manned by 70-year-olds and their grandsons. The rest sign on for the *tonnara*: it assures them of sixty days' economic certitude among three hundred of often profitless chance. The two-month tunnery contract pays them about L120 in a lump sum; for the rest of the year, gales and the frequent scarcity of fish even out their earnings to perhaps a pound a day.

So each April the tunnery becomes reanimated, an event as familiar in the island's year as the flowering of the wild caper in May, or the darting of the migrant quail among the crops before and after each summer, or the happening of San Giuseppe on March 19. It's a thing pre-ordained by the island's past like setting out figs in the sun to dry in late autumn, like eating *spince* at Christmas (the same sugared fritter as the Arab *sfinch* in North Africa). The nets are reconstituted and the boats reconditioned and hauled down the ramps from their winter berths ashore; and, with the resumption of these age-old processes, the same exactly as the year, the century, the millenium before, the beat of the whole island's pulse seems to quicken – for the tunny season isn't merely an incident that occurs every year like cutting the corn or the farrowing of the sow: it's a kind of communal galvanisation, a sharing of a sense of adventure among everybody. The fishermen turned *tonnaroti*, from being a miscellany of contentious egotists, suddenly assume the unity of paladins and even their way of walking, usually a sulky slouch (disgruntlement is a fisherman's hobby), seems to be touched with the heroic. The whole island suddenly gets keyed up like a crowd of fans before a football match – and from the day of the first *mattanza* people are daily asking in the streets "Quanto?", "How many caught today?" – as men in England ask each other the day's score during the cricket season.

Ernle Bradford is rightly esteemed as a navigator and a writer on sailing around the Mediterranean, of each of whose countless islands, almost without exception probably, he's had at least a cockpit view. A yachtsman's vision is notoriously circumscribed: his curiosity doesn't look much beyond sea and sky or his own moorings and the jetty in whose lee he's lying – it's surprising how often a visiting yachtsman is disinclined to see something more of the place he's visiting than the harbour or the wine shop nearest to it. Mr. Bradford, in *Ulysses Found*,[22] makes a number of assertions about this island, examined in another chapter, which closer observation would have corrected. Mr. Bradford throws off a curious aside about the very tunnery here being discussed; remarking on the occurrence of sea mist in these waters, he quaintly says: "On another occasion when I was giving a hand at a *mattanza* – the tunny netting – off Favignana ..." *Giving a hand!* Nobody "gives a hand" at the *mattanza* or in any other operation of the *tonnara*; a stranger who wanted to "give a hand" would be dismissed as a dotty tourist by anybody who heard him make the offer. The *mattanza* is fought out by a hundred-odd professionals who perfectly know the disciplines and drills and knacks and signals and practices of it, as well as its risks. It's the professionalism of apprenticeship from boyhood and the professionalism of heritage; the idea of being "given a hand" would sound like a silly joke to the *tonnaroti*. What Mr. Bradford doubtless did was to bring his boat to a spot just off the rectangle of lighters which, for the *mattanza*, frame the "camera della morte", from where he could watch; yachtsmen are generally shy of lying alongside one of the heavy lighters – when a good north-wester is beating up the waves, these bounce and grind like erupting rock.

In the same sentence Mr. Bradford reveals a second misapprehension: the word *mattanza* has nothing to do with "netting" – you can "net" a million tunny but that won't make a *mattanza*. For that you've got to kill them; the word means "slaughter", and is a Sicilian derivative from the Latin/Italian "ammazzare", to kill, murder, destroy. And that's what the *mattanza* is: the mass-slaughter of two or three hundred great creatures within a

---

[22] Hodder & Stoughton 1963, Sphere Books 1967. [Author's footnote]

tiny arena of space and time – and by extension the word has come to mean also the results and the freight of the slaughter. While the procession of boats are rowed or sailed or towed into harbour and up the factory creek, tarpaulins spread against the sun over the stained, convulsive corpses, watchers say: "The *mattanza* is coming in" – "sta entrando la mattanza" – as a citadel's civilians once proclaimed: "The army is returning."

Each morning, roughly from mid-June to Midsummer's Day, breaks upon the question: Will there be a *mattanza*? The answer hangs in such matters as current and force or direction of wind (scirocco from the south-east holds the fish off; a brisk north-westerly brings them hurdling the rollers into the *tonnara*) and on the numbers of fish reported by the look-out men who daily peer down into the guide-nets deep in the sea. The *Raïs* alone decides; he is like a medieval admiral who founds his expectation of the battle upon the weather, his instinct for the fishes' habit, and his knowledge of the enemy's deployment. When his fleet and crews are in position, and he has himself seen the state of the *tonnara* beneath the surface, he'll choose the moment to order the engagement.

If there were indications the night before of a "big *mattanza*" – a catch of two or three hundred fish weighing some quarter-ton each – the boats would be moving out at first dawn: about twenty long black wooden lighters, enormously heavy and stable, to form a solid rectangle round the periphery of the *coppo* or "chamber of death". Other crews will have sailed or motored out to the *tonnara* to operate the "doors" connecting the intermediate "chambers", by means of which a large shoal is corralled by stages along the guide-nets and into the execution trap. It's amazing how man learned almost intuitively from earliest times and using the simplest of primitive apparatus, to manoeuvre fifty tons of thrashing leviathan for a massacre in a pool of bloodied sea. It's sentimental, no doubt, to observe that the massacre is performed when the fish are within sight of their goal after a three-thousand-mile nuptial swim.

The arena, to begin with, measures about a hundred yards square. It looks like a swimming enclosure, walled by rows of long black lighter barges. They are moored round the perimeter of the *coppo* net, close-woven as knit armour; their gunwales are manned by the *tonnaroti*, grasping the net's edge and waiting for a sign from the Raïs, to haul in. The Raïs's place is in the middle of the *coppo*, standing up in a row-boat, a tough boat, heavy and durable as a small barge – when the fish are powerful, it's got to take a battering.

The Raïs gives the signal, and the circle of men take up the weight of the net; a bellying, reiterating chant, like a litany, comes from them all, and the Raïs begins sweeping forward his out-stretched arms like a man waving on a tug-of-war team. The harping, vocative chant, and the slow urging of the man's arms begin to work on the nerves like a pendulum ticking off the approach of the unbearable. Two hundred hands are hauling on the net. Inch by inch it's brought aboard; inch by inch the encircling lighters are drawn inward; inch by inch the *coppo* shrinks in area and, imperceptibly, its depth decreases.

With the first orison (for the chanting is a prayer: a demand in mediaeval Sicilian for the backing of the Mother of God) one feels a tremor of excitement – a warning that something tremendous and terrible is going to happen. One watches the dwindling surface of water with a fascinated horror – and a feeling of exquisite suspense: it's the *surface* one's eyes are glued to by both dread and a breathless expectancy – watching for the first tiny ripple that will show how near the climax is.

A slight ruffling of the water, as if a stone had been quietly dropped in or a bubble puffed from below: the sight of it sets one tingling with a suspense – this is the moment, I think, when excitement begins to bestride all feeling like the mounting dementia of orgasm and nothing exists but a terrible impatience for the final, enthralling horror. The unending monotony of the men's voices acts on one's mind like wizardry; suddenly one notices that the *coppo*, just now as big as a football field, has shrunk to the size of a back-yard swimming-pool. Soon, looking down at the water, one's aware, though one still can't see what it is, of a liveliness like that under a ship's stern when, at her moorings, the propeller's just turning over; and suddenly you see a fin cutting the surface – dorsal or tail, like an axe-head; and then an anguished fish's face, the size of a buffalo's, leaps dolphin-like clear and dives again – anguished, because suddenly one senses down there in that frenzied water the kind of terror that goes with stampede. Mere liveliness turns to commotion, the pool to a choppy sea: waves smacking up the barges and throwing spray over the *tonnaroti* and us watchers behind them; in the boat in the middle, straining and jumping at the warps fore and aft, the Raïs and his two mates pull on their oilskins. He is still waving on the men hauling on the net: inch by inch the circle of the *coppo* contracts, and the dwindling pool whips into a boil as more fish are squeezed into less water. Apart from the chorus of chanting, which seems by now to have soared or sunk to some unhuman pitch, the scores of human beings looking on are dumb with expectancy: each one is oblivious to everything except the dreadful turbulence of that patch of reddening sea. For by now the *coppo* is spotted with wisps of scarlet, as if paint has been spilt – wildly thrashing against this terrifying constriction, the titanic fish are ripping and flaying the flesh off each other, and the shrinking circle of their death trap is becoming a basin of blood. Now the catch is gaffed aboard the low black lighters; using long poles clawed like harpoons, three men to a fish, and grabbing fins or gills for the final hoist over the side, shouting triumphant laudations of the Madonna (or perhaps one or other of her predecessors), the *tonnaroti* must, besides the Herculean work of hauling in half a ton of fish at a time, dodge a lethally flailing tail. Once aboard the fish are rolled to the bottom of the lighter where tails frantically thump out a rhythm of death and beat up a spray of blood.

When it's over, and the perimeter of boats is being broken up, tarpaulins spread against the sun, sails set or towropes made fast, a delegate of the *tonnaroti* goes to the Raïs – or, if he is grandly present, the Genovese owner of fishery and factory – with a length of knotted cord – the tally of the catch – each knot marking 50 or 100 fish. A catch of two or three hundred big fish in one *mattanza* is a triumph which occurs but once or twice in a season; fewer than 100 is like one's favourite team being beaten. A satisfying season's catch is from three to four thousand; two thousand is bad. An inscription inside the factory gates commemorates the record catch of all time in about the year 1770 – ten thousand tunny in five or six weeks of fishing. "Probably small fish", comments the Genovese *padrone* of the tunnery, who likes 500-pounders and more.

From earliest times, and in Roman days too, the tunny-meat was salted, using the splendid sea-salt from the pans spread along the flat between Trapani and Marsala. But since the second half of the last century, when Ignazio Florio, a Palermitan tycoon who made a fortune from the wine, shipping and fishing trades, bought the tunnery (without however the feudal rights and marquisate enjoyed by Pallavicini) and built the charmingly old fashioned factory whose elegant buildings run like a dado round the foot of the mountain on the west side of the bay, the fish have been tinned in olive oil, and "Florio", still today the trademark of Favignana tunny, has always on the European market been a name for superiority. Through the nine months of the year outside the spring "campaign", the factory was kept running at full blast with shiploads of "yellowfin" tunny - a much smaller fish - caught in the Atlantic by Japanese, Scandinavian and German vessels specially designed for deep-sea tunny-fishing with the "long line". Tins containing fish caught in our own waters were distinguished from those of imported tunny by a guarantee. In addition to the 100 or more fishermen who each year turn *tonnaroti* for the season, about 400 people were employed full-time in the factory - skilled women who packed fish, oil and salt into the tins; men and boys who worked the sealing and sorting machines and who handled the many commercial byproducts got from these huge carcases. The *stabilimento,* the factory fed by its own fishery and for the rest of the year by foreign vessels, was until 1968 the economic heart of the island; one couldn't see how life could go on should it, inconceivably, stop beating. Many boys leaving school expected as a matter of course to follow their fathers or uncles into the *stabilimento* - about all that was open to a boy short of emigration or washing-up in a coffee-bar.

And then the inconceivable happened: in 1968 the padrone announced - from Genoa: he didn't come to tell the islanders in person - that henceforth the *stabilimento* would close down for the rest of the year after the season's catch was exhausted - and, as time was to show, a good deal even of this would be shipped to Trapani and even Palermo for sale or processing there, so that earnings here were also lost to the island.

The island was stunned; and then burst into a frenzy of useless demonstration and protest: a general strike, with all shops shut for a morning, mass meetings outside the *municipio;* and finally, as a sort of desperate blind swipe at authority, half the population marched one morning to the port and prevented the mailboat from Trapani from mooring – a piece of pathetic bravado which, of course, harmed only the islanders.

10. Il Giardino

There has to be real strength in the sun to start the reptilian summer; so it must have been late in May or early June when I opened the back door of my little house early one morning and found a long black snake at my feet, like a loose coil of licorice on the stone. It seemed unalarmed; but a current of silent motion began to flow through its length, and elegantly it slid, undulating, over the dust towards the wall opposite, with the bashful bravado of a couple of fornicators caught in the haystack. Then it poured itself up the wall like a fluid, trickling through a gap in the stones. And I thought to myself: "So I have my House Snake." This gave me pleasure, and a sense of comfortable security: a kind of antidote to the creepiness I sometimes fancied in my tangled, haunted garden or down in that greenish grotto. I liked to think that my House Snake was really an antique good fairy, as old as the fossilised shells embedded in the stones of my house. I saw him four times again that summer, each time cosily beside my back door.

I was scared that first morning, almost tripping over it, although I've often encountered the same sort among the stones and thistles and furze of different parts of Sicily and in Calabria (I remember one, on the shore near Crotone, which settled down among my clothes while I was bathing). They're a breed of *coluber*, black-brown and slim and four or five feet long; they eat mice and small birds and, I expect, lizards if they can catch them, which I doubt. Also, about the reptiles of Goat Island, I'd been reassured by one Salvatore Struppa who, writing just one century ago (1870) observed: "Benevolent Nature has not chosen to stain the soil of Goat Island with the venomous slime of vipers."

The islanders, however, won't believe you if you assure them their snakes are harmless. They'll stroke the underpart of their chins with the back of a hand, like an Arab stroking his goatee. *Sono cattivi*, they insist, "they're evil."[23] Not though, they'll

[23] This ubiquitous Sicilian gesture has something of the meaning of the French exclamation "la barbe!", and, sometimes, a little of Mr Barzini's

concede, as evil as lizards, which (called in Sicilian *serpe*) are obviously the heirs of the dragons. I don't mean that, in their minds, there exists a knowledge of the dragon, or its image, or its name – they don't think "dragon" when they see a lizard. Yet, deep in the age-old Sicilian awareness, there's felt a presentiment of menace when the tiny dragon of today darts like an arrow across their vision – the elegant and appealing emerald lizard or his drabber square-faced cousin, the gecko or "salamander". Once the yellow glare of summer has turned full on and the lizards come out from their winter lairs to hunt and bask and endlessly watch, then small boys from the *paese* creep like guerrillas along the rustic walls of stacked loose stones, catapults at the ready – these walls are the lizards' playgrounds. Happily, a hit is a rare occurrence. Our little Duzzo, at five years old, even four, walking out with me to my house, would freeze like a pointer at sight of a lizard, stealthily stoop for a stone, and hurl. I've never seen him score – but to try is a matter of honour. Yet if you ask anybody *why* a *serpe* is evil, he has no reason to give. "It's bad, one knows that it's bad": in the same way that any local custom can rarely be explained – and how could its origins be known. "That's how it's done", you're told, "it's the proper thing to do" – like mourners turning up their jacket collars at a funeral.

People interested in dragons and their baleful regard, their connection with fountains and water-holes and the part they may play even in earthquakes and such catastrophes, should make sure of reading chapter 14 of Norman Douglas's *Old Calabria*, one of the greatest of travel books.[24]

Myself, I welcome the lizards for their beauty's and charm's sake as well as for the summer they emerge with. On the high wall of loose stones outside my back door, and poised over the big stone washing-trough there, I can generally find one or two familiars – through that inflexible stare they can give an absurd

---

interpretation "I couldn't care less"; but almost always it's a warning of danger or at least unpleasantness. It means, according to the context: "Keep clear"; "Don't touch it", "He's no good," "I don't like it," "You'll be the loser." Its eloquence is infinite [Author's footnote]. By "Mr Barzini's interpretation", Davidson means the explanation given by the journalist Luigi Barzini in his book *The Italians* (1964).

[24] First published 1915, reissued Penguin 1962. [Author's footnote]

illusion of friendliness; there was one, in 1966, large and a specially bright green, perhaps because of his diet, which used to be waiting each morning for the last drops from the milk bottle of the day before. And there were others, down in the garden: this must have been in July, for "the season", as we call it, had already dessicated the ground into dust and burned the undergrowth brown. When, in the evening, the heat cleared a bit and I went down to water my tomatoes and some young lettuces I was trying to rear, half a dozen of them would be there, lurking under the shadow of a pomegranate or among clumps of wild-growing parsley. With the first trickle from the can they'd come darting out as if roller-skating on those microscopical basilisks' feet, and be lapping like dogs from water caught in the curling leaf of a baby salad. At this time of year the pomegranates were in flower; sometimes, a scarlet blossom, shaped like a tiny chalice, would have dropped, and a tiny dragon would be drinking out of that – there's a pretty piece of Beatrix Potter whimsy!

But it was in eastern Sicily, not in my garden, that I learned how mad for cheese the Sicilian lizard is. This adventure had occurred six years earlier, on the sea-shore below Noto: a stretch of dunes in sight of Cape Passero and beside the florid, rotting derelict of an inchoate casino begun under Mussolini thirty years ago and never finished or demolished. Here at Noto Marina, with beside me this monument to fascist sterility and high on the hill behind, above its skirts of olive and citrus, that perfect archetype of elegant town-planning (Sicily's Bath), I watched a pack of lizards fighting each other for my picnic cheese. The arena was a square metre of stony sand beneath the low wall I leaned over, with encircling coverts of scrub and palmetto; each time I dropped a piece into the sandy patch, half a dozen *serpi*, large and little, shot out like darts and tussled over it; but it was always the biggest, a dragon of a fellow, who got the lot. When I tried them with bread, not one bothered to give it even a sniff. Norman Douglas says that the uromastix lizard of Asia Minor – the true heir to the Homeric dragon, he suggests – is vegetarian; our Sicilian, of the genus *lacerta* (whence the Italian *lucertola*) is plainly carnivorous.

When fighting, they're apt to lose their tails. Some years ago, on the island of Lipari, north-west of the Messina Strait, I used often to see – this was in April – a bigger lizard pounce out from under a rock at a smaller, seize it by the tail and apparently drag it off, like a young Sicilian ravishing away a bride denied to him. It happened like a rapid-motion film, and the exact movements were difficult to catch. The first time, I thought it must be a case of nasty bullying; then, seeing it repeated almost daily along the mountain footpaths, I assumed that April must be the season of reptilian rape.

The *Encyclopedia Britannica* says that each of the small Mediterranean islands has its own form of *lacerta*, recognisably distinct from the others. On Lipari one blinding white summer day, climbing towards Quattr'occhi (whence one has such an astonishing view of Etna, fifty miles away), I saw on the steps ascending to the church of the Annunciation, which clings steeply to the mountainside, a sky-blue lizard: about five inches long and blue as the sea below me. It stayed quite motionless and I looked at it a long time; I'd read that blue-spotted lizards are to be found in the Mediterranean, but had never heard of one overall azure. If, however, the zoologists declare that no such creature exists, I repeat firmly: *I've seen a sky-blue lizard.*

The island's eastern wing, that reaching towards Sicily, which extends from the body of the mountain a little above sea level like a bread-board from under a big brown loaf, is pittied with quarries – not quarries as one thinks of them in England, dug into the side of a hill; but quarries carved downward from the surface of the land, by the process of cutting stone for building, block after block, layer upon layer, until an area of thousands of feet square has been excavated, up to fifty feet deep. Such precision has this work always had, that the walls of the quarry, twenty or thirty feet high or more, stand square and true, and the floor is level and carpeted with a rich tufa-gravel and clay. Once a quarry is worked out and abandoned, its soil after the rains blooms into a luxuriant garden – these gardens of Goat Island are miniature likenesses of the famous *latomie* of Syracuse.

At a lower level still, a little above the sea, the island's foundations are honeycombed with channels and reservoirs of water-wells, springs, pools, subterranean rivers, Stygian brooks: from a few comes water as cool and pure and sweet as anyone could wish to drink, others are brackish or rank. The sweet water must, I suppose, seep from the mountain heights with the rains and pass through the natural filter of the porous tufa. I have five wells sunk here and there in my garden; of which one, even through the summer drought, throws up water as fresh and sweet as any from Mount Helicon or the London Water Board.

The cutting to classic measurement of the local tufa-stone and its export to Sicily has been one of Goat Island's three industries for two or three thousand years (small-scale farming, and fishing and tunny-pickling are the others). Some of the bigger quarries, especially those which, started from higher ground, have immense resources of depth, are still being worked – indeed there's a steady trade in the stone by sailing barge across to Sicily. Electrically driven saws are used now in place of the old hand-cutting tools, but the formats immemorially used are still the rule. Most of the smaller quarries, however, carved out through the centuries almost to water level, have become sunken gardens, ten and fifteen metres below ground, lush with fruit and vegetables. Some of these old quarries must have been worked in Saracen, Roman, perhaps even Phoenician times – all these needed stone. In my own man-made cavern, thirty feet below my house, in whose floor the round head of my fresh-water well is built like a Roman's private bath, the walls, which in the half-light appear ghostly green beneath their patina of fungus-growth, are criss-crossed with the grooves of the cutting-tool of some old stone-hewer of a bygone day; and scrawled at even intervals and at various levels are obvious tally-marks, like a score on a blackboard, recording no doubt the production figures on the final day. When was that record made? A thousand years ago? Two? But the most ancient workings, I suppose, still to be clearly seen but daily eroded by spray, weather and wave, are those I've already mentioned, standing in the sea's verge between my "Roman road" and the outer reef. What else is the "Roman road" for along this shore but the transport of cut stone to "Cavallo"?

The tufa is cut to a standard size generally used for building, and three smaller variants; all four have ancient Sicilian – or rather Goat Island – names and have descended from forgotten times. The standard block is roughly the size of a hefty squared-off bolster – one can count one's walls being at least a foot thick. It's a soft, friable stone, composed of an infinitude of petrified shells and miniscule fragments of marine life; but, exposed, it hardens and endures. Its colour is what one expects of fossils, a whitish off-grey – a workmanlike colour for houses, and perfectly suited to our harsh, stony, staring landscape; but it hasn't of course anything of the romantic beauty of the golden stone quarried around Noto and Syracuse in south-east Sicily. Many of the stones forming my house-walls are embossed with big, perfectly preserved scallop shells, as good as new, so to speak. I believe geologists might say they've been embedded where they are for a million years, and could be a hundred million old.

The house, seen from some distance and in profile against the bare brown mountain, might be taken for one of those tiny Saxon churches in East Anglia: the stubby square tower flush with one end wall; while from the other end of the terrace-roof, an outside stone stairway sloped down, vaguely disguising, one might imagine, the rump of an apse. But looking up from the sunken garden, forty feet down from the top of the tower, you'd think you've got a mediaeval castle with its crenellated masonry reared up sheer from quarry-edge and half-veiled by the spring or summer foliage of a huge fig-tree whose roots, now at right angles to the sturdy trunk carrying its mighty load above, had somehow originated deep in the quarry-face underneath my flooring. But it's no castle: two small stone rooms with small windows of boarding, as most Roman windows were, doors that fitted badly, and no bog.

The house door opens east, on to a rural "strada" linking the *paese* with the southern coastal road. At the back, one looks full on to the long brown flank of the mountain, and the house wall is built flush with the quarry-side, as if it were a prolongation of the cliff of tufa. I told myself that every sunk garden had its house on the brink; that this kind of construction had been the island's architectural habit for untold time and that no house that I'd heard of had ever toppled over. Yet I had qualms when the winter scirocco, blowing from the southeast with a typhonic ferocity, puffed off a hundredweight of masonry from the coping of my garden stairway; and during that terrible month of almost daily earthquakes at the beginning of 1968 I couldn't see how the house could escape being shaken over the edge. But Papà assured me that this manner of building had always been the right one and therefore had always been safe. And, by God, it was; though frightening.

My house was built only twenty-five years ago. An old man stopped me in the strada one evening to tell me how fortunate I was to be living in it because he had been one of the two masons who together made it. But it conformed, of course, to the pattern of all houses in the *campagnia*: the Saracen pattern of near-cubic structure looking inward rather than out; and having, indoors, vaulted stone ceilings - exactly, incidentally, like those in the village of Forio on Ischia in the Gulf of Naples (only here our rooms aren't washed over with "Forian blue", which is native to that corner of Ischia). The pattern is defensive: the tower a look-out and also a refuge to which the family can retreat when the ground floor is attacked. This style naturally persisted, as everything proved serviceable persists, after the Saracen occupation disintegrated before the Norman and later dominations through the eleventh and twelfth centuries; the style persisted - but two or three hundred years later these little family fortresses were turned no longer against the enemies of the Arabs but against the Arabs themselves; they'd become the shelter of Goat Island's peasantry from those terrors from the sea, the Barbary raiders, the "Turks", of whose splendidly buccaneering captains Red-beard Kheir-ed-din Barbarossa and his brother Uruj were, at the time of Charles V, the greatest and the most terrible. My house, therefore, though built a century after the "Turkish" menace was finally removed from the Mediterranean by steam-power, has the characteristic outside stairway, subtly defensive, by which tower and terrace are reached: the width of steps spacious at the top, but narrowing between converging balustrades towards the bottom, so that people are forced to start mounting in single file, and a pretty tight fit at that. Thus I can, if unwanted visitors try to join me on my roof, hurl stones at the intruders jammed at the bottom of the steps.

There's another stairway at the back, but no need for defence here - it leads down to the sunken garden. Twenty-five stone steps cling diagonally to the face of the quarry like a companion-ladder aslant the side of a ship. Below the stairway, reached through a tangle of unpruned vine and some clumps of feathery fennel, there's a low-hanging entrance to a cave – you have to stoop for the sake of your head: inside, sombre and suddenly chill, a fifteen-foot scramble down boulders and trodden tufa-gravel brings you to the floor of the grotto where the fountain is. It would be easy to cut steps and save the scramble – but why bother? This has always been the way down: one can see how the same footholds have been worn hard through the treadmill of time, and these footholds my feet take too, with a surprising agility when I'm carrying the full pail. One's eyes need a couple of seconds to focus to the gloom; and then they find a vast chamber nearly forty feet high, with sheer greenish walls notched by the old stone-cutting. A faint twilight enters from another orifice in a second cave turning off the first; and this light receives from the lichenous walls an eerie viridescence, as if one were looking through a piece of bottle-green glass. No lizards are here, for here no sunlight or its heat ever comes; one may, perhaps, beneath some vestige of mouldering rubbish, find a nest of young rodents or the crumbling remains of a toad. The well has been cleverly opened in the floor of the grotto and built up into a shallow circular basin in which water from a stream flowing under the rock collects. Once or twice in summer drought I've sadly found a dead fledgling on its surface, impelled I suppose into this dungeon by thirst and have queasily bucketed the corpse out. Was it all right, Gigi asked his father, Michele's finding drowned birds in his *acqua dolce*? Why not, answered Tommaso, it's *living water* isn't it? So once again I had Papà's assurance that all was well; and sure enough my well water remained for ever sweet and immaculate. Living water it was, scrupulously filtered by the tufa pores through which it had come; yet often when I tipped my bucket on its rope into the basin, a flutter of moths rose silently from the shadows into the uncanny greenish half-light; I was always glad to reach the reality of sunshine again.

And the garden itself, sunk twenty feet and more below the workaday, rational, human levels of house and roads and farm animals; blanketed from sight and sound of the sea and mountain and the distant mutter of the *paese* – the garden never seems entirely earth-bound. One feels plunged into an underworld, secluded by these stone cliffs from all evidence of mundane life above, and alone and hushed in a violent unruliness of over-lush greenery or burnt, dessicated brown, according to season; while, amid a paradisal abundance of all sorts of fruit, or promise of it, one is assaulted on all sides and at every step by the tripping tendrils of vine, the thorns of lemon, pomegranate and wayward rose, the bodkin spikes of the almond, the claws of knee-high thistles and the odious miniscule spines of the clownishly stylish prickly pear. In this jungle of bizarre and even cruel beauty, the most frigid breast will surely recognise something oddly fictitious or mythic; while anybody with the appropriately romantic temperament can plainly hear the notes of Pan. (It's a long time, however, since there were goats on Goat Island.)

There are three hectares of the garden, more than seven acres: two gardens really, shaped together like a stone-age arrow-head and separated near the point by a high "cyclopean" wall, across which a whole spinney of ancient figs and pomegranates lean their weight. To get from one garden to the other, one squeezes through an absurdly narrow hiatus with, balanced above for transom, an immense stone slab. The inner garden beyond the wall, where Duzzo won't venture alone, is in part as dense as a Malayan jungle; in an extreme corner, within a kind of magic cincture of stones, rears up a grey-bearded thicket of prickly pear, a clump of old lags hanging round each others' shoulders and thrusting out hideous, treacherous green hands as numerous as the heads of Scylla at any intruder rash enough to go near – lucky, I always feel, not to have been devoured by these man-eating menaces, the intruder returns with every inch of his exposed flesh agonised by those tiny maddening prickles. Only Damianina can conquer them, like St. George killing the dragon; she puts on gloves and goes in with a hatchet and gets bucketsful of fruit for the pigs (the Indian figs in my garden are too old and rank to make fruit even for the children). Elsewhere in this curious orchard, at once so prodigally fruitful and so desolate, there are small groves of a hard, rough-flavoured nectarine (*nocepesca* in Italian, *speglio* locally); bushes bearing a vaguely cherry-like red berry from which Damianina makes a kind of jam; patches, among the spring profusion of waist-high marguerites, of delicious fennel with its sweet bulb and cypress-green feathers; and, after the rains, carpets of close-growing parsley – Duzzo takes home bundles of this for Damianina's cooking. In the honey-season, wild bees have their combs on the stubby short stems of grape-vine that sometimes stand alone like dwarfs.

I've two dear lemon-trees, boxed into their own small stone-wall enclosure to shield them against the killer-wind from the south-east; even down on the floor of the garden they need this extra shelter. They're old, sporadically pruned and for too long denied water between the rains; until I came, the roving undisciplined vines climbing over their six-foot walls did their best to strangle them. Yet for these three years with daily watering they've ploddingly blossomed and fruited and mellowed – those tender white flowers seem to come without regard for seasons; the fruit, though small and inelegantly dappled dark-green and yellow, is juicy and sharp. Scarcely once since I've been here has Damianina needed to buy her *limuni*: such precious and indispensable things in the house, they are: especially as a kind of panacea for the sort of troubles people have. When Maria has her indigestion she doses herself with fresh lemon; and for headaches Damianina does the same. When Duzzo, then five, became suddenly feverish and began whimpering with a pain in the groin, Maria scolded: "Too many *caramelle*! Too much chocolate has given you worms! Lemon for you!" Of course, when the doctor came, it was appendicitis. Poor Damianina became hysterical: "He's so *small*", she wailed – "*he's so small*!" But some blessed modern drug averted surgery; and Damianina went about the house gently invoking San Giuseppe and "Madre mia" or Maria, the great mother.

Four sour-water wells in different corners of the garden are handy for irrigation of a modest kind; the best, tunnelled out of the tufa wall and giving the cleanest water, is close to the lemon enclosure.

But the most curious thing about this well is that the bucket in late summer is constantly bringing up the dead bodies of black-beetles that had committed suicide. During what appears to be the mating season, the mouth of this well becomes an Eiffel Tower from which no end of them fling themselves into the abyss. There are hordes of these beetles in the garden (Italian, *scarafaggio* – the same word as scarab) and I've a constant struggle to keep them clear of the house. For some reason, during the mating term, they almost daily choose the head of this well; two of them I find apparently welded together in an inseparable embrace and then plop! – down they fall through twenty feet to the water; and shortly after I bring up their distasteful corpses – which I hope will at least be useful as manure.

Through the long dry months, April to September, I work an hour so each evening hauling up buckets for my lemons, which for Damianina and our family possess some mystic value beyond their worth as fruit – as bread has for the Moors of Morocco. And for me, too, a delicious satisfaction comes from this work: each day I can almost measure the swelling and register the change of complexion in a dozen or more lemons I've been watching, almost nurturing, from the day when the falling of their white petals made way for the tiny green nipple till they've become jaundiced and cushiony enough for picking. Two or three kilo every week or two I take down to the house in the piazza; and felt, I suppose, the same inner glow of pleasure which a man must have experienced when taking his offering to the earth-goddess Demeter. Taking fruit from the garden to the family is much more gratifying than bringing them stuff bought in a shop – even an expensive melon in the first days of their season: it was a contribution of my earth and my labour to the well-being of the family – the very act of gathering into the basket seemed part of a liturgy. In 1966 I must have taken a hundred or more kilo of figs – small, green mostly, the best for drying, and some larger black; from about September Damianina and Maria start slitting them open like oysters and laying them out on the roof top to dry in the sun; at Christmas, minced into a paste with orange and lemon rind and other condiments, they'd be baked in rings of pastry and eaten in between meals. That same year was a lavish one too for almonds – we shook them down in showers; yet in 1967 there was little blossom and hardly fifty nuts. In 1966 all the grapes shrivelled up long before maturity – there was a vine disease all over Sicily that year; but the next I got some fine big bunches. Pomegranates are the last fruit to be harvested; soon after the scarlet blossom, the dark russet "grenades" form and harden like croquet balls, but it isn't till late September or October that they start to crack and show that their flesh inside is crimson – then picking them becomes a race with the birds. But the pomegranate is a tiresome fruit, more romantic than practical and not much relished, even by the children.

The garden became mine (by virtue of paying L36 a year for house and seven acres of fruit) in early April; it was, after the rains, a turbulent green jungle, run wild and untended for years. Thistles and tall yellow daisies standing as close as corn strangled and smothered the fruit trees and turned an acre or two into fields of weed. We started to clear; Gigi came after school and we rooted all this rank growth over a useful area between an avenue of vine, fig, and pomegranate as far as the dividing wall – we never got to clearing the inner garden. I don't think Gigi enjoyed this hard labour much; his taste and talent went more for the working of a motorscooter then husbandry; but he came simply because his sweet nature sent him – knowing I was working, he came to work too. But we had some fun making huge bonfires of the rubbish we'd uprooted, with flames licking fifteen feet up the quarry sides. Then I started out to *zappare* all the soil we'd cleared – to break it up and turn it over with the *zappa*, the great heavy hoe that's used here instead of a spade. A long-handled pointed shovel like a tongue is used for jobs like road-making; but for what we call spade-work the *zappa* is the thing: it's back-aching work but wonderfully satisfying: you raise the mattock high over your head and the weight of the great iron head does more than your muscle to ram it deep into the earth. But not always so deep: after the drought the earth's like rock and has to be gone over twice; what's more, half what you hope is "soil" is made of stones or small boulders, which have to be thrown out by hand. That's why stone-walling is the natural form of fencing: the material's lying there to be picked up.

I found this heavy hoeing not only backbreaking but also unexpectedly sexual. I wonder if men who ordinarily work on the land see some copulatory imagery in this act of thrusting into mother-earth with each downward stroke – which, after all, is done for the purpose of fecundation; working in this way, I felt I'd hit on a kind of primal sexual symbolism. And then I had a wonderful brainwave: *zepp*, I excitedly said to myself, is North African Arabic for penis; may not the word *zappa* have derived from the Arabic since the two hundred years of Saracen occupation – especially as nearly all today's irrigation terms are Arabic, and even the word *sceco* (shekko), Sicilian for ass, donkey, is said to come from the Arab. But alas for my theory: the dictionary told me that *za* and *zappare* are good Italian words in use where no Saracen ever set foot.

When my ground was ready, I was eager to get on with propagation: Damianina got me seed – tomato, lettuce, and broccoli (which here is a form of cauliflower); I sowed, obeying the rules I'd been given; I toiled night after night carrying bucket after bucket; I watered and weeded and cultivated and transplanted – I was a mother to my plants. But my lettuces, long before they were big enough to eat, ran to seed in flowery spindles – I was told I'd sown too late; of my sixty lusty young broccoli, forty were cut off at the stem as if with scissors – I was told this was the work of some sort of slug; my tomatoes, puny, greenish things made about twenty kilo all told, which I thought was a crop to be proud of, but Damianina told me they were all right for the pigs – and thereafter *i pomodori di Michele* were a family joke.

After that I gave up my plans to make a living as a market gardener.

11. La Pecorella

The land next my garden belongs to an old man who walks bent right-angled from the waist like an old-fashioned starting handle. He must be nearly ninety; so he must have passed nearly eighty years stooped over his young broad beans or other crop, hoeing between the plants. No wonder he's bent. He has watery blue eyes and a toothless smile, vague and sweet, which he uses for concurrence when he doesn't understand what you're saying. Duzzo and I call him the "vecchietto", the little-old-man: he has the gnomish look of a Disney dwarf. Duzzo spends most summer afternoons in my garden; or on the roof looking out for the *vecchietto*'s cow or for his donkey. When he sees the old man leading one or both, he squeals with excitement: "la mucca, la mucca!" or "la scecca!" – all donkeys are feminine to Duzzo.

Ploughing animals here, when two are used, are yoked – they don't pull on collar and trace; and the *vecchietto* yokes together his cow, old and bony with an empty crumpled udder like a squashed balloon, and his donkey which is about half the cow's height. The two incongruous creatures work in perfect harmony, straddling the previous furrow faultlessly and leaning all their weight on the small steel share while the old man, driving with a single rope, heaves or hangs on the long wooden haft. T. H. White, who wrote *The Once and Future King*, apparently saw a man in Scotland ploughing "with horse and cow" and oddly remarked: "It is not a laughable spectacle really. There is something horrible about it...."[25] I can't think why he should have reached such a curious judgement, except that T. H. White was an odd man. There is nothing either laughable or horrible about this rather touching triplet of the double-bent ancient and his quaint team; instead, there's nobility about it. He uses his two beasts alternately to work the creaking wooden apparatus that raises water to fill his *gebbia*, the big rectangular cistern in which a species of carp or roach swim like shadows and keep the surface clean of mosquitos and their kin.

---

[25] Biography of T. H. White by Sylvia Townsend Warner [Author's footnote]

At sun-up the *vecchietto* is already at work among his tomatoes or salads or broccoli or beans, according to season; about eight he backs the donkey between the shafts of the "trap", a vehicle of varnished wood sprung over two high wheels - an easy-going vehicle with adjustable hood which in England would be dated about 1880; and loads the back with garden produce for sale in the *paese*. The old man is back in his fields by ten, and works there till dusk; with a short break for the old man and his beasts, around midday; the famous "siesta" is more legend than fact, except perhaps on Sunday afternoons.

Two men on this island own horses: lightweights of under fourteen hands which are yoked in with donkeys for ploughing. But the island's beast of burden and draught, and saddle too, is the donkey - the big, upstanding ass of Pantelleria: as big as a mule and more intelligent. He's an animal that will do anything: the blindfolded treadmill of the *gebbia*, round and round drawing the pole that rotates the chain of buckets; the plough, singly or yoked - he knows every trick; between the shafts of trap or farm "box-cart", at the gallop or at hearse-speed; saddled for paniers or rider (the saddle's a pad, without stirrups). The donkey of Pantelleria is a splendid animal, and on Goat Island he's a treasured one, well fed and cared for: you won't see animals in better condition anywhere. Every farmer has a good mare; in the summer a foal is running with its dam at nearly every farmstead, long-legged and childish; I've seen a donkey-foal chase sheep just for the fun of it. Sardinian donkeys are a very different animal: the size of a Shetland pony and as stolid. We've two on the island, used to pulling hawkers' barrows and wearing shabbily sandy "Sicilian" harnesses.

Any visitor to Naples who looks twice at a horse will notice how the animal pulling his cab is bridled; he'll be struck by the absence of any sort of bit. And if he goes southwards, round the coast as far as Taranto, and keeps his eyes open in all the towns he visits, he'll see the same thing: bridles without bits. It's the same in Sicily (except in Palermo where a good many cab-horses are bitted). For several years I puzzled over this; it couldn't be a Saracen custom: leaving aside the fact that Naples wasn't a Saracen city, I knew from first-hand that the Moors ride and drive their horses on the bit, and a severe bit too. Then I found that this mode of bridling with nothing in the horse's mouth was peculiar to the areas of the ancient Greek settlers - to Magna Graecia: the coastal towns of southern Italy and Sicily.

This type of bridle is simple and, in principle, everywhere the same; varying though between severity and laxity. It can be fierce, with a refinement of leverage to make a metal curb-chain bite under the jaw; or it may be no more than a twist of rope and a slip-knot. The idea is to put a squeeze by means of the reins, exerted through the rings of the cheek and nose straps, beneath the chin and round the bones of the nose - a sort of half-nelson round the muzzle.

A stay in London in 1968 allowed a good look at the Greek vases in the British Museum, and this dispelled all uncertainty. The way our donkeys are bridled on Goat Island is how most Greek horses were bridled in the fourth century B.C.; now and then careful scrutiny of the vases will reveal a bit, but by far the greater number of chariot scenes depicted show leverage from the cheek straps working on lower jaw and nose. And if one looks carefully at the holes bored in the cheeks of the Parthenon horses displayed in the Elgin room, it's clear that they're too high above the mouth for a bit; I take it they're for the fastening of a bridle.

In this detail of horse-furniture the Greek seems to have outlived the Roman and not to have been ousted by the Saracen - except in Palermo, which was more Arabised and less under Greek influence than anywhere in Sicily.

Soon after dawn I hear the sheep coming. From far down the road from the sea comes the soft melodious jangle of their bells; and then when they round the curve below the house, the chorus of them suddenly bursts like a fast-bubbling brook over a stony bed; and the multitude of their hooves scuffles like a wind through the dust. This flock, one of two on the island, passes each morning to what pasture there is on the stony foothills of the mountain, above the *stabilimento* and the football field; and late afternoon they pass again, going back to their fold for the night by the sea. Their shepherd is a small boy who spends ten or more hours of every single day in the absolute solitude of the mountain, with no companions but the sheep he watches; during the rains he carries an immense umbrella like a flower-woman's in an old engraving; He looks about ten years old, but must be more because in so small a community he couldn't escape the schooling law. His daily wage is about six shillings. These sheep are small, neat, rangy animals with wool off-white with the dust; they seem all the year to be lambing, except in late August and September when the flock looked mean and wizened for want of grazing.

Half a dozen goats run with this flock – sometimes a kid or two more, sometimes an old goat less. An enormous billy, nearly as big as a Sardinian donkey, leads the whole band, with a matted hairy coat like a yak's and enormous spiralling horns; and the genitals of a silenus.

A little after the sheep have gone by, a boy brings the cows, four or five of them, out from the farmstead down the road. They'll be taken a mile or more to graze on the higher ground above the sea beyond "Cavallo", where they can just pick a living among the rocks. But even in late summer the cows look well fed; a green fodder is grown in spring, and the richest dairyman brings in hay from Sicily – he may own a dozen head. There's generally a bull, perhaps two, running with five or six cows and heifers; sometimes a bull scarcely more than a calf. Owners don't seem to trouble much what their cows breed from, so long as they breed; perhaps because of the cost of a good bull – and there's no government stud animal on the island. I think it's likely I've watched a mother being served by her son.

By seven-thirty the sun is high and half-right from my door; by then I'm sitting on my doorstep feeling its early glow. This is the perfect hour of a Mediterranean day in summer; that little lively spell while the sun tingles the skin but doesn't yet dehydrate the very blood. I hear what I'm expecting in a moment – the tut-tut-tut of Gigi's motor; and then he comes scooting down the straight lane from the *paese*, or round the crooked lane opposite if he's already been to feed the family pigs. He comes every day on his way to school – to do a last-minute piece of homework, or wash down his scooter, or read the Italian football news in the *Giornale di Sicilia* he's brought if the *aliscafo* had come in time. Gigi never fails; I go to his house for dinner, and after that he comes to mine two or three times more – to fetch Duzzo home on his pillion, or stretch out and dream on my roof-top, or wander round the garden in his grave silent way; and later to bring me a billycan of supper his mother has cooked for me.

In March 1967, when lambing was in its peak season, Tommaso bought a *pecorella* for Duzzo; he paid about 12s for a female very recently born. At this time, lots of children in the piazza possessed a lamb: one couldn't find more proof that Mary's little lamb was sure to go everywhere that Mary went. There was one boy whose lamb followed his bicycle like a dog all the way between the *paese* and Punta Lunga, where the family boat lay, a good four miles there and back. The *pecorella* lived at first in the abattoir, where Tommaso was master under Don Pino, and of course was fed on the bottle. At about six weeks, when it ought to be learning to crop, Papà brought it to my garden – the natural place for it, offering pasture enough, as he thought, to fill its belly all the year. But I soon discovered two facts. First, a sheep should never be left in solitude – it requires emotional companionship, not necessarily of other sheep but of some substitute mother-figure; and secondly, when one small sheep and the Sicilian summer are in alliance, the rough grazing provided by three hectares of fruit-orchard means starvation fare.

Our lamb was known as the *pecorella,* "little sheep", because that's the word for it on Goat Island. At the butcher's, one asks for a cut of *agnella* if one wants a bit of lamb (which isn't often eaten); and "Agnallo di Dio" is the phrase for Lamb of God, a phrase not often used by the ordinary people of the island. But a lamb running on its four hooves one called a "little sheep", *pecorella.* Duzzo referred to it conversationally as the *pecorella,* but for direct communication with itself he named it Ninuzza – "little Nina" (the terminal "uzza" being a Sicilian diminutive, the equivalent of *uccio* on the mainland). When we knew the *pecorella* was somewhere alone down in the jungle of my garden, and Duzzo and I came down the road in the afternoon towards the high stone wall which ran along the edge of the garden cliff, Duzzo would start calling in his sweet child's shout: "Ninuzza! Ninuzza!", and almost instantly, the answer would come: the pecoralla would start frantically maa-ing and baa-ing and would be at the top of the garden steps, pounding with its front hooves on my back door, by the time we had opened the front one. The pecoralla was "furba" - a nice word akin to, but less derogative than, the French *fourbe*; she was "clever" in the sense of artful or cunning - often, when I've needed to go down to the grotto to fetch water, I've descended with the utmost stealth, literally on tiptoe, while she's been at the further end of the inner garden; but I could never fox her - she'd come pounding up the stairway, knocking my bucket almost upside down, nearly knocking me sideways as she grew bigger and heavier, and flinging herself at my door at the top in the frenzy of her insatiable, and unsatisfied, yearning for mother-love.

For several weeks, of course - two months perhaps - I went down morning and evening to give her milk: half a litre a day taken from a baby's feeding bottle. She wriggled furiously at the bottle as any lamb does suckling her mother; sometimes she'd pull off the rubber teat and get it jammed in her throat, and I'd have to pull it out. Very quickly she learned to graze, though she had no dam to teach her - this was in April and May when the earth was still alive from the rains, and there was young green grass for her to nibble.

Her harrowing, pleading cry began every day before dawn, unceasing and insistent; I found myself counting half-seconds to the next plaintive bloat. There was no more dozing once she began crying for her mother. I was her mother.

As the *pecorella* gained in weight, power and obstinacy, a new problem arose: how to keep her from kicking down the wooden door at the top of the garden steps. She had been pushed down from the top so many times that she had long understood she wasn't made welcome there; now she began trying out what size and strength could do. When I went down to fetch water, or to feed her milk, or gather lemons, she would wait meekly at the bottom of the steps till she saw me opening the door: than she would come charging up as heavily as a medieval war-horse but with the speed of a fawn; I'd pelt her with stones I had piled for the purpose or meet her nose head-on with the sole of my foot, and when I'd managed to turn her round and shove her down again, I'd get in when I could a sharp kick on her backside (I was barefooted except for single-thong rubber sandals). She came back for more; and when I'd squeezed myself and my buckets through the door and shut it against the *pecorella*, she'd begin to pound it to bits with her front hooves. Soon when I was carrying a bucket up, she was adding cunning to courage; she'd be cropping innocently at the bottom, as if she hadn't a notion of climbing the steps – and then, the instant she thought I wasn't looking, she'd be flying up like a toboggan in reverse.

When we were together in the garden, her pleasure and devotion were touching; where I went, she went, as faithfully as a gun-dog at heel; if I took the watering-can to same plant, or started wielding the *zappa*, she'd take it for a game and start gambolling in eurhythmical leaps or galloping crazily round a clump of pomegranate like a puppy chasing its tail. Or, if I was sitting on a block of stone against the lemon-trees' wall, watching perhaps Duzzo playing with his imaginary animals, the *pecorella* would push her head under my knees, and want me to tickle her beneath the chin or fondle her ears or rub her belly, as a dog wants one to do. And then I knew that no matter how often I threw stones at her, or kicked her, or clipped her on the jaw, nothing could diminish her filial adoration. I could do no wrong. The trouble was, I didn't want to be just an old sheep.

Then came another anxiety. Duzzo, then aged six, who was her owner and had named her Ninuzza, adored her when she was small and toy-like and tractable: but as the *pecorella* grew and, to her, Duzzo diminished in size, she began to feel she'd found something about her own weight; and by the time her head was on a level with Duzzo's, she thought he was another *pecorella*; as soon as he came down into the garden to play with her, calling "Ninuzza! Ninuzza!", she would lower her head like a billy-goat and charge, butting poor Duzzo head-over-heels. Of course he got frightened; and he could only show off his ownership from a distance. I should never have guessed that the care of a "little sheep" could bedevil one's days with so many perplexities, psychological and physical. Yet I became enormously fond of our *pecorella*, and fussed over her as maternally as any old sheep.

Duzzo, through 1967, used to come every day, after his morning at the "asilo", the nursery school where he wore a dainty white pinafore and a huge blue bow under his chin, to my garden, except when a winter wind was too cold or the rain too heavy. Round the hem-line of the garden, where cliff-wall and soil meet, there's a series, all the way round, of small grottoes or scraped-out shelters, four or five of which have been at some stage excavated or built up with masonry into sties, pens, hutches – a variety of shelters for exactly what animals it's hard to guess, besides pigs: the oven-airlessness down there in summer would make the toughest fowls wilt. At first, when I explored the tangled, and slightly eerie, wilderness of the garden, I'd found these caverns forbidding – I didn't know what I might find inside: a man-made enigma is more sinister than a natural. Duzzo, too, wouldn't go near them alone; but after a few days, when we'd together made sure that none contained skeletons or bogeys, he took possession of them. In one he kept his donkeys, which were apt to foal (in litters of five or six at a time) nearly every day; another was full of pigs, all of them constantly farrowing; in a third he kept some rather shadowy cows which he remembered now and then to provision with imaginary feed and water. But it was the donkeys and pigs which were completely real to him; he could spend a whole day quite happily, as long as I was there to do his bidding when help was wanted, counting them and feeding them and moving them about, tying them and untying them – and then starting all over again.

It was over animals that I was taught, twice, that a child's imagination is inviolable: you can't alloy it with reality. I had found, while clearing a plot of undergrowth, an old iron trough so rusted it was dotted with holes. One day, while Duzzo was laboriously going back and forth to pour imaginary water into an imaginary trough for his imaginary donkeys, I said: "Duzzo – I've found something splendid for your donkeys, just right for watering them – look, a real trough!" He looked at my trough and then, pityingly, at me. "Michele", he said, "you are silly. Can't you see all the water would run out?"

I got the other lesson much later; when the rains of November had come with a scirocco cold wind. From a window, I could see the *pecorella* cringing, as sheep can cringe, against the best sheltering wall it could find – few animals look as dismal as does a cold sheep.

When Duzzo came that day, I said: "Duzzo, the poor *pecorella* was so unhappy in that cold rain, she ought to have some shelter. The handiest shelter for her is where you keep your pigs – the one beyond the almond trees. D'you mind if we leave its door open all the time, so that she can go in?"

"Oh no," he answered with awful seriousness, while his big blue eyes filled with reproach, "we can't do that. If we leave the door open all my pigs will escape. You must arrange another shelter for the *pecorella*." And that's what I did.

The ravens which came soaring down from the mountain on their huge wings, fitfully giving a few lordly strokes and uttering that sad, ominous double-croak, were a great worry to Duzzo. They always hunt in pairs – was it T. H. White who said somewhere that ravens mate for life? – and when they're overhead he looks up at them frowning and shaking his head, like a seaman who sees a storm coming up. "Sono *cattivi* quei," he says "they're *wicked*, those are – they'll eat my little pigs if I don't get them under shelter." And he starts rounding up his visionary herd and shouting, "ava–a–a––, ava–a–a–––!" (avanti) ...

But when, about March, the goldfinches are dancing and flashing in the fig-trees, he squeals with delight, and tries to chase them as he does the pigeons in the piazza. In April the quail come, but rarely into the garden: they swarm and flutter in the fields, among the young corn; and, I'm glad to say, are generally too cute for the absurd "hunters" who come from Trapani and even as far as Palermo, dressed up like Red Indians going after buffalo.

In early summer, after the rains have brought the snails to maturity and they're clustered on every vine or twig like limpets on a rock, Duzzo will collect a bucketful – sometimes Maria and Caterina come too to harvest them: the family love them boiled for supper, though ours are on the small side – hardly as big as marbles.

Or he pulls up young fennel to chew the sweet yet pungent tuber; or gathers parsley to take back to Damianina – Duzzo knows better than I where the clumps of parsley are hidden. But as the summer gets its grip on the island, squeezing the land harder and harder till, like a vampire, it's sucked all the moisture out, the parsley gives up the fight; and then the only green to be seen in the garden is that of the foliage of the fruit trees. Everything aloe dries and crumbles to dust; even the stalks of the old daisy plants become as brittle as twigs. The garden turns as brown as the bare brown mountain.

By August, perhaps before, the *pecorella* had eaten the ground bald. She was chewing the vine-leaves off to what height she could stretch up to; even earlier she had cleared the lower almond branches of green. Fig-leaves, though, she had no taste for. So to keep her fed was now a problem. We gave her a daily feed of oats or maize, which delighted her; and kept her water-bucket full and fresh. There's a belief that sheep, like goats, can get enough moisture for their needs from green stuff, or most of it; and it's true that a flock can go through a summer day without watering. But I found that our *pecorella* was constantly picking her way over the paths she'd made from one end of the garden to the other to her pail of water in the shade of the lemons. She drank as often, I'd say, as a dog.

There was another reason for the grain; she was being prepared for maternity. Tommaso had arranged with the *padrone* of the flock that passed my door for Ninuzza to join them, after she'd been judged by some expert to be nubile (though she was only nine or ten months). So in October, when there was pasture again on the foothills of the mountain, I had her one morning on my doorstep when the flock came, and handed her over to the small saturnine shepherd. Next morning, I couldn't recognise her, among fifty or more identical sheep; and she, swallowed into the companionship of a host of her own kind, didn't give a thought to recognising me. I hoped she might already be having fun with a young ram or two.

Each day or so, when I heard the bells rippling up from the sea, I went to my door and asked the boy: "Coperta?" Had she been covered? This laconic little solitary could distinguish any one ewe from the rest as easily as pick his own mother from among a hundred others; and it was his job to register mentally the flock's fornications. "*Niente,*" he said dully but authoritatively. "She's timid yet."

This went on for a month. But one morning, he nodded his head. "Si," he said. Properly "coperta", was she? I asked. Was he sure? Had he watched? "Si," he repeated obstinately. So he cut our *pecorella* out of the flock, and I manhandled her through the house and down to the garden. From that moment she resumed her enslavement to me and seemed to have forgotten all about the flock and any experiences she may have had with them – she didn't even lift her head when the bells tinkled and jangled by in the morning.

Then the tantalising question in the family was: Is Ninuzza "incinta" or isn't she? Duzzo's questions had to be answered every day: Now that the *pecorella*'s been "coperta", will she have little sheep tomorrow? How many *piccolini* will she have - a lot, like our pigs? I found that an ewe's time for gestation is five months, which made the deadline March. Now, fortunately, there was again plenty of grazing in the garden; but, wanting to keep up the *pecorella*'s strength, I continued her ration of grain. Every day I scrutinised her figure, praying for signs of a swelling belly. But the weeks, and then the months, went by; and there wasn't the slightest change. "Feel her 'mammella'", Papà said; and each morning, I fumbled round poor Ninuzza's udder. By the time February came, we accepted the truth: our *pecorella* wasn't "incinta".

And then a decision I had to make helped to hasten the doom that inexorably awaited our *pecorella*. I was to go to England for a few months; and that meant I'd give up my garden. Where could Ninuzza go?

Over dinner, the talk was no longer of breeding from the *pecorella*, but of eating her. I said "Don't you dare talk in front of me about eating her - I gave her the bottle, for nearly a year I've been a mother to her, it'd be like eating my own child.... Duzzo! Would *you* eat our *pecorella*?" And he answered emphatically, bursting with laughter, "*Si!*", though I knew he was teasing. Then Damianina would join in: "Michele's too soft-hearted to eat the *pecorella* - but, Michele, you'd eat pasta with her *brodo,* wouldn't you?" And they kept on joking about how the *pecorella* was going to be cooked; and what a feast I was going to miss.

Next, I was haunted by a new spectre of horror. I was the only person whom Ninuzza would follow; she was far too heavy and intractable now to load on to Gigi's *vespa* or Tommaso's *motoretta.* She would have to go on foot to the slaughterhouse - and that was well over a mile, instead of the few feet between the condemned cell and the gallows.... And there was one obvious man to be asked to take her there: myself, because she would follow me with absolute trust wherever I went....

During the days leading to my going, I waited in a sweat for Tommaso's demand that I should lead my lamb to execution.... Of course, it never came: Papà and my family don't do things like that.

When, a few months later, I came back, I asked about the *pecorella*. It had been sold to Don Pino, and never came near their house. Of course they didn't eat it. I'd known they wouldn't.

12. Jove

About dusk on March 20th (the evening, that is, after St. Joseph's day) everyone on the island who can walk accompanies San Giuseppe back to the tiny fifteenth century chapel in the outskirts where he spends 355 days out of each year. (This sanctuary is always called "San Giuseppe's", although it's dedicated to Sant' Anna – his mother in law, after all.) I first formed part of this exuberant escort in 1966; and suddenly, amid the roars of "Viva!" and the whanging of the church bells and the waving hands of people trying to catch San Giuseppe's eye – suddenly I saw in a flash who it was we were taking home. We were taking Zeus home, or more likely Jove.

"Viva San Giuseppe!" went the cry: a long crocodile of cheering through the narrow streets. Now and then somebody called, almost apologetically, "Viva Maria!" – she couldn't be ignored altogether, for Mother and Child are inseparably part of the simulacrum of which Joseph is the chief figure. People at the head were scrambling to touch the image, ablaze with candles and festooned with flowers, as it was wheeled along on its ceremonial chassis, or were blowing it kisses with their fingers, making it the "*ciao*" sign, or asking its favour with a hand raised in salute ("There was a temple of Apollo near the theatre.... I lifted my hand and invoked a blessing," says a character in Mary Renault's novel *The Mask of Apollo*[26] – and that's just what people throughout Magna Graecia do today when they meet one of the *santi* (as today they're called).

St. Joseph was being taken back to his own little temple, after the annual ten days' stay in the mother-church. Now, as the procession came into view where the road fell towards the shore, the boys waiting on the chapel roof, bell ropes in hand, burst into a terrific clangour of welcome to the *santo* and warning to his enemies. Then he was carried into the whitewashed glare of the little nave with its avenue of homely rounded arches and eased on to the plinth where he'd stay another year. Before the little

[26] Longmans, 1966. [Author's footnote]

church could be emptied and locked up, there was a bit of a scuffle while people grabbed for a few petals or a leaf from San Giuseppe's tabernacle.

Any of the four or five "saints" whom the people honour through the year get most of this treatment; but none is escorted home after his *festa* as San Giuseppe is, and no other *festa* has the same note of fervent solemnity in the festivities. And now suddenly I'd seen why there was this difference; why the feast of St. Joseph here outranks in the people's eyes any other in the year; why his Day seems to retain more religious fervor than Christmas or Easter, but of a kind not concerned with hearing mass or going to church; why even the Madonna, in the two or three disguises she appears in here, and *u signuri* ("The Lord") – the mediaeval crucifix of the island's Patron – are less highly esteemed.

But first let's look at the *festa* and what happens during it; and in what detail it differs from the ordinary run of *festa*. On the evening of March 10th, Monsignore and Father Scoldi, with the men and boys who've volunteered (a privilege of course) to handle the travelling shrine (an old motor-chassis specially adapted and dignified to the needs of saints), and a good few of the populace, go to St. Anna's at about six o' clock and fetch San Giuseppe through the streets to the piazza, where he's set up in his place in the sanctuary of the Mother-Church for the *novena* before his Feast Day, the 19th. (In 1968 I went with Damianina and the children to bring San Giuseppe in to the *paese*: I was leaving for England next day, March 11th, and felt it would be wise, as I meant to come back, to be in Jupiter's good books.)

A day or two before the 18th, the eve of San Giuseppe, each household, if it's properly native to Goat Island, starts preparing its own family temple for San Giuseppe. In our family Maria is the altar's creator – she creates a masterpiece. The front room where we generally eat and which opens on to the piazza, is cleared; all the furniture, ornaments and toys go into the family bedroom where four sleep in the vast "matrimonial" bed and sometimes five if there's somebody extra in the house; while Gigi's bed stands beside it. Even the television is disconnected and put away. A small table from the kitchen is added to the big – there are guests for San Giuseppe; ten people can just squeeze round and eat their dinners, bathed in the glory of the "altar" as everyone calls it.

Along the wall facing the front door the altar has been raised against a reredos of long, coloured hangings. On the altar stands the big framed lithograph of San Giuseppe (with Virgin and Boy) which for the rest of the year hangs in Maria's little room; flowers and greenery deck the frame. The altar has an ecclesiastical air, with cloth, frontal of decorated material, and strips of white silk hanging vertically over its edge. A row of tall votive candles is burning; on both sides loaves of bread are piled and basins of oranges stand. An expanse of floor in front of the altar, forming a sanctuary or chancel, is covered with a carpet of cut grass, and white daisies arranged to form a pattern with, in the centre, done in yellow marguerites, three splendid initials – G. M. G. – Giuseppe, Maria, Gesù. Even if her devotion to Mary weren't implicit in her name, our Maria has lived beside this picture for all her eighteen years and though her temple is San Giuseppe's, she can't leave out the initials of Maria and Jesus.

On the 18th, Damianina is busy making and baking an enormous *torta* of sponge and blancmange and suger-icing; while everybody is paying a round of visits to the San Giuseppe altars set up by their relations and close friends – there's a ceaseless coming and going of admiration and comparison; something like the visits paid by the faithful on Holy Thursday to the *sepolcri* arranged in most Southern churches, which represent scenes from the Passion. That evening Damianina walks up to the prison-gates laden with bread and oranges for the "lifers" inside.

The biggest meal of the year is eaten at midday on the 19th: the women and girls of every household are working at it all the morning. And to this *pranzo* come special guests – it's a tradition on Goat Island to share the San Giuseppe feast with some "poor". But there aren't really enough poor to go round; and Papà for several years has bagged the three most neglected children on the island: two half-brothers and a half-sister, aged perhaps twelve, eleven, ten – who have had several older half-sisters and brothers, offspring of a Neapolitan immigrant who for twenty years had been getting pregnant by mistake.

The meal begins – naturally, because it is a *festa* – with *past' asciutta*, spaghetti and tomato sauce; then roast pork, and round hoops of bread like scooter-tyres which are special to San Giuseppe; then veal cutlets and lettuce followed by boiled artichokes; then two kinds of highly dulcified *torta*, fruit, coffee – with throughout wine and marsala flowing and finally *biccherini*, "little glasses", of *strega*. When the three guests left, a little tipsy, they were embracing three two-pound loaves and three oranges each and, besides, had in their pockets money for the cinema.

I've found this scene each time wonderfully moving: the three children stuffing themselves in a kind of ecstasy of pleasure, made dumb not by shyness but by total concentration on physical luxury – but even more touching was the sweet tenderness with which Papà and Damianina waited on them and lavished food and drink on them and finally loaded them with gifts. How, I wonder, did this theme of charity (the offerings to the prisoners, the feeding of the poor) come to be centrally, and uniquely, a part of this festival? I don't think St. Joseph, in his shadowy appearances in the Gospels, had anything to do with charity; and "charity" isn't a virtue that comes to mind with the names of Zeus and Jupiter. Pitrè says that at Pachino, in south-easterly Sicily, the same feeding of the poor takes place on St. Joseph's day.[27]

The rest of the day's rituals follow the lines of any other's on which a saint, one of the Madonnas or "the Lord" – our tutelary crucifix – "comes out" (*esce*) from the church for a circumambulation of the town and its outskirts. The difference is that there's *more* of everything – more enthusiasm, more people, more band-playing, more bonhomie. The principal Mass of the morning attracts, naturally, all the Church's devout; and also a large number of the younger unbelievers because this is an "occasion" for seeing and being seen, and because it's always as well to insure both ways. In the afternoon the ritual games are held, of course: Father Scoldi has organized a boys' football match – and Gigi scores a goal in the god's honour. But the cardinal business of the day, the most vivid highlight and the most personal, especially for the simple pagans or those anti-clericals in whose ken endure the vestiges of an older religion, is the evening's

---

[27] Giuseppe Pitrè, *Usi e costume del Popolo Siciliano*, 20 vols, Milan, 1850-70. [Author's footnote]

progress of the saint through the streets; when the saint, or rather *deity*, comes out among the people on their own level, so that they may have a little chat with him as well as acclaim him; blow him a kiss and ask him to do them some little favour instead of only listening to Monsignore talking about him (and Monsignore's really talking about somebody quite different). Sicilians like to touch their gods, not merely pray over their heads.

Damianina the day before had washed her hair and fluffed it out – she had soft brown hair which in summer she wore short and in winter drawn back into an oldfashioned bun. And then, before the procession, she did a thing I'd never seen her do before: she rouged and powdered her face and lipsticked her mouth as if she were going to a ball. She wore a black lace Spanish-style mantilla, a new flowered frock she'd specially made, and carried a candle three feet long tied with a pink ribbon. Little Caterina and Duzzo each had small candles – ribbons for all ages were pink for female and blue for male. It was astonishing to see the devotion of Damianina, who stubbornly refuses to go to church and to whom therefore Monsignore hardly concedes a "buon giorno". For the time of the procession, Monsignore found himself almost on a par in importance with our Papà, in charge of the little squad of devotees who were propelling the saint round the street. Papà's was the admired task, piloting the saint round the *paese* (it was fully two hours before the image was back in the church for the night); while Monsignore, wearing his little purple tippet and a *beretta*, vaguely arranged the throng at the church-door into a candle-light procession of two lines, now and then raptly intoning Ave Marias. At the very head, bossy young Father Scoldi was severely calling: "silenzio! silenzio!" at a crowd of infants rapturous over their candles. A column of little girls, last year's first communicants charmingly dressed in their bridal white of muslin and satin were followed by red-cassocked acolytes; Dr. Baffi, the mayor, and self-important councillors like Signor Alcamese walked just behind the saint's carriage with the Marshal of Carbineers (the saint's personal escort of carbineers wore their Napoleonic full dress). Then came the band, the joyless, wooden-faced deaf-mute who played the big drum, his front legs gleaming with gold braid; and after the band, nearly every inhabitant of the island, all carrying long candles which, going out, they earnestly tried to relight from their neighbours'.

San Giuseppe and his crawling, twinkling, solemnly jubilant retinue passes along almost every street in the *paese* and circles most of its periphery; and long before the end of the tour, lots of parents have an exhausted infant slung over a shoulder or carried in aching arms. Though San Giuseppe's follows the lines of other saints' processions, his is the most exhilarating of the year; even a cynical foreigner is infected with a feeling that what's going on is something out of the ordinary.

Joseph was the husband of the Queen of Heaven; so was Zeus/Jupiter, whose consort was Hera/Juno.

Joseph was the "Father" of the Holy Family, the visible paterfamilias of the divine kindred; Zeus/Jove was overlord and "father" of the gods.

Joseph was named (by Pope Pius IX, in 1871) Protector and Patron of the universal Church; Jupiter had been proclaimed, by Caesar Augustus about the time or Christ's birth, "Protector" of Rome – the concept of "Rome" as an ideal and an establishment being then the equivalent of a Church.

Joseph, unlike both Zeus and Jupiter, didn't marry his sister; but it's always emphasized that he and Mary alike belonged to the House of David – a flexible state of consanguinity which can, at will, echo the incestuous tradition of Olympus or accord with the Christian rules of marriage.

The glaring similarities between the names Giuseppe/Joseph/Jove, Zeus/Giuseppe/Jupiter/Joseph, can escape no-one, even if the etymologists, which seems unlikely, can unanswerably explain them away. And in import these names seem to arrive at the same general notion of creativity: the classical deities have the attributes of a generalised "fatherhood" (Jupiter = Jovis Pater) over the gods and mortals and, through the lesser gods and goddesses who all have their own jobs, a general lordship over the seasons and the earth and its increase. The name Joseph, according to the dictionaries, means "the increaser".

I can't see any way of tracing back the buds which sprouted

from Joseph's rod to Olympus; but in some temples to Jupiter the god was portrayed grasping a rod - and there's always the thunderbolt.

These are "facts": drawn from the fragment of St. Joseph's life which can be discovered in the Gospels and in the later "traditions"; from what the Church (and above all, I believe, an impelling popular urge) has done for St. Joseph in the last five or six hundred years, or more; and from classical mythology. The Gospels tell almost nothing about St. Joseph, beyond his conscientiousness as paterfamilias and his reverent credulity regarding the things he was told about his step-son (if that's the word). After Jesus' twelfth or thirteenth year, Joseph fades out of the narratives and the Church has assumed that he died before Christ's ministry began; indeed St. Joseph is counted an "Old Testament saint" - that is, a pre-Christian; a fact which tempts one to try, if one thought one could, to discern some fascinating indicator. What then were the influences that induced Pius IX, just under one hundred years ago, to appoint St. Joseph "patron" of the Church - not, surely, the influence of what's known about St. Joseph, which is little more than that he was persuaded against his will (over the age of eighty, according to the "traditions") to agree to become Mary's husband ("I'm too old", he objected, "and people will laugh at me")? Surely Joseph himself, or what's known of him, didn't provide the energy which two or three times in the five centuries before 1871 has moved the Vatican to upgrade him repeatedly in the hagiarchy?

Donald Attwater, the Catholic encyclopedist, writes that the "unerring instinct for sanctity of Christian folk at large" has in the past 400 years raised Joseph "to the highest rank of the Church's saints"; and defines this popular movement as "this increasing devotion". Addis and Arnold's Catholic Dictionary speaks of a "general manifestation of this devotion". The devotion, the authorities say, seems to have begun in the East - presumably Greece - where in the Middle Ages the nineteenth of March came to be the day the cult was celebrated; by the fourteenth and fifteenth centuries it had spread to certain Orders in the West. Two popes in the seventeenth century declared March 19th a feast of obligation, and one of them made it a "double of the first class". For a time after 1871, St. Joseph was celebrated as

Patron of the Church on a second day shortly after Easter; but today March 19th is firmly and - on Goat Island unchangeably - the feast of San Giuseppe. The absolute immutability of this date on our island must, surely, be of great interest; and was demonstrated in 1967 when San Giuseppe fell on Palm Sunday, which that year also came on March 19th. The Church decreed that the celebration of St. Joseph's Day should be postponed till May 1st. The image wasn't brought from Sant' Anna's that week; there was no procession. But this wouldn't do for Damianina and for other island families: for them, March 19th was the day of San Giuseppe - who was the Church to say that it wasn't? So that year, as usual, Palm Sunday or not, San Giuseppe was celebrated in people's homes with undiminished ceremony: the three little guests came to dinner, were filled with food and drink and sent off laden with presents; the "altar" had been prepared with customary care. And when the Church's official solemnisation of St. Joseph came, Damianina and the rest took no notice; neither the Church nor anybody else could play about with San Giuseppe.

It may perhaps be preposterous, though I don't think it is, to suggest that this "increasing devotion", this growing popular pressure from below which, apparently, had been nagging for centuries at the Church and finally obtained Joseph's elevation to the rank of supreme patriarch, was the consequence of the almost total disappearance from the Catholic escutcheon of God the Father. In southern Italy the "Almighty", "God" with a long beard, the first member of the Trinity, hardly exists at all. Nobody uses "Oh God!" as an expletive, nobody invokes "Dio" in moments of stress; ecclesiastical furnishing and decoration hardly ever provide a representation of the Almighty, and he'd seldom be recognised if they did. I can only remember once seeing in Sicily a portrayal of God Almighty (which doesn't of course mean there aren't others): a side chapel by the Serpotta family in the exciting Carmine church among the "Albergheria" slums of Palermo: the Almighty is rather cynically looking down from heaven's top at the unhappy humans striving to climb unscathed the hill of life.

The Church has allowed God the Father to wither away in order to make room, one may suppose, for the tide of Mariolatry which has flooded over Italy, and especially southern Italy – the Madonna has to a play a number of diverse roles which on Olympus were delegated to a number of assistants and she is constantly taking on new burdens; as Norman Douglas pointed out in *Old Calabria*, she is ousting a lot of the old rural saints from their immemorial niches. Some centuries after the demise of the old religion (when did the pagan gods finally die out altogether – towards A.D. 500?) there must have grown in the collective popular consciousness a need for the father-figure that had been lost; but the "folk-memory", what Jérôme Carcopino calls the "archaeological memory"[28], of the father-god Jupiter or even Zeus lingered and the people were looking for a successor. They recognised one in Joseph and the pressure from below, the "increasing devotion", the "unerring instinct" of the mass, began.

Presumably it's the kind of people who've never heard the names of Jupiter or Zeus in whom that "archaeology memory" of their existence survives most strongly – people like Damianina and Papà and the inhabitants of Goat Island. The peoples of the North who ages ago lost what folk-memory they ever had, and those cultured clerics who know the pagan classics backwards, don't confuse St. Joseph, if they believe in him at all, with anybody else, mythological or not; people like our islanders, intellectually restricted by isolation (it's amazing what twelve miles of water can do) to their inherited traditions and credences and relying on their "unerring instinct" to adapt the precepts and practices of the Church to their ingrained needs, can believe in St. Joseph only in the image of the cloud-gathering, thundering all-father, the patriarchal disposer, which they carry somewhere deep in that memory like a forgotten word on the tip of the tongue. These were the notions which, suddenly crystallising that night in 1966 into conviction, made me see in a flash: "It's Jupiter we're taking home!"

God the Father, one may assert, is hardly known at all to the ordinary southerner. The Son, too, doesn't appear often and

---

[28] *Daily Life in Ancient Rome,* tr. E.C. Lorimer, Penguin Books. [Author's footnote]

hasn't much of a following, except at Christmas, in his shape of Gesù Bambino – "Baby Jesus". But Jesus the Man, Jesus the teacher and even healer, isn't generally thought much of or felt much about; unless, as on Goat Island, circumstances have turned him into the local Patron – and then he ceases to be Jesus the Son of God (even perhaps the Son of Maria) and is simply "The Lord", a fourteenth century wooden crucifix with a magical history. There are some places in southern Italy where Jesus appears in his role of Christ at certain seasons, Holy Week and Easter especially. At Taranto, the Agony of the Passion is portrayed in a procession which lasts for sixteen hours, bare-footed members of the hooded confraternities staggering along under the weight of huge wooden crosses while others go along flogging themselves. Some ten years ago, the present Archbishop of Taranto (tall and patrician, a splendid mediaeval prince when in full liturgical panoply) forbade some of the unorthodoxies of this manifestation; but he had to give in to the pressures of a succession of deputations from the faithful. On Palm Sunday evening 1962, I was in the big church of San Domenico, built by the great Hohenstaufen in the early fourteenth century. I was there to watch the fantastic auction sale of the right to take place of honour (front right, I think) among the bearers of the Madonna in this procession. Once he's bought the right, the highest bidder may, if he's obese and ageing, delegate his son or anybody else to do the actual bearing – his glory is drawn from the sum he pays. That year it cost the winner the equivalent of L300. Afterwards I asked my companion Ugo, the owner of a trattoria, if the winner expected his lavishness to earn him heavenly privileges. "Oh no", said Ugo, "it's done for social prestige." The floor of the church was packed, mostly with businessmen, shopkeepers and the like; they lounged about on the altar rails of side chapels, spitting on the paving, flicking cigarette ash about and lighting fresh ones from the votive candles. The archiepiscopal power was represented by a minor cleric; the auction was invigilated by a committee of the confraternities and conducted by an auctioneer as professionally brash as any in the metropolitan salesrooms.

The mature Christ – indeed the Risen Christ – appears in an unusually touching charade performed on the island of Lipari on

Easter Sunday, at midday after the popular Mass in the Cathedral. But the Christ's emergence among the people in this ceremony isn't so much for his own sake as for his Mother's, the "Addolorata", the Madonna of Sorrows - a popular manifestation of the Great Mother often portrayed with a dagger in her heart. On Lipari, at Easter, two processions leave the cathedral, separate beneath the acropolis and follow different routes through the town to converge on the little piazzetta of the Marina Corte, the old fishing port, for a "surprise" meeting - the timing of the two trains is admirably done. The Madonna is shrouded from head to foot in a black mantilla; when the two figures, surrounded by prelates and dignitaries and guards of honour, approach each other from the two opposites of the piazzetta they halt and seem to hesitate: then recognition comes, and they gravely bow; the Mother first three times, and then, in acknowledgement, three times the Son. This little scene, though the "bows" are a stiff inclination of the images, platform and all, is charming and moving. At the last of the six obeisances, a tape is pulled and the Virgin mourning mantle falls to her feet and she's revealed radiant in blue; an enormous crashing of fireworks starts up from the sea-wall, all the brass of the town bands blow their hardest, and a flock of pigeons whirr up into the sky from a couple of suddenly opened baskets. And that's the end of Easter.

"Gesù bambino", the Christ Child, has a procession of his own in some places, Taranto among them, where children wearing angelic wings escort him round the town on Christmas morning; here on Goat Island his small pink image, like a bouncing cupid, is hoisted above the high altar in the mother-church for Christmas Mass, but he doesn't receive much more attention than that. The place where people expect him to be, of course, is on his mother's knee: in that traditional posture, so familiar in Italian painting of Virgin and Child, which was familiar too in antique Greek painting. I remember especially a vase of the fourth century in that wonderful museum on the acropolis of Lipari which portrays Aphrodite nursing an infant Eros, hooked into her left arm, exactly like innumerable Mothers-and-Child.

But in Sicily it's the island's most hallowed deities, Ceres and Proserpine (or Demeter and Persephone) who provided the prototype of subsequent mother-and-child representations.

Legend has always put the scene of this myth, and the first cultivation of corn, at Enna (also called Castrogiovanni) in the central Sicilian mountains. And Ceres/Demeter is still a dominating force in the "archaeological memory". Some quotations from Douglas Sladen, who was exploring Sicily at the beginning of this century,[29] will illustrate this: at Castrogiovanni (Enna), Sladen wrote:

> They show you a statue of Ceres holding the child Proserpine in her arms, belonging to the Roman era, which was used for centuries as the Madonna and Child Jesus, in spite of the child being a girl. It is not the only statues of the two goddesses used in Castrogiovanni in this way. And it is of enormous interest as being clearly the source from which the favourite Italian type of the Madonna holding the Child was taken. When we remember the fact that Proserpine was called the Saviour by the continental Greeks and that she had a resurrection,[30] this extraordinary historical fact is emphasised.... The Arcadians call Proserpine the Saviour.... Pausanias mentions this in his account of Megalopolis in Arcadia, the other famous seat of Ceres and Proserpine. Pausanias also tells us that the Arcadians called Ceres the Mistress, which exactly corresponds to Madonna.... Ceres' temple at Enna was one of the most famous of the antique world.... The people of Enna could only be converted to Christianity by the identification of Ceres with the Virgin Mary....

That's what Sladen wrote nearly seventy years ago. I have only passed through Enna and can't vouch for his story of the girl Proserpine's doing duty for the Christ Child although, in view of the liveliness of the Demeter/Persephone myth about Enna, I can see no reason to disbelieve it. It's unlikely, however, that tourists today would be told about it; the Church in the South, with great good sense and tolerance and some humour, accepts the paganisms in the religion of her congregation - but she doesn't go out of the way to point them out. Indeed, the Church sometimes secures a tactful adjustment: the Madonna who naturally assumed the place left vacant by Venus Ericina and her predecessors Aphrodite and Astarte on the top of Eryx, somehow moved down the hill to Custonaci when her resemblance to these goddesses looked like becoming too close.

---

[29] *Sicily*, Methuens, 1905. [Author's footnote]

[30] "resurrection", of course, refers to Proserpine's return to earth from Hades after her abduction by Pluto. [Author's footnote]

Custonaci is a *paese* lying in a valley between Monte Cofano, a headland rising from the sea like a spear-head, and the north-east flank of Eryx, on top of which this most famous Venus had her shrine overlooking Trapani and the islands. In her service a retinue of priestesses was as well known to any sailors whose ship called at Trapani as the goddess herself was throughout the Roman world. Venus Ericina was her title; "The Lady of Eryx," Ovid called her.

The Madonna of Custonaci, as so many other Madonnas have, arrived miraculously by sea; come in the form of a picture painted, as so many other pictures of the Madonna have been, by St. Luke. Legend landed her there and raised her church on the spot she chose; what legend doesn't explain is how she became the patron not only of Custonaci but of all the mountain and commune of Erice or Eryx; nor why, when some calamity comes or is threatened, she is taken up to the summit of Eryx and deposited in the Mother-Church after a perambulation of the tiny toy streets. If it's drought, the people shout at her: "Acqua, Maria, acqua!" - Water, Water!; or if it rains too much they cry "Basta, Maria, Basta!" - Enough, Enough!

There was, it's said, a Madonna at Custonaci before the arrival of the thaumaturgical painting by St. Luke; she, perhaps, was the authentic heiress of The Lady of Eryx, but since then the two have acceptably fused. There are two facts which seem specially relevant to this discussion: the Child, who in St. Luke's painting is carried at his mother's breast, holds in his hand three ears of corn - a symptom of confusion, perhaps, into one personage of the two great goddesses of Sicily - Aphrodite/Venus of Eryx and Demeter/Ceres of Enna. The second fact is this: rich men's wills, dated early in the fifteenth century, have been preserved in which bequests are made to the Madonna of Custonaci - doesn't this recall the legacies which Cicero said were left by rich Romans to Venus Ericina? The last Sunday of August is the Custonaci Maria's *festa* - like the feast days of an immense number of local saints, it won't appear in the regular Catholic calendar. During several days of ceremonies and celebrations, she's carried up to the summit of Eryx, the historic seat of her authority.

The Madonna of Custonaci, here on Goat island, has become the obvious person to cast in the role of Demeter/Ceres - the only one, indeed; since over there on Eryx, beyond Trapani, she's become merged in the twin deities of motherhood and earthly increase; and here Venus has retreated into the shade of the earth-goddess.

On the last Sunday in August 1966, when the Madonna of Custonaci had climbed Eryx and was playing Venus there, we were having a *festa* too – that of a Madonna I haven't heard of anywhere else: the Madonna Campagnola, the Rustic Madonna, the Peasant Madonna, Mary of the Countryside. For her, the "musica" was out at 7.30 in the morning, blowing its way round the town till about nine; for dinner Damianina made home-made macaroni and chicken stew. Papà was in great form and afterwards the whole family drank several glasses of a sweetish liqueur called *zambuco al' caffè*. In the afternoon the "Games", a component of any classic *festa*, were held in the middle of the piazza; obstacle races on bicycles, trick-motor-scooter riding round a cunning chalked course – Father Scoldi was the organiser, and had collected from the shopkeepers a fine sum for prizes; our Gigi won ten pounds in those Games.

Towards dusk the Rural Madonna "emerges": an artistically inferior effigy, life-size, of Mother and Child, the latter in the customary lap position, held by the left hand; they were festooned with flowers and greenery and the fruits of the field. But this "emergence" wasn't attended by Tommaso, our Papà, nor by the usual handlers of the chariot: the Madonna was escorted by *contadini*, and the principal peasants propelled her: the man with the most cows acted as master of ceremonies and headed the procession behind the "saint"; and though nearly everybody on the island followed the Madonna round the *paese*, it was gardeners, dairymen, vine-growers and cultivators generally who composed the leading contingent. Monsignore didn't wear a coloured cape; he appeared, as if to emphasise the basically unconsecrated nature of the event, with nothing but a little lace cotta over his *sottana*.

I was watching, I knew, a goddess's procession: Ceres, the earth-mother, the lady bountiful of corn and everything one can grow to eat, with the little Proserpine on her knee. Even on Eryx, Aphrodite seems to have yielded ground to Demeter, Venus to Ceres. There was bound, I suppose, to be a tussle for man's memory between the two great goddesses of Sicily; and on Goat Island, insulated (until the era of hydrofoils and television) by its moat of dancing sea from a wider world, the more useful of the two has won the place in the collective memory; when Damianina, or any other islander, exclaims "Madre Mia!" she's invoking the mother of all eatables, like broad-beans and parsley and the corn that makes bread and pasta rather than the mother of "amore" (which is all very well in its way, but doesn't fill the family's stomachs).

The Madonna is a hard-worked personage; she's always being called upon to deputise for some defunct or deposed predecessor. But it was left by all past history to Pius XII, in 1950, to put her in the position of being asked to replace a Roman emperor. In 1950, Pope Pacelli established as a dogma of the Church the Assumption of the Virgin Mary, and named August 15 to be a feast day in honour of her reception into Heaven. Now, August 15 is *Ferragosto*, the chief day in the *feriae augustae*, the feast in honour of Augustus Caesar. It's a day when, throughout Italy, everybody gets away for an outing from wherever he may be: Rome empties of Romans and becomes filled with (besides foreign tourists) local provincials. On Goat Island nobody stays in the *paese*: great-grandparents are driven or carried into the country, though most of them are game enough to walk. One is almost disgraced socially if one stays at home on *Ferragosto*. So in 1966 Father Scoldi organised Games in honour of Maria Assunta. Outside the cemetery, about two miles from the *paese*, there's a small chapel dedicated to Maria Immacolata; here, in an open space before the chapel, the games proceeded – on the same lines as those in the piazza. Father Scoldi, an aggressive young man, ran the Games with alarming energy and ignored his superior the Archpriest, Monsignore, who, sweetly vague, was doing his best to contribute some saintly jocosity to the day; he would break off a gentle crooning of Ave Marias to intone a would-be jocular announcement of a Games event which had already started. Or, as I found him, he'd be sitting on a wall surrounded by a group of eagerly inquiring boys: "Padre, padre," one would be saying, "how can I enter for the obstacle race?..."; but another would interrupt, "You mustn't call this one 'padre' – this one's called monsignore". "Well then, Monsignore, how can I enter...." And the Archpriest's sweet insubstantial voice would reply: "St. Paul was a glorious man, a gentle saint – if only, boys you'd read what St. Paul...."

But Pope Pius XII didn't ordain that Games should be held to honour the Assumption. Games were held in honour of the earlier gods, and Augustus had proclaimed himself divine....

A "saint" who has nothing to do with the old religion, and for whom the Madonna isn't asked to stand in, has his festival on September 14th, the feast of the Holy Cross and St. Saviour (it's thus the name day of anybody called Salvatore). He is the Patron of the island, "The Lord"; a wooden crucifix found in a cave in the year 1402 by a deaf-mute who was chasing a rabbit. The man instantly regained speech and hearing. The grotto was near the northern seashore, among a warren of caves in the rocky wilderness beyond the cemetery. It's within the cemetery that "Il Signore" resides for the rest of the year – he's brought into the *paese* for his festival; a rich man from Trapani named Coniglio in 1820 become a devotee of the miraculous *crocifisso* and built it the present sanctuary: Coniglio means "rabbit".

Il Signore is highly revered and very often invoked for help. His procession in the evening, since he's the Patron, becomes naturally a municipal affair, with the "autorità" there in force; Dr. Baffi, the mayor, walks immediately behind the Cross with an air of knowing The Lord's secrets and sharing with him the whole burden of communal politics.

It's not surprising that a deaf-mute found the magic crucifix; there are so many of them in Sicily. We on Goat Island at the moment have five, including a child of about nine, the front of the big drum, and the extraordinary gyrating scarecrow I mentally named St. Vitus. In Palermo, not far from the harbour gates, there's a hostel or college outside of which group of *sordomuti* generally stand arguing with their hands. In Trapani I used to know a leathery old lady who wore tattered clothes and huge man's boots, with a black madonna's mantle encircling her gaily grimacing face. I thought she was a beggar, until I found she was always in wine-bars, swigging down a glass and carrying a huge shopping-bag; they told me she was well-to-do and always in good spirits. She wore a large episcopal cross on a chain, which she would show to people while blessing them as if she were the Pope. Sometimes men would bring in small children to be kissed by her.

Why are so many born deaf-and-dumb in Sicily? Is it a curse left by an age-old heritage of malaria (now broken, thank God), or of under-nourishment, or of hereditary syphilis or some other malady – though I don't believe there's a formidable history of venereal disease in Sicily. What wicked godmother commits at birth this brutal sabotage of happiness so often? Not many can come upon a miraculous cross.

Christmas and Easter, in the hearts of most people, are "holidays" rather than "holy days": occasions for family rejoicing. Ten years ago, in Italy, Christmas was a purely religious feast, marked only by Midnight Mass for the faithful and in some places the procession of Gesù Bambino. But in these ten years the commercial blight has descended from the North: we now have "Babbo Natale" (Father Christmas), plastic fir-trees and artificial snow. Well, that's all right: the children enjoy it, except that none of these teutonic things seems here authentic. The children *certainly* enjoy it: Christmas has become a third occasion for their being given presents: on November 2nd, All Souls' Day, the *Giorno dei Morti* or the Day of the Dead, they received toys as from defunct family members like grandparents ("What have the Dead given me?" a child excitedly asks on the morning of All Souls); and on January 6th, Epiphany, they'll get more presents – this being the traditional children's day before ever Christmas was boosted by the Milanese shopkeepers into a festival of money-splurging. Even here, on Goat Island, the commercial magnates have got the better of Christ, and Christmas has become a vulgarism; even here post is clogged by "greeting cards".

Paradoxically, the Day of the Dead, though a day of mourning or rather of communion with the dead, is the happiest festival of the year, when family parties set out early for the cemetery two miles away to spend the day sitting on the grave-stones of departed relations, bringing them flowers and sharing with them picnic meals. This custom is a legacy of the Roman cult of the *limures,* the ghosts of the departed, which were visited and feasted in just the same way. Here on my island *I Morti* is peculiarly a children's festival: the presents they get "from the dead" (including, for some reason, a great number of top firearms) are in answer to requests they write to them, as our children write to Father Christmas: I have here a scrap of paper on which my "grandson", aged about six, wrote: "*Cari Morti* (Dear Dead), I would like a horse tricycle and an infant school satchel and I promise to be good. Duzzo." He got them, of course; and now, years later, he's still being good.

Easter has a traditional importance which, I suspect, goes back into the past beyond its Christian foundation – or rather Easter Monday has, *Pasquetta* in Sicily, which extends over into Easter Tuesday. Even more than at Ferragosto, it seems almost a social solecism if one doesn't spend Easter Monday out picnicking in some rural glade or at least by the seashore; this custom, as old as the hills, must descend from some rite connected with spring. What's historically interesting is that it was this Easter Monday (and Tuesday too) custom of the outing into the countryside that provided the concentration of ordinary people without which, on March 31st, 1282, the Sicilian Vespers might never have ejected the Angevin French from Sicily. Those lovely fields on the banks of the sweet river Oreto, where today the great Palermo cemetery of Sant' Orsola stands, within the golden circle of the mountains behind the city, would obviously be the scene of the family picnics at Easter of thousands of Palermitans living in the old slummy quarters of the Albergheria and the Kalsa; they didn't go there in the evening for Vespers, as most writers on the matter assume: they'd gone there for the whole day, to have a good time with the family – which is just what their descendants have done at Easter ever since.

13. Monsignore

Somewhere in life I had picked up the belief, never since let fall, that a monsignore wears purple stockings. So positive was I about this – on what authority I've long forgotten – that when, coming to this island parish a few years ago, I found our archpriest, an undoubted monsignore, with socks of a slightly dustier black than the skirts of his soutane, I felt the shock of one who suddenly finds he's been done. But faith disdains facts, and I couldn't admit to myself that all these years I might have been wrong. Monsignore's fusty ankles worried me; yet one can't go up to a man with whom one's on little more than bowing terms (extended now and then to a formal invitation, gravely declined, to an *espresso* at Uccio's bar) and ask: "*Why* aren't you wearing purple stockings?" or even "*Oughtn't* you to be wearing purple stockings?"

One day, surely, a flush of imperial violet would glow beneath the drab hem of Monsignore's frock as, crossing the piazza with that measured ecclesiastical stride which decades of ritual progress from sacristy to sanctuary had made his habit, he carried his shopping bag in his left hand and, with his right unsmilingly greeted acquaintances with that weary flap of the hand (descendant of the street courtesies of ancient Rome and unwitting prototype of the fascist pantomime) that is the usual Sicilian salutation. But it never happened; the only semblance of relief from the monotone charcoal of Monsignore's walking-out garb was the yellowish discoloration round the edge of his clerical collar, above which his sad grey features gently bowed with the melancholy of one of those nodding Chinese figures one used to have in childhood. All else was dingy black, from biretta to galoshes – all faintly grizzled, perhaps from long wear or want of brushing, as if patinated with a sprinkling of fine ash. He was a small man, with a long pallid face sanctified by self-restraint and the habitude of devout disciplines, beautiful white fingers delicate as tapers, and a spare frame, almost youthful except for an unhealthily hummocky paunch which gave his skirted figure the profile of a woman eight months gone.

Monsignore was a solitary man whose face, though it could momentarily light up with a smile of great sweetness, was generally grey with the sadness of disappointment. I doubt whether anybody had been able to know him intimately during all the thirty-five years he was parroco here and archpriest of our tiny archipelago; so nobody had really seen the nature of that disappointment. I suppose it was a recognition of failure: a puzzled realisation that against the inherited paganism and innate anticlericalism of the mass of his parishioners he had through all these years been ineffective. I remember one Sunday afternoon, not many weeks before Monsignore's death, when he came out on to the church steps after ringing the bell for the afternoon office. He stood in the warm sunshine and scanned the piazza for the approach of any faithful; and the forlorn expression of his face turned to delight when he was suddenly joined by a group of adolescent boys, four or five of them, who for fifteen minutes stood with him, chatting, joking, teasing; while Monsignore was clearly congratulating himself secretly on this nuclear congregation and perhaps even on the reclamation to the fold of a sheep or two wandering since First Communion. He was patting the boys on the back, clasping them youthfully round the shoulder, and telling them some of his best stories about St. Paul, always with him a favourite topic. And suddenly they gave him a cheerful *ciao*, and ran off laughing across the square to our village cinema, just then opening its doors; and Monsignore was left alone again on the steps of his church, gazing hungrily down the length of the piazza....

When Monsignore died he was only a little over sixty, but he'd been here a very long time and was as much an organic part of the island, and especially of the piazza, as the eighteenth century church he had devotedly cherished for three and a half decades. He'd been as familiar a feature, and almost as disregarded, as the tall palm tree that stood by the ingress to the harbour. Had that tree been suddenly felled, its absence would have shocked most of us who had never thought about its presence. Monsignore's availability had been as much taken for granted, and as unremarked, as the tinny clang of the bell he hopefully tolled four or five times a day; he was like the doctor when one isn't ill, and became a family necessity only when there was a child to be baptised, a daughter to be married or a dying grandad to be provided with the insurance of the viaticum. On Monsignore's death he suddenly became acutely missed by people who, before it, hardly knew him by sight. The whole island woke up to the news as awed as England on the death of a king.

But although Monsignore had been an island institution for thirty-five years, he had never, I think, managed to take it into, so to speak, his spiritual confidence. People didn't bring their troubles, moral, spiritual or mundane to his confessional; women didn't confide in him the arcane perplexities of their souls and none was cosily prompted by a feeling of spiritual affinity to knit, perhaps for his Name Day, a pair of purple stockings. Yet he impressed me as a man of great piety and even sanctity – solemnly but seldom affably chatting about his health, or repairs to the church, or even the unpleasantness of the scirocco wind, he seemed always, though meeting one's eyes and talking to one's face, to be peering behind one towards some immanence out of reach of one's commonplace perceptions. Yet, paradoxically, Monsignore's inner spirituality was manifest outwardly in a meticulous attention to ritual formality and observance of the liturgical rules; he seemed much more concerned that his faithful should perform the routine religious duties than that they should worry their consciences about faith, charity and purity. His sermons, brief and admonitory, dealt with matters like eating meat on Fridays, the confession of sins, even perfunctory attendance at mass, and the repetition of Hail Marys; he seldom ventured among the mysteries of Christian doctrine and the Church's interpretation of it. I used to feel that his priesthood belonged to the tradition of that which served the ancient gods: the Old Religion that the young emperor Julian romantically tried to restore, in which the exact performance of ritual detail was more important than the purpose of performing it. Thus, at an old Roman sacrifice, if anything went wrong, if priest or acolyte or the attendants on the bull made a mistake, they all had to go back to the beginning and start again – otherwise the rites would lose their validity and be unacceptable to the god.

I saw Monsignore for the last time, only a few days before his sudden death from serious stomachic illness, at a baptism; the rite was performed by his young assistant priest, while he himself, in his musty black soutane, fussed about the font, looking ashen-faced and sepulchral. There came a point in the ceremony when the young priest had to do something with a candle; and at this moment Monsignore's wan cheeks suddenly flushed with anger: he grabbed the candle from his curate's startled fingers and, his lips a taut thread of vexation, did with it whatever ought to have been done. It was the young priest's turn to blush, and for a second he lost his liturgical place; but by now Monsignore's features had recovered their melancholy calm – a serenity born, I supposed of his belief that his opportune interference had, in the nick of time, snatched the infant from the very jaws of perdition. Poor Monsignore! Not only had his lot been cast, for a third of a century, among an islandful of pagans, but he had to keep a sharp eye on his own subordinates, lest their technical mistakes let the devil slip in sideways.

The pagans of his parish – those, I mean, who while expecting his services at birth, death and for the intervening rite of marriage, never went near mass or the confessional – made up a good two thirds of it; them he regarded with a sorrowful tolerance, for he knew by now there was nothing he could do about them. Meeting our Damianina, mother of our family, he would shake his head sorrowfully, saying it would soon be time for her youngest to come to catechism, and adding: "And when shall I see you at Mass, Signora?", knowing that he never would. And he knew all about Tommaso's, her husband's, remark each saint's day when he appeared at the church, as his father had in his day, to take a leading part in manhandling the saint's image on its annual peregrination of the *paese*: "I do this in the service of the saints, not of the priests" – "saints" here being Tommaso's modernism for "gods" – and Monsignore admired the gusto with which he performed this task, though perhaps the Madonna, towards the end of August, carrying a sheaf of corn, might in some people's eyes be Ceres, and though Jupiter, on March 19th, might be disguised as St. Joseph.

As the Church's representative vis-à-vis the State in the island's official Establishment, Monsignore couldn't escape some social collaboration with the local politicians, particularly the Christian Democrats, since they monopolised the Establishment

– doubtless he sometimes dined with the mayor just as he played an official role on such occasions as the Day of the Armed Forces. But Monsignore seemed to have little truck with the policies of politicians of whatever colour; his principal social relaxation was a visit, perhaps once a week, to Uccio's bar where, sitting under the shade of the mulberries, he would gossip with a few old cronies of twenty or thirty years' standing, and even allow himself a few good laughs. Gentle and kindhearted, yet oddly unapproachable; the sternness of his piety softened, when it came to human beings, by a sorrowing indulgence; withdrawn, rather unworldly, that's how the people saw their archpriest – and humble, they added: he was the simplest of men and quite unmindful of the lofty position in the island's social hierarchy which his incumbency gave him. Wasn't it perhaps this humility, I thought to myself, that stood between him and those purple stockings? He wasn't a man to flaunt the emblems of rank.

* * * *

The news that Monsignore had died hit me, as it did everybody else, like a blow from behind, so impossible did the removal of such a permanent fixture seem. And yet, almost before I'd recovered from the shock, an irrepressible thought jumped disrespectfully into my mind: surely they'll bury him in purple stockings? Surely, I thought, now that his self-effacing modesty can no longer protest, they will send him on his last journey dressed, so to speak, in full uniform; if purple stockings are his due, he will be wearing them….

He died in the evening of a Friday in mid-July, when what in Sicily is called the *Gran Caldo*, the Great Heat, has set in for the next two or three months. Next morning, we learned that the Bishop, and a party of Monsignore's diocesan colleagues, would that evening cross over from the Sicilian shore and accompany his body into the sanctuary of the Mother Church, the shrine to which he'd devoted half his lifetime, where it would rest until the Sunday morning. That Saturday was to be the Church's day: when the Holy Family of Christ, Monsignore's closest friends throughout his life, would, through these prelates, priests and priors from all over his own diocese, pay him every possible unworldly honour and speed his soul off to Paradise. But on the Sunday he was to be turned over to the politicians.

That Saturday afternoon the diocesan *curia* chartered an *aliscafo* for the transport from Sicily of the Bishop and his funebrial retinue; and at six in the evening more than twenty clerics - secular and regular, of high degree and of humble - were gathered in homage round Monsignore's catafalque in the sanctuary of his church. It was impressive testimony to the regard and affection in which he was held throughout the Province. There must, I suppose, have been a few monsignori among them; but all - except the Bishop who was in his full splendour of scarlet and magenta - were clad uniformly in white with a kind of stole over the breast and reaching to the feet; and if there were any purple ankles among them, they were kept out of sight by those long snowy petticoats.

I had hoped he would be brought that evening on a bier, dressed in full canonicals, so that he could lie in state in full view of the faithful while he received his last Benediction on earth. But, instead, they carried him in from his lodgings behind the sacristy in a closed coffin (though not yet screwed down); and I realised that if any chance still existed of my seeing what Monsignore was wearing on his feet, it would occur at the morrow's Requiem Mass.

I went into church next morning a half hour early; the prelates and the priors had departed, whisked away last night by the *aliscafo* that had brought them. Monsignore was to be sent on his way by his young assistant and - as it turned out - by the local bigwigs of the Christian Democrat Party. Already there was a congregation bigger than usual awaiting this special Sunday Mass, mostly, so far, women; but the first thing that caught my eye was that Monsignore's coffin, standing on its catafalque amid a galaxy of candles, was wide open: there, for anybody who cared to walk up and look, Monsignore lay revealed from head to foot. The second thing I noticed was that at the head of the coffin stood an outsize electric-fan which, whirring at speed, was gravely turning its face from side to side, like an aged auctioneer, and keeping the air above Monsignore moving.

Busy in the sanctuary, seeing to small procedural details and checking the wiring and plugs of the electric fan, the Municipal

Secretary was daintily moving about, genuflecting each time he passed the Host and whispering instructions to the Municipal Constable who had brought in the island's heraldic banner and set it up near the pew where the mayor would be sitting. The Secretary was an indefatigable master of ceremonies at any civico-ecclesiastical function and a pillar of Church, State and Christian Democracy. Years before, soon after I'd settled on the island, I asked Damianina who was the elegant *signor* that so often paced the piazza with hands clasped at his breast as if holding secrets not to be shared with the vulgar. "E' una persona distinta," she answered; and indeed he never forgot, and never allowed anybody else to forget, what a distinguished personage he was.

From the piazza outside there came the tramp of military feet and a word of command; and the Guard of Honour marched in and took up their stand on either side of the chancel - a squad of prison warders, heads encased in steal helmets and each carrying a Tommy gun: the guns which are a constant warning to the convicts in these young men's charge.

Warders for Monsignore? Surely, good God, *prisoners* would be more apt if Guard of Honour there must be - more in harmony with Monsignore's profession and his Master's teaching? It was enough, I thought, to make him turn in his coffin already.

Meanwhile, a pilgrimage to the coffin was proceeding. Women, mainly women, some with an infant held by the hand, were walking the length of the church to stand beside Monsignore's couch under the electric fan; most would touch him, some would bend and kiss the cold hand, and some even hold up a child so that it could stretch out a finger and touch.... Monsignore overnight, and in death, had become a thaumaturge, a *marabout*, as the island's Saracen forbears put it - from his corpse, through touch, issued that same efflux of magical holiness that Muslims find flows (in the form of *baraka*) from descendants of the Prophet and other holy men or their shrines.

Now, an inner voice kept nagging at me, *now* you can go up and see whether he's wearing purple stockings. Yes, and so I could, easily - and yet I was held back by a kind of shyness, or perhaps decency: I felt it would be impertinent to go peering into Monsignore's coffin just to see what he had on his feet. And, I must say, that supporting this diffidence was the thought of that electric fan. ... The mid-morning heat was immense, even in the church's shade, and a great crush of people clustering round the doorway adder to the stuffiness....

The mayor arrived, like royalty, a minute before the celebrant issued from the presbytery for mass, and briskly walked, with that air of self-deprecatory self-importance common to public men, up the central aisle to his foremost pew. With his presence the Christian Democrat delegation was complete: all the councillors of that party whose majority on the Council ruled the Commune; and all the shopkeepers, landowners and so on who, supporting Christian Democracy, had voted these councillors in. The opposition councillors, and their supporters, if there at all, seemed almost quarantined among the congregated throng: it appeared that somehow Christian Democracy had managed to hog the day for itself – an appearance which became even clearer when, the Requiem Mass over, the cortège had started across the piazza.

Outside, ranged against the wall on either side of the west door, leaned a galaxy of wreaths – those splendid Italian floral offerings, framed in laurel, four or five feet high, and garlanded with a broad black ribbon emblazoned in gold with the names of the mourning donors. When mass was over, men and boys went to seize these, two to each wreath, and formed a long file of flowers stretching far into the piazza. Behind these came the priest and his acolytes carrying cross and holy water; then the coffin borne on the shoulders of young men of the prison service (Monsignore, always courteous, would have gently thanked them – but is that what he would have wanted?); followed by a group of family mourners and then by the mayor, the representatives of the State, flanked by the escort of *carabiniere* in splendid Napoleonic uniform, and the leading lights of local Christian Democracy – after that came the rest, including no doubt politicians of other shades who felt admiration or affection for Monsignore. And finally, in the rear, the municipal motor-hearse into which, at Sant'Anna's on the other side of the village, Monsignore would be transferred for the drive to the cemetery.

Coming from the shadows of the church into the heat of that flaming July sky was like moving from the sultry gloom of a public bakery into the full focus of the open oven. The sun was beating on the flagstones of the piazza like drumsticks; a boy, carrying a cone of ice-cream from Uccio's, was trying to pour it down his throat like milk from a coconut before it all trickled through his fingers. Into this sizzling heat, Monsignore was obsequially borne: he had been dead for nearly two days.

The cortège advanced slowly through the piazza; but when the head of the wreath-bearers had arrived at the further end of it, and the coffin the centre, the procession suddenly stopped; and Monsignore was deposited upon the almost glowing stones.

People like myself, who were forming a sort of popular guard of honour each side of the piazza, for a second felt aghast – had some catastrophe occurred, something which made one quickly cross oneself – had Monsignore started knocking with his bony knuckles on the side of the coffin, one old lady near me breathlessly inquired?

But then it became clear what was happening and remained clear for the next twenty minutes: I timed it. A *professore*, headmaster of a senior school across the water, brother of our Municipal Secretary and a devoted advocate of Christian Democracy, was pronouncing a eulogy. For twenty minutes the periods of his encomium sounded a splendid literary dirge for Monsignore and his long and admirable ministry on the island and I must say that I admired the *professore*'s delivery: he did the whole thing without a note. But it lasted for twenty minutes; and all that time Monsignore's coffin was on the ground under the full ferocity of that July sun.

The piazza is large; and there was that rustling murmur inevitably engendered by a crowd of a thousand or more people, however cowed; and I found it hard to catch the *professore*'s words: I cannot assert, therefore, that for twenty minutes he electioneered for Christian Democracy; but I'm ready to bet that for a number of those minutes he did.

At last the oration ended; and the orator, as modestly as any headmaster after addressing the assembled school, withdrew to his place among the island's bigwigs. Monsignore could move on again: the prison warders picked up the coffin – even the wood must have been hot to the touch by now – and shouldered it with sweat running down from under those incongruous steel helmets. The sun blazed down, and the coffin itself seemed to glisten. I watched Monsignore off on his last lap: at the other end of the village he would transfer to the motor hearse and be whisked to the coolness of his grave. And as I watched him go, before darting into the shade of Uccio's bar, I thought: "Well, if he was wearing purple stockings, surely the colour must be running by now. ..."

* * * *

This story has a sequel, though really inconsequential: just as Monsignore had to have a successor. For two or three months after Monsignore's death the rituals of the church were performed by a devout and kindly old priest who, one supposed, had been brought out of retirement. In those months rumour followed speculation about whom would have entrusted to him the cure of our island's souls; the old gentlemen at Uccio's bar gossiped and wagered daily about it. And then it became known that certain "regular" priests, monks, were to take charge of the parish; and then – in late autumn – came the day when the Bishop and prelates of the *curia* were to come for the ritual institution of the new *parocco* and his assistants.

It was a stormy morning, with a northwest wind blowing viciously on to the jetty. But half an hour before the Bishop's *aliscafo* was due to arrive, the mole was crowded with people eager to welcome him; and especially the contingents of the young which the old priest had ushered down to the port: galaxies of sweet young girls who, chanting orisons, hymns and psalms, were mainly kept busy holding their skirts down which the wind was furiously lifting; and the party of little boys in cassocks and lace collars who, after looking up the girls' skirts, were to bow to the prelate. The wind blew and the water swirled; the important people of the island and the leaders of local Christian Democracy stood on the jetty with their umbrellas spread and their legs taut against the wind. And behind, the old priest was bravely urging on the singing of his girls and boys – and when the *aliscafo* carrying the bishop, who showed himself on the top deck in the glory of his proper canonicals, seemed to be approaching the jetty, everyone joined in a great cheer and the old priest goaded his boys and girls into ever louder panegyrics, and the whole waiting crowd, as crowds do, trembled with anticipation, – but the *aliscafo* came no nearer to the jetty: in a violent sea it plunged and rolled just off the jetty, but suddenly the *comandante* decided that mooring was impossible; and away went the *aliscafo*, carrying bishop and all his entourage. (We are, on our island often cut off from Sicily by weather).

But on the jetty I found myself standing, just as the bishop's craft stood away, beside a [short plump man in his early thirties, who, to judge from his garb, was unquestionably a priest, though how he had got there I couldn't fathom. He was gazing out over the sea at the now distant *aliscafo*, so it was without embarrassment that I lowered my eyes and beheld below his frock, at long last, a pair of purple stockings.][31]

[31] The manuscript breaks off suddenly after the words "beside a", and the following words in square brackets have been hesitantly invented by the editor to avert a lame ending.

III. THE SEQUEL TO *THE WORLD, THE FLESH AND MYSELF*

Davidson's plans for Sicilian Vespers *suddenly changed in February 1975, when Quartet Books of London commissioned him to write a sequel to his autobiography,* The World. *This necessitated both writing about his life between 1958 (with which year* The World *ended) and 1965 (when he first visited Favignana), and changing the focus of* Sicilian Vespers *to be more autobiographical.* My Sicilian Vespers *continued to be his tentative name for the book, but has been dropped here to avoid confusion with the pure travel book he wrote in 1969-72.*

For reasons explained in the Editor's Note, the sequel as presented here ignores the slight redrafting of Sicilian Vespers *and is restricted to the new material he wrote in the months preceding his final hospitalisation in September 1975.*

I

My amour with Sicily began in 1951 when, from Robin Maugham's yacht *Clio*, after a night's passage from Capri, I first saw a September dawn break over Palermo and its gigantic reredos of gilded mountain; and then, spellbound, discovered that fabulous treasury of art, architecture and adolescent beauty that lies almost secretly behind the ferro-concrete modernities of this exquisitely paradoxical city. Infatuation, a week later, mellowed to romance when, sailing round to Messina, I watched, before another dawn, the dim, brooding shapes of Homer's "Floating Cliffs" drift by to port, as if they, not we, were moving – the Aeolian Islands among which, twelve years later, I was to pass a summer, voluptuously commuting between the sensuous, cushiony beaches of volcanic pumice on Lipari (myriads of tiny pumice pebbles floating on the cobalt sea like the Milky Way in a southern sky) and the brazen black sand of flaming Stromboli; and became a love affair when, turning south into the Strait towards Scylla and Charybdis, we ran full into the sun just as it topped, on the Calabrian side, the peak of Aspromonte and, on the Sicilian, illumined with Canaletto clarity, the pert maritime profile of Messina and the bruised and fissured cliffs of the heights beyond. Suddenly I knew that here, somewhere on this island of Sicily, I should find what I'd been looking for all my life: here, in this land of staggering scenic beauty, birthplace of so many of the gods and a nursery of creative man – here surely there must be all the ingredients of love.

Besides, I had some familiarity with a highly pertinent aspect of the Sicilian style. I had on board a Sicilian boy: a Palermitano of sixteen called Angelo. Robin had been cruising gently southward from Villefranche since August, putting in each night at some agreeable port and stopping the engines every midday for a swim over the side: a lotus-eating life, the parasitic vocation of the idle rich, yet neither of us was that, and we both had our work: I think only Anthony Trollope can have outstript Robin for industry and output. Because of some mechanical trouble, we spent a few days in Genoa, where I had found Angelo in the chief *piazza*, solving his own fraction of the national unemployment problem by peddling black-market American cigarettes.

At that time – and for another decade into the early 'sixties – almost any Italian street-corner was the "pitch" of such flouters of the laws that protect the government tobacco monopoly; while revenue officers zealously smelt out smugglers at the ports, the civil police seemed to turn a lenient eye on the street-hawkers: probably this "self-help" was considered a useful contribution to the country's economy. But today, twenty-five years later, it's almost impossible to buy a black-market Lucky Strike, and the trade from Tangier in yachts wearing the Red Ensign has about petered out for want of takers. Yet smuggling of a kind is still rife in Sicilian waters – the armed revenue launches are always on the prowl; and twice in the last year or so I have watched from this stone cabin where I've been living for six years a "foreign" boat steal into the deserted cove below my garden, hurriedly land a man carrying a hefty suitcase who made off on foot inland, and then head back for the Sicilian "mainland". Contraband? A fugitive? An escaped prisoner? Something fishy, certainly; the *Guardia di Finanza* never visit this spot two miles remote from their harbour headquarters.

But Angelo, up there in the "foreign" north, was homesick; and jumped at the idea of a passage south in *Clio*. Bureaucracy, though, intruded: without a passport he couldn't embark as a friend, or, without a seaman's ticket, as crew. So I put Angelo on the train, sent postcards to his Palermo address from Portofino, Livorno, Elba, Anzio, Ischia and Capri – and there he was on the quayside when we berthed that September morning. Angelo lived aboard the week we lay in Palermo and then, the Sicilian *capitaneria* there being less strictly canonical than the Genovese, sailed with us round to Messina. Thence, sadly, I had to send him home, for we were bound for Malta. And, sadly, I have never seen him again; though on later visits to Palermo I have haunted the Via Orologio where he had lived. His was my first Sicilian friendship, and a happy one. He combined a gentle and guileless nature, generous with affection and avid for it, with a honey-pale and rather gangling charm and a lazy enjoyment of ithyphallic posturing. I can see, as vividly in my mind today as then in my eye, the golden down on his cheeks glinting in the sunlight. Dear Angelo – can you really have passed your fortieth birthday?

Then, over the years, as my comprehension of Sicily broadened and deepened, this passionate attachment to her seemed to become even physical – a sense of personal absorption, sensual and mystical, into the primeval texture of this most ancient of lands: into its mythos and the aching melancholy of its cruel and splendid horizons and their wryly beautiful people. One can fancy, on this island, that one's standing on the oldest spot on earth – a place older even than the gods that still haunt it; nowhere else can one feel so close to the beginning of things – partly because of the primordial aspect of these landscapes, partly because the dramas of history, legend and myth that compose this people's prodigious antiquity seem today more alive and contemporary against this ageless scenery than the benumbing solecisms of modern living.

This implacable landscape of brazen yellow-grey stone, of vast inimical mountain and black, razor-toothed, coastal rock, a landscape ineffably sublime yet vibrant with malice – product of titanic tellurian convulsions down the geological ages; these beautiful saturnine people with sweet rueful faces and eyes brimming, beneath the ready surface laughter, with that inherent Sicilian sadness that must come from an infinite heritage of tragedy.... Land and people seem to carry one back very close to the prime. Perhaps that helps to explain, in Freudian or some such terms, the almost somatic enchantment in which this island can hold one: perhaps this sense of proximity to genesis can assuage a nostalgia for the womb?

And finally, just ten years ago – in 1966 – this steady devotion, often agitated by phrenetic spasms of infatuation, reached its consummation in a decade of elysian contentment – adopted by a fifteen-year old (as Gigi was then), by his family, his village and his whole tiny world on a miniature island off the west coast of Sicily. With him and with all of these I fell and remained in love; and have ever since been loved by them in return – the younger children, when I'm away, write to me as *Carissimo Nonno*, "dearest grandfather".... I had found, right at the end of my life, absolute human goodness or the nearest thing to it, and the happiness that such a frank and simple goodness must confer. "Goodness" is thus defined in the *Concise Oxford Dictionary*: "virtue; positive or comparative excellence; benevolence, kindness, generosity; what is good in a thing, its essence or strength...."; if to that is added a selfless and unfailing affection, what other favour can a man ask?

This is my ninth year on the island, and my sixth in this miniscule stone house. It's my ninth, too, of membership of a perfect family and of devotion to Gigi, the elder son. He was fifteen when, having fallen in love at first sight with the island, I fell in love with him in his father's butcher's shop. Now he is a carbineer and engaged to be married: I know that his first son will be called Michele.

At lunch with the family one day after I'd been on the island a week, I felt suddenly so dazed with happiness that I blurted out: "Why are you so kind to me? Why are you all so good?" – and Tommaso answered: "You love our son, so we love you."

II.

This matter of boy-loving is no longer wholly unspeakable; even the hyper-orthodox have come to realise, against their volition of course, that it's an endemic phenomenon in human behaviour that can neither be abolished by judicial abhorrence nor swept under the social carpet. It's probable that television comics are able nowadays to make little jokes about curates and choirboys without exciting puritan protest. Quite naturally, ever since – and probably from long before – the arrival in Sodom of those handsome young angels tantalized the men of the place, great numbers of people have been puzzled by this phenomenon (more or less, according as native temperaments at different points of history and geography have been modified by varying degrees of socio-religious pressure). And when people of small imagination are confronted by a thing they don't understand, their puzzlement often turns to resentment or horror or aggressive execration.

I can hear of no Greek author, writing before Pauline prudery turned Christianity into a Watch Committee, who condemned paederasty or even was perplexed by it; the cult of boys was so closely woven into the social and educational tapestry that it was taken as a matter of course. But Cicero, a man of intellect, being a lawyer, if not very imaginative, was puzzled by it although he must have been familiar with its ubiquity in the Rome of his day where, debased from Hellenic idealism to the standards of the 'Dilly, it was a popular pastime. In a rather obscure reference to paederasty (Latinists will find it in *Disputationes Tusculanae* IV, xxxiii) Cicero doesn't seem to know what he wants to say about it. While he does imply some disapproval of the cult of nudity, he doesn't on moral grounds pass judgement either way on the love of boys but rather on grounds of convenience: "And though such loves be, as I see is possible, within the bounds of modesty, yet they bring anxiety and trouble and all the more because they are a law to themselves and have no other restraint." Some of us in XXth century England will agree with that. Cicero, in this passage, asks rhetorically, and irrelevantly a question that shows his ignorance of these matters: "Why is it that no one is in love with an ugly youngster or a beautiful old man?" The answer is, of course, that the plainest youngster may appear beautiful to somebody and that beauty and old age are irreconcilables.

It would be odd if ordinary people were not puzzled. Male and female created he them – what could be plainer than that or more logical? How can that right-minded majority of men whose wholesome lust is aroused by mammiferous rondures and pelvic curves be expected to understand a miniscule minority's erotic interest in the gangling tenuity of an adolescent male? It's unnatural!

But to that minority, hardly miniscule, it's perfectly natural; what seems unnatural to them, and distasteful, is the majority's fancy for the female. (I recall how, in the early 1920s, a little old poet named Charles Dalmon, a relic of the *Yellow Book* and the *Savoy*, used to exclaim indignantly, when he saw near his home in Ebury Street a red-coated guardsman with a girl on his arm, "the *pervert*!".) What's more, that majority may be unwilling to believe, to great numbers of boys all over the world it seems perfectly natural to be loved by a man, despite the cannonade of opprobrium or ridicule about poofs, queers and child-molesters to which they're exposed from the "media" and their butchier coevals.

There was a time, and quite a long time, when I was puzzled by my own temperament. I cannot, of course, explain what strange cerebral or neurological eccentricity, what quirk of heredity or infantile circumstance it was that has made me love boys and shrink from girls, makes me see exquisite beauty in male pubescence and the antithesis of eroticism in maturity, makes me prefer the bud to the full-blown flower; but I have, through many decades of living side by side with this temperament, discovered a social purpose in this widespread sexual heresy. I believe there may be a Darwinist reason for the obstinate persistence with which paederasty appears, and always has appeared, throughout human history and wherever mankind makes love: that it is a selective consequence of the evolutionary process seeking to rectify certain anomalies in the emotional growth of the young that the increasing complexities of modern life are increasingly creating. One aim of this book will be to bring evidence in support of this theory.[32]

III.

The decade of the '50s concluded the first instalment of my life: my book *The World, The Flesh and Myself* brought the story of it up to 1958. In that year my active, adventurous, politically wayward career finished, after the Korean war, the Suez "troubles", and those turbulent years on Cyprus – with a last foray to Aden and my second journey to Timbuctoo, this time with Robin Maugham. 1959 saw me back in Sicily; now was begun a fresh instalment: a dawdling, hedonistic, lazily wandering life – a visionary aspiration, with little or no money and no aptitude for earning any (but I've always been a talented scrounger); all I wanted, I told myself, was sunshine, wine, the Mediterranean blue, and the companionship of a boy. Now, with oncoming age (sixty-one in 1958), my erotic avidity, though hardly languishing, was becoming less impetuous; while I had always sought to signpost my path with a sequence of small loves rather than dot it with heartless pick-ups (though it would be dishonest not to confess to plenty of those too), I now found myself moving away

[32] Alas, Michael left no notes upon his ideas [footnote in pencil to the original manuscript by Colin Spencer].

from promiscuity and aiming at passionate attachments lasting as long as circumstances or the transient bloom of adolescence allowed. (Enduring affection has, I'm happy to say, often survived the sexual in these affairs - often indeed into the boy's adult and married life; but inevitably the sexual interest evaporates with the phenomenon of the beard and the symptomatic Adam's apple.)

But, before Sicily again in 1959, I must go back a couple of years to a chance meeting at a party that was to initiate one of the three most important adult friendships of my later life: a friendship still as happy today, praise heaven, as staunch and as amusing, as it has been through these last eighteen years. I remember almost nothing of that Chelsea meeting; and more than a year passed before I saw Colin Spencer again - chance again, or perhaps this time destiny, found us together early in 1959 in the saloon bar of the King's Arms in Sloane Square. I hadn't long returned from Timbuctoo and the Niger River where the bronchitis which has dogged me ever since first laid me low; I was ill and sorry for myself and staying dejectedly in a small hotel and yearning to leave England again; but that evening with Colin, drinking quantities of beer and delighting in his wit and imaginative agility, was as good as a course of antibiotics as well as being hugely enjoyable. Colin wasn't then much over twenty; his rather impish good looks and smile were the externalities of an innate charm which, scarcely less youthful, he's kept to this day - yet even then I saw signs, behind his young and irreverent gaiety, of, a mature and thoughtful melancholy. At that time he was known only, and to a narrow public, for several short stories of striking merit in the *London Magazine* and - though perhaps these were of slightly later date[33] - for a series of line drawings in the *Times Literary Supplement* of contemporary literary swells like Rebecca West and E.M. Forster: portraits of a brilliance that pointed ahead to those superbly authentic architectural cartoons (the Curwen Press has issued a volume) that some consider his finest work. I used to say, when I knew Colin and his work

[33] They were printed in that summer of 1959 [footnote in pencil to the original manuscript by Colin Spencer].

better, that he was a better painter than writer (which doesn't diminish my admiration for his best writing). Perhaps he is; and yet critics and public alike have steadily ignored his marvelously perspicacious portraits as well as his fastidious line-drawings and those fantasies of his dottier moods which largely decorate his Islington home.

As for his writing – I cannot understand why these remarkable autobiographical novels (I think the fourth in the series will appear soon) haven't been more loudly and widely acclaimed: so funny, so readable, so percipient of the comic and the tragic in ordinary people's dealings with each other – these books give one a vastly entertaining, and often very moving, pasticcio of human tenderness and human perversity within and around the family; they also graphically document a period and a *milieu* of English life in the middle decades of this century. In the theatre Colin's assured gift of ridicule guided by intelligence makes him both a hilarious and a biting satirist. Yet his plays don't run. I believe perhaps his weakness in art (in all three of his arts), as often in his life, comes from a craving to shock for shocking's sake, at all costs to *épater les bourgeois*.[34] The public, I suppose, enjoy the outrageous when it comes to them as mindless entertainment: but not when it hits them on the funny-bone.

I thought of him at one time as England's young Leonardo: with his virtuosity, his flair and his taste, he would (given a sufficiency of income) have felt more at home in classical Athens or Rome, in Renaissance Florence, or the London of Hogarth, Swift and Smollett, than in the England of pop, plastic and package; his versatility and the impudent sense of the comic that gives the real flavour to his writing and painting, and to his talk, have been among life's chief pleasures ever since that evening in Sloane Square. Elegant, debonair, Colin touches everything with the fastidious finger of the artist – cookery, horticulture, the furnishing of a room, or the tilt of a hat. And he's so *funny*: and

---

[34] We used to discuss this, for I would deny that I felt any such urge. But I believe there was in Michael a residue of the Edwardian gentleman that felt some of my satires were perhaps not perfectly 'playing the game.' [Footnote in pencil to the original manuscript by Colin Spencer]

like all genuine artists, he finds "copy" in his own private miseries and sees what's ludicrous in them.

I have gone on a bit about Colin Spencer because he's one of the three adults who have most influenced my life in the last thirty years, because I believe he's an important producer of art and literature – and also because, all through these years, he's been an unfailingly precious help to me, as writer and as person; his affection, like mine for him, has been fathomless, his criticism and counsel inexhaustible. And how we've laughed together! Another of these three friends – first, of course, in seniority – is Robin Maugham, for almost three decades a devoted friend and ally in all sorts of literary and exploratory ventures – from our first journey together in 1947 down to the northern marches of the Moroccan Sahara to our last journey in 1958, to the southern Sahara and the upper Niger River. The third friend I shall call "Q"; my reputation is so murky and "Q"'s so distinguished in the higher reaches of public service that I'm not going to embarrass him by proclaiming our acquaintanceship, much as I should like to sing paeans of gratitude for his unfailing kindness and good counsel, and for his friendship.

I told Colin, that evening at the King's Arms, that I was off to Sicily in April – if I found a passable habitation, it would be nice if he could join me there? Thus we parted, in a beery haze of friendship and intellectual excitement. And next morning I thought, What a hope, to see Colin in Sicily!

* * * *

As I recall that April of 1959, both sky and sea of Catania were of a steady lustrous blue and the air was as dry and warm as in July. By the rules, the last rains fall in April, which can be a month of any climatic vagary. From January through into April the Sicilian weather is likely to be a kind of battledore and shuttlecock from north-west and south-east of bitterly cold gales and black seas and skies – yet the mood can change overnight and the sun blaze out like a roll of drums. I've seen boys bathing in Palermo harbour on New Year's Day.

But Catania's winter climate is specially benign: tucked, on the island's east coast, under Etna's skirts she is sheltered from the north and west and is really only open to the vicious scirocco from the Libyan desert in the south-east, ice-sharp in the cold months, enervating to mind and muscle, exacerbating to the nerves, through the rest of the year. (It may seems odd that Norman Douglas, so scrupulous an observer, so meticulous as to detail, should have called his novel *South Wind*, when the wind was the scirocco; but, after all, no novel could survive, or rather be born, under the name of *South-East Wind*!) That April Catania basked; and on the *playa*, as her southern beach is called (an overlay of Spanish influence in Catania on top of the main Hellenic and Byzantine), the boys were basking too. I'd chosen Catania this time because, I knew I must avoid Palermo's heady temptations, man-made and god-made; I knew that, if I were to find that emotional and mental sangrail that I was seeking, I must savour every part of the Sicilian anatomy. Confident of finding it, I knew I had to look for it. So I started with the plain of Catania beneath Etna and the legendary Greek city of Siracusa; it wasn't long before I recognised that what I sought wasn't here. It was another six years before I did find what I wanted - and it was at the opposite extremity of the island.

I found a flat at Acitrezza, a romantical suburb built on lava (all the environs of Catania are founded on Etna's black spewings): a picturesque "resort" whose romance derives, apart from the awe-inspiring immensity of its hinterland, from a group of *faraglione* offshore: lofty peaked rocks that legend identifies as boulders hurled after Odysseus by the enraged Polyphemus - but also, by other authorities, as those thrown by the same Cyclops at the young shepherd Acis, his successful rival for the love of the nymph Galatea. (The Acis story lives on in place-names along this reach of Etna's coast: Acicastello, Acitrezza, Acireale.)

Catania is a glum city, for a southern one: shabby and slummy and dirty; it lies too close under the foothills of Etna for the mountain's splendour to be felt - it's as if a midget, crouching near the big toe of a gigantic Apollo, can see no higher than his knee. Like Messina, Catania is a "new town" raised on the rubble of the old and the dead; the vantage is that the earthquake here preceded Messina's by more than two centuries (1693), with the consequence that Catania has some superb buildings of the best period of Sicilian baroque enlivening the general dinginess of its commercial streets.

Like a nail to a magnet, I'm peremptorily drawn to the waterfront where there is one; and I had of course early found the harbour and the *playa* beyond. I got into the habit of taking a bus each morning, with a couple of boiled eggs and a banana, into Catania and then walking down through the meat and fish markets to the harbour and the *playa*. The "official" bathing season, with its *stabilimenti*, cabins and gaudy umbrellas doesn't begin till the summer solstice; but the boys start theirs unofficially when the sun's strong enough to warm sand and rock and they start it, as a rule, in the nude. So that April, when I arrived at the *playa*, still in out-of-season slumber, I would find over that broad expanse of sand a scene resembling an Athenian *palaestra* or *gymnasion* – a kaleidoscope of naked ephebi running, leaping, wrestling; and among the rocks that support the harbour wall, a colony of basking forms supine in luxurious postures of hedonistic susceptibility (just as the Morning Glory opens wide at daybreak to inhale the whole flavour of the sunlight). But here a meddlesome natural law, a part of the alchemy of adolescence, asserts itself: a chemical (or rather somatic) reaction as predictable as that to the formula H_2O is one engendered by the conjunction of hot sunshine, euphoric indolence and juvenile nudity – the result is a spontaneous eroticism as natural as the mixing of yellow and blue paints into green. Let a boy put his clothes on or rouse himself from his torpor, and the magic will be broken and the strange involuntary carnality languish; but given the coincidence of these three factors, the product is invariable. It's this law, operating round the Mediterranean littoral, that may any moment present the unsuspecting rambler over the more secluded reaches of these coasts with a surprising sight: a non-stop display of unabashed boyish sexuality. And nowhere can this display be more ostentatious than around the harbour of Catania.

I made no friends during my stay there, but I found myself daily becoming more fascinated by the spectacle offered almost round the clock by these shameless young satyrs; I found myself at night re-running in my mind the film I'd watched all day; I found myself hurrying in the morning to catch an early bus. In other words, I found myself on the brink of becoming obsessed; and obsession of any kind means atrophy of mind and spirit.

There are, I dare say womanizers - "mulierasts", to borrow Robert Ross's famous coinage - given over to the exclusive pursuit of fornication; but the boy-lover, perhaps because of the impermanence of his amours as well as of the social hindrances in the way of his having any amours at all, is specially prone to the malady of obsession - paederasty becomes paedomania and, as the alcoholic's mind is dominated by his need of liquor, so the paedomaniac is driven by his compulsive craving for pubescent novelty round an endless circle of prowling in the wake of his sexual curiosity - without love, without emotion, without joy, without satiety, and to the exclusion of every other interest. It's the paedomaniac that "gives buggery a bad name" (to quote a "source" who shall be nameless), using that word in its general saloon-bar sense. I saw the danger signal. You're here, I said to myself, to explore the Sicily you fell for eight years ago - not to be mesmerised by a row of frigging boys. I took the train to Syracuse - Siracusa, once the proudest city of all Magna Graecia; once, briefly, capital of the Byzantine Empire; twice, briefly, the residence of Plato. Three days were too few for the discovery of the three thousand years of history that Siracusa today is the living monument of: nearly a millennium of Greek glory and Greek barbarity; Christian ecstasy raised with delicate insolence upon the pagan columns of Pallas Athene - the extraordinary cathedral synthesis of Doric and Norman and Baroque; the Catalan charm of Ortygia that not even the dead hand of Spanish colonial rule through two centuries could coarsen. And then, seen through my own eyes, the latest Weeping Madonna; alas, no tears rolled down those plaster cheeks for my heretical benefit, but already her unauthorised cult was attracting swarms of devotees and countrywide publicity. Four years later, on my next visit, she had been given a temple and attendant priests of her own, although the Vatican hadn't yet given its *imprimatur* to the miracle (Sicilians don't wait for the Vatican). Then on to Palermo - and, after a day or two, to take ship for Sardinia - I felt, I think, the need of a great distance between myself and that creeping obsession.

I remember almost photographically that departure. For an hour before it was time for the *di Cagliari* to sail, in late afternoon, I watched with abhorrence the loading of twenty or more horses and mules; one by one they were hoisted, slung on girths under the belly, to the height of the ship's foredeck: dangling, kicking, squealing. With the fo'c'sle bulkhead their only shelter, closely picketed in a bunch, they continued to kick and bite and squeal through ten hours of sea-voyage. They were a poor lot; were they being shipped for slaughter? I don't know if the Sardi devour horseflesh as the Apulians do on the Adriatic: in Taranto, if you order beef you're likely to get horse (perhaps a vestige of the Tarantine devotion to his god Poseidon, to whom the horse was sacred – perhaps a wry tribute to that sturdy breed of cob which is the pride of the Murge hills of Apulia?). The lights of Ustica: the tiny island three hours north of Palermo where the international aqualung desperadoes annually compete for the honour of slaughtering the most fish. (Driving in Sicily some years later with Robin Maugham, we passed one of those hideous road-side advertisements which, with the cars on them, disfigure Italy's roads: it proclaimed the delights of fish-spearing in the waters of Ustica. "Ustica", Robin drily remarked, "an' I'll stick 'im.")

In a golden daybreak the *di Cagliari* steamed into that city's harbour, an impressive waterfront skirting the town which, climbing the hill behind, rambled decoratively over it. "Where there is judgement there is injustice", Tolstoi wrote; and nowhere is this more true than in those generalized judgements we so glibly pass on peoples and places of which we are wholly ignorant. My fleeting impressions of Cagliari were quite superficial and probably refutable: the people of course, like all Italians, were kind and friendly; yet, after a week or so, I felt somehow that the people here, not being natives of the "Two Sicilies" were "foreigners"; they hadn't the warm, ebullient, unpredictable dottiness of the Sicilians or Calabrians. They seemed to me both in feature and mind to have inherited the long nosed severity of the Arabs and Spanish and to lack the glowing spark of poetry that comes in the blood of the Greeks and the Phrygian East. No: for all its wild loveliness, I at once saw that what I was looking for (what was I looking for?), was not to be found on Sardinia, so antithetic to Sicily, whose siren voice kept up a soundless cannonade of subliminal tantalization.

I took the mail boat across the Tyrrhenian to Naples where I'd lived for a large part of 1957. But I didn't stop there; I went straight to the station and took the first train down into Calabria. The six hour run landed me in Reggio at midnight and a cabman took me to just the kind of modest hotel I wanted.

Reggio di Calabria, like Messina across the Strait, was totally destroyed by the earthquake of 1908 (I remember gloating, aged eleven, over the lurid descriptions in the old *Morning Post,* and thinking: Oh well, it can't happen to *us*); I can't remember seeing any building of the old Reggio that was still standing. (On the island of Lipari, a few years later, I was to meet a man not much older than myself who had been a schoolboy in Messina when the earthquake struck. He had survived (not many did), alone of his family, and managed to get a passage across to Lipari, where he came to own a pumice-grinding plant: the product is exported to Sicily and the "continent" for mixing into mortar. He used to tell me about those terrible days while we sat on the feathery shingle of his beach.)[35]

Calabria is a cruel country of high, rugged mountain where men, year in year out, are pitted against the rigours of their own birthplace. Congregated, through the centuries, for security from brigands, in townships dizzily perched on mountaintops, the Calabrians endure winters of an appalling alpine severity. Somehow they survive by sealing themselves into the fug of their archaic homes; and in the pitiless southern summer they contend with the relentless dessication of land and stock. From birth to death their lives are a battle against climate and geology. Calabrians, therefore, are a harsh and rugged people: at once ruthless and sly, brave and capricious, often brutish yet passionately devoted to family and friends. They are obedient Catholics, in the superstitious southern way, but scarcely Christians and certainly not Pauline Christians; that proto-puritan's bigotry about the abominations of carnal pleasure would have

[35] Norman Douglas visited Reggio and Messina both just before and just after the earthquake. See *Old Calabria,* paperback edition, Peregrine Books, 1962, pp. 248 ff. [Author's footnote]

earned their contempt, though not their comprehension. Enjoyment of their sexuality is obviously the only apology fate can offer them for the hardships of their earthly existence: who is this Paul, they would indignantly ask, to tell them it's a "sin"? Their promiscuities are restricted by the taboos of their inherited system, not by conscience. How bored the Calabrians would be if St. Paul appeared and started preaching at them; they wouldn't be able to read any epistle he might write to them. We know from *Acts* XX, 9 how desperately he could bore his contemporary congregations: "... there sat in the window a certain young man named Eutychus ... and as Paul was long preaching, he sunk down with sleep, and fell down from the third loft, and was taken up dead." At least St. Paul was shamed into restoring the young to life.

Compared with the Calabrian highlanders, the population of Reggio were, of course, an effete lot of city dwellers. But one thing they had in common: a Greek heredity, however tenuous, and with it an amused, almost jocose sensuality and a seemingly guileless charm.

So here I was standing where George Gissing was standing at the end of *By The Ionian Sea,* published near the beginning of this century: looking across the Strait to Messina and its sickle-shaped harbour rampart, with, high behind the town, the black range of the Peloritani hills; following with the eye the high cliff coast of Sicily southwards to Taormina and round to Catania; and finally, though of course one's imagination is held by it from the start, the vertex of Etna, now, in late May, still gleaming with its cap of snow, rising like an astonishing waterspout from the foaming dark waves of Sicily's mountains: a splendour that's unfailingly fresh and astounding and exquisite every time one sees it anew. *Sicilia, Sicilia,* our Gigi used to sing when he came home from school when he was in the primary, a song of praise for their island, which the kids were taught. *Sicilia!* I too felt in my heart, as I looked across at that fabled coastline (how is it, I've often wondered, that none of the old gods, Olympian or lesser, ever set foot on or dipped wings over Calabria or Apulia, though both were colonised by Hellenes from almost Homeric times, while Sicily absolutely teemed with them?).

A day or two later I took the ferry over to Messina. About 100,000 people were killed in and around Messina (not counting Reggio) that December of 1908; a mere five hundred or so died almost exactly sixty years later in the earthquake of January 1968, which destroyed a dozen or more villages in western Sicily, cracked some buildings on our island and scared the wits out us for a week or more. But there was an illuminating analogue to be seen in the aftermath of both catastrophes. In *Old Calabria* (first published 1915), Norman Douglas wrote of his visit to Messina just after the earthquake:

> ... I was thinking, too, of those still stranger dwellings, the disused railway trucks which the government has placed at the disposal of homeless families. At many stations along the line may be seen strings of these picturesque wigwams crowded with poor folk who have installed themselves within, apparently forever. They are cultivating their favourite flowers and herbs ... along the wooden platforms of the carriages; the little children ... play about in the shade underneath. The people will suffer ... There will be diseases .... If, as seems likely, these rudely improvised sheds are to be inhabited indefinitely....

Indefinitely? Some weeks after the 1968 earthquake, I went by train from Trapani to Palermo and passed, towards Alcamo junction, rows of such railway trucks, shunted into sidings, in which hordes of the homeless had made their "homes". Here were the rows of flowers and herbs, here the children playing beneath the trucks. What's wrong with that, you may ask? The government was right to place railway trucks "at the disposal of the homeless". Of course: but *two years later* the trucks were still in those sidings and the homeless were still living in them. Bureaucracies!

Even Bognor Regis would be beautiful if it were set on the edge of those classic Straits, at the foot of the Sicilian mountains and in face of the Calabrian mountains, a setting that surely can enter against Sydney harbour, the bay of Naples and Hong Kong for the scenically spectacular contest? But Messina, though hardly a stone in the whole city survives from before its holocaust, has urban attractions quite independent of its superb situation; it's a pleasant town to live in and walk the length and breadth of, and I became very fond of it.

I quickly found a small furnished house in a "housing estate": drab and old-fashioned, it looked as if it had been raised, as it probably had been, to house the homeless. Rent was L20 a month; a Messinese would doubtless have been asked half that (Sicilians are an honest people, but in the matter of rent foreigners are fair game). An ugly, cramped house, yet opening in the rear to a *terrazzo* almost bestrode by the splendid arch of the railway viaduct some hundred feet high, from whose massive lower piers cascades of Morning Glory fell in huge gossamers of glowing blue. This soaring span of masonry, and, too, some delicate wrought iron stairways decorating the houses opposite, atoned for the dinginess of the place. I was perfectly happy with my new dwelling, my first Sicilian *home;* and I wrote to Colin that he had somewhere to stay.

I have always loved sea ports ever since, as a boy, I used to bicycle into Southampton to spend the day mooching round the docks and looking at the ships and the men working them. (I think I've always wanted to live by the sea more for the traffic of the sea than for the sea itself: after all, navigation is a human venture, and it's mankind we're interested in.) Messina harbour is a fascinating one, exciting and versatile: emigrant ships to Australia, the liners to the Orient, local craft from the islands and the "continent", those puissant harbour tugs, immensely proficient in the skills of probing and pushing and coaxing huge dead weights just where they're wanted and bearing such deliciously virile names as *Vigoroso*, now and then one of the swordfish fleet from up the Straits at Scylla: strange craft with masthead lookouts (often a wheel rigged to the helm below) and in place of bowsprit, a long protruding gangplank at the pulpit of which the harpooner waits (the craft, and the principles of fishing, recall the old whaling before the days of steam, but of course the swordfish boats are power driven). And the busy to and fro of half a dozen train ferries that assure our railway traffic with Italy and Europe (except during strikes). The nauseous proliferation of the car ferry that now pollutes every port in Sicily ensures that pestilential traffic is already choking the roadways of the island; God be thanked that political and capitalistic rivalries have so far scotched the perennially revived design for a bridge across the Straits....

The harbour curves round on its southern side in a charming hemicircle, culminating in the sickle-shaped spur which gave the haven its antique name of Zancle. At the end of this spur, facing the city, is the statue of Our Lady of the Letter *(Madonna della Lettera)* forever renewing her pledge to watch over the city and its people. The pledge was originally given in a letter to the City Elders written in the Blessed Virgin's own hand. Unfortunately this precious letter somehow became lost; and there are those who attribute to this piece of municipal negligence Our Lady's failure to avert the disaster of 1908.

It was under the eye of Our Lady of the Letter that I made the acquaintance of Carmelo. At a point of the *Passaggiata* straight across the harbour from the Madonna, I happened to look over the sea wall just as Carmelo was wringing out his swimming trunks on the rock ledge below. From above, I had a foreshortened view of his long, lean, white body glistening from the sea; he looked up at me, staring for a moment, unabashed, of course, by his nakedness, and what I saw was an upturned face, the face, perhaps, of a lost child at once perplexed, hurt, resentful and wary: unbeautiful in any conventional way yet, as I saw it, enthralling. He dressed lazily, the trunks, still wet but no longer dripping, under dark shorts, and a dirty white vest; then climbed up the iron ladder to the promenade. There was a hint of challenge in his stance as he leaned, scowling, against the wall, his long glabrous legs white beneath the short knickers: *Che vuoi?* he asked, "What d'you want?", using the familiar "tutoyer" form. In age, he was a lanky sixteen. That day we remained acquaintances, and rather stand-offish ones, though he consented to come to a bar for some food. It was a day or two before he lowered his defences and allowed warmth into our acquaintanceship: then, suddenly we were friends. And four years later we were again friends, until at the age of twenty the *militare* claimed him and he disappeared into the navy. And he turned out to be all the things I'd seen in his upturned face that day: puzzled, rejected, suspicious, a lost child; yet when given the things he was lacking – affection, care, acceptance as a compeer – he blossomed into something like happiness, although the gentle expression of his face

Editor: Here the manuscript suddenly breaks off, probably due to the author's final illness.

Synopsis of the rest

What follows is half of a finished document which Davidson called "Synopsis", written in 1975. It would seem to have been a prospectus of what he intended to write about in the sequel to The World *commissioned in February that year. It thus reveals all that is known about the parts of the sequel he never wrote.*

Omitted here are what he described in greater detail in the foregoing finished part of the sequel (his earliest experiences of Sicily and his impressions of Colin Spencer in 1959) and his summary of "some special subjects" in his portrait of Favignana, which he thought distinguished it "from anywhere else", but which can be read in Sicilian Vespers.

Two parallel themes run through the book: parallel, that is, in that they are the twin rails which carry the story from beginning to end; but also, are constantly meeting and crossing and merging into one. First, the love affair with Sicily, and quite a few Sicilians, which began a quarter of a century ago and reached its culmination in this last decade of astonishing happiness on a tiny island off Trapani and Marsala; and, secondly, the formulation of a philosophy, so to speak, of pederasty, the discovery that modern society must sooner or later understand that the boy-loving instinct and practice can be more valuably used in one social context than a battalion of psychiatrists, welfare workers and the rest. If a hefty lesbian makes an ideal hockey mistress, then surely the pederast must have an intrinsic aptitude for the comprehension of boys and their minds; often he is uniquely qualified by his own nature to diagnose and meet the emotional requirements of an adolescent boy in want of sexual understanding and sympathy, not to mention just simple affection. And all over the world there are millions of boys thus deprived. [...]

The treatment in this book of the latter theme, the anatomy of pederasty, is necessarily introspective, egotist, subjective; that of the Sicilian, on the other hand, is mainly objective and graphic: the fruit of long observation of land and people, of habits and credences, taboos, behaviour and tenets. Although this observation was made over the years through the Two Sicilies (Apulia, Calabria and the island itself), the bulk of the findings come from "my" island of Favignana, in the Egadi group off the West coast, a mountain in the sea five miles long with some four thousand inhabitants. These sections of the book might be called "Portrait of an Island", for that is exactly what they make, and especially a portrait of "my family", the family of Luigi, a boy who from 15 to his 25th year, at the present day, has remained my dearest love and friend. For these nine years, they have loved me and regarded me as one of themselves. "You love our son," said Luigi's father one lunchtime, "so we love you," and in all my life I've never known another love and loyalty so true. I was then sixty-eight. The 1966 paperback of *The World* and Bashlow's commissioning of *Some Boys*[36] in 1967 allowed me to spin out my first stay to nearly three years; 1974 was the first year in ten that I didn't see my island. […]

The portrait may reveal a saddening deterioration in the quality of the island's life, a coarsening of its innocence and a corruption of its guilelessness. […] This defilement of my island is mainly the work of the accursed car-ferry, put into service about five years ago and setting us at the end of a main motor-way from Turin, Milan, Genoa, Rome – the great northern sources of Italy's most strident tripperism (not to mention the foreign caravanners and car-tourists, and the local excursionists from Trapani and Palermo.). *Traghetto* (car-ferry), Tourism and TV are the three Ts of this spiritual pollution. Our old way of life is being vulgarised; even our local idiom is changing. Old, customs are vanishing – *carnevale* in 1973 was a shadow of what it was in 1966. Blocks of

[36] Robert Bashlow was the founder of the Oliver Layton Press in New York, as which he wrote to Davidson in August 1966 asking him to write an explicit book about boy-love, and sent him an advance of $1000 early in 1967. *Some Boys,* was the eventual result.

"holiday" flats are springing sky-high, overpowering our old 18th-century streets; huge "touristic villages" are rising round our coasts, and we have become something in the travel agents' brochures. We are, of course, merely taking our place in the general contamination of the Mediterranean littoral, which is vulgarizing its people as swiftly as it is poisoning its waters. [...]

There will be, on the pederastic side, an interlude in Tangier: the story of an Arab waif which perfectly illustrates and sustains my submission that the lover of boys has a specific social function which only he can perform. This sweet and pathetic fifteen-year-old was "normal" really sexually (he went to the whores when his pocket money ran to it); yet he desperately needed not only the security, material and emotional, which a pederast lover could give him, but also the affection, tenderness and understanding that couldn't be gained from ten minutes with a harlot. And, as important as anything, the homosexual lover was able to give also the *motherliness,* as well as the paternalism, which this Arab ached for. And it isn't only waifs in Africa that need this kind of "care"; all over the world, in all walks of life, there are to be found unnumbered youngsters whose adolescent unhappiness and emotional vacuum could be at least alleviated by just such a companion. Between a boy's pubescence and, let us say, his first girl-friend, he goes through a bi-sexual period and a sort of emotional limbo during which his blossoming sexuality is bringing up with it a variety of new and scarcely comprehended sensations and curiosities, aesthetic or intellectual; it's during this phase that, unconsciously perhaps, he longs to *share* these tumultuous emotions as he needs to share his new-found sexual self-service – and it's just in these blushing years that he's expected to hide this lovely eroticism under a blanket of furtiveness. Of course, a great many adolescents share their bursting sexuality with their best friends at school or down the street; but how many millions are there across the world who need a deeper, wider understanding of the turmoils of flesh and mind within them, and who need to blend their sexual discoveries with somebody else's experience – someone who will give them *love,* so often dangerously lacking, combined with sensible advice. This is where the pederast should come in; one may foresee the day when the enlightened Authority will be advertising in the *New Statesman* for properly qualified pederastic recruits to its Welfare Services.

That interlude occurred in 1974. There had been an earlier trip to North Africa in 1963, from the island of Lipari, north of Messina, where I was then living: Peter Benenson, founder and then director of AMNESTY International, asked me to go to Morocco (where I knew a number of political figures such as the late Sultan and Ahmed Balafrej, foreign minister at the time of this visit) to report on the imprisonment of a dozen or more Moroccans who had turned "Baha'i" - had renounced Islam and adopted a curious new religion which had originated in Persia and been taken up in a big way by Americans. My job was to see these people in prison and argue with the Moroccan Government about the "Human Rights" aspect of their incarceration for a matter of "conscience". Later that year I went to Geneva to attend a sitting of the UN Human Rights Commission.

From Morocco I went on to Algiers, to see Ben Bella, then President of newly independent Algeria, and ask for his backing for an international Amnesty conference on "prisoners of conscience" to be held in Algiers - an idea he welcomed as giving kudos to the youngest of the new independent countries. But before the conference could be called, Ben Bella was the prisoner of his rival for power and had vanished from the political scene (a pity; a man of humanity as well as charm and intelligence - and humanity is a rarity in African politics). I returned to Lipari by way of Tunis and Palermo; this was my final excursion into the political world.

[...] That summer [of 1959, Colin Spencer] came to stay with me in Sicily - a visit echoed in one episode of his first novel, *An Absurd Affair.* [...] This book will [also] describe (with Colin's permission) how a flippant and rather tipsy remark of my own, at a party, ridiculously found a prominent place in the divorce proceedings which - fortunately in my view - came within a few years of his maleficent marriage; and to this day is used by his former wife to barb his relations with his son.[37]

An important time for me was the six months of 1961 I spent at Piggots, Eric Gill's Catholic "community" in Buckinghamshire. Gill by then was dead, but his daughters and old Mary Gill were there and a number of delightful arty-crafty people. I'd been introduced to René Hague and his wife Joanna Gill by that distinguished yachtsman and ex-pupil of Gill's, Michael Richey. The Hagues gave me a cottage on the lovely Piggots estate; and here I wrote the first half of *The World, The Flesh & Myself* (the second half was done that winter at Taranto, in Apulia). And at Pigotts, I (a heretic) learned to revere, and indeed love, the extraordinary sense of absolute goodness – a kindness and tolerance which must be the core of what Christianity is meant to be – that English Catholics of a certain type give one. And yet this feeling of saintliness is slightly comically linked with an air of conscious superiority – as if Catholics in England, especially those imbued with the traditions of the Penal Times, were of an aristocratic texture and a cut above those rather common protestants. I loved, and still love, the Hagues and all of Piggots – now, alas, dispersed and dismantled and, for all I know, given over to the property developers.

The foregoing indicates, I hope, most of the chief headings of the book, as I see it so far (writing a book, to my mind, is rather like taking out a single-handed sailing boat: your port and general course are plotted but an awful lot depends on wind and current). There will be, of course, sketches of many people I've loved, liked or mildly disliked (I don't think I've ever really *hated* an individual – I only hate categories, such as property developers); and anecdotes about such dear, doomed and inimitable friends as John Davenport and Gerald Hamilton – as well as homage to such a splendid friend and man as James Cameron.

[37] At a party in about 1969, Spencer's nine-year-old son appeared, and Davidson made a good-humoured and amusing quip about him being too young for him, which caused laughter at the time, but was brought up by the boy's mother in her divorce proceedings against her husband as evidence that he had brought him into bad company.

But the only piece of personal comedy I can think of is my appearance in a television play as a Nun, clad in white habit and winged headdress, telling my beads and reciting my Marys, in a television play for Harlech. I never knew what the play was about.

THE END

IV. CORRESPONDENCE

On 7th December 1975, a fortnight after Davidson's obituary appeared in The Observer, *his great friend Colin Spencer announced in it that, "as Michael Davidson's literary executor I should like to compile and edit a Volume of his Collected Letters." He went on to request that any such correspondence be posted to him, noting that "of particular interest would be any letters which still exist from the years between 1935 and 1955."*

This section is the present editor's attempt to fulfil that promise nearly half a century later, done from the surviving archive which Colin has entrusted to him. It includes most of those down to 1930 (all in fact to one couple in the years 1926-30), as these are particularly witty and evocative of a lost age. Colin's special plea for letters from Davidson's middle years sadly elicited only one, produced here as the lone representative of the years 1931-57. The surviving correspondence from his last seventeen years, 1958-75, is massive, but much of it is to do with mundane practicalities, so only a small selection of the most interesting is being presented.

1. Letters to Boris and Phyllis de Chroustchoff, 1926-30

Boris de Chroustchoff (1892-1969) was a Russian who was sent to England for his schooling, attending Harrow and Oxford, and then remained there. By the time Davidson met him, following his own move to London in 1924, he was an antiquarian bookseller in Bloomsbury and married to Phyllis née Vipond Crocker (1900-38). They were at the centre of a vibrant social circle that included Christopher Millard and other writers and met at a pub called The Plough. Davidson describes them all at length in the ninth chapter of The World, The Flesh and Myself, *to which the reader is referred for information about many of the people alluded to in these letters. Phyllis killed herself, but her husband re-emerged as one of Davidson's greatest friends in the 1960s.*

i

GRAND CAFÉ ORIENTAL
13, Cours Mirabeau, 13
ELIE DALADIER, PROPRIÉTAIRE
Aix-en-Provence

The Eve of the Nativity [24 December 1926]

My dear Phyll & Boris: At this moment, I suppose, you are drinking pernots in Rouen; I am drinking them here. Being weak by nature, I stopped here today instead of going on to Fuveau as I meant to; result: I'm getting blind and wasting time; for, alone, the place is as dull as Drinkwater, in the evening. I may perhaps go to the Casino later where there is a Variety show, and a dance starting at midnight; but there will be nothing to suit me!

I am enjoying my walk enormously; the country is quite marvellous: you are right. And things really are frightfully cheap. If it were not for these bloody extras (wine on the road, wine before dinner, wine after dinner, and so on) I do not spend more than 15 frs a day - often less. I did 20 miles the first day,

20 the second; only 10 today – heels a bit sore, Christmas Eve, and a pleasantish looking town. I wish now I had gone on today; only spending money I could better dispose of in Toulon. Really one is imbecile: I am not enjoying myself in this place, and yet – one sits and drinks gloomily, and longs for one's friends; and tomorrow one will not feel as well as one expected, and will regret money one no longer has. Raving mad.

There is a café here (I forget the name at the moment) kept by a v. handsome couple (man & wife) behind the bar; with the children playing the parts of garçons: three *marvellous* girls about 16, 13 & 11; and boy of 10. A pity the boy is 10. But *marvellous*! And dressed wonderfully – skirts just below their behinds, and jumpers of flaming colours.

I think I will now go to the Casino. I don't know why [the bottom of the page is torn off here]

Cuges-les-pins Dec 26th

I'm simply speechless at the loveliness of everything. You have not lived until you have walked from Aix to Roquevaire, and thence to Cuges. This is the coloured country now: villages in blue and orange, and evergreen covered mountains. Although I have come the most direct way, I doubt if it were possible to find better walks anywhere. In some ways these stony ranges remind me of Zululand; their tremendous sweeps, and their wildness, and the outcropping of stone are similar, but of course the vegetation is different. I don't know if you have been this actual way; if not you *must* do this walk next year when you come. You *must* do the walk from Aix to here through Roquevaire. You enter Roquevaire through an enormous ravine, and come suddenly on the *place* which is too lovely for words; fronted by a vast pile of rock falling sheerly to the river; then the square planted with pleasant pollarded trees, and then the circle of crooked yellow houses. Marvellous. The hotel is good, but more expensive than most I have stayed at – 20 frs room and repas. Here, the best room I have had so far, 5 frs only!

I spent last night (Christmas) at Roquevaire, and got *blind*.

Toulon 29th Dec:

Really this is an amazing town! My room costs me 6 frs, and I eat for 5 – by far the cheapest place I have stayed so far. Only, of course, these everlasting cursed cafés and a drink every time you sit down. What to do in the evenings without spending money is the problem. Last night – well! The weather is *marvellous.* I'm sitting now, outside on the quai in blazing sun, and as warm as summer. You've probably sat on the same chair, which is a pleasant thought.

Well, last night: One walked from Cuges (where I stayed two nights) about 24 miles, and arrived here at 5 p.m. Found a room at 6 frs at once, ate for five, and proceeded to get blind for about fifty – economy! Then one got into a bar on the quai – the Cecil – which is entirely given up to homosexual sailors who dance lasciviously together, and do monstrous things in the rooms upstairs. One very queenly young sailor had rings on every finger and jingled bracelets. Eventually one only just managed to escape the advances of two colossal great beefy sailors. It is a pity they are all so big and, for me, elderly. I have discovered nothing young as yet: one can only hope.

I can't say I eat well for five frs: but I eat. The best cooking possible [bottom of page torn off and missing]

ii

Jan: 21 [1927]

My dear Phyll: I cannot rest till I have told you of a most *marvellous* place I found yesterday. I went first to le BROUSSAN – *not* the fosty place we found, & I *was* wrong about the name – you go the way we went till you get to the bridge place where was that rock shelter (where we waved to the hilarious young men) turn to the right a little way & then to the left up a rocky track. le Broussan is a tiny, v. primitive, hamlet: about 5 aged houses grouped round the Café des Lilas, and a crumbling church the size of a Maples pantechnicon pushed well to one side. The café is kept by a dirty old dame like a sack; her legs come squarely out from her skirt as if there were two feet between them all the way up. Hoping to find a cheap room I asked if there were any. "Not here" answered the cunning cynical old bitch, "but lots at EVENOS." So I went to Evenos, about 4 kilos on, and found the *most* incredible place – but not a room! I do wish we'd found it together. Perched frightfully high up; on the edge of a sheer precipice, and overlooking a tremendous view of the sea, right over to Bandol. Behind, mountains; and within ½ a mile, a fort full of black soldiers. But the village is the incredible thing. Shaped rather like Revest, with a tower on top; but *completely in ruins*. Like a dead thing; all crumbling and decayed. The only living thing I met with was a mad dog who grinned and sniffed and slobbered, and then, to my relief, ran away like a frightened Saracen. I wandered about the place feeling like a spectre in a tomb-ful of bones. Marvellous.

Eventually, outside the dead village, I found a café, kept by a lovely old woman with an apparently half-witted brother. She talked about the poetry of Nature, the beauty of mountains, the glory of the sun and air, and all that sort of stuff. She had lived on the same spot all her life. (She was about 60.) I sat talking to her for about 2 hours, drinking her v. excellent wine (at 4 frs a litre!) of which she was v. proud. She made it herself. I asked why the village was in ruins. She lifted her shoulders and depressed her mouth: "Oh," she said, "they've just let it fall." And that's as near as I could get to the mystery. Then I approached her on the subject of rooms. Oh no, impossible! Not a room within miles! C' n'est pas la peine! Could I, I suggested, live in one of the less ruined ruins; they were empty and dead; and eat with her? Oh, Mon Dieu! they'd think I was mad, and lock me up! I said I was mad, and liked living in ruins. Eventually, after more discussion of this insanity, she said she would make enquiries about ruins, if I would come back. So I shall go up there again – on Sunday probably; and perhaps I shall live in a marvellous ruin, high among the heavens. Tho' how I shall do it I don't know; I can't afford to buy blankets, and they're necessary these nights!

I'm leaving here. Pierre is so fosty (altho' he *did* stand me a petit verre when I paid his prodigious bill. He's frightfully expensive: about 18 frs a day for my one fosty little meal and modest ration of wine. I don't know where I shall go; but I shall go to our old dame at Dardennes this morning, & see if she'll work out cheaper. In addition to the enormous hole made in this coming month's money by Pierre, I *lost* nearly a hundred francs yesterday; just lost it, how or where I don't know. A bunch of filthy 5 fr notes given me in change. So I'm feeling v. fosty and depressed, and the future frowns.

<u>Evening</u>

I have just eaten a thrush, a robin red-breast, croûtons and dandelion salad. Marvellously good. This was Pierre's way of celebrating my good-riddance; and no doubt I shall have a thumping bill tomorrow! Pierre has a habit of producing delicacies as if ordinary: and then charging like hell. The poets, no doubt, would squiver at the idea of eating a robin: but thank god I am sufficiently far removed from a poet to appreciate & relish its flavour: twice as subtle as a thrush's; tho' only one mouthful.

I have arranged with Madame Dugecis (I think, tho' that may be all wrong! the name I mean) to go to Dardennes tomorrow. Room 4 frs: much cheaper than here. It's much too civilised for me; but economy must be my chief motive nowadays; and in any case it's pleasant to have human, kindly people about one. I'm there for a week at least; and after that I may be in my ruins: I don't know. Meanwhile my address will be: Chez Mdme: Décugis, (DÉCUGIS), Restaurant

Quartier des Dardennes
Le Revest-les-Eaux
Près Toulon (Var)
France

At least I think that's it. That *is* it.

This morning, talking to the old lady at Dardennes, we got on to the subject of Christinel's. She said, what did you eat in the evening? I answered, Monsieur generally ate rouget, or bouillabaisse, or something like that. Her scorn was withering.

What! Fish in the evening? Jamais! Fish only à midi! Never in the evening! and so on.

Yesterday, she told me, a party of Russians came to eat; and ate .... I don't know what; she spoke too fast & too excitedly! But apparently it was one of those occasions that will go down to posterity, like the red-faced people who ate 65 birds that we were told about.

I went to Toulon this afternoon; and I visited all the places: Coq Hardi, La Rade, and so on: sentimentalist at heart am I! I went primarily to have a bath & to get a balm, a salve, for a certain parasite that I have acquired: a gift, I suppose, from my Italian, blast him. An expensive lad, that. I do loathe those sorts of things. And just now, especially; with all these difficulties.

I came back by the 'bus; and at the 'bus met *our* policeman who, crowned in a shining best cap, gilded and grand, told me that he had come to Toulon with papers: *very* important, *very* secret; quite staggering under his responsibility, and various *avis*. I said, No, really? Come & have a drink; which he did with eagerness. On the way up I told him I was going to stay at Dardennes. "Ah," he said, "you're going to Mdme –, where you all had lunch the other day!" I asked how he knew we had lunched there. "Ah," he answered, "I know *everything*!" and wagged an omnipotent forefinger at me! Dear, charming policeman!

Alors, à demain!

By the way, coming back in the bus were three most wonderful young girls, who got out on the way. They were about 15, had short frocks, short socks, and bare knees. But why are the young French knees, girls & boys, so thin & skimpy, – like hotel banisters? Not the good, thick, oak-table leg knees of English boys.

There is a wind blowing now – a full-grown gale – that has probably made my ruins into a heap of rotting stones – not that stones can rot, but they look like it.

À demain –

<u>Saturday</u> <u>Dardennes</u>

I think that even my ruins won't drag me away from here. Madame is evidently going to make me frightfully comfortable. I told her, rather tremulously, that I was very poor, and did not eat much. Would she mind? Not a bit, she said, eat what you like.

I hope the chit-chat of Dardennes Valley doesn't bore you too much.

Write if you have a moment: anyhow a post-card to say if your head is alright. I'm worried about it.

Love to you both, and Salut! to the Ploughshares.

Michael

[*front of envelope*]
[missing line]
20 Bury Street
Bloomsbury
London, W.C.1
England

[*back of envelope*]
On top of the hangover two brandies and a beer have made me completely roaring ga – [*illegible*]. Bitte schön

iii

chez Mdm Décugis
Quartier des Dardennes
le Revest-les-Eaux
près Toulon (Var)

Monday 31.1 [1927]

My dear Boris: *Delighted* to hear this morning, and such fun to get a letter by air – the facteur was so impressed, too! Yes, your song has made me quite sentimental again about my Italian! but I am glad to say that le bataille has been fought; and won by me.

I'm feeling *v.* shaky this morning; I got *blind* y'day at my ruined village Evenos – for the first time since the night with

Irving[38]! It was a marvellous day & I went up in the morning; had half a bottle and casse'd a croûte at le Broussan, and then with my old lady at Evenos drank six demi-litres straight off in a row. She left all the bottles as they were finished on the table till I was surrounded by a sort of palisade of bottles. Some sailors from Toulon arrived and got blind and recited and sang. Another demi-litre at le Broussan, an anis at another pub on the way back, and a litre here. It was pitch dark before I got back and I got lost and fell about mountain paths but *this* time I have nothing worse than a cut across the bridge of nose and sundry bruises and tendernesses. Really it is most dangerous to get blind about here.

Listen, I've got a *marvellous* idea. I'm going to *buy* a ruin at Evenos. It appears that one can get one for about 100 frs: or 200. So I'm going to interview the Maire who lives somewhere at the bottom of the mountain; and I shall then be the owner for ever of a *house*! With a little patching it could be made quite habitable and one could live incredibly cheaply. And what is more, *there* would be a *permanent* headquarters for all of us. It would be yours and Phyll's and mine; and could be used by other specially selected people. Don't you think it's a wonderful scheme? A gorgeous place, with a v. pleasant pub kept by the poetical old lady; and about 5 or 6 miles from Toulon. Unfortunately I haven't got a hundred francs at the moment, so I shall have to wait; but I shall certainly do it the moment I have. I'm so excited about it. If ever one made a little money one could do some renovating. One might even hire a builder's lad who of course would sleep on the premises. Any amount of wood to be had for the gathering; a casserole, and a few vegetables; – and there is Arcady!

Phyll will remember Mdme Décugis telling us of two English girls round here. They turned up for coffee on Sat.. Very chic, one tall and good-looking with Eton crop and no hat; the other ugly and older, but v. well dressed. I suspect lesbianism. I was just going to talk to them when two monstrous nouveaux riches, man and wife, (English) whom I had the misfortune to meet once before, arrived, and I had to talk to them, which made me wild.

---

[38] Presumably Joseph Irving Davis (1889-1967), the partner of Boris de Chroustchoff as a bookseller in Museum Street, Bloomsbury, and the step-father of his wife Phyllis.

The man foully vulgar, like the least pleasant of the Plough brokers. The sort of man who refers to the French as "these Froggies," and who goes for excursions. Horrid. But next time I will investigate the two girls.

Madame Décugis is completely charming: will do anything for me, and cooks marvellously. I find it a little difficult to live properly up to her cooking; as I have to discuss everything minutely, which I am not competent to do. She is looking forward eagerly to the expected visit of you and Phyll some time in the future, and is going to do indescribable culinary things for you. I have made you a Count, so don't forget your rank & title. Also a man of vast erudition and culture; and an epicure of international repute. But she becomes sometimes a little boring. Every day I must listen to the same recital of her maladies and of her past glories - avant la guerre [before the war].

But it is the son whom I would like to murder. He is cretinous. He sits vacantly about all day. And when I am working he puts his filthy bottom on the chair next to mine, and spits and picks his teeth and watches me. After ½ an hour he speaks. Are there cinemas in London? No, say I. Another ½ hour. What is the title of my story? The village idiot, say I. Another ½ hour. Is it about love? Yes, say I, "the love that dare not speak its name" (Alfred Douglas). But of course he does not understand. M. Décugis is a marvellously handsome old man of about 70, with one leg that won't work; and every morning at 5.0 he goes out and sits on a mountain and returns at 6.0 in the evening with 3 or 4 *grives* [thrushes]. Mdme Décugis works all day and has heart attacks.

I find myself repulsive just now. I am growing a beard! The 19th Article of my Faith reads: "He that hath not looked fully upon the horror of his own beard shall not enter into salvation." So it has to be done. When it has reached its maturity I shall get myself pictured in it and send a copy to you. Then I shall bribe M. le Coiffeur here to remove the offending growth.

Ah - la Maison Blanche. Downstairs things were elegant and utterly respectable: dancing, drinking, and mildly lecherous talk - nothing to which Anna B. could take exception. Eventually I said to the two harlots, If we go upstairs will you two perform together? They said the French equivalent for not 'alf, and we trooped joyously up. Arrived, they stripped naked, and one yelled down the stairs for a dildoe. It was brought by a maid. A marvellously virile affair: accurate in every detail with hair and balls. They had each other in turn with this, which wasn't frightfully exciting. Then they sucked. Each in turn. This was marvellous. The suck*er* worked like a Trojan, while the suck*ee* squealed with delight, gasping and rolling about on the bed and whimpering. The crisis came; and they lay, clasped and slobbering, panting and content. A good scene. What Irving did I don't know; I left him there, but he said the next morning he had done things but was very reticent and remorseful about it.

And the dog. It happened this way. (I have never before met with so salacious a beast). I was sitting on a stone up a mountain; my thoughts were inclined towards shameless things. Always I like pee-ing sitting down so I decided to pee. I produced to the air of heaven my penis; and at that moment the dog, gambolling innocently by, caught sight of it. He gave a bark; and, frothing at the mouth, he leapt. He took it in his mouth, licking and sucking. It was marvellous; I have never before, I think, experienced so great, so intense a tumescence. The dog sweated, and so did I. I grasped his tool, and started to masturbate him. In a moment his slim, scarlet spike was out; and that round lump in it swollen and hard. He wriggled and thrust; I did the same, and in an incredibly short time he shot all over me. Then I: right in his mouth. He lapped it up, and licked everything down. All the time we were both squealing: the exquisite agony of it all. I have never imagined so perverted a dog. The worst of it was that ever afterward he made a bee-line for the junction of my legs whenever he saw me. Most embarrassing some times.

By the way, in one of The Houses a marvellous notice something to this effect was displayed:

Chambres	
Un Moment	5 frs.
Demi-Heure	10 –
Une Heure	12 –
Toute la nuit	20 –

I should not like to experience those sheets after a succession of "moments"!

The other day I found the most marvellous wild mountain walk that led me right to the very top of the buttock-shaped mountain (Mt. Caume). This is about the highest here; and the whole prospect was incredible. And everywhere the ordure and other evidences of *sangliers* [wild boar], but I have not yet managed to see one. Also I found a way up to Phyll's rock-shelter: quite easy, & very good.

I have not yet managed to achieve Méounes, a village about 12 miles due north of here. I was going y'day, but rain the night before would have made the narrow, breast high paths too wet. It appears that for the first ten miles there is not a *single* house or human being to be encountered; and everybody here tells me that the right path (there are a thousand similar) cannot be found by anyone not knowing it. And no one here does know it! The young Décugis has lived here for 20 years and has never been further than Toulon! They are an unadventurous race. But I shall do it one day: stay the night and return.

I have never eaten *some* haggis. I hope you enjoyed it. I wish I'd been there. Tell Gray that I hope he will visit me in my *house* at Évenos one day. I think La Maison Morte would be a good name for it, or do you think La Charrue? Or perhaps Le Chenil ?(!) La Maison Morte, I think. I dream about the day when you & Phyll come to stay in it. It will be *our* Mediterranean home.

By the way, I had an incredible dream about you the other night: incredible, I know, tho' the details are lost. Something about cutting up babies. I dream terrifically here; perhaps it is the wine; I don't know. Marvellous semi-nightmares. I have written a story about a man who liked killing boys, which, like Kubla Khan, had its genesis in a dream. That was in Toulon when I was sharing a bed with a million fleas. I wish I were not feeling so ill today; I find this wine, tho' excellent and exalting, is v. bad the next morning if you have drunk it really in quantity. Also it turns one's urine greeny-orange, and one's ordure black, which is depressing. I have here a marvellous stony hollow near the chapel where I deposit my ordure every morning.

Yes, I think Ross[39] must be going mad. How does he reconcile

---

[39] Presumably, "Amyas Ross, collaborator in intellectual socialism with G. D. H. Cole, and briefly, before dying of an overdose of pills, a Labour Party

his lofty spirituality with such preposterous behaviour? A cretin would know better.

Millard[40] sent me a cutting of the Plough fire. I feel it is an act of god. Do please let me have detail about the new people and their attitude to our corner. And do the brokers still go there? And can one eat tolerably?

Yes, there are many moments when I yearn for a pot of honest beer, and for boiled beef such as you gave us those Saturdays; or some roast with some of Phyll's Yorkshire pudding and horse-radish sauce. – or for some frizzling sausages and mashed and onions. And what wouldn't I give for an afternoon in that hot Petronian tank in Holborn small baths? Here I am reduced to occasional sacrifices at the shrine of Onan.

The Brémonds at le Revest are become decidedly frosty. I don't know why; but behind their superficial politeness there is a defined lurking frost. I think it must be due to M. le Boucher, who quite decidedly hates me for some obscure reason. But Brémond has qualities: I find that at one period of penury he sold papers in the streets of Paris. But I shall see him this afternoon. I shall go up to Revest to post this: one can't get stamps in Dardennes.

The other day I went to Toulon to have a bath, a real one; and there were great things going on. Soldiers marching everywhere with trumpet squeaking bands. The black men blowing trumpets with all their faces blown out marvellously, and with agonised expressions. And everybody who could raise one dressed in their grandest uniforms, with gold swords and yards of medals. I don't know what it was all about.

Will you please tell Irving[41] that I'm so sorry I didn't write as I promised; but I lost all his addresses. Also that I couldn't send the 50 frs I said I would because I lost a 100 and so on. I hope he'll forgive me.

---

politician and husband of Phyl's sister Joan Crocker" (*The World, The Flesh and Myself*, p. 143).

[40] The writer Christopher Sclater Millard (1872-1927), highly revered by Davidson and others in their social circle, and frequently to be referred to long after his death.

[41] Again, presumably the Joseph Irving Davis of footnote 38. The left-hand side of the last page beginning with this sentence is taken up with an ink sketch of a man blowing a trumpet.

How is Chang? And Uno? – and the Monico[42]? Lord I'd like to turn out of Coptic street at six this evening into the Plough; and find Gray nodding his head, and Lambert waving his arms, and Johnny picking and mouthing, and Rodker moaning, and Ross frowning, and Nina obscening, and Pops shouting, and Jellinek bragging, and Millard grumbling, and Eileen powdering her nose, and Judy talking about the Café de Paris, and Tasha belching, and Chamberlain haw-hawing, and Roman dithering, and Mrs. Stan Harding being vague, and Back paying for Johnny's beer, and Moeran reddening, and Irving sagging, and Al smiling, and Pigs sulking, and Mrs. Dagnall abusing, and Phyll Philling, and you gazing with a pint-pot of bitter, and God in his heaven.

I'm glad my letters don't bore you; but you've no idea what pleasure yours give me. You can not guess the joy with which I got yours this morning. So please write, both of you.

Love *Michael*

iv

28 Worcester Place
Oxford
8 January 1928

My dear Boris: A week's residence in this admirable city has convinced me that I shall never leave it. I shall grow old here, and eventually, I suppose, impotent; and Oxford shall know my grave; though there's no hurry for that, for: "The grave's a fine and private place, But none, I think, do there embrace..."

Mrs. Heritage has given up ginger wine; she has returned to gin (taken hot), and finds her conversation more satisfying in

---

[42] The Monico was a café in Shaftesbury Avenue, from which Davidson, who had frequented it, was expelled for good by a doorman when a jealous page-boy of 15 "narked" on him for having flirted (or more) with two others there (*The World, The Flesh and Myself*, p. 145).

consequence. Dolly (the little one: Aet: XVI) is marvellous. I asked her to come to a film, but Mrs. Heritage forbade her. And I so harmless and all.[43]

I have redeemed THE PIPE from Colin Lunn[44]; it is a marvellous pipe: it has all the qualities.

Now, I must tell you about my lodgings. I have a large sitting-room, comfortably if a little lodging-y furnished with large bookshelves already there; a large bedroom with double bed; unlimited coal piled on fire at all times; light; bath; bromo; and unlimited food of the first quality; good ENGLISH food, well cooked. All this I get for £2 a week. A marvellous landlady (Mrs. Wrighton yclept) who *cannot* do enough for me, who gives me lemon in my tea and crumpets to eat, and whose husband is a *little* inclined to get blind. If ever and whenever you or you-and-Phyll come to Oxford I can put you up at any time with ease, comfort and pleasure. I have a sofa on which I can sleep downstairs; and my chaste bed upstairs is at the disposal of you or anybody good who will come. So remember that.

A thing has happened that is really rather humorous ... I have been asked (and have consented) to teach the 'prentice boys English! It will be an emotional strain, but rather fun. Altogether everything is fun; I'm enjoying life; tho' continually I want you to share the enjoyment; and Oh, how I long to tell Millard all about it. The whole place is so full of him; today I went to see our boat;[45] it has survived the floods and other furies of Zeus.

Last evening I went into the Clarendon, and Millard and I drank a pint of BASS on DRAUGHT each. But it's a bad pub in other respects. I go also sometimes to the NEW INN (Simonds' Reading Ales) where there is something incredible behind the bar. The CHEQUERS is always unbearably crowded. The DRUID'S HEAD back room sees me not infrequently. I have

---

[43] Especially when considered in conjunction with the reminiscences of Leslie Bearock presented in section 5, this might be considered as evidence that Davidson had not in his youth been as impervious to the charms of girls as he much later made out in *The World, The Flesh and Myself.*

[44] A tobacconist in Oxford.

[45] Millard had died seven weeks previously, but - not long before then - Davidson "had one golden interlude with him", boating on the Thames up from Oxford (*The World, The Flesh and Myself*, p. 146).

discovered a PLOUGH (nr: Folly Bdge:), but I have not been into it. It sells 'All's Ales – "'Allsop's they calls it now" – which is of course the most frequently found brew here.

I forgot to say that included in the £2 a week is the use of a rear, which however, in spite of the fact that it has two doors and two windows, is a little primitive.

From the point of view of horticulture this city is in the first rank; the genus παις [boy] is particularly abundant and of a high quality. I have hardly seen one specimen that might not be pleasurably plucked. But so far the blooms have been beyond my reach.

I sent you a postcard the other day to thank you *frightfully* for the map of the river: it is a dear and rejoices me enormously. You have a genius for getting the precisely right things. By the by, the photograph of Millard was so unsatisfactory that I am having the other one done (the Godstow one); it will be ready next weekend, and I will send it then. Will you tell Al and Irving (and give them my love) that I will send them a copy too.

I long to hear about your Christmas. Was it good? I heard that Nina[46] and her young man went too to Rouen, which sounds a rather incongruous mixture. I suppose it was a vast blind? What else in that ghastly weather. The Backs may have told you of our Christmas: did you hear that I was beaten up by a gang of roughs – a most undignified and disquieting experience. I very bravely went to the police-station. The inspector asked "Have you been on the booze?" I replied "Yes, for 3 days." He then said: "Well, you know, at this time of night the streets only contain policemen and sinners", which I thought rather good for a police-inspector.

Do let me know if anything good happened to you and Phyll. I have not yet heard even, if you are back; and I am quite anxious about you.

I have come by chance upon some lines of Beaumont that are I think quite appropriate in connexion with the Annual CHRISTOPHER SCLATER MILLARD dinner. They are:

---

[46] Presumably their artist friend Nina Hamnett (1890-1956), also referred to in letter xxxiii.

Fill me this day with some rare delicates
And I will every year most constantly
As this day, celebrate a sumptuous feast
(if thou wilt send me victuals) in thine honour!
And to it shall be bidden for thy sake
Even all the valiant stomachs in the court;
All short-cloak'd knights, and all cross-gartered
gentlemen;
All pump and pantofle, foot-cloth riders
With all the swarming generation
Of long stocks, short-pan'd hose, and huge
stuff'd doublets;
All these shall eat, and which is more than yet
Hath e'er been seen, they shall be satisfied!

And this is rather pleasant; it is an American hobo song, addressed, of course, by a "jocker" to his "prushun":

Won't you come down to the jungles,[1]
Come with me down to the camp?
I'll buy some punk[2]
And other old junk,
And toppings[3] that's sweet for a tramp.

I'll buy candy and whiteline[4] and smoking;
I'll fill your coozy[5] with joy,
If you'll only come down to the jungles,
And say that you're my little boy!

[1] Hobos' camp
[2] Bread
[3] Luxuries
[4] Pure alcohol
[5] Can you guess?

Do, Phyll-and-Boris, come and stay with me here some weekend. And I'll tell the Backs (I hope the fast is over?) I will gladly put them up.

Love

Shimmihl*
Albanian for Michael*

V

25.10 [1928] bei Biela

Savignyplatz 13
Berlin – Charlottenburg

My dear Phyll & Boris, Irving, Jonny & Gillie, and Leo: Thank you so frightfully for the really marvellous time you all gave me that weekend; it was so good – one of the best times.

Forgive paper & pencil; I'm in a pub – a low pub and like most places the low pubs are more fun than the high pubs. I achieved sobriety 2 or 3 days go after finishing a prolonged blind by drinking a whole bottle of very inferior vodka one evening & it nearly killed me; now I drink vast quantities of the helles bier [pale ale] which is excellent at 3d a pint.

Up till today I have loathed this place: it is inhospitable and the cheap food is porky mess (tho' I had a really marvellous steak today – even Millard would have liked it) and the first adventure I had stole my pocket book containing what little money I then had and, what was worse, some very precious photographs. Today I had a marvellous adventure – 16 & charming in every way – it will be repeated on Saturday. The 'places' are amusing to see once but dull after that; they can always be recognised by being painted black outside & windows heavily curtained. Inside shaded lights & walls curiously decorated. Bald-headed stockbrokers holding hands sentimentally & elegant powdered youths dancing & feeling each other. There are dozens of them. Perhaps I shall find some more amusing places. Everybody here are such rogues & thieves that one can rely on nothing. For instance at one place a decorated youth asked me to hire him for the night; when I told him I liked them younger he said he would give me addresses for 5 marks. I gave him m.5, but when I tested the addresses they contained the same sort of stockbrokers. Also I was offered cocaine. I said wieviel? – two marks a packet. I thought at such a price the stuff must be chalk. But I shall find out more about such things when I have got a better hold of this stinking language which is infernally difficult.

In a day or two I am going to a thing which advertises itself as 'Cabaret Erotik – Sadism, Masochism, Exhibitionism, etc faithfully reproduced.' But it will probably be very dull. All the picture papers on sale on the streets are full of completely nude men & women being very hearty with each other. The boys' schools play football in the public playgrounds dressed in nothing but bathing drawers – this in the cold and rain.

It is quite evident that *all* the boys here *know* things; some will & some won't, that's all. Most will, I think.

Today I went to the headquarters of Freundschaft – books incredible, but photographs disappointing – my own collection is much better.

But I am so inarticulate as regards language that I cannot do all the things I want to do or say all the things I want to say, & it makes me so angry. I'm coming home as soon as I have learnt the language & have finished an exceedingly silly & obscene novel I am doing.

Don't any of you come out here till I know more about it & find it more tolerable. I long for you all but I feel you would loathe it. Somehow it isn't friendly and cheerful like France & Paris and even London. Perhaps its atmosphere can be tasted in the fact that all the pubs look difficult to get into, if you know what I mean. And everybody is out to do you, which is tiresome. I'm being done 10 times a day because I can't yet speak the language.

I mean to bring you back marvellous drinking receptacles – stoppered bottles of vast size for fetching the family beer in, and an amazing goblet thus [little sketch of goblet] about 9 inches across, out of which people drink weissbier – a thin kind of beer. I haven't yet had time to sample all the local drinks. And as for food the bill of fare is always totally illegible for me & I never know what to eat. Vegetables are good, but this everlasting fleshy porky muck makes me sick. I bathe a lot – good baths, full of creatures, but oddly modest; things of Igor's age[47] go through incredibly elaborate processes to prevent the middle parts of themselves being observed. Of course that's a sign of the times, – but when I think of Long Bridges, Oxford ....

The cove who keeps this pub is called Joseph. He is large & hairy & fat. 20 years ago he was a waiter in Whitechapel & he loves to talk in English. By the way, *all* the owners of the 'places' are large & fat & hairy & have wives; it's most amusing to observe the supercilious way they look at the decorated youths & elderly stockbrokers. But they love to take their money.

I must go to the police tomorrow which is a little terrifying. I have to get registered.

My dears, I wish I were with you; I'm rather lost here. But I hope to back in 2 or 3 months – when I've learnt the tongue.

Write to me, all of you, *please*. I will write again soon, when I have more details of the social conditions of Bairleen.

Always
M.
Savignyplatz 13

I have just said to Joseph – 'You are very empty tonight.' – 'Yes,' he says – 'There are five days to the first of the month.' Isn't that pathetic? – this in a working men's pub you see.

The *next morning*: I got vastly blind last night & finished up in a place called the 'Adonis' where elderly gentlemen were playing about in short knickers & sailor suits. This was after being forced by Joseph to eat what he called a very special dish. It arrived and showed itself to be a leathery pancake made of eggs & potatoes & very salty. On this I was ordered, tho' protesting, to spread jam & sugar. Then I was nearly sick. I'm going to be sick now. *Please* write everybody.

---

[47] Igor was the seven-year-old son of Boris and Phyllis de Chroustchoff.

vi

[Envelope addressed to B. de Chroustchoff Esq:, 20 Bury Street, Bloomsbury, London W.C.1, England. Postmarked 2 Nov. 1928. Two enclosures (tickets for shows).]

1.11.28 bei Biela
Savignyplatz 13
Berlin - Charlottenburg

Dearest Phyll & Boris: This is a pub near my house where I have been often before and generally blind; and just over there I can hear the frau telling some cronies that I am a sad English case and that I DRINK. This is a little embarrassing.

However, the point is that I am married. To a Lettlander. Will you please tell me at once where Lettland is: is it more Slav than Teuton or the other way about. Anyway meine Braut [my bride] is not at all the Teuton type.

D'you remember, Boris, saying to me, just before I left, that here one made *friends* - that sort of thing. I said pooh-pooh! that sort of thing don't happen. Well it has! An unbelievable creature aet: XV, with masses of black hair, huge eyes blacker than I've ever seen before, and the brownest slimmest body - a Lettlander, Berlin-born but Lettland parentage. It wears the shortest knickers, open shirt, gay jumper; and if you could have seen me careering down Friedrichstrasse (a sort of Piccadilly) into Unter den Linden on the back of this amazing vision's bicycle you would have gone and had a drink. His name is Walfried Reile-Reiljon and he calls me mein 'hosbent' and he loves drinking cognac and this and that & we roar round Berlin with our arms round each others' necks and we swim eagerly and heartily every day and when I am broke he shares his last cigarettes with me saying 'Was ist mein ist dein', and we're going to buy a lute and go walking (he loves walking) in the forests singing lewd songs. He plays the lute. And he can't speak English and I can't speak German and we get on marvellously. And he's far more sophisticated than I am about everything and is utterly marvellous and I'm going to bring him to England and to the Plough - in his short knickers.

I've been starving for a day or two – nothing to eat – and Walfried has shared his cigarettes with me; but today I am rich again and have just eaten verily, and behind me are people singing political songs and over there people saying what a sad case I am. How odd it is. And Walfried is making clothes in his father's tailoring place; but tomorrow evening he and I go swimming and then we go home and play a little and then we go out and drink and sing and amuse ourselves. And at this moment (7.0 p.m. mid-European time) you are thinking of going to the Plough.

Walfried has shown me a marvellous swimming place called Luna Park (*not* Tottenham Ct. Rd) where a mechanical contrivance makes real waves and the deep end is like mid-atlantic and the shallow end like Brighton beach.

And all round is like the Lido; for the rank & fashion of Berlin sit round all day drinking and looking fascinating in bathing dresses & the men & boys wear nothing but tiny drawers, and the girls not much else. And Walfried & I sit & look fascinating too – at least Walfried does.

I have also discovered a marvellous bathing place where they are not so modest as they had seemed to be in others. That is where I met Walfried.

I have just bought my landlady's child a doll. The shops here display, besides the usual sets of toy toilet things, sets of toy medical instruments of obscure kinds. I haven't yet seen toy french letters but I expect there are. By the way Boris pfeife [pipe] is more colloquial than nüler[48].

It's odd that a year ago today Millard was alive but that 3 weeks hence he was not. Personally I've not been able to believe he's not still. How he'd hate this place – why don't they open the WINDOWS; This cutlet's cooked in BATter – almost as much as I do – except for Walfried.

I saw a place in Friedrichstrasse this evening that you would have loved. A really marvellous youth of about 17 in chef's cap etc. was doing incredible things at a grill – as Christnich[?] does. Terribly efficient and marvellous to look at. I shall eat there tomorrow – with Walfried.

---

[48] Perhaps a misspelling of "nille", which, like "pfeife", is slang for a penis.

Shall I send you some examples of the illustrated papers?

It is incredibly warm still. This evening, after dark, (Nov. 1st) I sat drinking in the open air in Unter den Linden. Very entertaining and pleasant, and warm.

I find that the nicest people here are the policemen, the pawnbrokers and the bathing attendants. The publicans all treat you as if they'd rather you didn't buy their stinking beer which is horrid. – their attitude I mean, not the beer.

Next day

After that I went round the city. And to cabarets (here with) – nackt [?] females with swaying breasts – very dull. Alkasar is the swanky cabaret of Berlin. You pay a mark for the privilege of going in. Then inside – enormous with 2 bands – people who are *dressed* and drink champagne have the front tables; behind them are a row of tables labled WEIN, and behind them the mere beer-drinkers are allowed to sit; & you pay a mark for a glass of beer that in a pub costs 15-20 pf. I was livid with rage at such stinking snobbery. Please try & keep these tickets – they are always amusing to see afterwards. Then I went to various odd places – of that kind – all a little dull & was persistently importuned & was kept busy refusing. In one was a large gentleman rather like the late Mr. Wilde surrounded by a bevy of fairies who was known to all as Der Englander. My god! Finally I tried to acquire cocaine but apparently the vendor had gone to bed or something – anyway it's all a put up job and idiots like me are done right and left.

By the way I am furious because a new edition of the Priest & the Acolyte[49] is out here advertised as by O. Wilde. I am livid for Millard's sake – you know the trouble he went to to show that it is *not* by W. If he were alive I would start a campaign to EXPOSE it, but what's the good. And anyhow they know it isn't true, but Shaw, Galsworthy and the late Mr. Wilde are the rage here.

I asked (see above) about O but got vague answers so far as I remember. But it is obviously to be had – like everything and everybody here.

But I shall learn the tongue – if I can – & come back as soon as

[49] *The Priest and the Acolyte* was a short love story by John Bloxam published in *The Chameleon*, December 1894.

possible because I am really unhappy here – except for Walfried. But I shall bring him with me nicht wahr [is that not so]? Of course not. 11.0 a.m. I am drinking coffee and cognac and the publican hates me. They are like that here. Last night I dashed about in taxis; they go at a million miles an hour and cost a mark for 5 million miles. And to go through the Tiergarten at night is great fun. The Tiergarten is a park in the middle of Berlin through which runs a straight road 2 miles long. All the Tiergarten is carefully darkened so that the less affluent Berliners may have their fun in peace. It is a considerate country, I will say that for it.

This evening – Walfried. You would like Walfried.

Write for god's sake or rather for my sake. I long for letters & I long for you. And I long for England. Really this is no better than London for certain things. It's all a put up job. But Walfried!

All love

M

WRITE

vii

Thursday [Nov. 1928]

Bln – Chlbg
Savignyplatz 13
bei Biela

My dear Boris: A large number of drunken people are making a large noise on a piano and with their mouths, so it is difficult to write a letter and shortly I must go to hear Mozart (which I don't want to do) with a Turkish mädchen [girl] who prefers wearing trousers to a skirt and who hates men. She is a sculptor and speaks Russian, German, French, Italian, American, and I suppose Turkish.

Your incredible letter today convulsed me; but I'm afraid you've all gone very bad since my restraining influence was withdrawn. Rest peaceful about the Jack o' Newb'ry letter: it arrived without let tho' I expected the police to follow it, but so far they have not done so. But I expect the König of Albania will prosecute – and poor Chany[?] will go to gaol; how sad.

I love your description of Back dishevelled and without his usual aplomb! I think I have once only seen him approaching that condition. What does he say about Jonny & Irving? He does change his co-respondent a lot of times. But please don't any of you do anything really bad: I don't want to find you all at The Scrubs or anywhere when I come back.

I had a temporary row with Walfried because he smiled at a man in a café. It was really tempting providence, because we went to a *queer* café full of old men & fairies and of course Walfried was the beauty of the place, besides being the only junge (large notices prohibited anybody under 18 – W. is 15) which delighted me enormously, till I found all the old sods were goggling at W. & when I found W. smiling back at one of them I divorced him on the spot. But it was all made up the next day & he's better than ever and on Saturday he's bringing his particular friend (er macht mit – if you get the phrase) to see me. Same age.

Werner is a new acquisition: best German type – we go to spend the day at Luna Park on Sunday. Hans came last night, but I'm a little bored with Hans; but his friend Max is rather remarkable (16); he is able to perform an action upon himself which has hitherto been the privilege of dogs.

Hitherto I have eked out a meagre living teaching in a sort of tutoring establishment that has now gone Kaput – the manager having disappeared with the week's takings which is awkward, and leaves me out of a job. But I am hoping for another job: it depends on whether there be a vacancy & I should hear any day. If this don't come off I don't quite know what will happen; it's very worrying as I *must* stay out here till I've learnt the language properly. I *can't* come back before and don't want to as this place is so amazing.

Tho' I'm made frantic by the meal you & Jellings had: this food makes me sick tho' I *did* have some miraculous goose's liver done with onions & potatoes the other day and {the pianist has just fallen off the music stool} not so battery as usual. But the other day I *craved* for poached eggs on toast and I asked for zwei Spiegeleier mit tost which according to the rules of the game should have produced poached eggs on toast – tost being the accepted word. But *fried* eggs and sauté potatoes arrived. Why? Ish weiss nisht [a slurred "I don't know"].

And they're such devils; you have to watch them like s[??] {tho' in reputable pubs & restaurants they are as honest as day}. The other night, a little so-so, I went to the Kant Casino (in Kantstrasse, and so far as I know not patronised by the philosopher. It is a sort of pub-cum-brothel. I was talking to a hoo-er, when the owner whom I knew before came up & asked me to have a drink. I said it could be done & he ordered 3 cognacs – me, himself, and the hoo-er. I thought I'd better return it and repeated. When I got the bill I was charged for *six* cognacs. That's the way they do it.

I will try to find out about Gross (or Grozs) but so far have not succeeded. The Well of Loneliness[50] (English Edition) is to be had here for M. 33 but I can't afford it at the moment. I have an incredible book called Neger-Erotik which has marvellous detailed descriptions of methods of masturbation among Nandi boys with photograph of junge [boy] in act. Also of mädchen [girl] (without photograph). And other things. When I come back I shall have a vanload of prohibited literature and indecent cartoons besides a pound or two of O. & C. How to deal with it?

auf wiedersehen [good-bye]

M

viii

RESTAURANT "SCHAURTÉ"
Inhaber: Josef Schaurté

Restaurant Schaurté
Steinplatz 14155

---

[50] *The Well of Loneliness* was a lesbian novel by Radclyffe Hall published in London in July 1928, but condemned as obscene in a trial the following November.

Charlottenburg
Bleibtreustr. 49,
gegenüber Bahnhof Savignyplatz

den 19. 11. 1928

My dear Phyll & Boris: For this 22nd of November I cannot write to Millard because the letter would not be delivered; therefore I write to you. Let me know about The Wake. How Millard would loathe this country; how he would damn it. He could eat *nothing* here, unless possibly he ate at the Kaiserhof or the Adlon or somewhere like that where meals cost about 20 m. But there is one aspect of life here which he would probably have tolerated – genug! Gut, gut, gut. Ja. Ich habe viele! Aber es ist gut – sie sind so freundlich.[51]

Since last writing to you I have added to my collection the following: Walter (16), Kurt I (14), Kurt II (14), Willi (15), Rudolf (14). I would describe in detail these creatures if I had not to go to bett [bed]. Kurt I is completely glabrous & terribly proud because a sprout occurs on either side. He describes marvellously things that occur am schule [at school]. So does Kurt II & Rudolf. It is incredible. There was once a cove who said he would always possess the 30 BEST Japanese swords in the Welt: When he found a better one than one of the 30 he then had, he discarded one other very reluctantly. I am like that man. Every other day I find a better one and have to determine which to cast away: it is very difficult. One never knows at any moment what one is going to run into. Leo would go mad.

This afternoon I left Rudolf to meet my everlastingly marvellous Walfried – my Lett who is always incredible and FAITHFUL. We went to a Cognac (nur [only]) pub in Friedrichstrasse & drank many cognacs; then we went home mit bottle of wein & drank & I drank wein out of his vorhaut (verstehst du?)[52] and do you know what he did this weekend? Saturday evening 7.30 he

[51] "genug … freundlich" means "enough! Good, good, good. Yes. I have so many! But it's good – they are so friendly."

[52] "mit bottle of wein & drank & I drank wein out of his vorhaut (verstehst du?)" translates fully into English as "with bottle of wine & drank & I drank wine out of his foreskin (do you understand?)".

with the walking Klub started, mit Mädels [with girls] and walked throughout Saturday night & Sonntag until 7.30 Abends – 24 hours and they all bathed in a lake – terribly cold – completely nackt [naked] – mädchen [girl] for every boy – Then back to drinking & wichsen [wanking] & so on – That is German decadence! – The most virile race in the world surely – and I adore it. But you ought to drink red wein out of Walfried's vorhaut. And this evening, on our way home, we were walking along Berlinerstrasse and Bube [lad] tripped along past like any little fee [fairy]. I said 'Ein schön Knabe de nicht wahr?' ['A handsome boy, isn't he?'] to annoy him because he always go raving mad if I refer to another boy; and he said – Ney, ney! weibisch [effeminate]! And certainly it was weibisch!

But next Mittwoch [Wednesday] is a public holiday for some obscure reason so neither Walfried nor Willi work & they both come mit mir [with me] and we will have a marvellous time because Walfried & Willi do quite unnameable things together & will do so in my room. Willi although the same age is about a year younger in development and it is all marvellous.

But things are schlecht [bad]. Because the job I was out for has no vacancy until January; and I don't know how I'm going to carry on here, but I hope I may get one or two private pupils. I told this to Walfried tonight and he said 'Seid gut?' ['Be good?'] & I said Wie? [How?] & then I realised that he thought the pupils were Jungen [boys] & told him that they were old men & all was well. He goes mad if I refer to any boy.

Also my suicide is continually about to commit suicide again which is terribly difficult – especially in a foreign country & I don't know what to do about it. Today she was raving mad talking utter gibberish & it is very difficult. God knows what is going to happen & what I shall do & what it will all end in.[53]

But this is Millard's death-day & I will not tell about schlimm [bad] things: let's talk about Millard – my darling Millard whom I've believed yet not to be tot [dead]. I expect always to get a letter from him; but I don't. And when I think about all the old

---

53 Presumably this refers to his close friend and sometime fiancée Felicia Browne (1904-36), who had asked him to come to Berlin. Her attempt at suicide in Berlin is described on p. 155 of *The World, The Flesh and Myself.*

days & up the river & Bury Street & The Bungalow & the Great CENTRAL HOTEL and a STEAK at the HORSE shoe – or a Made up FISH DISH with a Pint of BASS on Draught – and I can't Drink this BEER and why don't THEY OPEN the WINDOWS? – and YOU BORE ME! – what am I to do? – I'd give the world to be told by Millard that I bored him – instead I must try to deal with my suicide who is literally at the moment raving mad and also I must deal with Rudolf tomorrow. Mittwoch [Wednesday] with Walfried & Willi & tomorrow after Rudolf I ought to deal with Kurt No I & so on & it's all so difficult. And all the time I don't know what is going to happen. But it remains the most amazing place.

Oh yes. I have an elderly lover who until last Saturday night had only offered to take me to the Zoo for which he had free tickets. I refused. (Alas he asked me to meet at swimming baths: also refused). But last Saturday I met him here late & he said 'Kom mit mir nach Friedrichstrasse (Come with me to Friedrichstrasse).' I said Ney ney! and ordered another beer. Then I said I WILL go to Friedrichstrasse – & we went & the cove *insisted* on paying for everything, and evidently hoped to take me home afterwards. And we both got very besoffen [drunk] in various very odd pubs & then he said we will go back home & I said No! No! I will not go home – When I go *out*, I go *OUT*, & I spotted two boys, having already that day dealt with Walfried, Willi, and Kurt No 2, & he went off in a huff and I got done by the boys and altogether it was a peculiar evening. Then I went to a pub near my haus [house] & found an admirable fight progressing between the landlord & another gentleman (It was about 4.0 am). So I, in the best manner divided the combatants. Always after 12.0 midnight there are fights in pubs.

They fight like hell here, but are otherwise charming: it is a very odd place. One ought never to drink anything really: only devote oneself to my Buben who are unspeakably good. Today im Schwimmbad [in the swimming-pool] I saw Rudolf & said to myself I must have that child; When dressing, a Mensch [man] (auch [also] dressing) got a foul erection & Rudolf & I both caught each other's eyes about it. Then I asked him to have a cigarette, then we went to a café & drank Kaffee & he ate a kuchen mit sahne (*sahne*!) [cake with cream (*cream!*)] and I said you don't drink cognac do you? – 'Ach ja, ein bisschen [Oh, yes, a little bit].' he said – and this was a 14-year-old schoolboy! So we had cognacs arranged for tomorrow & then I rushed off to meet my incredible Walfried, who becomes more marvellous every day. And if I so much as look at another Bube he goes mad; and of course he *doesn't* know about all my others – and I go raving mad if I think he has another friend; but I know he hasn't, and so I go on being unfaithful, knowing that he is faithful, which is marvellous. Exactly five boys, including W., have determined to come to England with me; it is very difficult.

Phyll, darling, write *please*, because one does not know what is going to happen to one & everything is pretty bloody. Enormous debauches occur; unnumbered Buben; & all the time suicide suicides – this is literal; and all in a foreign country. How very odd it all is! And one longs for letters. So good. You've no idea how good. Everything is so obscure; but one lives only for the moment & tomorrow is Rudolf; & Mittwoch is Walfried & Willi & Donnerstag [Thursday] is at the moment I've forgotten & so it goes on. Drink a Bass on Draught for me at the Wake & always my love to Millard.

Love, Michael.

'I don't WANT your LOVE' – C. S. M.[54]

ix

RESTAURANT "SCHAURTÉ"
Inhaber: Josef Schaurté

November 24 (?) [1928]

My dear Phyll & Boris: I have this evening inquired (not having before found anything out) about the works of Georg

[54] The initials of Christopher Sclater Millard.

Grosz, and in the next few days the bookseller concerned is going to send me a complete list of his published drawings with prices; I will send them on to you immediately.

I have been hoping for a letter from one or other of you; but it is possible you all died on 22 November; I hope not, and I hope that I may hear shortly that you only nearly died.

After the end of this month {that is in a week's time I think} I leave my present Wohnung [abode] for one costing just half as much I hope. At present I pay RM.60 per month for the privilege of living in select Charlottenbursch: in the much more pleasant district of the slums round Alexanderplatz (in old Berlin, beyond the top end of Unt' d'n Lind'n) I can get a Zimmer mit Frühstück [bed and breakfast] for RM 30 - at least so Walter says and Walter & I are going to search for one on Monday. Walter has just left me. He is a distinctive youth, 17 last Sunday (when I first met him) but in appearance is 15 in every way. Speaks Russian, Polish, German, some French and ein bisschen [a little] English. Was until recently a pageboy at the Vaterland Café, - Leipzigerstr; now an apprentice painter.

But Walfried! - Walfried is really the only one. I am gradually getting rid of Hans, Max, Kurt I, Kurt II, Werner, Rudolf, and all the rest - and devoting myself to Walfried & his friend Willi. Willi is 14 ½ and *incredible* in behaviour - spass [fun] is not the word. He & Walfried are lovers and the two together are unbelievable; I have never known such a pair of miracles - Eric & Curly are left far behind. Last Wednesday was Busstag [Day of Repentance], and so they had a day off, and spent it with me. We bought wine and food & went to my Wohnung, and there unbelievable things happened - ganz nackt [completely naked] all three - and lots of red wine to give colour to the proceedings. Then we went to a very expensive café in Friedrichstr. and behaved monstrously, kissing and dandling all over the place. Really you are wrong about Letts unless my Lett is an utter exception - Anyhow he is like nothing that has ever happened before - in looks, in personality, in faithfulness, in everything. Willi is echte [real] Berliner and not anything wonderful to look at - just young and glabrous - but spass! and passionate as hell. Walfried is terribly jealous about my dealing with him even all together but as they are lovers he allows it.

This is certainly an odd place. Last Tuesday I had to meet

Rudolf at 2.0 to take him for a swim. At 6.0, I had promised to meet Kurt I (14.1, Schüler [schoolboy]). At 1.0 I arrived at Unt' d'n hin'n Ecke Friedrichstr (sort of Piccadilly Circus) & went to have a P. there; I ran into a red-headed, freckled child there (15) and soon was dealing with him (in the place) and all the time was aware that an elderly gentleman was having a quiet rub in a corner by himself. After some time a paroxysm in the corner implied that the elderly gentleman had achieved the climax. He went off to his office or whatnot & Freckles & I finished things off. As a rule, when one goes into this place in the middlest of Berlin one finds things of that sort going on. All very odd.

I've had a hell of a time lately because my suicide has been a complete raving lunatic, literally. It's been a very difficult time. But now things are better in that direction. But schlimm [bad] as regards the future, for I am out of a job except for a few pupils who never dream of paying for their lessons. But there are one or two jobs in view & one hopes for the best.

Monday
Café Leon, Nollendorf Platz

Enormously pleased to get record of the First Millardian Commemorative Dinner. Marvellous! I would have given a million pounds to have been there. I don't think you could have included anybody else - except Harry Cohen! - or excluded anybody. I'm surprised Al didn't come-up for it - and most amused and rather pleased that FRED was there - how did you get into touch with him? I suppose the last time you saw him & certainly the last time I did was when C. S. M. & you & I were at Thame - Do you remember Millard riding through LONG WICK on your bicycle, head in air, smoke curling upward?

The food was perfect - but I think you should have had a MADE-UP-FISH-DISH to be tasted and refused by everybody. And why is M's name not BASS ON DRAUGHT? Thank you for sending the everlastingly precious Bill of Fare. Next year I hope I shall be there.

x

1 *hour later* [26 November 1928] Potzdamer Bierhaus, Grolmanstr

I went to the Leon to see the president of the Englischer Klub, to whom I intend to give lectures. A good idea, – but what the hell shall I lecture on? – Walfried? or Millard? or English food? – that's a good idea.

I got so blind y'day that I can hardly write. Sunday is always pretty bloody here, & y'day was Totensonntag[55] which made it worse because everyone was conscientiously gloomy. Also it rained like blazes & was cold & miserable. I had arranged to meet Willi at 3.0 & we were both to meet Walfried at 8.0 – he had to go to a meeting of his Klub. And Willi did not turn up which made me raving with rage and gloomier than ever. So I went home & drank some cognac & three whole bottles of Weisswein [white wine] & at about 7.0 went to Leipzigerstr to meet Walfried. Was too early, so went to a pub in Manerstr where W. & I often go. Drank beer, came out, was sick all over Manerstr & staggered to the trysting place. There were my miraculous Walfried – the shortest of shorts & the openest of collars & Willi – the latter very apologetic; had been kept by his Eltern. We went to a café & drank & hailed a kleines [small] taxi & bribed the drive to allow 3 in it which is illegal – and drove to Savignyplatz & Walfried's knees were very fascinating. Bought wein & went home – there were *all* my landlady's family and I, swaying gently to & fro, explained that these were my Zöglinge, Schüler [pupils, students] come for an English lesson, while Walfried waved a bottle of wine & yelled for a corkscrew & Willi (14 ½ – looks 12) had reached the giggling stage. Then we drank wine & played unbelievable games & the English lesson was over & I went to Josef's round the corner (Schaurté) and danced with Frau Schaurté, and a whore & Josef himself. Then I roared in the Stadtbahn [light railway] to Friedrichstrasse & can't remember what happened there, but eventually arrived at the Kleist Casino which is one of The Places. Full of fairies & stockbrokers, and a very fairy-

[55] A German religious holiday in late November, commemorating the dead.

ish and beautiful young waiter (achtzehnjahrer [eighteen-year-old]) with whom I got on marvellously & he was incredibly fairy-ish and amusing till I murmured 'Ich habe kein geld [I have no money]' – and he faded away with the agility of any Oberon. {That is rather a good joke – waiters are always here addressed as 'Ober'}. Then I went to small pub on the way home & made peace in an avuncular way between two gentlemen who were trying to ring each other's necks. Reached home about halb fumf {Berliner = fünf} [half past four], and this morning am dying.

Until further notice please write bei Flu Browne Grolmanstrasse 4, Bln-Chtbg, as I leave Savignyplatz this week & have not yet got a new address. Do *please* write fully about the Millardian Dinner in all details. What was the EGG BOY like; what time did you all go home & how? How did you find the Prospect of Whitby?[56] Please every detail.

I'm going to be sick.

x x x

I have been sick.

Ever
Michael

xi

12 mars 1929

Rue des Alpes 12
Genève

My dear Phyll & Boris: I have just eaten snails followed by Frankfort sausages, and feel very good; with ½ liter of white wine on the table & ½ inside me. Last time I ate snails I had pigs' feet to follow: also very good. But neither of my snails

---

[56] The Prospect of Whitby was an old pub in Wapping, and presumably where the Millardian Dinner was held.

here had the flavor quite of yours. Have you got a small black pan with 12 delightful indentations, for cooking & serving 12 delightful snails? Would you like one? Tonight my snails cost 1 fr. 60; the Frankforts with pot. salad 1.80. = 3.40. I might have had the diner, vin compris 3.50, but the menu was horrible. To eat cheaply one must sacrifice quantity for quality - and it is terribly difficult here to find a cheap place where one is allowed to choose one or two pleasant dishes; in most of the cheap restaurants they thrust a horrible menu at you which always includes either beef or veal. I have been trying to eat for 2.50-3 fr, being considerably broke till the 20th, but it is impossible.

I walked to Annemasse on Sunday for lunch, and ate quite pleasantly at the Café du Commerce for 14 fr (French) which included an extra ½ litre, so that was very cheap. It is out of the question to live there or anywhere in France: (a) it is too far away & (b) in France I would have to pay income tax, but here I am diplomatically immuned. I get a marvelous diplomatic passport which takes me anywhere, and makes the customs bare their heads & the police flinch!!

Rue des Alpes 12 is my address: a quite pleasant room, utterly clean for 40 fr a mouth which is very reasonable. Owned by a charming old couple who keep a tabac underneath & supply one with my monter leger: I smoke nothing else & look forward to sending you some. *Don't* send any sausages yet: there's nobody to cook them & I must look round a bit before I go camping. I hope to walk this weekend, but don't know where yet. But if you send the book I will fill it with monter leger.

The work[57] is incredible: leisurely, comfortable, every kind of convenience & courtesy: an enormous building built specially for the Office with every kind of modern comfort producing contrivance. Hours slack, plenty of time for lunch, and more mid-afternoon at tea-time. Everybody charming & so on. BUT, my God, the smugness, & respectability & bourgeoisie of the place & of the whole town. You know it: how I shall survive the tedium I

[57] Work just begun as a "Proof Reader" at the International Labour Office, an agency of the League of Nations in Geneva.

don't know. And apparently the conduct of the League people outside the Office is noted by the Heads. Recently I understand a man was sacked on some minor technical point: really because he was known to go whoring!

At present my spirits are not too horribly low because of the incredible sunshine & warmth, and I look forward to bathing &c. But what of the winter?

In my room at the office (central heating, sun blinds, telephone on each table, armchairs cushioned &c &c) there are a Frenchman, a German, a Swiss & an Englander). The last is terribly common, & collects stamps & books on cricket: of these he has over a 1000 volumes, so if you have any cricket incunables here's a market!

They've given me 40 fr. expenses for the journey, & as I only spent about 100 fr (French) in Paris & nothing anywhere else I've not done too badly.

About Easter: I get Friday, Sat: Sunday, & Monday: I could be in Dijon early Friday morning, but would have to be back here on Monday night. The trouble is I don't know what I can afford. I don't know how much I get on the 20th (which must last me a month) & I don't know how much the fare would be. Anyhow if it works out that I am rich I shall come & if possible send you something. Also how much would one want (French money) to 'live' during that time? Let me know what your ideas on the matter are.

This town teems with s.bs, mostly very decorative – but never a glimmer; however – exercising extreme caution – we shall see.

The chief material difficulty here seems to be the problem of getting a bath. Every time I have one it costs about 4 francs: soap extra, towels extra tip for attendant, &c., and the privilege of sitting for a little in a little hot water 2.50! And in Berlin or London 3d for unlimited time in unlimited hot water plus swimming belt plus s.bs. Really!

And this stinking hole has no water swimming bath. It is scandalous.

Also there is great economy in the provision of pissoirs, but those I have found are inscribed with very peculiar things so apparently all the Genèvois do not die quite innocent. But I think that most do. As you know the quartier reservé is abolished, but there is considerably nocturnal movement to be observed round my street.

I hope you had some tea on Sunday: I thought of you reading the N. of the W. in bed as I was going to Annemasse.

I want to say things about letting me live in your house all that time, but I can't – but here's to you!

I have no news: and nothing ever will happen here, I believe.

Where is your house, Boris? I want to look at it.

I shall devote the rest of my life to THE HEALTH

Ever

Michael

Did you & Maude & Roman get postcards from Paris? I can't remember posting them.

xii

17 mars 1929

Rue des Alpes 12

[…] I have decided that this place is the most horrible place on earth. The Bureau and the work I even mildly enjoy; the town drives me mad with boredom. The only thing to do is to sit about in cafés & get mildly muzzy (or sometimes blind, as last night). […]

If I have had one or two I sometimes go to the Café de Tonneau, a lowish pub kept by an incredible old Italian female who looks like one of the Medici, is enormously fat, has a misshapen body & legs of different sizes, a husband who is generally logged; she plays a mandoline terribly badly & sings Italian songs in a deep & voluminous bass. She has also a superb s.b. of about 12 who sits about all night. Also an s. g. of about 14 who plays the piano stolidly & looks completely Chinese, with a squint. There is also a young waitress with a face like a black haired Gish[58] girl who seems to think it might be profitable to sleep with me. Last night at 1.0 a.m. there were 3 s.bs in there, and the s.g. There was the s.b. belonging to the place; another (about 14) who with his pa and ma sat watching a drunken man mucking about a drunken woman; and a German-speaking baker's apprentice (very ugly) who told me about his girl.

But the chief attraction is the Café de l'Europe, a second-rate brasserie. There is there a miracle of an s.b. 15 or 16 who flirts outrageously with me across the café & keeps blowing kisses at me from the kitchen door, while he polishes glasses. It all started with an exchanged wink the other evening, but what it will yield I don't know. If things went well I might without difficulty drop into love. But so far I've hardly exchanged a word: but there is lots of time.

The Code Pénal is being revised: see cutting enclosed. Finally the age was fixed at 16, but article 169 was sent back to the committee for further report.

If we meet at Easter I shall try to bring large numbers of Montheys[59] with me.

love
Michael

xiii

BRASSERIE BERNOISE - GENÈVE
[printed description omitted]

Genève, le 20 avril 9.0 pm [1929]

[...] The last week has been mostly given up to the most outrageous blinding and Midgin'. On Sunday evening last I met, as arranged, the man from the Bureau: he is 32, a Jersey-

[58] Lillian Gish was then a prominent American actress.
[59] A brand of cigar.

man by birth, speaks French like an aboriginal, blinds *terrifically*, is completely comme-ça, has a horrible reputation at the Bureau & in Genève for general debauchery (tho' not (yet) for *that*), has been here 5 or 6 years. He took me that evening to all the really vicious & low cafés which are infested with thieves, murderers, blackmailers, souteneurs [pimps], s.bs of a certain kind, dope-merchants – and of course mere drunkards. We roared & screamed and eventually I took home an achtzehnjährige [eighteen-year-old] (from Lyons) who turned out thoroughly charming. This continued more or less (I mean the nocturnal blinding) until on Thursday we got so completely logged that I remember *nothing* until I woke up at home with a damaged leg, no money, my cheque book gone, and also an envelope with my name & address, containing most of Walfried's (Lettland) photographs, his letters, and the drawing of the 50-year-old German soldiers [?] undergoing medical examination. The Banks here never dream of scrutinizing a signature; they pay all cheques indiscriminately it seems, so probably the gentleman who saw me to my house will write my name on a cheque & receive many of my precious francs! Also my landlady was furious & said I made such a din that I must have woken the whole street up: it was lucky the monsieurs were kind enough to bring me home! I didn't know they had: but it explains the loss of my belongings.

Today the achtzehnjährige came for a couple of hours in the afternoon, and tomorrow he brings an s.b. three years newer. But I must get a flat at once. Life is too dangerous at present.

[...]

Sunday

He was unable to bring a newer specimen of Geneviève s.b. All to the good no doubt.

Hope the fungi arrive safely.

Grüss [Greetings] to everybody & all love to 20 Bury Street.

Michael

xiv

[Reverse of postcard postmarked Geneva 27 June 1929]

beloved people I am not yet im Gefängniss [in prison], but it might occur at any time. I will write at prodigious length the moment I get a few minutes free between love affairs. Forgive so lamentable delay. Has been much work, much bathing, much beer, and much love. Wish oh wish I were in London. *The* Camera is in full Action. Immer treu, Michael	B. de Chroustchoff Esq. 20 Bury Street Bloomsbury London, W.C.1 Angleterre

xv

CAFÉ-RESTAURANT DE LA MARNE
G. CARUGATI
GENÈVE
10, RUE DES PAQUIS

le[60] 27. 7. 29.

Darlingest Phyll & Boris: My neglect of you has gnawed at my liver daily ever since it began. It is the fault of the heat, the bathing (thrice a day in the insipid lake), and a very intense and distressingly *pure* amour. Also I struggle every month to send to you the 100 french francs I still owe you. But I am 400 swiss francs overdrawn, and every pay-day monthly I seem to spend

[60] A printed letter-heading down to this point.

in paying debts: I eat once a day in a workmen's café: I walk in the snobby streets of this loathsome parish of English-speaking aunts and civil-servants in the clothes of a Speckjäger [vagrant]. – no socks, no coat (how shocked you would be!) and the rest of my sous I spend on toy boats, trains, ice-creams, food, bathing expeditions up the lake, oddments of clothes and adornments, animals and chocolate for Victor Tullio Lapertose, Aet: 14.11, born in southernmost Italy with the perfectest face & figure that that fact can suggest, – hair the colour of cooked crayfishes, vast cat's eyes of greens and yellows like Russian cucumbers and pickled onions in aspic, skin the colour of a Cornish pastie and the texture of mushrooms, shoulders and limbs, emotionally speaking, like a shoulder of the exquisitest Home-Killed lamb; and with it all the most fascinating vitality and general lachendes leben[61] combined with affection that can be conceived. Also a most tantalising natural innocence. We spend every free moment together and he is amazingly content with my company. But I am amazingly successful at being violently active, at playing with trains (I love them) and at generally playing the gosse [kid]. In public life he's a butcher's boy: in private life one of the earlier gods – in fact eagles constantly hover round him.

Occasionally I go out and get blind. Last week I went out with a man in the Office (who knows Nina at the Dome and at Kleinfeldt's) and his wife of great girth and a female who had expressed a wish to get drunk with him & me. So we made her drunk, which took the form of getting gloomier and dismaller through the night till finally she was sick all over a café. We finished up by having a bagarre [fight] at Maxim's (a horrible 'lady-whore' dance place) because I danced in my blue-shirt and no tie or coat: blood, police and general upheaval.

I used to get drunk a lot before the arrival of Tullio, and finally had an awful row (quite justified) with my landlady because I took drunken and abominable youths home. So I fouted le camp pretty rapidly and took a horrible and expensive

---

61 "Lachendes Leben" means "laughing life" and was also, perhaps not coincidentally, the name of a monthly German nudist magazine which Davidson would surely have known of due to his involvement with nudism in Berlin the preceding year.

flat, where at any rate I am free, & put in essential furniture of loathsome quality at vat price on the hire purchase system.

If it were not for Tullio I should have been away from here long ago: never have I experienced such a horribly constipated town: the citizens have minds even flatter than their faces: the only outstanding thing about them is their navels. And what can you think of a confraternity that says 'Adieu' when they meet you, and 'Salut' when they say goodbye? I have come across one or two pleasant German-Swiss lads, one of whom I have occasionally and pay for his French lessons.

The other morning I arrived at the Office at 9.10 to be told that someone had telephoned to me, giving the name & style of the Grand Duke Boris Petrovitch or Detrovitch or Metrovitch. Knowing no grand dukes at all I wondered, but rather hopelessly, whether *you* could have rung me up from somewhere - perhaps France or Museum Street - God knows where you are now - perhaps you two walking in France, doing together the marvellous adorable simple things we did round Dijon at Easter. I have lived largely since then on those lovely days - and on the memory of the food we ate. D'you remember our Seat-pit?

I may, in November, go to Tunisia for a month, to indulge in an Arab or two: why not meet me in Marseille? I've got to take a holiday, though I shall have no money therefor - but the Banque Fédérale will have to finance that.

Next year I shall have to go to Berlin, and also I hope to bring Tullio to London for a week or two. One more year here after that and then I shall fout le camp, and come back to London for a bit.

Please oh please send me a Red-Green-and-Black Book, telling me all your news and that of everybody concerned with us: Do Irving & Jonny live in Paris, Bushey or Bury Street? How is Back? And above all how are you two, and where and why? And for *my* sake write so schnell als möglich [as soon as possible].

Genève is in a ferment because AL JOLSON in THE JAZZ SINGER is coming next month in the film Sonore!!!!!! *Now* d'you understand?

adieu

me Dr. Alfred Vincent 21
Genève (or always) B. I. T. e (enough)
Genève

xvi

18 January [1930, Geneva]

My dear Phyll & Boris:

[…]

I have been back here a fortnight. Since then I have been into no Kneipe [bar], have drunk nothing: all energies are concentrating upon paying debts and saving what is left from the ruin for next April or May when I shall bring Walfried to England for 2 or 3 weeks. Just now I am at home and am drinking red wine at 1.20 a litre and after a fortnight's teetotalisation the effect is rather pleasant. […]

You have never seen me in love, have you. Only in a quite gaga state of fleshly excitement. But now I am really entirely in that condition of emotional dither that is being in love. I have only one thought, one image, one longing. Everything else me dit rien [means nothing to me] and ist mir Wurst [I do not care]. But I will not bore you with all that. You will I hope see after Easter.

What are your plans for Easter? I would give everything to meet you again in France, but money – lack of it – forces me only to Berlin there to collect Walfried & then to England. You must be there when we come which will probably be in the beginning of May. I plan that we – yourselves, he & I, – will walk weekends in the country.

He is, by the way, a sadist – he's only 16 but knows all the technical terms – & goes mad to beat me & subject me to agonies, besides all *sorts* of humiliations! – but please don't utter this to the Plough n. s. w.

He is utterly marvellous: and the loyalist, truest, utterest, thing I've ever known.

It's quite possible I shall get the sack *before* April. My official reports (about work) have been marvellously good, but last summer sinister rumours were circulated (about me & Edmond); I got anonymous notes and horrid things like that (nothing *official*, but disturbing). Then my immediate chief went suddenly raving, screaming mad (he did it suddenly one day in the office all round me & I had more or less to deal with him: this was October). As I was the last person he saw there, he went to a lunatic asylum roaring that *I* (me) was the cause of all the trouble (we had actually been very good friends always). Just before he was led away he telephoned to tell me that I was "the dirtiest dog he had ever known, & he would like to see me at the bottom of the river." Nobody had ever said that to me before. And apparently (he is still *inside*) he roared this about so much that various friends of his chose to circulate a rumour that *I* (me) had deliberately and with malice aforethought caused the gentleman to go mad. [...]

You cannot conceive how good our walk in Kalkberge was. Such utter, bitter, white weather; marvellous caves; marvellous sleeps, and one or two incredible roars. They are probably still talking about our sojourn there. The stories we told some of the people in some Kneipes [bars]. (He has an agile tongue). He was aus Riga; I aus London. We told adventures that had occurred to us in all the corners of Europe, and the villagers gaped in wonder.

Berlin is amazing. Theatres, cinemas, zum Beispiel [for example]. One play we went to was about a school: in the second act a man starts literally to *have* a lad: the lights go out in time. In the 3rd act the headmaster says to a junior master (the hero) 'Sind Sie Homosexual?' Dramatic pause – 'Ja!' says the hero sharply.

And the audience was a packed one consisting of Berlinische Hausfrauen & their respectable families.

Then we went to a film called "Zwischen Vierzehn u. Siebzehn – Die Sexualnot unserer Jugend [Between Fourteen and Seventeen – The Sexual Plight of our Youth]" in which a 16 yr-old had a 15 yr-old Mädel: and later one saw a close-up of the damsel's face, writhing in agony, while she was undergoing an illegal operation!

The red wine is making me so agreeably blind.

But it is nearly at its end & I think I shall go out to a Kneipe which is *so bad*! [...]

love

Michael

xvii

Bavaria
Die Völkerbunds Kneipe La Brasserie de la S. D. N.
Renommé pour ses excellentes bières et ses spécialités
49, Rue du Rhône
et en face du Jardi Anglais
A. Neiger, prop.

Genève[62] [(about May) 1930]

Dear Boris: Weeks ago I got from you with immense joy two terribly funny letters: one from the Royal – do you remember? Phyll was at Worthing: what an odd place to go to. I shall show them to you one day.

I am now in this horrible pub drinking beer – the *first* for exactly a fortnight. It seems to taste rather nasty, and to swell uncomfortably the stomach. Since I gave up drinking (!) I am so *well* and *young* – unbelievable, – but tomorrow I must go out on what promises to be an enormous blind, so I thought I'd better try this evening to see what happens when one drinks alcohol.

Just before Easter I got a note from Irving thus: "Dr. M.: About a year and a half ago, I sent you £5 to Berlin. I did not say anything about it, because I thought when you were in a position to do so you would pay it back. Will you send it before Easter as I am very hard up -----" Of course I haven't got £5 and haven't yet answered. I shall send it whenever I can. At present I'm still paying off £50 to my mother & never have a penny. This year I can't come to England; no money. Nor can I go to Germany in summer for the same reason. So in the middle of July I mean to go to Tunis, to lie about among the Arablings indolently. Might even smoke a little φικ[63]. That about which I told you was brought from Algiers by a man I don't like: he wouldn't give me any so I stole some, and had a most astonishing evening. In Algiers he paid about 7.50 french francs for about ½ a pound of it! I am still awaiting your *Christmas* catalogue with excitement.

---

[62] Printed letter-heading down to this point.

[63] *kif* spelt backwards in Greek letters.

Why do you not send me one? Surely it is *out*? I *do* hope the shop is working well. Should love to hear about it. Of course here nothing ever happens. I live an eventless, chaste, sober, intensely boring life: and only am waiting to pay my debts to loslaufen [run off], and to become a Speckjäger [vagrant] in Germany.

Will you do me an immense favour, one that will involve enormous effort, and make you thoroughly angry? – In your writing desk in the Gods' room at Bury Street, is a typed story for a girls' paper about some s.bs. bathing in the Regents' Canal. Do you remember? If you could discover it and send it to me *in an envelope* I should be most frightfully grateful. I want to *adapt* it to something I am doing. I am sorry to bother you for this, and will forgive you if you fail to send it, but hope a lot that you will send it. Do you like the talkies? I have seen only two in my life – both German: one very good, the other rather stupid. I have nothing to say: but I wish we were drinking beer together – or walking down Commercial Road, E., or having tea on your bed at 10 a.m. on Sunday in Bury Street. How is The Back?

All love to you both –

Michael

2. Letter to Charles Elwell 1952

Charles John Lister Elwell (1919-2008) was, together with his wife Ann, an M.I.5 counter-intelligence agent, and served in Security Intelligence Far East from 1950 to 1955 in Singapore, where Davidson had stayed several times as a journalist in the three years preceding this letter. Security Intelligence Far East was at the time maintaining a file on Davidson as a suspected communist,[64] which may well have affected his relationship with Elwell in ways he was unaware of.

xviii

To Charles Elwell Esq, Office of the Commissioner-General for South-East Asia, Phoenix Park, Singapore.

c/o H.S. Cuttajar
CORFU
Greece

9 August 1952

My dear Charles,

No sooner had I written this address, than a savage Greek insect stung me on the breast. I thought I had left unprovoked terrorism behind; though people seem to get murdered here on the flimsiest grounds - little matters of a girl's virginity, and things like that.

Here I am in a tiny cottage looking across the Ionian Sea to the Albanian hills; I sit under a vine; great tumescent figs ripen within my reach; my almond tree has but to be shaked and almonds tumble; ancient olives give me shade. I drink masses of rough wine (or retsina from the mainland) and live on eggs and olive oil. Just below there's a tiny beach where I bathe. Now just

[64] [British} National Archives KV2/2976 219a.

think about all that as you stew in Phoenix Park compiling a report on Bestiality among the Annamites and its Significance in Relation to the Directive issued by the Far Eastern Cominform in 1899. The people of Corfu are charming, friendly, helpful and – to some extent – honest. The people of Athens were revolting, ugly, ill-mannered, rapacious, unfriendly, horrid and unclean. I LOATHED Athens, and fled at the first possible moment. Unfortunately the Mountbattens chose to arrive at the same moment as I; so the Embassy was submerged and of course I could not see the Peakes,[65] but your charming sister, who was kindness itself and so ridiculously like you to look at, as I told her, forgave me for bothering her (I hope) and forgave me too about the letters (of which there's been one so far – a charming one, utterly unexpected, from Malcolm MacD.,[66] which took a fortnight to come having, by the postmarks, hung around Athens for one whole week. Greece is just about as competent as most exquisite women). By the same post came a delightful letter from Lady Peake: she may be passing this way next month which will be fun, and expects to reach England about the time you and Anne do. She says: "Judging from his letters Charles certainly had very little affection for Singapore and I am glad that they are leaving the Far East – he is altogether too much of a Nordic for that climate and too much of an – Elwell? – for that society." Her letter took a mere four days (it's an hour's flight from Athens). So it is improbable that this note, will reach you before you leave for The Dear Old Country. But don't stay there too long; come and be Charge d'Affaires in Corfu: there are 2,000 subjects of Her Majesty here – of Maltese origin – and they are mad with rage because the F.O. closed down the consulate here about 18 months ago for "reasons of economy". Good patriotic Britons denied the protection of their own Sovereign by the parsimony of a callous, effete administration: the consulate here abolished

---

65 Sir Charles Peake was then the British ambassador to Greece. Earl Mountbatten of Burma visited Athens in July 1952, as Commander in Chief Mediterranean.

66 Malcolm MacDonald, several times mentioned in *The World, The Flesh and Myself*, was then based in Singapore where, as Commissioner General for South-East Asia, he was laying the foundations of the future State of Malaya.

so that gilded youths of the Foreign Office may dine their girls at the Sea View. That gives you something to work on.

I've got a spare room in my cottage, if you come this way. My book is going apace.

All possible wishes to you both; & thank --[illegible] being in Singapore.

Yours

Michael

3. Letter from Joseph Anthony, 1958

Joseph Anthony, a Maronite Cypriot, was described by Davidson in The World, The Flesh and Myself *as having lived with him in Cyprus for nearly three years, 1954-57, aged fifteen to nearly eighteen, "when I helped him into a career in England in which he immediately did brilliantly." It is evident from his first letter to Davidson, sent from Marlborough, Wiltshire on 14 June 1957, that that career was in the Royal Artillery. Apparently some letters are lost. Four survive, of which the following is the last, undated but sent in 1958 from where he was then serving, near Münster in Germany. All four letters end with the words "I kiss you" above a sketch of lips.*

xix

2347650 GNR ANTHONY.J.
38 Fld BTY 40 Fld Regt R.A
B.F.P.O. 17

My dearest Michael. You don't realise how happy I was to-day, when I got your lovely lovely lovely letter where I was waitting for so long. I knew that I was going to get it because I know you and when you I ask something where I want from my FATHER, but really want, He always helping me. For 4-5 months now I was waitting for your lovely letter, and I knew that something wrong with the post or anything else was going on. I was very happy because you were alright and you didn't change to me at all. This morning when I came for dinner I found your letter on my bed. When I oppened it and seen that it was from you I start jumping on my bed, laughing, and crying. I was very very happy, at last God gave me what I was asking Him for months.

I was thinking back the wonderful time where we had living together and my eyes filled of tears and I was giving everything to live that life again. Something telling me that we shall live again together but somebody else will live with us as well, and we shall have very good time again. This where I am asking our father.

I wish you all the best and God help you to finish your work where you are living and make you happy.

[Three pages here omitted describe what he has been doing, serving in the British Royal Artillery in Germany]

Well dear Michael thank you again for writting to me and please answer me and tell me your news. I shall write you more about me later. Thank you for always remember my birth day it's means that you think of me.

Dear Michael please write back.

Always the little Joseph
to you.

I kiss you
[ink sketch of lips]

Joseph

xxxxx

4. Letters from Eikichi Suzuki, 1960

Eikichi Suzuki was a boy loved by Michael Davidson while he was a reporter for The Observer *in Tokyo 1950-51, and is described in both his memoirs. Writing in* The World, The Flesh and Myself, *soon after they remet in 1961, Davidson said of him: "Of all the loves I've had, his has lasted longest; of all the boys I've loved, he, more than any, was the 'divine friend, much desired' – the perfect one. He was 15 when I met him in the Hibiya gardens in Tokyo; today, at 26, his affection is as perfect as ever; and mine for him, though changed in structure, is unalterable in strength." Five letters are preserved, dated 1960-61. Davidson quoted from the first two in* The World.

xx

My Dear Michael

You must be surprise to received letter from stranger? I'm afraid you must forget me completely aren't you? I'm one of Japanese, about nine or ten years ago. When you were in Japan I met you at Hibiya park and since then we were always together. You came every day for lunch and Dinner to my house. Now you remember me? I do hope you are!! and I was stay with you every day and night. First we were hotel then you found some house in Satagaya.

How are you Michael? since you left Japan I sent several letter and some parcel for you but, some unknown reason There wasn't any reply to me, so I wondered whether you are lived or not. of course I sent them to Observer which you were had your work. I was so very sorry that's time. I was hard to live alone I thought I'm going to mad? You can't imagine how I was mist you so.

Do you know, Why I'm writting to you now. because I had job of cause driving a car for "The Times" London I have been there about six and half years now. And some time ago my employer asked me that whether I had work for British people so I told him I had my nice English man before but unfortunately he has gone back to England and I don't know where he is now? So he felt very sorry for me that he helped me to find out of your address for me. he is very nice man also. he wrote letter to Observer and some others certainly he wrote letter three or four times. So I was very grateful to him.

If you even got this letter please reply to me soon as possible. I'll be most grateful if you can. I always happy to receive from you.

Yours truly

Michael (My Christine name) Eikichi Suzuki

P.S. Now I'm Christine so my name is Michael of course from yours.

xxi

26th May 1960

My Fatherly Michael

I must say that 23rd of May is one of happiest day in my life, because I received your letter. You do not realize that how I happy to hear from you. Frankly I did not expected to have reply so soon because I had awful travel to find your address. First I asked Mr. Hargrove (who is my employer) write letter to "The Observer" editor they said you left there long time ago, and they told me that, if you Ask Mr. …? (Oh I must forgotten) who was in the Africa last year you must know him, who also had injured that awful earthquake then he wrote again to him we got your address at last. so it was not very easy. any way that's all passed now. I can not tell you how happy.

On the other hand, you remember me very well. I was not very nice to say that wether you remember or not. You must offended aren't you? Will you please forgive me.

Since you left Japan, I felt very lonly and sorrow then I became very norty boy but I have grown now.

My family are all well, especially young brother who is attending high school, and we still have resturant downstairs, but bigger than that time. I told my mother that I got letter from you, she was so surprise and she also she is so pleased. My mother always asked me what was happen to Michael-San. almost every day. When she ask me that I was hard to explane to her and I felt very sad which I couldn't say anything to her. but now I got letter from you so easy to explane.

My Dear Papa (you do not mine to call you?) my family are very anxious to see you, especially I want to. I might able to come to England? I'm sending photograph which with my motorcycle but this motorcycle is second one. I bought one last November exactly same one but unfortunately I had stolen by somebody at that time I thought I'm gone to completely mad. Just three month after I got it, then my employer help me to buy again, I'm quite crazy about motorcycles. I'm useing every morning and evening.

[Presumably the page ending the letter is lost]

xxii

Mon père. I hope your health are better. You must have been very hard time after 1951 but, are you still travel your chest? Oh I wish I can look after you. it will be very nice isn't it?

My employer suppose to leave Japan very soon. it not very definitely. but, he told me in six months he will be. I have been to "The Times" almost six years now. he said if you want come with me to Germany you can. but I do not want to stay with him anymore. then I told him if I can go to United States in stead. unfortunately bit difficult in to U.S. it not possible but only six month. I thought only six month to on broad that rather not to go. because his sister married with an American who leaving in Washington he said that his sister wants me to came her her house 30 $ a week. I didn't reply yet. but now I found you that I want to go to England. suppose if I paid my travel expenses, Do you think you can find job for me?

if it's possible, will be splendid isn't it? didn't I ask you to take me with you but this visa made us not to wasn't it? at that time we were still not peace treatment[67] that why but now, seems quite easy to go except U.S. I know lot of people in Embassy. of cause my employer help me if I ask him. if you think about this matter I should be very grateful to you. Nothing worry about money. I have been very good boy. I save money quite lot. ...

I wont write more and more but I'll write to you again.

If you make me happy that please write to me as soon as possible. I can almost read by heart that letter from you.

Thousand kisses and Much. much. much much much much much love to you.

From your son
Michael Jr.

P.S. will you please send me your photograph also. I'll be very pleased.

xxiii

17th July 1960

My Dearest Michael

Did you ever get my letter which I sent to you on last June? I suppose you were not? because I never receive your reply since then. Do you know how I get disappointment. I thought you don't like me any more. those sort of silly imagination make me so illitate. I use to be very patience but unfortunatly since I got this job getting worth and worth. My dear Michael, please write me a letter to me as soon as possible, and please do not let me drop. I'm waiting your letter about month. What was happen to you. I hope you are not ill again as you tell me before. It was very suffering for you. I'm also getting worry about you, so please please, a reply to me.

---

[67] The Treaty of San Francisco ending the war between Japan and the allies did not come into effect until 28 April 1952.

In Tokyo, getting hot and hoter especially this most uncomfortable dampness make me illitate me grote suffer. I was told by my employer that summer in Europe are much more comfortable than Japan, because, air are much much more dry.

I'm going to have my summer holiday week next about ten days, so I had a plan for trip on Hokkaido by my motorcycle it will be very nice? if road are good even more but, this is more hopeless. if you are in Japan, we could go together that's will be a vest, don't you think? Oh I wish you to be in Japan how about your holiday? You are already know lot of country almost around the world aren't you? You are lucky I hope you can understand that letter before, how I get miss you and lonely but I am seriously thought so please you too take seriously and also it my most desire. otherwise I wouldn't be happy. but I'm not insisting you so please do not think I'm forceting [?] you. but I hope I have one's desire fulfilled.

I'm sleeping in my employer's house because, they are having their holiday in Karuizawa. do you know this place call Karuizawa, in NAGANO prefecture. Now this place are very popular since Prince Akihito got marrage. reason why that they met in Karuizawa and played lot of tennis so they start love each other. of course very comfortable in summer air are dry and not so many people nice view of Mount Asama. I drove there just last night come back today by car. soon as get Tokyo weather was so different I found it while I'm driving.

My dearest Papa I hope I can see you soon? might end of this year? as I said again please write me as soon as you got this letter. Madly love and thousand kisses look forward to seeing you.

Your's son
Michael

The final brief letter in the archive from the younger "Michael", undated, was sent from an address in London after Davidson had telephoned, and was about their reunion planned for the coming Friday: the young man had somehow come to London with an employer. They apparently met up on 31st March 1961, as Davidson wrote to Boris de Chroustchoff on 6th April to say that last week he "got up to London to see my Japanese SB-that-was – after just ten years. All the sweetness and charm of before, and the same steady devotion."

5. Letters to Boris de Chroustchoff 1962-66

Davidson's old friend Boris De Chroustchoff, the recipient of his oldest surviving letters, had long disappeared from his life. Commenting on his life following his return to London in 1942, Davidson wrote: "Boris and Ida King, his sweet new wife, were remote in Wales". In October 1960, however, they suddenly reactivated their friendship, and thereafter maintained a massive correspondence until de Chroustchoff's death in 1969. During this time, Boris and Ida lived in a house called Woodcock in Oxfordshire.

Three letters to de Chroustchoff later than 1966 are presented in a later section of the correspondence.

The first letters quoted from here were sent from Taranto, where Davidson had settled down to write as soon as he received an advance from his publisher to finance his doing so.

xxiv

Albergo Vittoria,
via Cariati,
Taranto

28th July '61

Dear Boris,

[…] This isn't an awfully good place for salamini[68] – they don't really understand that they're good to eat: not a bit like Sicily, where they grow, so to speak, on every tree and are ranged along the sea-shore like the upstanding pommels of cacti; but I've found two quite agreeable specimens; aet: (as they say in the local dialect) xiii and xiv. The first isn't really quite mature – that *pelo* [hair] which, as you know, is a sign of ripeness is only just beginning to show in a few dark strands. The 2nd though is

[68] A *salamino* is a cyclindrical Italian salami, and Davidson's code word for a boy's penis, popping up frequently in the letters of both men in his later correspondence with de Chroustchoff.

very well developed and of excellent shape; flavour pleasantly acrid. A problem, though, is where to eat them; it's embarrassing taking a salamino back to one's hotel. But I'm really quite glad they're not easily obtained; if they were, my appetite would be so constantly whetted that I'd never do any work, which is the vital thing. [...]

XXV

Albergo Vittoria
Taranto

30th July 61

You dear kind people, all three of you:[69] [...]

Did I tell you my daily programme? Up at 6 sharp, and out to the bar round the corner for two cappuccino (that's breakfast); work till about 8, when to the sea to bathe. I do this from the rocks of the molo [pier] which is one of the arms of the mercantile port – alas, a totally moribund port, which is disappointing as I love shipping. Generally two or three boys are bathing too; and today one of them introduced me to an excellent salamino, real casalingo [homemade], & quindici anni [fifteen years old] when, they say, they're in their prime. A magnificent specimen, on which I feasted my eyes in anticipation of feasting in verità. [...]

[69] The three people addressed were Boris, his wife Ida and their fifteen-year-old daughter "Datila". To judge from two letters before and after this in which her father showed himself anxious to preserve Datila's sexual innocence, one presumes she was not expected to guess the double-entendre of the word *salamino*. Unsurprisingly, it did not work in the long term: on 4 September 1966, Boris wrote to Davidson: "Recently Ida found one of your more outspoken letters *to me* hidden away among Datila's clothes! One has to be very careful nowadays with her. [...] But how much does she know?"

xxvi

Albergo Vittoria,
via Cariati
Taranto (Puglia)
Italy

14th Aug. '61

My dear Boris,

[…] I've now got a *team*: rather like Corvo in Venice[70], I should think (I ought to write some *letters*): all coloured, with sun and sea, the brightest gold; and with features that show their lineage: a couple of pure Greeks (one with nose and brow in straight line, as one sees in some sculpture), a Saracen or two, some imperial Romans: Tonino, Aldo, Ninino, Dando, Mino, Gianni & c. […]

Tomorrow is ferragosto [The August festival] which means that everything will be shut (even my trattoria I think), and everywhere will be suffocated with huge families being screamed at by huge women with huge bosoms carrying huge bundles and baskets of provisions. I shall escape to my rocks and probably eat nothing but salamino. Talking about huge families, one of the punier hangers-on of my team has *25* brothers and sisters, all from the same mother. […]

xxvii

Albergo Vittoria,
via Cariati,
TARANTO,
Italy

[70] The writer Frederick William Rolfe (1860-1913), better known by his fictitious title of Baron Corvo, spent his last years indulging in liaisons with various teenage boys in Venice. His *Venice Letters* were about these boys and were written to another pederast to whom he offered to introduce them.

20th August 1961

Dear Boris,

I've just woken up to the fact, in considerable panic, that I shall be dead broke again in about a couple of weeks; one really can't live on less than a pound a day, and one always seems to be paying 50 or 100 lire to a purveyor of salamino, though I've cut those down to the two best, and sternly shoo off the others. [...]

xxviii

Albergo Vittoria, via Cariati
Taranto

21st Dec. '61

Dear Boris,

[...] I'm simply LONGING, dreaming night and day, to get away from this HORRIBLE place and these LOATHSOME people. I'm now having violent rows every day with my trattoria where the people have acquired a charming puppy which they torment unceasingly: they think it's a joke to pick it up by its tail or ears, swinging it until it shrieks; to kick it about like a football; hold its nose so it can't breathe; tease it to distraction when it wants to sleep; beat it when it wants to play. They overfeed it with fishheads & c (the English belief that dogs mustn't be given fish-bones seems to be unfounded – this one gobbles them!) and forget to give it water. I almost get apoplexy with anger. "Oh no", the filthy people say, "You mustn't be *kind* to a puppy, mustn't stroke it or make much of it – that makes it *soft*, makes a missie of it. You've got to treat it rough." Really, I can't describe to you how wholly base and boorish and vile and subhuman these Apulians are: I didn't know there *were* such barbarians; & I've seen a good many different sorts of the so-called human creature.

Alas, alas, I thought, as you say, that here at least I'd escape the horrors of the northern Christmas. But no: these imitative ignoramuses have allowed themselves to be tricked by their thieving men of commerce into believing that "Christmas" is *fun*: trees, tinsel, presents, festoons of festivity & c & c – and into tamely paying double or thereabouts the real price for *everything* in the shops. I'm simply dreading the next few days, and Christmas day especially: I shall have to go to my trattoria and join in their dreadful gaiety. What, indeed, would I give to spend it with you! [...]

xxix

Taranto, 1st April 62

Dear Boris,

I'm GIGANTICALLY grateful for your various letters, with fascinating cuttings, which I haven't lately had the courage (French sense) to answer; the last, containing requirements in ortaggi [vegetables], came last night; and at dawn this morning – a lovely warm April dawn exhaling the soft breath of summer – I hied me to the new town in search of seedsmen, but with doubt in my heart. You were bravely optimistic when you supposed that Taranto would have such merchants, who here know only about fish (price of). But I visited some half doz. flower-shops, with the result that I promptly posted you a pugnetta of packets: not one, I expect, what you wanted. Dark cabbage was the most difficult; it seems to be a "foreign" plant – "Tuscany? Oh, no, we wouldn't have anything from Tuscany here" – and regarded with suspicion; the only one I could track down appears to be of unknown origin. Ditto the only discoverable basilico; one of the chicories, I forget which, was guaranteed to be "Brindisi" but bore I think no marks of identification. I threw in one or two other things, like spinacci & peperone (probably won't grow in Oxfordshire) for luck. The postage cost just double the seeds (I sent it registered, because experience has shown that registered things get a privileged place in the slow postal caravan across Europe). But I do hope you'll have some success with them, and get some agreeable flavours from them, even if they're all the wrong kinds.

I haven't been able to bring myself to write, because had I done so I would have written nothing but MOAN, & that would have bored you to distraction. For weeks I've been in the lowest profundities of sag: not only because of the most agonisingly depressing weather – the WHOLE of March, snow and bitter winds; and because of recurring poverty and fear of more poverty; but especially because of two major calamities which fate has thrown at me with better aim than the Cyclops threw his rocks.

First, I got the news that that horrible old gargoyle Willie Maugham, aged 90, was publishing a "frank" autobiography[71] this coming June – the month mine was down for coming out; this after publicly vowing "for his daughter Liza's sake": formerly Pallavicini, now Ldy John Hope – that he would never do such a thing. But apparently his greed for money has got the better of his paternal sensibility. This news worried me terribly because, although our books won't clash – they'll be wholly different (& mine will probably be the better!) – his monstrous prestige and antiquity would be likely to awe the reviewers so much that, in their obsequiousness, they'd give him two columns and me two lines.

Next, because of this indecent and Maughamish intervention, my publisher decided to *postpone* my publication until the autumn – 28th September is now the date; thus losing me three whole months of fun and delaying for the same time any possible financial fruit.

Next, a couple of weeks ago, I was abruptly told that the paper-back payment, on which I'd been totally relying for getting rid of my debts and transferring me at least as far away as the Ionian coast of Calabria, wouldn't be "payable", under the contract between my publishers and the paper-back people, until paper-back publication: i.e., about 18 months or two years hence, when I shall plainly be dead.

The book is now being printed; proofs will be ready in May, when, armed with them, my agent can start selling American & European rights &c; but no returns from those scattered sources can reasonably be expected until July or August – leaving me with four or five months with no money whatever of any kind or from any quarter. Meanwhile, my publishers and agent write wonderful letters of enthusiasm not only about the literary and other qualities of my book but also about its probable *selling* potentialities – they apparently will be the ones who will reap

---

[71] *Looking Back* by W. Somerset Maugham.

the worldly benefits, not I.

I'm now trying to trying to raise a bank loan, to keep me for 3 or 4 months while I write another book, with if possible my rich and mingy brother underwriting it. But as my bank hasn't yet answered my preliminary inquiry and I haven't notion what my stuffy brother's answer will be, that's still very much in the air.

An earlier seat of intense pain was the necessity for cutting out some 35 or 40 thousand words of what I'd written – the publisher's "necessity", not mine. I expect the cutting has quite ruined the book – not really I don't: probably a lot of the cuts have tightened it up to its own benefit. But the loss of great deal is sad: especially a big slab of Millard which I had to dispense with, including the whole of the Blue Boar letter which I'd set out in full. (But I'll put it into my next book.)

You can imagine that after all these tribulations I've ceased to draw the slightest bit of pleasure from this beastly book; in fact, I'm hating the whole business, and the worry of it has made me constantly ill. I've had a whole series of indispositions, largely the result of the weather, but mostly I believe of a "psychosomatic" nature – I think that's the new-fangled word that's fashionable nowadays.

Well, that's enough about me. Today, this April Fool's day, the sunshine and the air are full of the hint of blessed summer; and I'm hoping that you too at Woodcock, dear Woodcock, are feeling the beneficent change. Your sudden cry for seeds suggests that you've a notion that Spring's round the corner. I shall think a lot of you working in the garden, and watching lovely things coming up and breaking into bud and putting on leaves; and carrying cans of water from the kitchen and spraying the good thirsty earth. What, I wonder, can you do about the moles? Such nice creatures: it'd be horrible, one feels, to massacre them with venom; but I suppose if given their head they can tunnel ruin through the garden?

Oh dear: it's such s such a lovely day – it really looks as if that Hexe, who's been flying her malicious course over my head as well as yours, had at last departed; but I don't like the appearance of this happening on April Fool's Day!

Violet Hunt? Vaguely that name seems familiar; but I can't pin it down. Was it a good book? Did you read, when it came out in

England excellently translated by Archibald Colquoun (how can one spell it?), a Sicilian novel by Giuseppe di Lampedusa? I think it's TREMENDOUSLY, ENORMOUSLY, HUGELY, good. Oh, it's called in English "The Leopard" – Il Gattopardo in the original.

By the by, if when you're next in Blackwell's or Parker's you ask to see the Arthur Barker spring list you'll find a blurb about my wretched book on p. 18.

If I can raise my bank loan – familiar with the sfortuna [bad luck] that dogs me I don't suppose I shall – I'm thinking of moving down the western coast of this Gulf into Calabria, to try out a place called Crotone, about half way as the train crawls between here & Reggio di Cal. It's where Pythagoras taught (as if that mattered), and it's whence a great number of champion chariot-drivers went to Olympia &c to win races (also doesn't seem important as far as I'm concerned); and it's now an ugly little modern town, with however a good little port and some wonderful beaches – and the Calabrian salamini are especially plentiful and of very high quality, as I found in Reggio three years ago. I shall, I feel, never be able to afford to reach Sicily – and anyway, Sicily is so dreadfully *crowded*: there's barely a bit of coast that isn't bagged by a hideous villa and a stabilimento balneare [bath-house], striped umbrellas & wireless machines and all. I don't suppose, though, I shall ever afford to get as far as Calabria.

Of course, another thing that's reduced me to pathological levels of depression is my inability to get out of Puglia. I feel constantly like SCREAMING, and lapse frequently into tears, I hate so violently this odious stretch of Adriatic earth and more still its brutally barbarian population. I walk about this horrible place muttering aloud obscene imprecations against these repulsive people, with their cozze [mussels]-laden bellies and fish-head mindlessness.

One of my standby items of diet has become an enjoyable ricotta – great curds, country made, one of the few agreeable things that these foul contadini [peasants] produce (besides, of course, their wine). And I've been taught that the way to skin a pip of garlic is to give it a sharp blow on the back of the head: the hide then almost falls off. And that *young* garlic isn't in pips at all, but a long root like a robust spring onion.

I'm wondering if the three pregnant cats have dropped their

litters yet; and how Datila can think of new names for them all as they multiply like recurring decimals. Poor Datila; on 27th Mar. you said her exams were on; I hope for her sake they're by now done with. I suppose you'll be going to Dol for Easter?

You've never told about Ida's birthday, and what you did.

love to Woodcock

Michael

XXX

viale Mario Nicoletta 38,
presso Barone,
CROTONE

29th May 62

Dear Woodcock,

[...] Robin M. wrote to me about his Maugham book.[72] What an extraordinary thing to do! Who on earth will read it? The dullest family, I'd say: petit-bourgeois solicitors & schoolmasters. He told me he couldn't get back further than 1764. Why in the world is he getting a lot publicity on account of it? – but of course trust him for getting himself publicity.

My regards to His Honour when he comes to stay; what does he drink – barleywater?[73] [...]

---

[72] Robin Maugham, 2nd Viscount Maugham (1916-81), often referred to in Davidson's correspondence simply as Robin, was a great though sometimes trying friend for the last thirty years of his life, and, like him, a writer attracted to male youth. *Somerset and All The Maughams*, his history of his family, was published in 1966. While it is true that some of Davidson's ancestry was classier than Maugham's, it has not really been traced back any further than Maugham's in the male line (see the appendix), and the criticism is anyway somewhat ironic since many readers find Davidson's lengthy description of his own family in his just-finished *The World, The Flesh and Myself* to be much its least interesting part.

[73] Maugham, who had succeeded his father as Viscount Maugham four years earlier and was usually a heavier drinker than Davidson, was going through a teetotaller phase.

xxxi

presso Mazzarese
FAVIGNANA (Trapani)
Italy

27.i.66

Dear Boris,

Here is a new address; & here I am ecstatically content (this awful January apart) on a magically lovely island with a magically lovely name – say it over to yourself a few times, to flavour its perfect beauty. D'you remember years ago writing to me the suggestion that I should try the Egadi islands? Well, I've tried them & found them to be a paradise, & peopled with angels. I pay *three pounds a month* for the Palazzo Michele – it is rather like living in a garage: two large bare compartments, but with well and bog and cortile. I have sparsely furnished it, and do my own cooking – I have excellent meat (a rarity in Sicily) because my boy-friend's father is a butcher. Next Sunday I am lunching with my boy-friend, his father & mother and six brothers & sisters: rather an alarming prospect.

[three paragraphs intervene that are of little interest]

This is but a hurried line to tell you that I am in the seventh heaven. The people are so nice here, nicer even than in Trapani, & have beautiful manners. [...] And the young are so beautiful, displaying a lot of Saracen influence.

love to Woodcock

M

xxxii

Michael Davidson
FAVIGNANA (Trapani),
Italy

17. ii. 66

Dear Boris,

It pleases me to know that this address above is all that's needed; the postman knows everybody, of course; - one doesn't need a letter-box - my house hasn't so much as a name & number - one simply meets the postman in the street.

Please thank Blobji[74], for whom my respect & affection are undimishing, for the Victim taken from his own august person & assure him it will be received with the greatest pleasure by Poseidon or Amphitrite or the Old Man of the Sea - whichever may grab it first. The sacrifice will be reverently offered, with libations, as soon as the present foul scirocco, which is cold and grey and wicked, has blown itself out; it would only blow Blobji's belly fluff back to the North again & I'm sure he wouldn't want that; I shall wait for a gentle & balmy tramontana which shall carry his offering fondly to the South.

At the moment the scirocco has brought a deluge of thunder of thunder-rain, and my roof is pouring water on to my paved floor - fortunately in places where no damage can be done. I have just had an excellent lunch of pasta al' burro followed by a kind of Bauernfrühstück [farmer's breakfast], sent me by the mother of my GrecoSaracen s. b. whose name is Luigi. For elevenses I had a taste of my usual salamino; it is one so exquisite in form & flavor that the memory of them linger on in the mind after each savouring until the next one. It seems to me quite extraordinary that I should find at the very end of my life one of the very best & choicest s.b.s I've ever known throughout it;

[74] Blobji was the de Chroustchoffs' marmalade cat.

indeed it's extraordinary that I should find one at all - let alone this superbly beautiful creature whose face & figure almost make me swoon when I see him naked, & whose nature is sweet & simple & frank. How is it possible, I have to ask myself, that any form & face, human or divine - even an un-ageing 15-year-old immortal - can be so supremely lovely?

On Sundays I lunch with the family: Tommaso, the father, good-natured, kind, loving to his family, bluff & blunt, a native of the island, an executioner in the communal slaughter-house & a chopper-up of tunny in the season; La Mamma, a sweettempered Pugliese by birth (from Lecce), ageing before her time, wrapped up in her children, showering kindnesses on me; a rather brooding, darkly-looking daughter of about 17; the dazzling Luigi, 15; & two piccolini of 6 & 4; femmine & masche. We have of course pasta & various forms of meat, mostly horrible; Sicilian meat is always tough - they say it's because they eat it too soon after killing; the only way I can devour it is by simmering it for hours - almost melting it away.

The backbone of the island is the limestone mountain, north & south, about 4 km long & very steep on all sides. It has 5 peaks or humps, the highest of which, 302 m, a proper peak, has a Charles quint castle on its topmost tip. I haven't been up there; it's too damned steep; but I've crossed over between the two northernmost humps, whence you get a wonderful view of Marettimo away to the west.

East & west of the mountain are two "wings" of level plain, made of solid tufa; the western is fairly ordinary & devoted to cattle pasture and some plough for grain; the eastern is a strange Cyclopian country of tortured & writhing tufa, with gigantic boulders balanced inexplicably on top of each other, or being hewn into vast arched gateways by heaven knows what forces. Vast areas of this eastern wing are pitted with extraordinary excavations which, in fact, are merely quarries where for centuries the stone has been cut out for building - miniature versions exactly of the famous latomie of Syracuse.

A certain S. Struppa, writing in 1877, lists these as flourishing: vine, fig, mulberry, apple, apricot, pomegranate, almond, pear, peach, orange, lemon, olive, carob, cactus, wheat, barley, maize, cotton, seakale, wild watermelon, rue, mushroom, black salsify, caper, asparagus, yew, saffron, chicory, hembane, hemlock. Of course there are unnumbered other plants, including the enclosed - which Luigi says is "menta"; or is it wild thyme?

There are plenty of snakes & toads but, says an old writer "benevolent Nature hasn't chosen to stain the soil of Favignana with the venomous slime of vipers".

Yes, the tunny fishing will be trying - & the *tonnara* is quite close to my house, just across the end of the harbour. I shall go & look at the "mattanza" once. Apparently it's not too bloody; from what I hear they "dry" them to death - assiugare - which sounds more cruel than ever.

The tunnery here & on Formica is centuries old. The Pallavicini of Genova bought the island & the tunnery in 1648; Florio, also of Genoa, is the present owner; I don't know whether he's the same Florio as he of Marsala.

So far there've been no foreigners at all but I'm told that "many" come in the summer - pray not too many. I think most must be day trippers for there's no-where for them to stay; there's a minute & horrible hotel (I've been inside only once) which holds about 10 people & could feed about a dozen - there isn't a trattoria on the whole island. (The Hotel Paradiso is on Levanzo)

I too would like to see Pantelleria; but it's eight hours by steamer from Trapani & in winter one never knows whether one's going to be able to land or to re-embark. And in the summer I should begrudge any time out of the sea & sun away from Luigi.

I wonder what Papà really thinks or suspects - or cares? He says blandly over lunch, of me & his son: "lo vuole bene Lei and therefore we want to be nice to you" – which means nothing less than "you love him".

I wonder how the Back visit went; is he becoming more irritable & obstinate & self-centred? Poor Jellink; I'm sorry about his Ball. Did you send him the appropriate Greek Epigram?

Love to all, love to Woodcock

M

6. Letters from John Davenport, 1962-63

John Lancelot Agard Bramhall Davenport (10 May 1908 – 27 June 1966) was a highly-regarded critic and book reviewer. He first wrote to Davidson in admiration of his book The World, The Flesh and Myself. *They very soon found they had much in common, though, as Davidson put it in a letter to Boris de Chroustchoff, "he is by no manner of means a woman-hating homo – he's had two wives and has four children and an assortment of concubines." A warm friendship sprung up, leading not only to their meeting, but to Davenport getting to know Davidson's greatest friends and his sister.*

Their frequent correspondence continued until at least a few months before Davenport's early death, but though all Davenport's letters are infused with his warm humanity and intelligence (an "entirely charming person as well as an extremely witty and highly amusing one", Davidson told de Chroustchoff), once they knew each other well, his letters inevitably tended to be taken up with daily news and other mundanities. Presented here are most of his early letters only. For the identity of some of the mutual friends referred to briefly in the first letter but who do not recur, the reader is referred to The World, The Flesh and Myself. *The footnotes about them here are restricted to shedding light on Davenport's comments on them.*

xxxiii

DUXFORD GRANGE
DUXFORD
CAMBRIDGESHIRE
FOWLMERE 292

6.xi.62

Dear Mr. Davidson,

I have just read *The World the Flesh & Myself* with the greatest admiration. So beautifully written, so absolutely straight. We seem to be opposites: myself a widower with four children, a Papist; but with so many friends in common, dead & alive. It is odd that we should never have met in any of the places, the many places, where our paths have crossed. I have edited literary reviews with Eden R. & Jack Lindsey; was a pupil of van Dieran's …. Well, perhaps we *did* meet, & you preferred not to repeat the experience. I am sure that Nina H. never committed suicide. She had broken her thigh previously & lacked balance.[75] Tommy Earp was an intimate friend. It was I who proposed him for that absurd Authors' Club. And Brian Howard, whose death you have described inaccurately (although not essentially misleadingly).[76] Mary Butts, John Rodker…. & Norman Douglas[77] I knew for most of my life & half his. Did he ever till you about his first boy (1904), whose wife later offered him (N.D.) their eldest son: 'Ecco, carissimo Signor Douglas: we have been keeping him for you.' This I have always felt justified Norman's tastes; & your own, although they are alien to myself. I was at Cambridge with Bill Empson, & was a close friend of Dylan's, whom you should have met *in Wales,* not in Soho.[78] And of course of Augustus John's, whose last letter was directed to me. Michael Richey sent me your book. Mamaine & Celia Paget I knew since they were children. James Cameron & I were friendly neighbours for years; Dick Wyndham was a cousin. All this is babble, but admiring babble. I was even taken by Hugh Kingsmill Lunn to see Millard when I was an undergraduate. Please accept a dull extrovert's handshake & admiration. I have asked the B.B.C. to let me review your book. Sincerely,

John Davenport

---

[75] Nina Hamnett (1890-1956) was an artist friend of Davidson, who fell to her death from the window of her upstairs flat. Davidson had also doubted the rumour it was suicide (*The World, The Flesh and Myself,* p. 142)

[76] Brian Howard (1905-58) was a poet friend of Davidson, who committed suicide not in Spain, as stated in *The World, The Flesh and Myself* (p. 208), but in France, as Davenport explained in his next letter.

[77] Norman Douglas (1868-1952) was a much-admired writer and a boy-lover, who had been a close friend of Davenport and visited by Davidson at his home in Capri. Generally henceforth described simply as "N.D.", he is one of the main subjects of Davenport's letters to Davidson, which are thus a valuable source for his life.

[78] Davidson knew and disliked the famous Welsh poet Dylan Thomas in Soho in the early 1940s. (*The World, The Flesh and Myself,* p. 208). By contrast, Davenport had been a close friend of his and co-wrote a novel with him.

What happened to Charles Ashleigh?[79] Wilfred Macartney knew him but has no information.

xxxiv

DUXFORD GRANGE
DUXFORD
CAMBRIDGESHIRE
FOWLMERE 292

19.xi.62

My Dear Davidson,

It was snowing when your letter arrived this morning. I was disputing a grilled kipper with three autocratic cats. Ten days ago I was in Tenerife, which I can heartily recommend for paupers like ourselves. At least I assume - hope - you're a pauper, too. The best climate I've come across; and like yourself I've tried a good many. One could I suppose become bored there, but if one is bored at 54 one deserves to pass on, as hospital nurses say.

Do you mind if I tick off some points you raise? (α) The BBC is inclined to hedge, but I hope to overcome this. It seemed to me that it might do more good than a written review. If they remain unimaginatively unresponsive there are other places - the Spectator for example.

The Observer have sent it off already, but I think to a good person. You will not misunderstand me when I say that it would be better for you to be reviewed by a fairly well known R.C. paterfamilias, however inadequately, than by a very well known, breathlessly enthusiastic homosexual. All too often, instead of being enthusiastic they are cagey. One doesn't want the book, *which is a very good book indeed,* praised, or chewed up, for what are after all irrelevant reasons. If you disagree say so: I am not

[79] The labour activist Charles Ashleigh (1892-1974) was described by Davidson as "one of my closest and kindest of friends" in *The World, The Flesh and Myself* (p. 143).

trying to be impertinent. What I mean is that the book is of value *to all of us,* not just to an esoteric group. I have a dread of group-whooping, with all the improper under- and overtones. I confess that when I was working in Hollywood (1936-39) I had my anti-Semitic moments! Not a pleasant thing to have to confess. Luckily I am a wretched hater….

β) I hope we can meet in the spring. My older daughter Natalie is living in Rome & I have promised to get there in May by hook or crook, & from there to Palermo is (from N.D's point of view) a short walk.

γ) Of course now I remember our meeting at Robin's.[80] The Bloomsbury meetings are hopelessly obfuscated in my memory. The area (not the company) always turns me into a despairing alcoholic. So many people I have seen through many glasses darkly.

δ) I'm so glad you liked the little preface to "Old Calabria".[81] I was supposed to write a biography, & that is the pathetic skeletal vestige of it. Still if has some useful *dates* – how he loved dates.! 1904 is the date of the affaire with the boy. The wife's offer took place in *1920,* when he was back in Italy.

ε) You are not precisely *wrong* about Brian's death, only it was in his house near Cannes, not during the disastrous Spanish sojourn. His father died, & BH inherited about £70,000, bought a house down there, & settled in with his mother & the young man Sam. Sam died (entirely by accident), Brian sent for John Banting, & took the pills the night he arrived, but not in such a magnificently Petronian way. Brian's tuberculosis was in any case incurable, but we all hoped he'd have a few happy years before he died.

ζ) Tommy Earp. What don't we all owe that man! I have some of his poems in MS., & endless letters.

η) Mamaine; & Celia, too; perfect, yes, but too VULNERABLE …

θ) I'm glad Ashleigh is still flourishing. I met him just after my first trip to America, & wrote to him about his book 'Rambling

---

[80] Presumably Robin Maugham, introduced in a footnote to letter xxix and referred to later in this correspondence as Robin.

[81] Davenport had written the introduction to the edition of Norman Douglas's 1915 book, *Old Calabria*, published by Secker and Warburg in 1956.

Kid', which Jim Tully had given me. I admired his courage, & he told the best prison stories I've ever heard; better even than W. Macartney's (whom I met long ago with my godfather, Compton MacKenzie.) The only thing that irked me about him was that whenever he borrowed money it was because he "just *had* to have a boy tonight." This I thought a gloomy approach.

ι) I often see Edgell, who now manages what used to be called The Bomb Shop (book shop in the Charing X Rd.) Pale, plump, diffident & fastidious as ever. He & Jonnie came down to Cambridge the other day.[82] I'll give them your message.

κ) How good to hear about Jimmie Cameron's autobiography. I haven't been in London much lately. As you probably know, he's just joined the Daily Herald. Lucky them!

λ) Don't apologize for typing. I should apologize for my handwriting, which was once that of a classical scholar & now looks like the wandering of an intoxicated beetle.

μ) Did you see anything of Archie Colquhoun this summer? He was a 'technical advisor' on the Lampedusa film. A dream job. Deserved, in his case.

I have now run through half the Greek alphabet & must stop. Thank you so much for writing. Your letter came at a good time for me.

Yours most sincerely,

John Davenport

XXXV

DUXFORD GRANGE
DUXFORD
CAMBRIDGESHIRE
FOWLMERE 292

---

[82] Edgell Rickword (1898-1952), a poet, communist intellectual and friend of Davidson from the days when his social circle met at The Plough in Bloomsbury in the 1920s, was mentioned thrice in *The World, The Flesh and Myself*, once with his wife Jonny.

26.xi.62

My dear Michael,

I quite agree with you: once the BBC start(s) hesitating it (they?) are likely to continue humming & hawing. I have written to the Spectator. I expect the Observer review is set up but 'held over' temporarily.[83] This has been happening a lot lately - pressure of space due to advertising, *etc.* The Wordsworth review is surprising. I know him well - a madly neurotic man who has been living as a poacher in the Welsh hills for years with a succession of other people's wives, the last one being Sarah Amberley, B. Russell's daughter in law. He is in his forties & quite indifferent to the snobberies of the London lit. scene. It's all very strange, as he is a brilliantly intelligent & *sympathetic* man; although off-balance, of course.[84] The Wordsworths are all melancholics or medical missionaries. Enough said. He - CW - got married once: 'I couldn't have made a greater mistake. It was George Gissing all over again."[85]

This money business is frightfully boring, isn't it? An exhausting - indeed almost totally debilitating - nightmare. I had plenty when young, nothing now! - better the other way round. Still, like the old whore in Hemingway's story, "I have my beautiful memories." But tell me, why is poverty supposed to be *stimulating?* What vulgarian started *that* canard? I suppose it would be true if one had started from scratch, so to speak; but that scarcely applies in our case. Thank God my children appear to be more pragmatic than their father: a common reaction of course. But it would be pleasant to be able to give money to one's friends

[83] The BBC was evidently uninterested in Davenport's proposal to review *The World, The Flesh and Myself*, mentioned in his previous letter. A review by him was published in *The Observer* on 9 December 1962.

[84] The journalist Christopher Wordsworth (1914-98) had just written a hostile review of *The World, The Flesh and Myself* in the *Guardian*. He had an adulterous affair with Susan (not Sarah) wife of Lord Amberley, the philosopher Bertrand Russell's son.

[85] The novelist George Gissing married a prostitute and went to prison in 1876 for stealing money from fellow students in order to keep her off the streets. She went on to become a hopeless alcoholic.

again: *not* loan it!!

The Dawkins book on N.D., described as a 'biography' by Penguin, is a timid little dissertation on some of his works, written under the pseudonym of MacGillivray.[86] The reason why I have never added to that preface is that Norman had really said all he had to a say about himself. All I unearthed was squalor: most depressing, I promise you. He let himself grow gross. Taking one's false teeth out in order to suck off a boy of 14 lacks Theocritan grace or charm. Something went wrong in the middle. This is interesting, but defies analysis; at any rate by me. In the preface I hint at the overstrong reaction – reaction from puritanism, I mean. Please don't think I'm a hopeless prig.

[…]

Yours ever J.D.

I'm glad you approve of "group-whoop": a word that belongs to you, as I invented it for your benefit.

xxxvi

[Plain postcard from John Davenport at the same address addressed to Signore Michael Davidson, Via Tunisi I, Palermo, Sicilia, and postmarked Palermo, 11-XII-62]

Dear Mike, I feel so ashamed of myself for having written such a lachrymose letter this morning. This is an apologetic p.s. Short, but not meant to be dismal, & containing two notes for your files. Hare you any files?

1) N.D. always said that Robin, born while the divorce proceedings were going on, was *not his* child, naming an Austrian cavalry officer. He loved poor old Archie, but not Robin, who is a

[86] Richard MacGillivray Dawkins originally published his *Norman Douglas* in 1933.

dreary business executive in Chicago.[87] When I met him on Capri he was having an affaire with his illegitimate daughter (married to a South African) in vain emulation of his putative papa's naughtiness.

2) Sylvia Gough was not Hugo Gough's daughter-in-law, but the wife of his cousin Wilfred. When I met her in Paris as schoolboy in 1926 she was one of the loveliest creatures imaginably. O quam mutate dum diddy dum diddy dum.

Love JD.

xxxvii

DUXFORD GRANGE
DUXFORD
CAMBRIDGESHIRE
FOWLMERE 292

Christmas Eve 1962

---

[87] Given that Davenport knew Norman Douglas well and is reporting what the latter told him, his information that he denied paternity of Robert "Robin" Sholto Douglas is a matter of considerable importance to understanding the elder Douglas's life, and one that was apparently not even suspected by Mark Holloway, author in 1976 of a fine biography of him that is widely considered definitive. Holloway reports that Robin was born on 20 August 1902 and that, according to his putative father's petition for divorce, his mother had had her adulterous affair with the Austrian Baron von Stengel (and miscarried his child) between February and May 1903, when she was living apart from her husband. Holloway further explained Norman's marked preference for his (undoubted) child Louis Archibald "Archie" Douglas (born in 1899) as partly because "Robin, who was born to parents who agreed to divorce before he was weaned, was a constant reminder to his father of those unhappy days." However, Holloway himself points out that the petition for divorce may not present a truthful account of what happened, so Davenport's account, implying that the adultery with Stengel began over a year earlier, seems to offer a more credible explanation of both the divorce and Norman Douglas's feelings for Robin. Davenport evidently did not think this information fit for public release, as he gave no hint of it in his description of Douglas's marriage and sons in his introduction to the 1956 edition of *Old Calabria.*

Dear Mike,

A delightful letter from Palermo to-day – once again 8 days in transit: too absurd. The enclosed bit of journalism[88] is not sent out of exhibitionism: it involves you in a rather curious way. It was written about a year ago as a BBC broadcast. It was published in the Listener, & then Harper's Bazaar in New York asked if they could re-print, & it was re-broadcast more than once. On one of these occasions Mike Richey[89] happened to be listening (at *breakfast* time!) & immediately wrote to me about your book. Not only wrote to me, but sent me a copy which was the one I eventually – after weeks of frustration – reviewed. Richey I had only met once, lunching with Robin & Terry Rattigan in Brighton. He is a true friend of yours, & I hope will become one of mine. I admire his generosity of spirit. He also knows when to produce a bottle of champagne; & he like myself is a papist. Many of my co-religionists are disagreeable, I fear: always in such a *temper!!*

So I thought you might like to have the first link in this chain, being yourself such a splendidly black sheep.

You are quite wrong about that review being only 10% right. I would say it was about 90% right. Had there been more space I *might* have made some criticisms, just for the sake of balance (like salt in oatmeal). Coleridge said that any bloody fool could see the faults in a book, but that it took a wise man to understand its virtues. I've always tried to be wise to that extent, even if a lamentable fool in most respects.

The melancholy is not due to bodily malfunctioning, except in so far that all illness is psychosomatic. It's a family failing. That's what the psychiatrists mean by en-dogenic: i.e. it is not brought on by external worries merely. It is not a gentle autumnal melancholy, which can be most agreeable, I agree. It is a state of total accidie – a sort of spiritual dysentery. In any case it has now lifted,

[88] Davenport's article "In praise of Black Sheep", which included an illuminating section on Norman Douglas, and was published in *Harper's Bazaar*, June 1962.

[89] Michael William Dugdale Mills Richey (1917-2009) was a sailing enthusiast and navigator who went on to become the oldest person to sail across the Atlantic on his own.

helped by children home for the holidays; and enormous quantities of rather bad wine; and the Brahms Crysander edition of Couperin. I ought to get married again. Five years of widowerhood is a little too long for an old-fashioned animal like me.

Yes: I *do* remember the exquisite Eileen Hawthorne - like a Hunter's gazette. She had a friend called Fry (what *was* her Christian name?) very tall, tubercular, with copper coloured heir and those pure *violet* eyes that go occasionally (not often enough) with that pale pigmentation. She died of tuberculosis. I once had the very great pleasure of making love to her in an open grave in Brompton cemetery. This tickled Norman's fancy, I remember. About poor old Archie Douglas there is awfully little to say. He is a great melancholy giant of a man who was in the Scots Guards in the 1914-18 (your) war, but who never recovered from shell shock. He was buried alive for 48 hours & suffered permanent damage. It was a great grief to his father. He lives with an American wife on Long Island. He's worth six of that little shit Robin, who, as far as I'm concerned, has no redeeming feature. Also, hopelessly americanized.

No, I don't drive about our concrete little island, but I do go to Oxford quite often to see my younger daughter Clare, who is in her 3rd year there - reading philosophy with Iris Murdoch. I should like very much indeed to see Boris de Chroustchoff[90] - a legendary figure. And the Hagues. We have friends in common. How I do rattle on. I do hope Arthur Barker[91] tries to shift the book. Am I right in thinking that he suffered so much in health as a result of being in a Japanese PoW camp that he has to winter abroad always? My impression is that he's in the south of France half the year, but I may be wrong. I don't know who else is in the firm. Let me know about this if you will.

Yours affectionately

J.D.

---

[90] This was quoted by Davidson in a letter to de Chroustchoff together with the admiring words about Davenport that have been quoted at the beginning of this section of the correspondence.

[91] The publisher of *The World, The Flesh and Myself.*

xxxviii

DUXFORD GRANGE
DUXFORD
CAMBRIDGESHIRE
FOWLMERE 292

4/1/63

Dear Michael.

Pencil & twitchy hand - writing not due to G.P.I. (I hope) but to British Railways. You letter arrived as I was leaving for a London weekend with young. Incidentally, it was written on Boxing Day (26 xii 62), & so made a record run - so far - of *nine* days. The soured (this looks like SACRED. Actually SOURED) menopausal spinsters are surpassing themselves.

Yes: my friend Peter Gunn has just got back from Naples & was appalled at the Teutonic jollifications. One is only pleased (and surprised) that they hadn't twigged earlier the commercial possibilities of the season, it's odd when you come to think of how long the Americans have been around; and how Easter has always been fun & fireworks & the Holy Ghost doing a high-wire act across every piazza in Italy. But these rather charmingly childish ingenuities were not co*mmercial* in intention. There was no *spiritual* vulgarity; or am I being intolerably priggish?

I certainly had no intention of being priggish about physical expressions of love like *fellatio* when I wrote of N.D. None of the sexual variations[92] shocks me; & I can even remember Theocritus's word - λειχαξειν - I think he invented it: the *word*

[92] [Note on the side of the paper by Davenport] We all do them in our different ways. And often wish there were more. The limerick "there was a young man of Nantucket/ Whose cock was so long he could suck it" drew from N.D. the comment that it was just as well the phenomenon was a rare one - "or most of us would be doing little else."

I mean![93] Nor does the removal (on insertion) of false teeth distress me. I remember the dusky ululations from Cornish hedges of dear old Cornish fisherwomen: "It's better with your teeth out!" *No.* I should have explained mere deeply. When N D was in Lisbon with Neil Hogg (1940/41) he had a last love affair. He arrived in London Christmas 1941, & Faith Compton Mackenzie - an *angel* - & I went to see him. {Many years before on Capri it had been his delight to make her sing in a shrill Cockney choirboy's treble endless Anglican hymns to his sensitive accompaniment on her Steinway}. He then said that he was now too old for these games, & was planning a final decade of contemplation - sexual but not active. When he went back to Capri in '47 after a - *not compulsorily* - chaste lustrum in London, he seized like an old satyr on the lost delights. Who shall blame him? But it was not pretty. The boy Ettore was a wretched spindly creature; there was little love or joy; there was (for the first time) a wretched chapter of blackmailing Neapolitan parents, and all the nightmare horrors one associates with our haunted Anglo-Saxon world.[94] His melancholy - N D's - saddened me. There was obviously no *reciprocal* love. It was as commercial as the modern Christmas we both deplore. It was then that he wistfully mentioned the teeth, *etc.* He could no longer have an erection: not surprisingly. I felt, and *he*

---

[93] In a letter of the 17th of the same month, Davenport explained that "λειχαξειν simply means licking &/ or sucking (it is only used in a *sexual* connotation)."

[94] Ettore, Douglas's last love, was a starving Neapolitan aged ten when Douglas first met him in November 1946; he lived with him in Capri from about August 1947 to February 1948 and stayed there frequently for the rest of Douglas's life (Mark Holloway, *Norman Douglas*, London, 1976). Holloway describes their relationship and the feelings of Douglas's friends about it in very much the same terms as Davenport, even quoting one of the friends as saying "Ettore was a little tart". In mentioning Douglas fellating Ettore, Davenport adds interestingly to what has hitherto been known or surmised. Michael Allan, in *Dear Doug! Letters to Norman Douglas from Eric Wolton, René Mari, Marcel Mercier and Ettore Masciandaro and a selection of letters from Emilio Papa* (Graz: W. Neugebauer, 2008, p. 135), after quoting Holloway, wrongly concluded: "Considering Douglas's state of health during the last years of his life, it seems doubtful that the relationship with young Ettore was anything more than sentimental."

felt, I am sure that there was no mutual satisfaction. Hence my own sadness about his rather bitter end. Incidentally, your simile of the horsey man sucking a straw deserves classic status. I shall do my best to see that it gets it - with due acknowledgements, of course!

Love J.D.

I am delighted that this correspondence shall have become "staggered," as they say. It means more letters in the post, a great pleasure to me. J.D.

You must think me excessively voluble - sorry, Bethnal Greek (POINTS)[95] - to scribble at you so endlessly. I like to receive & to write letters, but not in a neurotically compulsive way. Only to those - known or unknown - who can, as Wittgenstein once expressed it to me, "Say A true Word." No flattery intended. Certainly no Christmas after-glow! They are for igloos, not for leaky manor houses.

xxxix

DUXFORD GRANGE
DUXFORD
CAMBRIDGESHIRE
FOWLMERE 292

9th January '63

Dear Mike,

I got back from London last night to find your long letter of Dec. 30th. & this morning your change of address arrived. I wrote to Palermo from London on Jan. 4th. Will they forward mail from the via Tunisi?

I'm so glad you liked the broadcast talk. The voice is that of a

---

[95] Presumably meaning Davenport's train had just gone over the points, distorting his handwriting.

pedant who has done himself rather too well – husky with tobacco & alcohol & affected in a horribly dated way owing to a constitutional inability to roll Rs (at any rate in English); and TH tends to degenerate into a V, or an F. You know ve sort of fing: wahver fwightful, weally.

[...]

I am quite at a loss to understand what Guercio means about Nepenthe, which is a photographically accurate picture of Capri & its inhabitants – the decade 1904-1914, precisely.[96] There is nothing Sicilian about it. One might as well say that 'Vestal Five' is a picture of life on Barra. Incidentally, Compton Mackenzie is celebrating his 80th birthday in a week's time.

I look forward to meeting your friend Boris de C.[97] I remember after reading *Paneros* & the later Cook Book saying "But Norman, you don't seem to have much faith in any aphrodisiac. *Are* there any?" With a richly rolling Austrian R he said "VARIETY, my dearest boy."

I am *delighted* about the Arthur Koestler news.[98] Barker's really ought to go to town. Of course they may be waiting until the Christmas/ New year debris is cleared away. There is always a ghastly hiatus in the book-selling world at this time of year.

O excellent Saint Jude! How nice (and how *right)* of Alan Searle.[99] And there you are on Lipari! I don't know about the

---

[96] Nepenthe was the name Norman Douglas gave to Capri in his thinly fictionalized novel *South Wind* (London, 1917).

[97] Boris de Chroustchoff, already much described.

[98] This news was that the writer Arthur Koestler had named *The World, The Flesh and Myself* as one of the three best books of the year (1962) in the *Observer*. Koestler and his second wife Mamaine (mentioned in Davenport's first two letters to Davidson under her maiden name of Mamaine Paget) had become friends with Davidson in Israel in 1948.

[99] St. Jude was often considered the patron saint of lost causes. Alan Searle, the private secretary and companion of the writer Somerset Maugham, had written to Davidson on Boxing Day 1962 as follows:

> I have just finished your book, and feel I must write to tell you how good I thought it was, and how much I enjoyed it – beautifully written too. The last paragraph made me cry because it is my story also. Please don't be offended by the enclosed [$100]. I had a bit of luck this Christmas, and Robin [presumably Davidson's great friend Robin Maugham, Somerset's nephew] tells me that it might come in useful.

literature of the Isles of Aeolus, but the above-mentioned Ernle Bradford most certainly will, & I'll ask him to send you a book list. N.D. wrote about the Ponza Islands, but not (I am almost sure) about Lipari. He went there first in 1895 on leave from St. Petersburg. That was when he wrote an official F.O. report on the pumice industry, which led to the abolition of the child labour. I hope all goes well with you there.

Love J.D.

7. W. H. Auden, 1965

The English poet Wystan Hugh Auden (1907-73) had an intense and intimate, but chaste, friendship with Davidson for about two years, beginning in 1923, when Auden was sixteen and Davidson twenty-six. Evidently, however, they had different memories of whether the latter had ever shown any sexual interest in the former. Davidson wrote in The World, The Flesh and Myself, *that though romantically and passionately drawn to Auden, he never found the unboyish youth physically attractive. In contrast, Auden, writing about his boyhood friendship with Davidson for an article in* The New Yorker *of 3 April 1965, said:*

"Why he should have taken a shine to me I cannot imagine, since I was a very plain boy. He made advances, which I rejected, not on moral grounds but because I thought him unattractive."

This came to the attention of Davidson, who wrote to him, apparently challenging the truth of his assertion, and eliciting the reply presented here.

xl

W.H. AUDEN

July 18th [1965]
KIRCHSTETTEN
(WESTBAHN)
HINTERHOLZ 6
N.-Ö., AUSTRIA

Dear Michael:

I was delighted and touched to get your letter of June 15th this morning.

Sorry about the historical inaccuracies. I still seem to recall that some 'suggestion' was tactfully made (I was, after all, no innocent), but if have invented this, it is because I have reproached myself ever since for being such a pig [sic].

I am well and busy and enchanted with this house which I bought in 1957 to spend the summers in. My new book of poems which is shortly due to appear contains a cycle of poems about the significance of every room in a house. I am the first person, I think, to have written a serious poem about the Toilet.

As for my 'private' life, the poems overleaf may tell you something. Hope all goes well with you

love

Wystan

P.S. What an extraordinary address you have!

GLAD

Hugerl, for a decade now
My bed visitor,
An unexpected blessing
In a lucky life,
For how much and how often
You have made me glad.

Glad that I know we enjoy
Mutual pleasure:
Women may cog their lovers
With a feigned passion,
But males are so constructed
We cannot deceive.

Glad our worlds of enchantment
Are so several
Neither is tempted to broach:
I cannot tell a
Jaguar from a Bentley,
And you never read.

Glad for that while when you stole
(You burgled me, too)
And were caught and put inside:
Both learned a lesson,
But for which we well might still
Be *Strich* and *Freier*.

Glad, though, we began that way,
That our life-paths crossed,
Like characters in Hardy,
At a moment when
You were in need of money,
And I wanted sex.

How is it now between us?
Love? Love is far too
Tattered a word. A romance
In full fig it ain't,
Nor a naked letch either:
Let me say we fadge,

And how much I like Christa
Who loves you but knows,
Good girl, when not to be there.
I can't imagine
A kinder set-up: if mims
Mump, *es ist mir Wurscht.*[100]

AT GREY OF DAWN

At grey of dawn
He takes a street-car, happy
After a night of love.

Happy.
But sleepily wondering
How many away is the night

[100] This poem was written in 1964, but only posthumously published, eg. in Auden's *Collected Poems*, edited by Edward Mendelson (New York: Modern Library, 2007) p. 746. It refers to a relationship Auden had while living in Kirchstetten with a young Viennese auto-mechanic: initially Auden paid him for sex, but mutual affection developed and they ended up sleeping together for over a decade, even after the youth married.

When an ecto-endomorph
Coco-sucker must put on
The Widow's Cap.[101]

[101] This poem was likewise written in 1964, but only posthumously published, eg. in Auden's *Collected Poems*, edited by Edward Mendelson (New York: Modern Library, 2007) p. 746. In its case, it was there slightly modified and given a new title "Aubade".

8. Ida de Chroustchoff, 1966

Ida Vera de Chroustchoff née King (1909-72) was the second wife of Boris de Chroustchoff and Davidson's friend and occasional correspondent in her own right from the time of his reunion with Boris in October 1960. The letter presented here was sent to her after he received the sudden news that she was planning to come out to see him in Favignana on her own.

xli

Favignana (Trapani), Italy

10th Sept. '66

Dearest Ida,

I wrote to Boris a couple of days ago, brimful of excitement over your plan to sail out here. [...]

Now I'm writing quickly to you – in case you jump on a ship before I get any warning – because I want to ask you to bring me out a thing that won't take up much room in your luggage or be a bore – a pair of Beatle Boots!!!! These are NOT for me, but for my s.b., Luigi, who is longing to strut in the piazza wearing the first Beatle-Boots ever to be seen on this island. As he's now a g.f.-s.b. (a growing-fast s.b. – double the size he was eight months ago) the size should be 8 ½ or a small 9; anything smaller would be outgrown within a month. And they must be *black*; heels slightly high though not scandalously so. Do you know *how* to buy Beatle Boots? I'm sure you don't; but it's quite simple – I've done it. You go into one of those "popular" shoe-shops and ask for Beatle Boots, just like that. They'll cost between £2 10 and £3. I'll pay you here. It will be such a kindness if you will do this for me – he will get immense pleasure out of them, and I out of his pleasure. [...]

Eleven days later, Boris replied that Ida was leaving that day for Dol, but that she had already enquired about the boots in a boot-shop and it would be easy to send them by post. A week after that, he told Davidson that her planned journey on to Favignana was being abandoned, and on 3rd October Davidson replied, expressing great anxiety that the de Chroustchoffs should post the boots as soon as possible.

9. The Hoheit, 1967-68

Hubertus Maximilian Friedrich Leopold Ludwig Prinz zu Löwenstein-Wertheim-Freudenberg (14 October 1906 – 28 November 1984), a German historian and eminent political figure., was one of many whose first contact with Michael Davidson was to write to him in praise of The World, The Flesh and Myself. *Not unusually, their correspondence blossomed into friendship.*

xlii. From Hubertus v. Löwenstein to Michael Davidson

as from:
Bad Godesberg, Lahnstr. 50
(en route Paris – Bad Godesberg)
27 November 1967

Dear Mr. Davidson,

This is only a short, preliminary letter, intended to establish contact with you. I just finished reading your book THE WORLD THE FLESH AND MYSELF. It moved me, and fascinated me beyond words – because of its own merits, but also for terribly egocentric reasons, because I discovered in it a truly amazing number of parallels, identities of problems, experiences, tastes etc etc Born in 1906 (you'll find my biography in the Who's Who). I was one of the young "Jugendführer" (Reichsbanner Schwarz-Rot-Gold)[102] fighting the Nazis – I camped at lake shores with "Werner" – with Klaus – Jürgen – Herbert – Heinz – (Where are they now – ?) –

I wrote (and write) books (my autobiography TOWARDS THE FURTHER SHORE will soon be published by Gollancz – who published my book on the Spanish Civil War in 1937) articles – etc. etc.

---

[102] In other words, he was a youth leader in this organisation set up in 1924 to engender respect for the new democratic republic, whose flag bore these colours. Its name translates literally as "Black, Red, Gold Banner of the State."

In the course of the last 7 or 8 years I have been many times to all the wonderful countries of the East - Japan with its Yoshihiros, Hiroshiis, Nubus, Singapore, K. L. (again this summer), Indonesia - with its "smiling brown creatures" - and to M. I know Cyprus very well indeed - having been (due to a lucky constellation) the initiator of Greek-Turkish negotiations in 1958.

Now I am lecturing in many countries (in England again last February - with very *good* impressions of the new English youth).

I feel like you - "nie ein Erwachsener - Gott sei dank, nicht!!"[103] I am on my way to Rome (for 2 weeks) doing some works for FAO - and to meet my young Greek friend Andreas.

Should you find time to drop me a line - I would be very happy indeed. The train is too jumpy - I better close now. I hope to be in England in spring.

Danke für Ihr schönes und wichtiges Buch.

Freundliche grüße

Von Ihrem[104]

Hubertus Löwenstein

xliii. From Michael Davidson to Boris de Chroustchoff

Boris de Chroustchoff, recipient of this and two further letters about the Hoheit, has already been amply introduced as the recipient in two sections of Davidson's correspondence.

Favignana (Trapani), Italy

[…] December '67 (Luigi's 17th birthday)

---

103 These seven words mean "never an adult - thank God, not!!"

104 These eleven words mean "Thank you for your beautiful and important book. Friendly greetings. From your"

Dear Boris,

Will you do me a kindness? Go to the nearest WHO'S WHO and look up PRINZ HUBERTUS ZU LOEWENSTEIN, and copy out all that's interesting. I've had a *fan-letter* from him - a very pleasant and intelligent letter indeed: mad about World/Flesh, saying the nicest things about it, and telling me something of himself - writes books, lectures round the world, now in Rome doing a job for the F.A.O.; has travelled all over world and knows and loves all my Far Eastern countries; then he says tantalisingly, "you"ll find my biography in Who's Who", and of course I haven't a Who's Who within miles. He writes almost faultless idiomatic English - he may well have been at school in England, I should think.[105] Sixty-one years old. So please rush off and let me know who he is - and who are the Löwensteins? It might be amusing to look at the Alm. de Gotha.[106] He doesn't, by the way, live in a Schloss, but at a street number in Bad Godesberg: perhaps he's a younger son, or the family's gone broke. I've got an idea from his letter that he's an awfully nice man.

I'm *hoping* to be in England before Christmas - but all depends on the American.

Love to Woodcock[107]
Michael

xliv. From Hubertus v. Löwenstein to Michael Davidson

532 BAD GODESBERG
LAHNSTRASSE 50
TEL. 7 4001

[105] The explanation seems rather to be that he had an English mother.

[106] The annual *Almanach de Gotha* gave genealogical details of world royalty and the high nobility of Europe. It had ceased publication in 1945, but this was not widely realised among the English.

[107] Woodcock has already been introduced as the de Chroustchoffs' home in Oxfordshire. Davidson had been to stay there many times.

18. Dezember 1967

Dear Mr. Davidson

last night, when I came back from Rome, I found your letter on my desk – amidst piles of Christmas cards, letters, etc. But I spotted it at once and it was the only one I read before going to bed. I am very happy that you wrote and that now we are in contact with each other. As I told you in my first (probably hardly readable) letter: It is absolutely amazing to see all these parallels between your life and mine!

I wrote my first editorial for Die Vossische Zeitung in July 1930 (I was then not quite 24), calling it "Das Dritte Reich" – there'll be another world war, should Hitler come to power! You can well imagine the outcry – not just among the Nazis, but among all those goody-goody conservatives, all diese wohlanständigen Leute [these decent people]! The scandal, that someone with my name should come out "für diese dreckige, Schwarz-rot-goldene Republik"![108] Then – to make things worse – I joined the Reichsbanner and organized and led its youth organization – boys between 12 and 18 – Vortrupp Schwarz-Rot-Gold. I wrote for the Berliner Tageblatt and similar papers. Of course, after the war, I was "der liebe, liebe Vetter Hubertus, der immer schon gesagt hat, was wir alle fühlten."[109]

Last year – I wonder whether you saw it – there was some real scandal when, found in the Nazi archives, a letter written by the chief of the junior branch, Fürst Karl zu Löwenstein-Wertheim-Rosenberg, was published – a letter addressed to the Nazi Foreign Minister, denouncing my brother Leopold (living in England) and me, in the vilest terms. That gentleman now wears for the year the black-red-golden ribbon of the Order of Merit of the Bundesrepublik – those same colours he and his kin were dragging through the mud in 1933.

Well, "Schwamm darüber [No hard feelings]"!

In 1933 I left Germany – the usual road of exiles – Austria, England, France, Holland, finally the USA. My first books were published by Faber in 1934 ("The Tragedy of a Nation", and

[108] These six words mean "for this dirty, black-red-gold republic".

[109] The quoted words mean "Dear, dear cousin Hubertus, who has always said what we all felt."

"After Hitler's Fall" - because of the latter Adolf 'expatriated' me). Some more followed, in England and America. I then had a Visiting Carnegie Professorship for history (though I had taken my degree as doctor of *law* in Hamburg, 1931) from 1937-1946, when I returned to Germany. Member of Parliament 1953-57, since then Special Adviser, Bundespresseamt, on foreign Affairs.

Unfortunately, I have never been in Bali - but my experiences - but one.. which apparently was planned, a political frame-up - on Java were very pleasant too!

My main love (and loves..) is Japan, "the only country" someone told me when I arrived, "where a man can afford not only to become older, but old, without developing inferiority complexes - the older he gets, the more will the boys love him!". Hiroshii - Nabou - Yoshihiro - Motoji .. etc. there is always a bit of "Boy Butterfly"-nostalgia in it - one never knows whether one will meet again.

I owe my introduction to Japanese life to Francis King, the writer whom you may know. He was then in Kyoto, with the British Council. I met him through the courtesy of a real institution - don't tell me, you don't know him! - Col. Thanos Veloudios in Athens - a war hero (Peloponnesian - Turkish - World War One - ? nobody knows!), and Lover of the entire Royal Hellenic Air Force.

Anyway, my "private" relations are most helpful for my public relations. Francis King introduced me to another youngish Englishman, charming, Lionel Thompson in Bangkok, and he in turn to Jim Bush in K.L. to Peter Mole in Singapore - and so on. There have been some parties in these two pleasant cities, which resounded through Asia - My book TOWARDS THE FURTHER SHORE is scheduled to come out in April, I am expecting the proofs momentarily. The German text - which I am now preparing (though I don't have a publisher yet) is more outspoken.

Cyprus: a friend of mine (life long friend!) and I were doing a book in NATO. In 1958 we were in Athens and met the Greek Minister of Defence the Chief of Staff and, most important, Panajotis Kanellopoulos (deposed by the Junta, this year). The Cyprus crisis had reached a climax. I said "I don't have to explain what I feel about Greece - suffice it to quote a line from a poem by Stefan George: 'Hellas, Ewig Unsere Liebe!' ['Hellas, forever our Love!']" Whereupon Kanellopoulos* recited the whole poem, "I studied under Gundolf in Heidelberg and as student translated George into Greek" he said. (The line in Greek reads: Aineion Eros mas he Ellàs") The atmosphere changed and I said, "Of course, you could have Enosis any moment, you just have to leave Nato and get Enosis in one vaste Soviet KZ, just as we could get that kind of 'Wiedervereinigung [reunion]' ". Thereupon, after a short silence, Kanellopoulos asked me to convey his greetings in Ankara to the Minister of Defence, Etem Menderes, "He will understand..!" He did, and within a few weeks the negoziations started.

There is one point on which I don't agree with you: Makarios. I don't like, I don't trust him. Ein böser, politisierender Pfaffe! [An evil politicising priest!] The London and Zurich Agreements were perhaps not the final solution - but they worked, until Makarios broke them. He is responsible for every drop of blood shed on Cyprus.

I was last in Greece for a few days in August - coming back from Ceylon (a lovely place too!), South East Asia, Japan (In April I had been in India - the gentle "Hindu Youths" - certainly!). I had met a young Greek (my present Ruling Friend), Andreas in Paris, 16. Oktober 1965. His father placed his boy's hand in mine and said "Na ton agapàs!" May you love him! This can happen only in Greece. Now André is in Rome, as a language student, very poor - his parents can't send him anything due to conditions and the Drachma is not being accepted abroad. I spent every free hour with him. Yesterday at noon we were on the Capitol together. In 1966 I spent a fortnight with him in England - but for a boy from the land of Helios it was too dreary. He looks 17, though he will be 24 tomorrow. (My "age of consent" goes higher, as you see!)

Have you tried the Stahlberg - Verlag (who publishes Peyrefitte. By the way, do you know his latest book "Notre Amour" - it is the most astoundingly open story one can imagine. He gave it to me on Capri, in August - he was there with a lovely young 'cousin'.)[110] For a German edition perhaps you

---

[110] Roger Peyrefitte's *Notre Amour*, published that year, was a lightly fictionalised account of his love affair with Alain-Philippe Malagnac,

would want to shorten the family background – it's important for the English, but the average German reader has no immediate contact with British modern history. And, instead, put in some of the stories I suppose you took out for the paper-back edition!)

I am sending you – it'll probably take a long time to arrive – one of my novels, in a way one of my favourites, which was a complete flop, in spite of good reviews – each one missed the point. It is neither a veiled autobiography, nor a "Schlüsselroman auf Bonner Zustände"[111] – it is sort of guide through the twilight realm of the soul ... between dying and death. Of course, there are some autob. elements – there was a boy by name of John, a poet – his poems were published later on by Harold Nicholson – THE great love of my life – he rests on the British War Cemetery near Anzio (I speak about him in "Towards the Further Shore") – who's image is reflected in "Lycidas" –

I'll be here for the next few weeks, unless I have to go to Rome (F.A.O.) once more, before flying to the USA on January 19. At the end of February, or rather, first part of March I will be in England. In summer, God willing, in Capri –

Merry Christmas and may we soon meet and exchange experiences.

Yours

Hubertus L.

*You must read his book "The Five Athenian Dialogues" – in each as representations of Eternal Hellas there appears a couple of young lovers, Dion and Diotimos. The most remarkable of the Dialogues is "Hadrian in Athens" – his conversation with those two youths. A very courageous work for a man in high public office!

How is youth on your island?

---

twelve when they met, fourteen when they became lovers according to the account in *Notre Amour*, and just over sixteen when Löwenstein met him in Capri.

[111] This expression means "A novel based on real events in the Bonn set-up but using changed names".

xlv. From Michael Davidson to Natasha von Chroustchoff

Natasha de Chroustchoff (born 1945), known as Datila within her family, was the only child of Davidson's friend Boris by his second wife Ida.

Favignana (Trapani), Italy

23.xii.67

Dearest Datila,

How awfully kind of you to go all that bother! I AM grateful. Such a lovely full dossier – it must have taken hours to copy out: how you must have blasted me! I'd no idea he was such a swell, quite apart from his Alm.-de-G. swelldom: historian, academic, literary bloke, politician, government official &c &c: well, he called W.F.&.M. "ein schönes und wichtiges Buch" – & that's enough to earn him my most distinguished consideration. But in one thing I'm disappointed: I'd been having lovely daydreams that my Fairy Prince would live up to the Renaissance principle of the noble Patron of Letters; I'd been hoping that he'd install me in the West Wing of the Schloss, with the run of the Library, a small staff of retainers of my own and, of course, a small but reasonable allowance of ducats, amount depending on the devaluation of the ducat. But now I find he's married with three daughters. Obviously the Prinzessin is fat and money-grubbing: watching every penny and devoted only to her schemes for marrying off the three ugly daughters. Where then is my dream of the Patron of Letters? [...]

Love to Woodcock
Michael

xlvi. From Hubertus v. Löwenstein to Michael Davidson

532 BAD GODESBERG
LAHNSTRASSE 50
TEL. 7 4001

January 10, 1968
My dear Michael,

of course you call me Hubertus! I've called you Michael in my thoughts ever since I read your book and discovered that we may have been camping at the shores of the same lake, and perhaps with the same boys! I was just about to get worried when you letter arrived – I had been afraid that perhaps you had gone to England and God knows, who might have read my letter..!

Over Christmas I corrected the proofs of my autobiography, making it more pointed here and there. You probably remember the German "Sprichwort": "Unter der Laterne ist es am dunkelsten!"[112]

There is an Italian edition of Kanellopoulos CINQUE DIALOGHI ATENIESI, Cappelli Editore, translated from the German version Fünf Athener Dialoge. I am referring to this book several times in my autobiography – for instance in the chapter "Through the Gates of Hellas":

Quoting: ""Viewed from the Akropolis, lands and continents are moving more closely together." I wrote this sitting at the foot of the Parthenon, in January 1960. "The borders of Hellas are one with the true borders of nature."

I visited Eleusis, the sacred place of the Mysteries, for the first time during this journey. Never were they betrayed, even

---

112 " 'Sprichwort ... dunkelsten' " means " 'Saying': 'It's darkest under the lantern.' "

though the number of initiates must have been very large. At Eleusis there remains one of the most beautiful statues of Antinous. Panajotis Kanellopoulos in his book The Five Athenian Dialogues makes Hadrian say that Antinous did not need a special rite of initiation, he was an initiate by nature. It might be, I suggested, discussing the Mysteries with the author, that Hadrian met Antinous again in Eleusis during the ceremony of initiation, after his death in the Nile. Perhaps this mystic meeting gave to the Emperor the certainty that Antinous was not dead, but alive on a higher plane...." (end of quote)

And in the same chapter I am saying:

Quoting: "From the human angle also Hellas has remained what it was in the days of Socrates and his disciples. *Na ton agapàs!* 'May you love him!', a Greek friend of mine said, when he entrusted to me his son, André who is now a student at the Sorbonne. Mary Renault, the excellent British authoress, has caught in her novels - The Last of the Wine, and others, the timeless spirit of Hellas - then and today!

Dionysus, according to tradition, proceeded to India with his retinue of bacchantes and satyrs. Alexander the Great followed. Eros accompanied him and the other Gods of Greece, Hellenic art and the philosophy of Plato and Aristotle. Traces of Hellenic culture have survived in Iran, Afghanistan, and certainly in Pakistan. The name of the great Macedonian has been preserved in many families in the form of Iskaner." (end of quot.)

I do wish I had met Eibo[113] - I would still cling to him! but unfortunately, I haven't. Nor do I know Braun[114] - he was not in

---

113 "Eibo", correctly Eikichi Suzuki, was the 15-year-old Japanese whom Davidson had loved while working in Tokyo in 1950-51, and described in *The World, The Flesh and Myself* as the boy he had loved longest and most. His own letters to Davidson have already been presented as nos. xx-xxiv.

114 An author's footnote added to the 1985 edition of *The World, The Flesh and Myself* reveals "Braun, Secretary of the International Red Cross", to have been the boy-loving "Swiss friend whom I'll call B---" of Davidson who "kept going a pied-à-terre in Berlin" in the last years of the Weimar Republic. Davidson had presumably told Löwenstein his identity in one of his letters. Why he should have been a member of a post-war German legislature if he was Swiss is not clear.

the Bundestag, when I was in, nor is he now. Or is he perhaps a member of the North-Rhine Westfalian *Landtag*? I wish I knew! It is always very amusing to know something about someone, who doesn't know about us (Really?? don't they know?! That's what we think!)

I had a pleasant card from Peyrefitte (with one of those pictures taken by Herr von Gloeden – "The little Flute Player" – decades ago (Peyrefitte wrote a story about him in "Amoures Singulières) – from Taormina, signed also by his lovely little "cousin" Alain Philippe. He is returning to Paris next week.

Now that the proofs are corrected and the German text completed (I still don't have a German publisher!) I am thinking seriously again of my book .. started years ago .. almost completed in a handwritten draft .. re-written again and again .. "The Death of Lucius Annaeus Seneca" – in the form of an autobiography. There are many interesting parallels between his time and ours. There was even a sort of "20th of July 1944" against Nero, the conspiracy, that failed and yet eventually brought about the fall of the tyrant. Seneca perished in it. Plutarch who is very anti-Seneca has things to say about him, which are just too-too-terrible .. namely, that he loved young boys! Just think of it. He even insinuates that he had an affair with his pupil, young Nero – then about 12-14 years old!

Of course, I knew Norman Douglas very well! I must tell you a little story, which is so British (I hope, you won't mind!). Once his young grand-son (son of his daughter)[115] came to Capri, a very beautiful boy. I thought Douglas would be glad to hear it, so I said it in so many words. Believe it or not – he was morally shocked and from that moment on hardly spoke with me anymore.

The gods of Greece never deserted him. You could see him every day on the Piazza, surrounded by scores of ragizzini ... until finally he would move along – slowly – followed by all the

---

115 Norman Douglas did not have a daughter, or at least neither a legitimate one nor one known to Mark Holloway, his most comprehensive biographer. Presumably Löwenstein was confused and the grandson in question was the son of a son. Or perhaps his having got the wrong end of the stick was somehow the cause of Douglas's coldness.

ragazzini. It is rumoured that he died in the arms of his latest lover – a ragazzino 13 years of age.

By the way do you know – do you remember – Platens beautiful poem: "Der Tod des Pindar"?".... ich will ja nicht im Leben oder Dichten/den groβen unerreichlichen erreichen/ Ich möcht', o Freund, ihm nur im Tode gleichen ../Doch höre nun die schönste der Geschichten:/ Er sass im Schauspiel, vom Gesang beweget/ Und hatte, der ermüdet war die Wangen/ Auf seines Lieblings schönes Knie geleget./Als nun der Chöre Melodien verklangen/ Will wecken ihn, der ihn so sanft geheget/ Doch zu den Göttern war er heimgegangen."[116]

On January 19 I shall be flying to New York, staying there 4 days and continuing for places north – across Canada, back to the States (San Francisco – where I know a number of pleasant people) – Miami – New Orleans – on the 26 February to Jamaica. Back in Europe, Deo Volente, in March – and then I hope to meet you in England.

People I knew so well ... Stanley Richardson, the young poet (killed in an air raid while on shore leave from the R. Navy), Peter Cornwallis (son of the ambassador to Bagdad, + als a RAF pilot) .. did you by any chance know them? And then, of course, John – and always again John "Who fell on the road to Rome that youth of all nations may become brothers" – this is the dedication ... I put it into my little book "The Child and the Emperor" (Macmillan, New York, never in England, it's the first of a trilogy)

---

[116] The German in this paragraph means: "The Death of Pindar"? ...
"Not that I would in Life, or in my Verse,
  With him, the great Incomparable, compare;
  Only his Death, my friend, I ask to share:
But let me now the gracious tale rehearse.
Long at the play, hearing sweet Harmony,
  He sat; and wearied out at last, had lain
His cheek upon his dear one's comely knee;
  Then when it died away – the choral strain –
He who thus cushioned him said: Wake and come!
  But to the Gods above he had gone home."

Well, my friend, and "Schicksalsgefährte [fellow-traveller by destiny]" - so long and "Auf Wiedersehn [good-bye]" for I do feel that we know each other for a long time. Bacci ed amore al tuo sugazzorgo[?][117] Favignanaense e ai tutti i belli ragazzi e giovanotti della tua isola! In amicizia

Sempre Umberto[118]
(Hubertus)

I am sending you a copy of my booklet A BASIC HISTORY OF GERMANY. This week it will come out in French, next month in Thai. There are also German, Spanish and Italian editions. The *Original* - almost 600 pages THE GERMANS IN HISTORY was published by Columbia Press in 1945. I rewrote it in German: DEUTSCHE GESCHICHTE (almost 700 pages) 4th edition 1962. The "Kleine Deutsche Geschichte", BASIC HISTORY etc. are the great-grandchildren of the 1945 Columbia Press book. Tens of thousands of boys and youths, in USA, England, Asia, Latin America, France, Germany, are drinking German history from my wells - a thought I find intoxicating!

xlvii. From Michael Davidson to Boris de Chroustchoff

Favignana (Trapani)

17. ii. 68

My dear Boris,

[…] You ask about the Hoheit: the answer is, HOW so can a man be? He specialises in oriental varieties, and is very romantic and literary about it all. You shall read his letters; and, since he's to be in England in March, we could all meet him. At the mo-

117 This word is illegible and its meaning unclear.
118 "Bacci … Umberto" means "Kisses and love to your Favignanan sweet-boy[?} and to all the beautiful boys and youngsters of your island! In friendship. Always Hubert."

ment he's in the U.S. on a German Govt mission.

[...]

Meanwhile best love to Cock[119]
Michael

xlviii. From Michael Davidson to Boris de Chroustchoff

120 North Side, S. W. 4

28.iii.68

My dear Boris,

Best thanks for your note. [...]

I have met the Hoheit! He seemed quite charming, bubbling with gaiety and good humour and entertaining talk, and very princely in appearance: a splendid parrot's nose, designed for haughtiness and the "let them eat cake" attitude, yet he's not like that at all! He was rushing off northwards to lecture some provincial university & I was running to do things in London, so I saw him only for a few moments, but we meet again tomorrow when I go to a German Embassy reception to celebrate publication of the hoheit's autobiography: Get it from the library – "Towards the Further Shore" by Hubertus Prinz zu Löwenstein (Gollancz), published tomorrow.* At the party I am to meet two more hoheits, his brothers, and the hoheit-ess, his wife (who has read my book!!!).

[...]

[119] ie. all the de Chroustchoff's household in Woodcock, Oxfordshire.

Love to Woodcock & all there

Michael

*I don't know what it's like!

10. To Tim Brierly 1969-75

Timothy Graham Brierly (26 August 1926 – 24 December 2010), a "notoriously undomesticated" bachelor, was a founding member of Oxfam's African aid team, based in Nigeria 1966-68, North Africa 1968-73, Saigon 1973-75, East Africa (Ethiopia, then Kenya) 1975-80 and Oxford 1980-87.[120] *The first letter quoted from below is the earliest preserved from Davidson to Brierly, and may really have been the first.*

xlix

91023 Favignana (Trapani), Italy

10th September '69

Dear Tim,

Very many thanks for your long and interesting letter from Oxford [...]

About property here: Certainly one can buy small houses & a bit of land for around £2000 or less or more depending on size &c &c – generally half-ruined peasants' shacks (solid stone) which require a lot of transforming. Generally therefore a lot of money is needed on top of buying price to make the place habitable & bring such things as water, electric, plumbing, baths &c – BATHS! – you see, nobody on this island has these newfangled refinements. BUT – I don't think you'd *like* this island; I don't think you'd want to live on it for a moment; & I don't think it has much future as an investment – I suppose property values will go up bit by bit, like everywhere else, but no faster than the values of everything else. This is no boom island. There's *nothing* here: no social life, so intellectual life, no any kind of life – one cinema, showing pictures nobody over

[120] Obituary in the *Independent*, 17 February 2011.

the age of eight wants to see. Population under 5000. I'm the only foreigner living here. I have lived here for most of the last four years because I have my family - Luigi's family - here & because I'm writing a book about the island & because I can be fairly content with NO comforts & NO pleasures & even NO decent food!!! Being an absolutely egocentric & in-growing creature who delights in solitude &, generally speaking, detests his fellow-men except as interesting spectacles or specimens, & who is quite content to sit only on a stone & never a soft chair & to have no bog & have windows that won't shut &c &c &c, I'm quite happy living this kind of extraordinary life (though I loathe the unending *wind* (it's the windiest corner of the Med.) & sometimes in winter *ache* for *warmth).* But even I, now, feel I'm getting a bit old for this sort of living - though I generally feel 53, I remember now & then that I'll be 73 in February next - how absurd it seems! And finally there's one other deficiency which, I believe, makes it an island where you wouldn't want to live: there's no "trade" here, in the special sense of that term: anything anybody does is known to the entire population within an hour of its happening. When we meet I'll tell you the story of my good fortune when first I came here - which is why I stayed here - & met Luigi & his father at one & the same moment - but if in these last four years I'd so much as raised an eyebrow at anybody else the whole thing would have been ruined & I'd have been removed from the island. The place is too *small.* My experience has been quite exceptional simply because I had an astonishing piece of sheer luck on my first visit - which is why I've been here ever since. Then I discovered that the island contained the constituents of a book, which is what I'm now finishing. Apart from these two things, which happened to suit me personally, the island has *nothing* to offer except dullness, discomfort & a rotten climate!!! It would be lovely for me to have you here, if I were still here; but I must in honesty say that I don't believe you'd like being here for a moment. But I'll send postcards when I can manage to buy some.

[...] I've got three books going, each of which in its way is *good,* I know, from other people's testimony as well as my own, & yet I can't get a *penny* from any! The American edition of life-&-loves[121] won't be on sale till towards Xmas; the German contract for same has been signed but the publisher is promptly breaking it by either falling through altogether (because of the Law) or being indefinitely delayed. World/Flesh, poor old hag, has almost dried up after 7 years' pretty good going, & her new pretty garb won't be ready awhile. And, the final blow, in the middle of my Island book[122] (which I know, & other people know, is excellent of its kind) the publishers which commissioned it changed managing directors & the new man is interested only in Sporting Books!!! [...]

Every good wish

Ever
Michael

1

Bath, 19. xi [1970]

Dear Tim,

[...]

Glad to hear that my first impression of your impressions was a wrong one: I felt – happily in error – that you'd read it chiefly with a fleshly eye!

Certainly I've corresponded with a few in my time, or kept up with them in some way or other. But by the nature of things it's not often practicable – numbers have been illiterate or the like, some without addresses; & there's an ineluctable financial element; in 19 out of 20 such letters one is bound to shove in a £-

---

121 *Some Boys*, published by David Bruce & Watson in London that year. The American edition was only eventually published by Oliver Layton Press in New York in 1971.

122 *My Sicilian Vespers*, of which this is the first edition.

note or thereabouts – & that, at your rate of ten or so correspondents, mounts up especially if one's "educating" & c the current one!

You say that anybody would assume "from your book, that all h/s relationships are equally ephemeral". Nonsense, my book deals with *pederastic* relationships, with pedophilic – a v. different matter; & 99 ½ % of pederastic relationships *are* equally ephemeral, because they're limited to an ephemeral fragment of human development - the 3 or 4 years of adolescence, & they're bound to be ephemeral because Tom Dick or Harry aged 15 is an *absolutely different* individual, in body & mind from Tom, Dick or Harry aged 9 & 19. "Boys" are a separate race, a distinct species.

The remaining *half* %, after the above 99 ½ %, is represented by such rare beings as my Luigi, or by the sum of the circumstances of my friendship with Luigi.

Next time you look round Foyle's for any book of mine don't *please* just satisfy yourself that it's not *visible*! *ASK* for it: that's the only way to create a demand & stimulate the market!

No I'm not going to make a penny out of it. The market's strangled & the publishers are amateurs. I think later it'll be paperbacked & that'll bring in a little. But the chief disaster is the U.S. market: I'd have had 4 or 5 thousand dollars by now if the American publisher had *published;* but he's inexplicably leaving the thing dormant. It should have been selling there *last autumn.*

Sorry about that handwriting. Typewriter out of order – and the catastrophe!

Ever

Michael

Where *did* you get the idea that I was pegged between 12 & 15? 12 very rarely, 16 or 17 very frequently.

li

B'Bugia [Birzebbugia, Malta], 25.ii.74

My dear Tim,

At LAST! At long long *last*! And - most miraculous of all miracles - your letter is postmarked Saigon 21st Febr & arrived here the 25th: I wish to God I could hope that this letter will go back to you as quickly - instead of having to fear it may never reach you at all!

But my dear boy - *what* a delight it is to hear from you, and to have such a long and interesting letter, I've been longing all this time to hear how you were enjoying my Far East - I envy you the pleasures of the Philippines: islands I never, alas, reached, just as I never managed to get Ceylon - these are the two countries which, from our specialist point of view, are unrivalled:[123] however, the whole of the Extreme Orient & SEAsia are pretty generous in that respect. I hope you get back to the Ph. soon: Vietnam, corrupted by war & GIs, must be saddening: I wonder if Tonkin comes into your parish? A place with a lot of charm, & charmers.

But Tim, my dear boy, don't you think that your lending me first this flat, & then your flat in Tangier[124] (& probably before long, one in Tibet) is generosity enough? Why, bless your heart, do you send me L50 as well???? (Aptly, your letter & cheque arrived le lendemain to my birthday - *my 77th*!!!). I'm not good at expressing gratitude in flowery fulsome phrases; but you can guess what I feel about it & about your characteristic kindness.

---

[123] "Our specialist point of view" is clearly that of pederasts. The Philippines and Ceylon were widely regarded by pederasts in the 1970s as the countries in which it was easiest for foreigners to find local boys for amorous liaisons.

[124] MCD had finally left Favignana, his home for eight years, due to severe flooding in December 1973, and had moved into Brierly's flat in Birzebuggia. Soon afterwards, he borrowed Brierly's flat in Tangier for a final stay in that old haunt of his.

Well now, I have today written off to Jim Skelton in Marrakech, asking him to be kind enough to let me know if the T. flat will be empty roughly 2nd half of March (I now plan to leave Malta about Mar. 10th, call at London for a few days, where I've got to see publishers (a new firm is bringing out a new edition of World/Flesh – & an old firm is trying to diddle me out of some loot), go on to Spain to stay with Robin[125] for a day or two, & then on to Tangier. My dear boy, what *fun* it will be to see Morocco again, & old Georgie Greaves[126], & to revive my Arabic (I've been trying to acquire at least an elementary use of Malti; but although the root is almost pure N. African Arabic, the pronunciation is baffling, & I haven't been able to find a young B'Bugian willing to become a conversational partner – in fact, the young here, tho' lavish with waves, smiles, & hearty Hullos, are highly standoffish & shy of the informalities; I'm really excited at the thought of going back there – & the thought of certain Moroccans....

[...]

You ask what Dr Bonnici stung me for? I promise you, I haven't been so *moved* (& surprised) for ages: In the grandeur of his Hilton "clinic", as he calls it, I performed all the formalities of a consultation in Harley street: he listened, he tapped, he squeejeed my arm, he prescribed (very effectively as it turned out), & he said if ever there was anything I needed, just telephone his receptionist at the Hilton – & I said, fumbling in my pocket, Now Doctor, your fee. . . .? – and he took me by the arm, led me to the door, & playfully grinned: "You couldn't afford my fees"- &, I protesting hard, gently pushed me out of the door. Then he & his wife sent me a Xmas card, & he steadily ignores my postal pleas for his bill for professional services. Now isn't that nice? Would you get that in England? I told this story to Molly & she said that the Bonnicis had always been who so kind. I find that everybody

---

125 His friend Robin, 2nd Viscount Maugham, introduced in note 71 to letter XXX.

126 George Greaves was an Australian journalist and MI6 agent in Tangier, and one of the most colourful characters in that city, described in *The World, The Flesh and Myself* pp. 195-7.

– the shopkeepers &c, & the families below & on either side, are quite charming. I get on very well with the neighbours, & have bought myself a little popularity by giving sweets &c to the various children (only very tiny ones!).

I've been to Gozo once – a friend of mine has a little house at Xlendi & soon after I arrived here I spent a couple of nights there – but my friend went back to Eng. & won't be out again till about Easter. Yes, I loved Gozo, what I saw of it & sensed quite a different "culture" so to speak: Malta I find ugly (in spite of all this top-heavy architecture) & very suburban – while politically . . . . [...]

I never got to Laos. My dear, I *hope* you're keeping a journal – I want to see a book out of all this; just as I want to see an African book from you. I've been *devouring* your bookshelves, & all your African & Muslim stuff: what a joy M. Perham's anthology of African travel is! But I want a book, or books, from YOU. [...]

Ever, and ever thanks
Michael

lii

9 St Simon Street, XLENDI (Gozo), Malta

22nd Febr '75

My very dear Tim,

[...] Gordon[127] is very nice & amusing until he's had his 4th brandy. Unfortunately, he's generally had his 4th brandy by about 10.30 a.m. & thereafter becomes somnolent, repetitive, mumbling & generally increasingly boring. What an awful pity it is: such a nice person, just gone to waste. And everybody on the

[127] Gordon Munro, frequently mentioned in the letters of Davidson and his friends in Gozo.

island expects him any day to have an almighty car-crash – yet there's nothing anybody can do. Poor Gordon keeps going into hospital with what he calls "bronchitis" – reappears "dried out", & promptly sets out to contract "bronchitis" again.

[...] You are, of course, absolutely & utterly right in your judgement of the relative merits of the two islands: Gozo is quite enchanting, & quite different in tone & texture from Malta; while the Gozitans are the nicest & friendliest of any people in the Mediterranean. I have an extremely agreeable & decorative Personal Assistant whose parents have also become great friends & who bikes the two miles from Victoria every day, bless his heart.

[...] I'm being commissioned to do another book, a sort of sequel to World Flesh & Myself; so if the advance is right – terms are being debated in London – I shall be secure here for a bit. When the owners of this house return in May, with various oddments of their families or friends, I'm hoping to move to Marsalforn where my Personal Assistant's parents have a tiny flat which they'll let me have. Xlendi is in most ways divine, but inconvenient in one: can't buy so much as a loaf of bread or a pint of milk, & in winter there's NO bus into Rabat; so shopping & transport are problems – generally, about twice a week, I manage to cadge a lift in, & walk back laden with my supplies.

What news of rue Dante? I haven't heard from James????? of Marrakech for many months, & wicked old George Greaves hasn't answered a single one of my letters.

Do please write again – I adore your postcards. Bless you, & my best wishes for all sorts of black & bronze delights.

Love

Michael

liii

9 St Simon Street, XLENDI (Gozo), Malta

25th March '75

My dear Tim

[…] My dear Tim – I *adore* Gozo: you always told me that Gozo was far more attractive in every way than Malta, & I find you're 100% right; it's an enchanting island & the people are the nicest of any in all the Med.; while the chickens (GG style) are most friendly & forthcoming & their parents seem to take it for granted that elderly foreign gentlemen should take an interest in their sons. I have a wholly delightful Personal Assistant (xv) who bicycles two miles each way to see me almost every day, & Mum & Dad are bosom friends.

[…] Of course you will see old GG if you're in Tangier: give him my love & tell him he's an Old Sod for not once writing to me in the last year. Thank you very much for offering me SHP if I find myself on Malta; but it looks as if, for as long as I'm in this country, I shall be on Gozo. Next month I think I'm moving to Alfred Arnold's delightful old farmhouse half way up the Rabat road from here – I think you've met Arnold, a very nice person who is the composer, begetter, executive, trainer, teacher & moving spirit of all the exciting musical enterprises, pantomimes &c, done at the Don Bosco boys' club at the Oratory.[128] They've just done a highly entertaining Robin Hood.

Finances in the long term are promising: I've been definitely commissioned by Quartet Books Ltd to write a sequel to World Flesh & Self; & am now writing it. Short term they're pretty dodgy, because except for a miserly L50 "commissioning fee", the publishers won't give me any advance until the MS is delivered & that won't be for about four or five months. So on paper

---

128 Alfred Arnold (died 1985), besides being a composer, had been Private Secretary to Viscount Brookeborough while he was Prime Minister of Northern Ireland and had then retired to Gozo. Davidson did indeed move into his farmhouse in July and stayed there until his final hospitalization in September.

I've got to live on ten pounds a month for the next five months or so! Added to this obstacle, is the blow that the publishers of Some Boys have gone bankrupt, so there's no more money from there. Publishing in England is in a very parlous condition, with firms desperately short of ready cash & increasingly unable to pay their printing bills.

I shall be fascinated to hear your account of Ethiopia, & how you find life there & the qualities & defects of the people. Also the quality of their chickens. It may well be an enthralling country, & much saner & morally healthier now that the old régime has been got rid of – let's hope it will be politically comfortable for you. But I can't think you'll be much enamoured of the old "East Africa" – as those traces & traditions of the "settlers" (tho' I believe they do the chickens very well in places like Nairobi & Dar-essalaam); & it would be nice to buy a suitable slave in Zanzibar.

[…]

Be happy, & may all good fortune follow you & protect you like Athene did Odysseus.

Much love

Michael

liv

5 St Katherine's Lane, XEWKIJA, Gozo, Malta

24th Sept [1975]

Dearest Tim,

How good of you to write on your return from Kenya (& on the back of such a decorative herd boy!). I always love having your news.

My own, tiresomely, are of the grimmest: my blasted spine is back where it was at the beginning of June: it's apparently re-broken itself unaided & I'm going back to hospital, probably today, in horrible pain, to start the process of mending all over again. I'm still trying to pay off a huge bill for the first time – but this time it will be cheaper as I'm going to the public hospital & not the Nuns.[129]

You'll be amazed to learn that Robin M.[130] bas appeared on this island – a mixed blessing for me, as you will guess: my one & only desire is to get on with my work, & neither Robin nor a broken back encourage industry.

I've seen Gordon a few times of late – *off spirits* & an entirely different person. But how long will he keep it up?

Poor dear Tim – you say the work is killing & you've no time to enjoy life! But if there are Masai herd boys around, they surely can relieve the gloom.

Yes, Xewkija has the church being built around the earlier, smaller. A nice village on the way to Mgarr.

Shall write again when I can: in hospital I have to lie flat on my back.

Love Michael

[129] When Davidson had first fractured his vertebrae in a fall in June, he had been cared for in a Dominican clinic.

[130] Robin Maugham again, often a trying friend.

11. On Michael Davidson's end 1975

In September 1975, the seventy-eight-year-old MCD had to go into a public hospital in Gozo, initially due to his fractured vertebrae. He went into progressive decline and died there on 19 November.

The recipient of all the letters in this section was the writer and artist Colin Spencer, the great friend of Davidson's old age amply described by him in Sicilian Vespers. *Davidson had originally come to Gozo to live in Colin's property there. Phyllis van Calle, author of all but the last letter, was a friend of them both who evidently took good care of Davidson while Spencer was in England.*

lv. From Phyllis van Calle to Colin Spencer

Colin dear,

Herewith a saga of visits to Michael.

Wed 22nd. Oct.

With Will[131] in the car at the ready, heated up the chicken broth and wrapped it in a jar with a towel round it to keep it hot. Drove post haste to hospital and arrived in Michaels's room with it satisfyingly hot. Michael was as to be expected following your departure in his worst grumpy mood. Having poured out half a mug of broth asked him to have it as I had promised you I would. "Later" he replied testily and left it for 15 minutes. During this time he demanded to know the gossip but also asked whether I should be there, ie. visiting and hoped I was resting enough. He said Gordon had been in, boring him to tears and then promptly told Will (to my extreme irritation) that if he went to see Gordon they could go to the canteen and have a beer. He then had one mouthful of broth, and refused more because it wasn't hot enough!

[131] Will was apparently Phyllis's husband or lover.

Alfred came in and brought two roses which Michael loved as he loves all flowers. They then proceeded to the 'Shoppings'. Alfred had not been able to get either chicken essence or egg custard, these Michael in a somewhat stronger voice said were the only things keeping him alive. Alfred somewhat plaintively pointed out that he had a houseful of guests and was extremely busy and had had no time to attend to his own affairs. Michael reiterated his disappointment. It was amusing for me to hear this directed at someone else. I made one or two moves to go but each time M. protested and I stayed over an hour but finally left him with Alfred saying that I would be in, probably Friday. Sister said Michael had eaten a boiled egg, but that he was still refusing food.

Thurs. 23rd.

Didn't go in but Will went instead and found Michael asleep, he looked in several times in between chatting to Gordon but Michael slept (or pretended to) right through the time. The previous visit Michael had complained that he had asked for sleeping pills to help him to sleep through the noise at night but that he had an altercation with a nurse who refused to give him the tablets at 7 and had had the insolence to insist that 10 p.m. was the time to take them. He had finally sent for Sister, who, said Michael, had the sense to see that he should have them when he wanted and had written it down on his chart! Michael very pleased that he had won this victory.

Fri. 24th.

On entering the ward, saw Robin, William[132] and Gordon looking rather solemn. Robin told me that Michael was sinking fast. I was surprised and Gordon muttered something about his heart, I said I had wondered about pneumonia setting in. Robin had arranged for the hospital to telephone him at any time, and was proposing to contact you. Michael had been quite aware of Robin and had greeted him. Went in to see Michael who al-

---

[132] Robin was Robin Maugham, whose arrival in Gozo was mentioned earlier, in Davidson's letter to Brierly of 25 September. William Lawrence was his much younger lover and personal secretary.

though deathly ill, still managed to mutter feebly 'You're late darling.' As he was so very low I merely said I was sorry and that he'd better get some sleep, he said in the faintest of exasperated voices 'That's what I'm trying to do' and I left not really expecting to see him alive again.

Sat 25th.

Went to the hospital in the morning and to my surprise Sister told me that M. was very well. Gordon then came on the line & said that M's one lung was not working, full of fluid from lying prone so long. Said I would visit at 3 p.m.

When I entered his room Michael immediately said 'Darling I am full of apologies for you, for being so rude yesterday.' but added that he just hadn't been able to do anything at all about it. He had been reading but wanted to tell me what the Dr had said and to my surprise said that he was meticulously obeying instructions, 'lying on my left side, which I hate to let the rt. lung drain and also doing my breathing exercises'. He asked Will to do some work for him, beating up an egg in milk which he then drank. He also recounted for my benefit what he had already had. I said that really after so long he should really treat himself like a Strasbourg goose and asked if there was anything at all he fancied. He said he would like some tongue. The Dr came to give an injection and I left the room, Alfred then appeared and was as surprised as I had been to hear his improved condition. Again Michael wanted me to stay on as he thought Robin would be visiting and for some reason wanted me to be there during Robin's visit, however I tore away saying I would go in in the morning.

We were at the Patrick's in the evening for Glen's mother's party and saw Robin and William there. Tom was sick. All of us stayed only a short time, as long as courtesy would allow. Arranged to coincide my Monday visit with Robin so that he could come on here to see the garden.

Sunday 26th.

To hospital at 9a.m with tinned tongue, product of Winterbotham Darby & Co., of Croydon as I later told Michael. His weary comment was 'Couldn't you get any of those nice packets of sliced tongue?' (As I had arranged a plate with cocktail paté mini sandwiches with small chunks of tongue on cocktail sticks I was not enchanted by that remark)

He was reading yesterday's Express and continued to do so during my visit, and fussed a great deal about getting the pages in order. He was querulous about the advertisement pages not being numbered. He was also cross about his watch, maintaining it wouldn't go in the night, and wished that he was on his feet to go to take Schembri to task.

He seemed very frail indeed, his body temperature was low and he seemed to have difficulty in following what I was saying. After ½ hr he seemed to drift off into a semi doze so I left so him saying I would visit again on Monday. Not very happy about his condition as he seems to have relapsed.

Monday 27th.

Michael seemed not so well at first, lying down and complaining of pain in his chest.. I think he looked worse as he had not been able to bother with his teeth. He now seems to be getting on well with the nurses, especially Sister and they are very attentive to him. He complained that he had not had his penicillin injection, but said that the nurse swore that he had been given it. Sometimes he seems to go off into a sort of twilight semi conscious area. Again he was cross about his watch which after taking home and checking is working perfectly, so I think he had forgotten to have someone wind it for him. Robin came in and was able make him laugh and also to reply very pertinently about Tom's swollen ankle (Ball). There was chit chat between them about men managing perfectly well with one & M claimed to have known a man with 3. There is no doubt that in his present weak state it is touch and go whether pneumonia will win. His spirit is still good, [...]

Love to you both, & excuse the rotten typing

Phyl

lvi. Phyllis van Calle to Colin Spencer

Fri Nov 14th

Colin,

[...]

I last visited Michael on Sunday – then the car which had been limping badly finally & totally burnt out its clutch. He was on Sunday so much more alive, interested & dogmatically dictatorial. I had made some jellied beef tea which he said was 'delicious darling, so nourishing & if only you had made it before, it might have saved my life – much better than the Brands'. The £50 I suppose is that which I have in trust. He has not mentioned money & I thought he was too ill before. Today I will tell him that Will has it for the hospital bill. I think the question of money came up as he has broken into his last £10 yesterday. Alfred has visited as Michael would put it "faithfully" and is a monument of patience & devotion. Michael is now having 2 eggs a day & a cup of concentrate beef & chicken jelly. It is now easier to understand him as he wears his teeth. Alfred came round for me yesterday as he & Michael were afraid the broken car was a 'cover story' for ill health. [...]

Then the next morning (yesterday) Will stepped on a scorpion & the little grey beasts do sting & badly. This was at 4 am in the dark. Will didn't wake me till 7 but sat in agony with his foot in a bowl of water. The cat & Will both limp badly.

If the car d*oes* come back at all life may become more organized. If not Alfred is going to fetch me to see Michael,

Lots of love

Phyl

Saturday

M has received a cheque from ?Addis Ababa which he said would pay the hospital bill[133] – then I told him the arrangement about the £50. He was in a Towering rage why the bloody hell can't people tell me things. I merely said he was very ill at the time, & left it at that. Alfred will cash the cheque on Monday. I

[133] Evidently from Tim Brierly. In his last years, Davidson became quite dependent on handouts from his friends.

think I will ask Sister how much the bill is & pay that off or do you think it's wiser to hang on to the £41 pro tem. M says Pace is 'very vague' about the possibility of flying back per RAF. M now *very anxious* to get to England & frustrated by getting no information from Pace. Perhaps you'd better write him direct any news Male Ward, Craig Hospital. He is much stronger but will need a stretcher. Love.

lvii. Phyllis van Calle to Colin Spencer

57, Munxar St.
Nov 20th.

My dear Colin,

So Michael died 'On my terms' as he might have said. Refusing all help from the nurses & refusing to let them wash him.

I visited him on Tuesday & he said he was a little bit better than the previous day. I stayed ½ hour & left when Alfred arrived. After asking me to beat up some of my jelly, he suddenly produced his 'hospital bottle' from under the covers & demanded that I empty it down the hand basin. I made towards the lavatory but raising his craggy nose he said peevishly & impatiently "No, No darling over *there*". I complied. "They'd be *furious* if they knew" he said with the greatest satisfaction & a slight grin. Having exhausted the small news I had & talked a little about the Duke of Bedford's biography 'Ah yes the Flying Duchess' said Michael I looked at my watch to see whether Alfred was nearly due. "Why do you keep looking at your watch' he asked. He demanded that I take away the Sunday papers. 'Too difficult to read them lying down darling.' He was on good terms with some of the male nurses, especially one he called Gigi (Geegee). I think he gave him a copy of his book, one day last week Gigi was accepting the book from him & Michael was instructing him to cut out the inscription 'with a sharp knife'.

Did I tell you that on Sunday he said Will you please thank Will for taking care of that money, although I was ignorant of it.

But please tell him that Alfred is looking after my other money & I would like to have all *my* money in the same place. Does that seem reasonable. So I took in the unopened envelope on Monday & he opened it & *counted* it! If Alfred had not been going to take charge of it immediately I would not have left it with him.

Gordon missed out on the death bed scene this time & learned the news from Alfred. He did come up though in time to stop me trekking off for my visit for which I was grateful, as with the dislocated cat & Will very unwell – it seems the toxic scorpion has affected his heart – I have enough at present. I hope that Will's complaint is temporary he is to have an ECG on Saturday. The Dr described it as an 'irregular beat.'

My plumbage is doing well thanks to you & everything in the garden here is flourishing including weeds!

Love

Phyl.

Received your cable but line was terrible & I'm slightly deaf so am asking Alfred to phone.

lviii. Phyllis van Calle to Colin Spencer

Fri Nov 21st
57 Munxar St.

My dear Colin,

Gozo being what it is your cable although urgent wasn't delivered to me until mid-morning Thursday. Your letter with the beautiful stamps arrived this lunch time.

I took the liberty (or presumption as per Michael) of making up a 'floral tribute' for you & writing on a card Love Colin. It looked rather good, trailing bouganvilea, red hibiscus, white daturas & bronze elmrysanthe all from the garden. Alfred Arnold & I also arranged sheafs & a nice gesture from Alfred a rose from Michael's favorite tree there, a perfect bud & Alfred had put a purple ribbon trailing from the stem.

It was all very simple & somehow fitting. David Leach said a few Latin words both at the hospital & at the cemetery. The age old prayer for the dead. I shed a few tears on the way driving in the procession of 4 cars & the clippetty clop hearse. Funerals are given such decent respect from the Gozitans. Michael might have thought it fitting that so many heads were bowed & hats raised as we travelled through Victoria.

I am sure that death was swift & surprising, as Michael had asked for a cup of tea & Sister went to get it – she says just & few seconds, & on her return he had gone.

He was so swiftly up & down the last month & I expect my letters may have conveyed this. Poor Colin, you must still have a letter or two to come which won't help as you read of the visits. The cortege was made up of Father Leach preceding the hearse Alfred, Gordon & me. Josephine would have liked to have some she said. It seems as though Alfred will have quite enough to cover the nuns & Josephine & please don't read anything into *that* rather unfortunate phrasing!

Alfred, I am sure, will take care of every scrap of paper but I will see him tomorrow. We find that we have a great deal (Will included) of common interests. Incidentally, I am saving your letters for posterity so you'd better make a note in your diary.

Apart from being bored with the hospital & with his body, the only thing that ever lit Michael up latterly was a mention of you. Of course no visit went by without something about you cropping up & always If you're writing darling – my love to Colin.

If Alfred has nowhere safe & dry then I'll convey the papers to No 9. Will settle that tomorrow.

There were sudden, vicious westerly squalls this morning, one of them at the cemetery so we all (Michael included with bearers) were put in a sort of semi-chapel cum potting shed. Alfred carried the bottle of holy water for David Leach which he & I thought amusing. Alfred cast the traditional handful of earth into the grave. All the graves are stone lined & there is room on top of Michael for two more, if any one wants to book a place.

[…]

Love

Phyl.

lix. Alfred Arnold to Colin Spencer

DAR IL-WIDIEN
XLEMDI ROAD
GOZO MALTA

21 November 1975

Dear Colin,

We buried Michael this morning, setting out from the Craig Hospital at 1030, and by 11 it was all over. I had already, some three or four weeks ago, sounded out Father Leech, who had secured the Bishop of Gozo's permission for him to officiate if it became expedient, the Bishop's provisos being that he should not cut across any claim the Anglican Church might have, and that Fr Leech should act as a simple Priest and not on behalf of the Church authorities in Gozo. So it was.

Phyl and Gordon Monroe and I met at the hospital gates. Phyl's Will is suffering from the after effects of a scorpion sting and did not venture forth. Henry, having no available attendant or transport, did not come.

We went into the nearby hospital mortuary building, and Father Leech said (in Latin) a prayer over the coffin & sprinkled it with Holy Water. (This he had prepared overnight: 2 pages of Latin prayers as prescribed, plus a pinch of salt - literally). The coffin was put into the marvelous old baroque hearse with flowers that Phyl & I had brought. I produced also a solitary pink rose bud, new that morning, from Michael's favourite rose tree at Xlandi Road.

It was blowing & spattering with rain by this time. No signs of anything from Interflora, but speculations as to whether the first ferry from Malta had run.

Procession into Victoria and out again to Xewkija burial ground (St Mary's): headed by car with Fr Leech reading his missal: the horse & hearse with remains of Michael: me in my car: Phyl in hers; Gordon in his. I had plenty of opportunity to study the trotting action of the old horse and the decorations & lighted candles on the hearse - all of which are remarkable.

At the cemetery we made at once for the little chapel, with the undertaker & his men & young nephew, and a Pater Noster and another prayer were said by Fr. David, - with response - in Latin - from the older generation of the Gozitans present. Then we went to the grave, taking refuge for 2 minutes foam a sudden squall of rain, in another little cemetery building.

At the grave, the coffin was lowered, Fr David pronounced a benediction & prayer & scattered more holy water. I threw a handful of earth on to the coffin. The grave was closed with stone slabs. (It's number 883, & Michael's for at least 3 years. They will let me know if & when the remains are removed to the ossuary). The rain stopped, but the wind was strong enough to blow inside-out the umbrella Gordon was holding over David. (David wore over his cassock the purple stole, but not the surplice). It was all like a scene from some Carol Reed film or Guthrie production, by now. I drove home with David, [...]

[Two paragraphs on petty financial matters ending:] unless something quite unexpected comes to light, Michael would seem to have died solvent! - which would have surprised him, I'm sure.

I have his ring, watch & typewriter here, & a few books, and of course his manuscripts; & propose to guard the lot until you next come, unless his brother wants me to send them to London.

I have a strange feeling of emptiness this evening, as well as relaxation. Obviously we are going to miss Michael an awful lot. [...]

I hope you would have approved the way things were done today. After reading p 243 of the 1962 edition[134], I think Michael would have been content. [...]

---

[134] "If I had belief I should want to become a Catholic - not too exact a Catholic;" etc. (*The World, The Flesh and Myself*, p. 243).

V. REMINISCENCES

Most and probably all of the reminiscences about Michael Davidson presented here were written in the two months following his death. The first was in response to the announcement of his literary executor, Colin Spencer, in The Observer *of 7 December 1975, that he was seeking Davidson's correspondence for a book. That by Spencer himself looks at least as though it was written at that time for inclusion in that book. The other two were not written as if intended for publication, but were given in the course of friendly exchanges about his death.*

They are ordered here according to when the writer first knew Davidson.

1. Leslie Bearock

In The World, The Flesh and Myself, *Davidson explains that on moving to London in 1924, he took a job as sub-editor for "a short-lived weekly called* By the Way & Interviews*", but he then says nothing further about his work until the end of 1927, when "I got myself a job at the Clarendon Press" in Oxford. Fortunately, Colin Spencer's earlier-mentioned public request for correspondence was noticed by one Leslie Bearock (1894-1990), who responded with information on his public and private life at that time which would otherwise be lost:*

71, EASTBURY ROAD,
OXHEY, HERTS. WD1 4JN

Dec. 16, 1975

Colin Spencer, Esq.

Dear Sir,

As an old man in his 82nd year I am well aware my former pelman-like memory no longer functions as it should; about forty years ago I ceased to subscribe regularly to 'The Observer', it is therefore remarkable that my wife should be perusing the Dec. 7th issue and have called my attention to your letter.

Like so many people I was very fond of Michael Davidson and made his acquaintance in the following manner. His doctor brother was a clever surgeon and performed a major op. upon a colleague who, in gratitude promised to do what he could for the alleged ne'er-do-well younger brother. At the time I was in charge of the reading dept. of Sun Engraving (now Sun Printers) employing some sixty correctors of the Press and the usual complement of female copyholders. The time was about 1926-27. The idea was to employ Michael as a corrector but difficulty arose through his lack of membership of the Typographical Association; at the time I happened to be the local branch president and was able to use what influence I had to persuade the committee to admit Michael to membership on the rather slim excuse that he had been a member of the NUJ.

Learning his literary inclination I at once put him in charge of the periodical 'T.P.'s Weekly'. He at once struck up a close friendship with the editor Caradoc Evans and his sub. Con O'Leary. This militated a good deal against the prompt production of the paper – the three of them vanished late at night into the local pub and comps were kept waiting for the foundry press proofs. I cursed him through having to divert other men on to the job he was supposed to be doing.

He fell in love with a comp apprentice, Ron Figg, a very ill favoured youth that subsequently became a six-foot inspector of gendarmerie in Palestine during the British mandate. Michael bought him presents that included a six-chambered revolver. But, at that time he was not only a paedophile but, coming in late one Monday morning he told me he had walked from London after a party with Augustus John[135], with a female, had slept part of the time in a field (they had no money for railfares) he had tried to smuggle the woman into his bedroom but had been thwarted by the vigilance of his landlady, so the woman had returned on foot to London.

It amused me to listen to his tale of how he sat on the veldt and had watched his cows die, he never appeared to me to be a liar, he regularly borrowed 2/6 from me and another comp every Monday morning and we were religiously repaid on the following Friday when he received his wage. He was extremely accurate and fast at proof reading, well above the average in regard to his literary knowledge which proved useful both to me and to the editors of our periodicals. He materially assisted in the production of a supplement to 'T.P.'s' in the shape of an outline of World Literature. He had also showed me various contributions he had made to 'The Bystander' and other publications. In his autobiography he makes no mention of his time as a corrector, seems rather ashamed of that very creditable episode in his busy life. He did write me once or twice for reference.

Somewhere about 1941 I met him in the Strand, he told me he was then working at Reuters, looked the same in his shabby flannel bags, blue shirt and sports jacket, cigarette in the corner

---

[135] Augustus Edwin John (1878-1961) was the leading British portrait painter of the day, twice mentioned in *The World, The Flesh and Myself.*

of his mouth. When he changed digs all his belongings went into a sandbag! I heard of him during the time he went native in Morocco for the 'Daily Express'.

I have no correspondence from him; he gave me two books: 'Love's Coming of Age' and 'Towards Democracy' by Edward Carpenter. In the latter there is a postcard from E.C. asking him to visit him again. During my activities as secretary of the local Left-Wing Group he got his friend Charles Ashley[136] to address a meeting for me but he was, at that time, not very interested in politics: beer seemed his greatest passion and he more than once told me he believed in a short life and a gay one. Evidently, from your letter I deduce he reached a ripe old age. At the parties with John he habitually sniffed substance peeled from a certain corn plaster and more than once arrived late, as usual, saying he felt twelve feet high. He is one of the personages never to be forgotten in my not uneventful life. Thought this screed might interest you. I am, Sir,

Yours faithfully,
Leslie Bearock
(Leslie Bearock)

PS. I was a patient of his surgeon brother. He left his practice, his wife and children to run off with a secretary so it is alleged!

[136] The labour activist Charles Ashleigh, already mentioned in letter xxxiii.

2. Walter Lucas

Walter Lucas, a fellow journalist whom Davidson had known in Tel Aviv in 1948, was described in The World, The Flesh and Myself *as "a gentle, languorous person who looked more like St James's than Fleet Street. [...] slow, indolent, stuttering slightly, his mordant wit emerging with the fruity leisure of a club steward bringing the vintage port. But [...] to me [...] adorable.*

33a The Avenue
Lewes
Sussex BN7 1QT

4/1/76

Dear Colin Spencer

I feel very badly that I have not before this thanked you for your news about Michael – but I have been in hospital & still, though freed, don't feel too hot. Your tale was most interesting & most sad for I always thought that one day he would write something worthwhile, he had mental agility, wit, perception, the power to express himself. We used to have wonderful evenings together in Tel-Aviv when we were covering the first French-Arab war; Arthur Koestler[137] always in my memory seemed to be there, adding to the fun & intellectual contest of the occasions. I suppose Michael was fundamentally lazy & could not drag himself away from what he was primarily interested in,

---

[137] The writer Arthur Koestler (1905-83), whose most famous book was *Darkness at Noon*, was described by Davidson in conjunction with Lucas. Koestler had a far higher estimate of Davidson's literary achievement than did Lucas, naming *The World, The Flesh and Myself* in *The Observer* as one of the three best books of the year, and describing it as the "twofold story of a courageous and lovable person's struggle to come to terms with his Grecian heresy and of a brilliant journalist's fight against colonial jingoism".

and get down to what he could have done & was even contracted to do.

I always wondered whether he was the "third man" in the Montague-Pitt Rivers case. I had seen him the day before; he said he was going down to Beaulieu to stay with Montague - we were to meet again in the following week - but he never turned up - the press kept on mentioning a third man. At the time his non-appearance did not worry me as he had the habit of appearing & disappearing as suddenly & inexplicably as the rabbit from a conjuror's hat.[138]

By the way was the Sicilian book ever published? & what is Luigi heir to - it sounds like Lionel Fielden[139] who lived up near Pisa with his Luigi - & died when he had run out of his considerable original fortune for which his Luigi had waited.

Once again thank you for letting me know about Michael. I'm glad he retained his wit & perception to the end. I must go to Gozo to die if it only costs 50p a day.

Best luck to your next book.

Yours

Walter Lucas

---

[138] It sounds doubtful that Lucas had actually read *The World, The Flesh and Myself,* wherein Davidson recounts his role in the Montague-Pitt Rivers case. It is hard to see how Lucas's information here adds anything to that or casts doubt on Peter Wildeblood having been the "third man."

[139] Lionel Fielden (1896-1974), founder of All India Radio, was an English writer who retired in Tuscany.

3. Nicolas Freeling

Nicolas Freeling (1927-2003) was Davidson's nephew, son of his beloved sister Nancy. A hotel chef and then a prolific detective novelist, his uncle described him to Boris de Chroustchoff as "awfully nice" and as one who "knows all about me and my way of life."[140]

N.Freeling
3 rue Twinger
67000 Strasbourg

Colin Spencer

28-xi-75

Dear Colin,

[…] Now that I think it over, I am much more saddened than I knew. To say that when one is fifty the older generation DOES disappear is pure self-pity, and despicable. I have though lost my mother, my eldest sister, and my 'uncle' (so stupid; he was so much larger than uncles) in one year, and the last, in a sense you will understand, almost the worst. Nancy was 'en sursis' for thirty years, and we waited almost daily for her to go. But Mike … I see him so vividly the last time I laid eyes on him: I watched him coming up the moving-staircase in Highgate tube station. He hadn't seen me; I watched him for a whole minute, a year long. We had a wonderful day: Mike stuffed in my car with several children on his knee: Mike drinking red plonk and eating shepherds pie in a pub in Hampton Court. Mike ashamed and crying rather (and me too) at my slipping him ten quid, and Mike so patient, good and sweet, thinking only of giving my children pleasure, in Windsor Safari Park (the two of us loathing it, catching one an others eye, bursting out laughing.) Mike so gay, gallant, funny, so tired and so undefeated. It is so stupid to say 'God rest you' – he so obviously will and has, and I am really awfully happy. I hope to go like that – don't we all … So I'll

[140] Letter of 18 November 1961.

phone you in London, and hope very much we can tie up a thread.

Yours gratefully and affectionately

Nicolas

Nicolas Freeling

4. Colin Spencer

Colin Spencer, the writer, artist and great friend of Davidson for his last seventeen years, has already been well introduced in the sequel to The World, The Flesh and Myself. *As his literary executor, he not only hoped to do the editing that was essential if the latter was to be published, but also planned a volume of Davidson's correspondence. In the archive preserved in Davidson's own battered last suitcase, he included two reminiscentary sketches, the first the rough draft of a preface to one of the two intended books (though it is not clear which) and the other a memo. Both are presented here.*

i. Roughs for MD Preface.

In England in those winter months, which he so loathed and fulminated against, at first glance his appearance might seem prosaic, just another elderly citizen in a shabby worn check coat, wearing beneath a variety of sweaters, cardigans and scarfs, carrying an M&S plastic bag which bulged with books and bottles of plonk; yet at second glance, an observer may well have been struck by the darting perception of his stare which would embrace both youths and architecture, or the tantrum of furious impatience he would succumb to if waiting for a delayed train or bus. I have heard him sigh on these occasions with such an expiring groan of deepest gloom that one might have thought Ganymede had been struck from off the pages of mythology; then he would stare upwards with a mocking glance as if to say that the Gods could not envisage a worst punishment for him than this.

His nature was certainly that of a manic-depressive, though such a phase he would have loathed as being a trendy description of a more complex condition; yet he was either in a state of exuberant joy or else sunk in melancholia, the latter state effected him more when for reasons of economy he lived in England. I would suggest that most pederasts contain in their nature more of the child than others and, apart from the fact that when Michael was with his youths he became their emotional age, applauding their gaucheness with delight and indulging their whims with the generosity of a loving Aunt, he lived, as children do, utterly in the present moment: he did not plan towards the future, he never for one second worried over the fact that he was almost penniless, only able to live in his latter years from the kindness of friends. But then he did have more than the talent to amuse, he had the genius to enlighten, or was this merely my own experience? A feeling that Michael endowed a conversation with a sense of magic, not only his wicked humour, his delight in a *bon mot* to be relished upon the tongue with as much fervour as a nubile and erect penis: but the manner in which he could destroy a cliché of thought, a spurious belief or a sham aspiration. Iconoclastic certainly, but oh with such enthusiasm, boomed out in the tones of a classical Don, but with such wild theatrical gestures, such animation of arms and hands and furious nodding of that lined head (sometimes likened to a camel or a turtle) that all hypocrisy, I felt, all illusions and self-deceit would scamper in fright and hide from his defiant scorn.

I have tried to indicate above that, often, his appearance was of such forlorn neglect, it almost bordered upon a wandering tramp; yet when the occasion prompted it, Michael could assume instantly an air of grandeur and majesty that was all the more striking because of its indigenous reality. He had, I believe, a secret arrogance which may be derived from his background and be true of the social strata he was born in; this natural superiority could be irritating at times, his detailed pedantry over syntax, his self-righteousness over pronunciation and his insistence on formal good manners in others when he so often lapsed himself. On other occasions this grandeur could be amusing, for it then turned into self-mockery, a deft and delicious gift he had. Once at Gatwick Airport, when he was waiting for a delayed flight to Palermo, due to leave at 7 in the evening and still at 10 non-existent, Michael carrying more paper and plastic bags than usual, exhausted and in a fury of impatience, and also suffering from a complete absence of wine in his system, walked into the only dining room that was then open in the Airport building. "I'm sorry, we're closed," a waitress told him. Michael saw people still eating and drinking. In a second he had squared his hunched shoulders and, fixing the young waitress with a formidable glare, he boomed at her: "Do you know who I am?" She retreated, full of apologies, and found him a table. It is interesting to note that she did not enquire who he was, or, either, suggest that, even if he was Queen Wilhelmina, it still made no difference to the fact that the restaurant was shut. Such is the power of the intonation and the belief in one's inherent superiority.

There was another time when Michael was staying at a kind friend's house on a Mediterranean island: the friend had mistakenly left Michael in charge for two weeks for a holiday in England. As soon as this happened, two youths took over the house and Michael played the maternal and over-indulgent figure to them, the part in life which gave him more pleasure and happiness than any other; unfortunately I could observe this villa slowly being wrecked around them all. The keys on the grand piano refused to budge after a few days, the record player died with a slow groan, the grocery stores were being plundered as the bottles of coca cola were thrown around the garden. I knew from long experience that it would be useless to point this out to Michael, my anxiety would merely have been for him trivial bourgeois reality that might poison his ecstatic dream. When the friend returned he was naturally distressed, but having a kind and understanding nature he forgave the broken grand piano, the record player and the violation of his kitchen; what angered him was a torn bedcover over his own double bed, a cover which had been ruined by the cavortings of the two youths when having their siesta which, from the evidence, was never enjoyed. The friend's amiability vanished and, dragging the torn cover out onto the terrace, he shoved it beneath Michael's pendulous nose and began a long harangue over the destruction he had discovered. After some minutes of this – the friend was naturally garrulous and in anger Michael obviously thought the tirade would never be concluded – Michael raised a hand, not unlike a cleric in the act of blessing, and with lofty tones he stopped the flow. All he said was: "Send me the bill."

It was at those moments I forgave Michael anything, it did not matter in the least how infuriating he had been, how much a sponger of others, how reckless he was with the gifts of money, for large portions of it went on his youths. The motor cycles, the wrist watches, shirts, suede jackets, the high heeled shoes purchased for boys all over the Mediterranean in the last twenty years must be enough to fill Harrods. If you had declared that he was buying his boys with gifts of money and desired objects, making them into prostitutes, he would have negated such a proposition violently and pointed out that in all sexual relationships, including that of marriage, there is an element of purchase by one partner or the other. My own view would be that such a state of affairs is a flaw in the arrangement, that love and sexual happiness is best sought when the partners are balanced in equality. Yet for pederasts this cannot be.

When Michael last journeyed to go the island of Gozo, he left with me several cardboard boxes. Several days after he died, I opened these boxes for the first time and found among many letters, photographs and rough pieces of typescripts, some letters from men who had, several decades before, been at one time Michael's boys. These men were now married with several children, their letters were full of ardent affection for Michael, still anxious as to his health, still anticipating a reunion. Not, I hasten to point out, a sexual reunion, for neither partner would have sought it. But there was no doubt as to the real love and concern which had spanned the years and the space that divided them. Certainly, this view of the boy's future was Michael's own, he maintained that he had never done a boy a wrong; no, it is true, that he would not have done any of his boys a wrong intentionally. Michael was not malicious, his nature was too generous and warm. Yet in the last year of his life I heard of one boy who had that summer committed suicide. I did not tell Michael, for fear of his depression deepening. The boy was English and he had become a male prostitute. So the exact theory that Michael's life needed to demolish was proved in this one case; I may be naïve, but I think the story of this sad boy would have been so if Michael had known him or not. If it has any relevance, it indicates what is wrong with our own social system and not with the concern and love given by an old man to a confused adolescent.

Pederasty, if not shocking to most people, is profoundly disturbing, sometimes to even the most enlightened and liberal of us; I have always thought this reaction stems basically from ignorance and an acceptance of a social myth which operates in the Judeo-Christian West. This is why I have always felt Michael Davidson's work to be valuable. In both of his books he made a genuine attempt to be honest, to state the facts of his experience; if, in the autobiography, he also judges himself and lets himself off rather lightly, that ethical self-examination is understandable in the social climate in which his books were published. For society had already judged him and found him obscenely guilty without even giving him the right to defend his case. It is an amusing irony that the character of Humbert Humbert has become a racy archetype in the atmosphere of the pub or the Sporting Club, while the homosexual equivalent is loathed and thought of as a threat to morality and the structure of our society. One would have thought that the seduction of nymphets, a corruption of the virginal mother, would have met far more with society's disapproval than the fourth form sexual play that boys and pederasts enjoy. But we are up against two conflicting myths. I don't think Humbert Humbert is endured with much patience by women, the fact that his compulsion is a source of salaciousness with men stems from their wish to dominate all women, and the seduction of the helpless and innocent one is the most potent symbol of all. When the seduction of boys is contemplated, then both sexes unite in disapproval; the men have some obscure feeling that their virility is being drained in a sub fusc manner.

His daily habits had become set in a pattern: he rose early soon after six a.m., made himself a strong pot of Indian tea which he drank without milk or sugar; if *The Times* had arrived and was delivered by seven then Michael would settle down to read it with detailed care, often giving expressions of fury and disgust at the news, but more often at opinions. Mr. Bernard Levin made his bile rise. The Leaders would be studied for trends of thought & subtle shifts of opinion; Michael might then conjecture, proposing a hypothesis which grew by sleight of mind into a comic satire on politicians, governments and celebrities. For breakfast, he merely ate one piece of toast with margarine, for I believe it was *The Times* he actually consumed. Once the shops had opened, he would take a walk and buy a few provisions, then, returning to his bed-sitting room, he would read and write for the rest of the morning; his writing depended on his reading, for he constantly checked facts & enjoyed making classical allusions. In those last years, writing was a dreadful slog for him (I suspect it always had been), so perhaps in a morning no more than a sentence might have been written and that one sentence would suffer rigours of revision in weeks, months and years to come. For lunch - his main meal - a few boiled potatoes were de rigueur (he expressed the utmost shock at my boiling new potatoes in their skins and claimed he hated them) with simple packaged foods such as steak and kidney pudding, fish fingers & sausages: these he would savour. He had a lifelong dislike of fresh fruit and never ate any. Though he liked cabbage and spring greens, he considered their preparation (far more simple than boiling potatoes, I would tell him often) too much of a chore: so where the vital Vitamin C came from in this diet is a mystery.

The afternoon might be spent, if it was a fine day, in walking through London: he loved walking and could manage many miles up to the last year of his life without exhaustion. In 74 he paused on Hampstead Heath to watch three boys fishing. Michael had always kept his hair cut very short, but at this time, to save money at the barber's, he had allowed his hair to grow long and his friends all remarked that it suited him, for the hair in length became curly and did somewhat soften the beaky shock of his face. He watched these boys not with any sexual curiosity, but rather with the pleasure of a Nanny watching her charges enjoy themselves, when to his complete Edwardian horror, one boy - they were all aged about ten - turned to another and said: "Look, there's an old poof watching us." The two other boys glanced up at Michael and one of them said. "No, it isn't, it's an old woman." They then began a fierce argument over the enigma as Michael hurried away and went straight to the barbers. Such stories he would relate with great pleasure, for they were not only amusing in themselves, but they also shed light on how society had changed from the era between the wars when he had walked over the Heath to solicit boys. In those days, he liked to recall, three ten-year-old boys fishing would have sat on the bank in total innocence and, if noticing his interest, would have merely thought it was a nice Nanny figure watching and enjoying their activity. They would have been right and the boys of today were almost wrong; the pendulum has swung too far and there are worse corruptions than that of the flesh.

At five in the afternoon, Michael would open a bottle of plonk, it was the time when he needed his friends, needed the stimulus of conversation and the luxury of being in affectionate company. But, if alone, miserably, he would still open the wine and, at six, possibly another bottle, for he retired to bed to read by seven, after a supper of either a boiled egg or biscuits and cheese. I have briefly mentioned this routine to show how both simple and extremely conservative it was. He maintained that he wanted twelve hours in bed every night and he was usually very angry if for some reason he did not get it. These were the days without a boy companion. When they existed, then the routine could be altered completely at the whim of the boy, for Michael was the boy's servant and, whatever the boy wished, if it was possible, Michael, like a very ancient fairy Godmother, would arrange it. Little work was done if a boy existed: his friends came second naturally, but so did everything else.

ii. Notes on MD

1st meeting. Autumn of '58 at Robin Maugham's house in Seaton Street. A party. I have a vivid visual picture. M roaring with laughter, his body bent over, his face like a caricature, very odd, it struck me at once of almost unique ugliness, but it was the way those tiny eyes gloated over JT of whom he thought - how did I know then - must be barely 16.

But when we met in the Pub in Sloane Square some months afterwards, we immediately felt a great rapport. Our correspondence began when he left for Sicily in '59. Acitrezza: 24: iv: 59. "I require sunshine and salacity, nudity and noodles." "The Sicilian nephew is without moral, scruple, loyalty or honour; in compensation he has beauty, good manners (he robs you charmingly), an unending capacity for lewdness, an unabashed desire to exhibit it, and an enormous pride and interest in whatever he may possess - generally something to be proud of." Goes on about nephews beautifully. The *weather:* a constant problem in M's life, generally it is bad, or if good, wrong in some way.

Messina: Sept 17th. Same old trouble that recurs. After about 4 months M has to leave because boys start blackmail.

Sept 9th: speaks of our time together "wonderfully restful companionship, as quiet and gladdening as the Calabrian Hills, yet witty and gay when we both felt like being witty and gay."

30th Oct 60: always anxious, in a perpetual fret over something! Yet what energy. Remarks on Corvo[141] are apt. Mentions Boris de Chroustchoff giving him his old letters and the C. Millard letters.[142]

Dearest Michael: I know this is absurd of me, but I must tell you that I can't find any letters from you from this year until 69 when, you will be delighted to know, there are about 3 thousand. Also, to enchant you, in my search I discovered an E.M. Forster letter in its envelope that I had not sold. So we shall see what T. d' Arch Smith[143] says about that. I want to sell a few letters so as to get a small sum of money out to Luigi at once. Knock five times if you approve! Our letters were so often silly in that way. And I'm feeling horribly sad and very silly now. Funny thing is, I never thought you would die, not this year, I expected the vigour of your mind to keep you going well into your 80's. So I feel a sense of outrage at fate and the beastly Gods.

He had no talent for fiction, a novel written in the 50's remains unpublished, for he was awkward in the mechanics of unfolding a story, or relating imaginary dialogue, yet the real incidents

---

141 See note 70 to letter xxvi for the writer "Corvo".

142 None of Davidson's letters to Colin Spencer are included in the archive kept in the former's suitcase, which is all of his correspondence that the present editor has seen. The "C. Millard letters" included letters from Millard to Davidson; the present editor does not know whether there were any the other way round. In any case, they were all returned to de Chroustchoff, a collector of Millardiana, in 1961-62, as is clear from Davidson's letters to de Chroustchoff of 3 December 1961 and 7 March 1962.

143 Timothy d'Arch Smith, author of *Love in Earnest: Some Notes on the Lives and Writings of the English "Uranian" Poets* (1970) and, more relevantly here, an antiquarian bookseller.

embedded in the novel spring out from the page with striking clarity.

Perhaps his greatest gift was the art of conversation, (which, with certain friends, was carried naturally on into letters), for every topic touched upon would be seen by Michael in an idiosyncratic light which extracted the important detail. He had an acutely perceptive eye for art and architecture placing them in their human and historical context. But perhaps his wit was the most exhilarating experience of all. It was not only a gift for the devastating *bon mot,* but also a gourmet's relish in the comical aspect of humanity. How well I remember his bubbling excitement before relating some saga involving an acquaintance whose pompous mask had been punctured by scandal or absurdity; yet a similar saga might well be told against himself, for he might fall back upon some *pretensions to grandeur* (J. D.'s letter) in a tricky situation which afterwards, with much chuckling, he would mock at.

He never, as we are told Joe Ackerley did, took painstaking care over a letter. They were like his conversation, a torrent of stimulation, one moment spitting abuse of such heightened vituperation it might have been Baron Corvo himself[144], the next moment adding a reflection of depth and insight, managing often with lyricism and always with wit to place the human animal in his warring social context with unique precision.

I loved him. The world feels smaller for his going.

[144] "Baron Corvo" was notorious for quarrelling with those who befriended him and then being extremely vituperative.

Appendix I. A bibliography of Davidson's writings

This includes all of Davidson's known writings except for the scores of newspaper reports he wrote during his time as a correspondent, whether as staff or freelance, and the newspaper articles (as opposed to books) he translated from German.

Published memoirs

1. "The narrative of my Moorish 'adventure' ", published with photographs in about nine consecutive daily instalments in the *Daily Express*, 1941.

2. *The World, the Flesh and Myself.* 1st edition, London: Arthur Barker, 1962; 2nd edition, London: Mayflower-Dell Paperbacks, 1966; 3rd edition, London: David Bruce & Watson, 1973; 4th edition, London: Quartet, 1977; 5th edition, London: GMP, 1985, reissued Swaffham, Norfolk: GMP, 1997. 1st American edition, Washington: Guild Press, 1962. Translated into Dutch as *De wereld, het vlees en ik,* Amsterdam: Nederlandsche Keurboekerij, 1964. A general autobiography.

3. *Some Boys.* 1st edition, London: David Bruce & Watson, 1969; American and only unexpurgated edition, Kingston, New York: Oliver Layton, 1971; 2nd British edition, London: GMP, 1988, reissued Swaffham, Norfolk: GMP, 1998. Sixteen independent short stories about Davidson's liaisons (or, in one case, chaste friendship) with boys in different locales in three continents.

4. *Sicilian Vespers.* First mentioned as being written in September 1968. Half written and delivered in April 1969 to a publisher who had commissioned it. Decommissioned 1969. In February 1975, Quartet in London commissioned a new book, a sequel to *The World, the Flesh and Myself,* name lost or undecided, which was intended to take in much of the content of *Sicilian Vespers.* First published in the present volume, 2021.

Published fiction

5. "A Sentimental Voyage" in *The Sketch: A Journal of Art and Actuality*, London: Ingram brothers, Vol. CXXXV, No. 1754, 1 September 1926, pp. 412 and 421. In Davidson's own words, a story about "a London docks ship's watchman who, never having been to sea in his life, swaggered in fantasy as a seafaring hero and became to everybody but himself a laughing-stock."

6. "Atti Innominabili" in *Jeremy* VII, London, 1970. A short story set in an Apulian fishing village, in which jealousy between a boy of fifteen and a loose girl of fourteen over the love of an older boy leads to a small fight and devastating consequences for all three when the police interfere.

Published translations of books from German

7. Klaus Mehnert, *Youth in Soviet Russia*, London: George Allen & Unwin, 1933. Revised by the author with a new chapter and translated from *Die Jugend in Sowjetrussland*, Berlin: Fischer, 1932.

8. Walter Schoenstedt, *Shot whilst Escaping*, London: Wishart & Co., 1934. A translation of *Auf der Flucht erschossen*, Paris: Carrefour, 1934.

9. Ernst Henri, *Hitler Over Europe?*, London: Dent, 1934.

10. R. Braun, *Fascism, make or break? German experience since the "June Days"*, London: Martin Lawrence, 1935.

11. Egon Erwin Kisch, *Secret China*, London: John Lane, 1935. A translation of *China geheim*, Berlin: Erich Reiss Verlag, 1933.

12. George Dimitrov, *Dimitroff's Letters from Prison. Compiled with explanatory notes by Alfred Kurella*, London: Victor Gollancz, 1935. Translated with Dona Torr.

13. Ernst Henri [Simon Rostovsky], *Hitler over Russia? The coming fight between the Fascist and Socialist armies*, London: J. M. Dent & Sons, 1936.

Other published writing

14. Various contributions to *The Bystander* and other publications (mentioned by Leslie Bearock as shown to him in about 1926-27).[145] *The Bystander* was a weekly tabloid magazine published in Fleet Street that featured reviews, topical drawings, cartoons and short stories.

15. Articles for the *Daily Worker* posted from Germany between February and July 1933.

16. "Schoolboys Searched for Arms by Nazis", "Deepening Discontent in Fascist Germany", "Secret Party Work in Germany To-Day" and "How Hitler Fears the Working-Class" by Michael, "a member of the German Communist Party who left Berlin this month," in the *Daily Worker*, 19, 21, 23 and 24 August 1933. A series of four articles about "working-class life in Berlin under the Nazi terror."

17. "Red Front Lives! A True Tale of Nazi-Berlin" in *The Daily Worker*, 9 December 1933. About a youth's defiance of brownshirt violence in the street.

18. "Three Pictures of Ernst Thaelmann" in *The Daily Worker*, 2 October 1934. Memories of the imprisoned leader of the Communist Party of Germany.

---

[145] See Reminiscence I in this volume.

Unpublished writings

19. A not quite finished book about Morocco written in 1938-40, which Davidson described as "a chain of sketches describing the things Mustapha and I did and saw – a sort of 'Stories Toto Told Me', only it was Mustapha who did the telling." The manuscript was lost some time after 1941.

20. *Love on a Greek Island*. Written during his months in Forio in 1953, he described it to a friend as "a frivolous frolic of a novel about a Greek Island – a kind of 15th-rate South Wind"[146] and in *The World* as "a little novel [...] founded upon an erotic drama I'd watched enacted next door to my Corfu cottage and containing in a central female character an infusion of all my Childers aunts and some of myself. It was barely 40,000 words long, but people who read the typescript were amused." It was nearly published, but finally rejected by Derek Verschoyle. Afterwards, "for four years I forgot all about it; and then a kind friend who had it sent it to Hutchinson's; whence I was told they would almost certainly accept it if I could stretch it to full length and buttress some of its debilities. After a couple of years, I did both; and ruined it; since when it's been resolutely rejected by half the publishers in London. I don't quarrel with their judgement."[147] The manuscript was sold to a private collector in 2017 or 2018.

21. A book about Cyprus written on the Italian island of Procida in 1957, "the heart of which was the study of a terrorist, Nicos Sampson. It wasn't a good book: it was too hot with recent anger, and the British reading public, exasperated by the wickedness of Greek Cypriot terrorism, weren't in the mood for a condemnation of that terrorism's attempted repression. Gollancz were probably right to reject it; Andre Deutsch later wanted to do it if I would put more 'balance' into it and bring it up to date: but by then I found it impossible to bring Cyprus up to date."

---

[146] Letter of 16 October 1960 to Boris de Chroustchoff.

[147] *The World, The Flesh and Myself*, p. 301.

Appendix II. Davidson's immediate ancestors

The following account of the last four generations of Davidson's ancestry is a tribute to the interest in his ancestry that he expressed in both The World *and some of his correspondence. The only difference found with his own beliefs about it concerns his male-line descent. He believed himself to be descended from the Davidsons of Tulloch Castle in Ross-shire, but that family only moved to Tulloch in 1762, while Michael Davidson's ancestry can be firmly traced back to the marriage of a London rope-maker (no. 16 here) in 1775. The notion of Scottish descent came perhaps from the romantic imagination of his grandfather, the first in the family to give his children Scottish-flavoured names.*

Details of the births or baptisms of the earliest generation have not been generally sought as this would be tantamount to having to trace the next generation back.

1. Michael Childers Davison, Writer
Born 24 February 1897 at 101 Warwick Road, Paddington, London.
Died 19 November 1975 at Craig's Hospital, Victoria, Gozo, Malta.

PARENTS

2. Walter Burn Murdoch Davidson, Timber merchant.
Born 14 June 1858 at Neath, Glamorganshire.
Died 21 October 1911 at Yew Tree Cottage, Bitterne, Hampshire.

3. Clare Mostyn Childers.
Born 3 May 1865 in Rangoon, Burma.
Married 29 July 1891 at St. Mary Magdalen's, Paddington, London.
Died 21 March 1941 at Kilahara, Dovea, Thurles, co. Tipperary.

GRANDPARENTS

4. Edward Davidson, Major-General in the Royal Engineers.
Baptised 17 September 1827 at Syston, Gloucestershire.
Died 1 November 1889 at Tudor House, Wandsworth, Surrey, aged 62.

5. Eleanor Maria Freeling.
Born 1 April 1833. Baptised at St. Botolph's Aldersgate, London.
Married 2 January 1855 at Allahabad, India.
Died 4 November 1859 in Calcutta, India.

6. Eardley William Childers, Major-General in the Royal Artillery.
Born 6 April 1833 at Enniskerry, co. Wicklow.
Died 1 November 1883 at Sutherland Gardens, Maida Vale, Middlesex.

7. Henrietta Mostyn.
Born 14 March 1830 in Dublin.
Married 31 December 1858 at St. Mark's, St. Helier's, Jersey.
Died 15 February 1909 at 145 Sutherland Avenue, Paddington, London.

GREAT-GRANDPARENTS

8. George Madgwick Davidson, Pin and Needle Manufacturer of London.
Baptised 6 March 1780 in St. Magnus the Martyr, London Bridge.
Died 12 July 1851 at Warmley, Gloucestershire, aged 71.

9. Elizabeth Francis
Baptised 10 March 1790 at Lambourn, Berkshire.
Married 27 April 1809 in Berkshire.
Died 8 June 1856 at 61 Cambridge Terrace, Hyde Park.

10. Sir George Henry Freeling, 2nd Baronet, Commissioner of the Customs.
Born 22 September 1789 at Peckham, Surrey.
Died 30 November 1841 at 7 Hyde Park Gardens, Kensington.

11. Jane Lang.
Born 21 December 1798 in Middlesex. Baptised at St. Luke's, Old Street, Middlesex.
Married 22 February 1816 at St. Marylebone, Middlesex.
Died 26 August 1868 at 2 Chandos Place, Clifton, Bristol.

12. William Walbanke Childers, Captain in the 42nd Royal Highland Regiment.
Born 15 May 1801, baptised at Cantley, Yorks.
Died 1862 in Jersey.

13. Mary Elizabeth Pentland.
Born 1802/3 in Dublin, Ireland.
Married 16 August 1826 in Dublin.
Died 2 July 1863 at Thames Ditton, Surrey.

14. Henry Thornton Mostyn, Army surgeon.
Born 28 May 1789 in Ireland.
Died 22 October 1848 in Norley Hall, Frodsham, Cheshire.

15. Cecilia Susannah Forbes.
Born 1801 in Stirling.
Married 3 February 1822 at St. Ninian's, Stirling.
Died 8 April 1882 at Cedar Lodge, Downend, Gloucestershire.

GREAT-GREAT-GRANDPARENTS

16. James Davidson, Net and Rope Maker of the City of London.
Buried 13 April 1829 at Bunhill Fields, Islington, Middlesex, aged 82.

17. Susanna Madgwick.
Married 1775 at St. Magnus the Martyr, London.
Died before 6 May 1828. Buried Bunhill Fields, Islington, Middlesex.

18. Edward Francis.
Baptised 17 February 1748 at Lambourn, Berkshire.

19. Mary Spicer.
Baptised 26 January 1758 in Lambourn, Berkshire.
Marriage license 31 January 1781, Salisbury, Wiltshire.
Living 1810.

20. Sir Francis Freeling, 1st Baronet, Secretary to the General Post Office.
Born 25 August 1764 at 24 Redcliffe Hill, Bristol.
Died 10 July 1836 at Bryanston Square, St. Marylebone, Middlesex.

21. Jane Karstadt.
Married 24 April 1787 at St. Clement Danes, Middlesex.
Died 5 May 1796 at Ramsgate, Kent.

22. Robert Lang, West Indies Merchant.
Baptised 1765 at All Hallows London Wall, London.
Died 16 March 1828 at Moor Park, Farham, Surrey aged 63.

23. Maria Francklyn.
Born 19 May 1777. Baptised at St. Marylebone, Middlesex.
Married 8 October 1795 at St. Marylebone, Middlesex.
Died 19 December 1846 at Sussex Square, Paddington, Middlesex.

24. John Walbanke Childers (originally surnamed Walbanke), Colonel of the 11th Light Dragoons.
Baptised 9 October 1766 at Little Ouseburn, Yorkshire.
Died 1 March 1812.

25. Hon. Selena Gideon (surname changed to Eardley 17 July 1789).
Born 21 September 1773.
Married March 1797 at St. George's Hanover Square, Middlesex.
Died 16 March 1851 at Hastings, Sussex.

26-29. [Not known; their children were born in Ireland, most of whose relevant records have been destroyed]

30. James Dugald Forbes, Bahamas Planter.
Born 5 August 1759 at Craignish Castle, Argylshire.
Died 9 September 1820 at Melville Place, Stirling.

31. Elizabeth Green.
Married September 1789 in Nassau, The Bahamas, aged 17.
Died 9 April 1811, aged 39.

Appendix III: Davidson's first meeting with Luigi

This alternate version of how Davidson first met Luigi, the love of his life, is found in two manuscripts written in 1972, and contradicts the account written in 1969 which was included in his main (also 1972) revision of Sicilian Vespers. *It is presented here in the interests of determining the truth about the most critical moment of his old age. "Totuccio" and "Tommaso" are the pseudonyms adopted in several (but far from all) versions for Luigi and his father.*

Within an hour of coming ashore, I was talking to Tommaso in his butcher's shop; and his son Totuccio, still a schoolboy, who had passed his fifteenth birthday a few days before Christmas. We went for coffee to Uccio's bar at the corner of the piazza; and, before I caught the *aliscafo* back to Trapani, I'd been given, by Tommaso, a promise that a dwelling would be found for me before the week was up and, from Totuccio, another that he would meet me at the boat on the day fixed and help me with baggage and the furnishing. This was how I became born, so to speak, into my new family; after so much wandering, I had arrived "*a casa*".

Comment by Colin Spencer

Written in pencil on one of the manuscripts giving the version above, and probably soon after Davidson's death:

M has simplified the first meeting with Tommaso & his son. He had always told me that the youth he calls Totuccio was on the jetty with other boys when he arrived. It was Totuccio who offered to carry his luggage to the one modest hotel & from this incident the friendship, or to state the truth, the main, most fulfilling & lyrical love affair of his whole life, began. However, Michael never wrote this scene as he told it, & there is another version which somehow strikes a more truthful note.

Editor's comment

The other version mentioned by Colin is the one presented here in the chapter "The Family" of *Sicilian Vespers,* and further strong evidence can be adduced in favour of his contention that it "strikes a more truthful note".

Above all, apparently not noticed by Colin and quite possibly forgotten by Davidson himself by the time he began writing *Sicilian Vespers,* there survives in his papers a rough diary scribbled in pencil and covering the days from 14 November 1965 to 2 January 1966. This shows that he first visited Favignana on 18 December, not "a few days after Christmas" as he remembered in every version he wrote for *Sicilian Vespers,* and it makes it clear that at least two (most likely in fact five) weeks passed between then and his second visit, rather than the one he recalled. Most pertinently, it records that on his first visit he was accompanied by a Trapanese boyfriend called Ignazio, which surely makes it even more unlikely that it was then that he struck up his magical rapport with Luigi and his father. Certainly also, it was a mere day visit and so unlikely he had baggage needing carrying "to the one modest hotel." Moreover, there was a second mention of Favignana in the diary: on 27 December, Davidson wrote: "[Salvatore, his current boy in Trapani]'s *ruining* me. Favignana?" This hardly fits with the idea he had already firmly agreed to return there on a fixed date.

It should also be pointed out that Davidson allowed himself considerable literary license in his late rewriting of his story. For example, in his partial rewrite of *Sicilian Vespers* adapted for inclusion in the sequel to his memoirs commissioned in February 1975, the year of his death, he describes himself as in Favignana in mid 1975 with thirteen-year-old Duzzo, but in fact he had not seen Favignana or Duzzo since December 1973, when Duzzo was eleven. (He could though have been writing in the expectation of being back in Favignana by the time his book was published.)

If one therefore accepts the earlier version as the essentially accurate one, there remain two as yet unanswered questions.

Why did he tell Colin that Luigi had been on the jetty when he first arrived and why did he find Favignana so "very alluring" (as he called it in his diary) that he soon returned to it with an evident determination to stay? Does not accepting the truth of what he told Colin provide the simplest explanation to the latter question? In other words, he had at least *seen* Luigi on his first visit, and it was the memory of that which hooked him. When he described how Luigi came into Signor Alcamese's shop on his second visit, he did not actually say it was the first time he had set eyes on him.

Appendix IV: The Odyssey's Goat Island

Though this was included in one of the partial drafts of Sicilian Vespers *written in 1969, it is far from clear if Davidson finally intended it to be included. It has been relegated to an appendix in this volume, as being valuable but esoteric.*

Whether Odysseus really lived or, if he lived, whether he set foot on an island swarming with goats, is here immaterial; what is certain is that Egusa is that very Goat Island of the *Odyssey*. The author of that work – Homer perhaps, or a native Sicilian poet, or Samuel Butler's woman of Trapani – must have visited the island of Egusa and known the coast-line of north-west Sicily pretty well; or if he was a foreigner, an eastern Greek for instance, he must have had it all described to him by some navigator familiar with these waters. Nobody who is intelligently acquainted with these shores and with the small islands to the west and north of Sicily and who reads the *Odyssey* with a thoughtful eye on topography can fail to see how the two perfectly fit together no matter who wrote the *Odyssey*, no matter how many more scholarly squabbles it may evoke in the future, one thing is undeniable: a large part of the voyage it chronicles followed a course round the northern coats of Sicily from Pantelleria to the Strait of Messina, and the island of the goats was the island to be seen today off the coast between Trapani and Marsala.

There are those who say that the name Egusa itself is evidence that the island is indeed the original Goat Island, since Egusa comes from the Latinised Greek Aegusa which was the Roman name for the island and means "goat island". But this is too facile: Aegusa came from Aetusa which came from the Greek Phaetusa – the normal sort of mutations that time accomplishes through unlettered generations. What a convenient adaptation to any old legend about a goat island "Aegusa" must have seemed! Phaetusa is Egusa's name in its second Odyssean role – Phaetusa and his brother Lampetia herded the cattle kept by the Sun-God on Sicily and unwisely slaughtered by Odysseus' men. From my house today (1969) I look northward over two and a half miles of sea to Lampetia – a tiny island with three hundred and fifty inhabitants, now called Forbantia.

This is how the author of the "Odyssey" portrays Goat Island:

> ... by no means a poor country, but capable of yielding any crop in due season. Along the shore of the grey sea there are soft water-meadows where the vine would never wither; and there is plenty of land level enough for the plough, where they could count on cutting a deep crop at every harvest-time, for the soil beneath the surface is exceedingly rich. Also it has a safe harbour, in which there is no occasion to tie up at all. You need neither cast anchor nor make fast with hawsers: all your crew have to do is to beach their boat and wait till the spirit moves them and the bright wind blows. Finally, at the head of the harbour there is a stream of fresh water. ...

One hardly needs to change a word of that today: even the grey sea seems too often to prevail over the gentle blue in this windiest corner of the Mediterranean. "Not far from the harbour on their (the Cyclops') coast," the *Odyssey* narrates, "and not so near either ... there lies a luxuriant island, covered with woods, which is the home of innumerable goats." That is a perfect statement of Egusa's deceptive adjacency to the shore of Sicily – "not far, and not so near either"; for, besides the tricks of light and distance which atmospheric variations play, our nearest point to Sicily is four miles off, while it's twelve miles from our village to the "Cyclops' harbor" – today the port of Trapani. It is still a luxuriant island; but our luxuriance is of fruit and corn and vegetables, for the woods have gone; the great bare brown mountain has scarcely a tree left on it, and on the plains the only foliage is that of vine and lemon, fig and pomegranate. Carthage, Rome, Byzantium, and the Bourbons of Spain and Naples each in turn cut out our timber for their navies; end this steady deforestation, followed by the consequent erosion, has left the mountain barren, though its bare slopes are still marked with the sears of ancient terracing. And there are no goats. When I first came in 1966 to my house outside the *paese*, I counted nine goats running with the sheep that daily passed my door. There weren't more than twice that number on the whole island. There's no grazing on the bare brown mountain now, no leafy young boughs to reach up to and nibble at. The sheep and those few goats herded with them, thin as rakes by September, find only a scanty picking over the foothills above the rocky shore. It's an island without goats, Goat Island is.

I rather doubt whether Odysseus found goats here at all. I think he and his crews ate venison, not goat-flesh – what they killed with their "curved bows and long spears" was a breed of mountain deer. The Arab geographer Edrisi, who compiled the *Book of Roger* of 1154 and was one of the brightest intellectual lights at Roger II's court at Palermo, wrote of the antelopes of these islands; while in Amico's seventeenth century *Dizionario topografico della Sicilia* reference is made specifically to "i cervi", the deer, of Egusa itself.

* * * *

Near the most westerly point of the island, beside the Cala Grande ("Great Harbour"), a circular cove about as big as half the serpentine in London, from which a lighthouse flashes towards the outermost island of Hiera, there's a hotel or holiday camp romantically named Approdo di Ulisse – "Ulysses' Landfall." It's a rather high-class agglomeration of little bungalows and central "services" which caters chiefly for middle-class holiday-makers from the Italian "continent". In July and August it's full of "foreigners", but the island itself sees little of them; the place is a good four miles from the *paese* by a bad road that circumscribes the mountain, and there's hardly any traffic to or from it. "L'Approdo", the islanders call it when they have reason to mention it; but it isn't often that they do.

If these holiday-makers were American ladies, one can almost hear them exclaiming: "Well, just fancy that – this is just the very spot where Odysseus landed when he came to eat the goats! You've heard of Homer, of course?" But – and this is where I differ from an authority so eminent in Mediterranean navigator as Mr Ernle Bradford – these ladies' pleasurable sense of being intimate with antiquity would be unwarranted: this point wasn't where Odysseus landed. Some familiarity with the topography of Igusa and with the physical detail of its contiguity to the Sicilian shore-line, and a fairly careful reading of Book IX of the *Odyssey*, must make it perfectly clear that from the Cala Grande it would be totally impossible ("looking across at the neighbouring land of the Cyclops", invisible from there) that "we could see not only the smoke from their fires but hear their voices and the bleating of their sheep".

A reader who, uninterested in Homer, must be bored by a plotting on this tiny corner of the Odyssean map, should skip the next couple of pages, in which I punctuate my dissent from the conclusion Mr Bradford publishes in *Ulysses Found*[148], an enchanting book which no lover of the Mediterranean should be without. I am neither seaman nor scholar, and Mr Bradford is both: I wouldn't dare challenge him in either's field. But I do know Igusa, having lived on this island for four years. Mr Bradford, writing of Igusa, says: "I spent a happy day here, spearing fish along the southern coast and anchored all night in Cala Grande" (from his earlier book, *The Wind off the Island*, in which describes a week or two spent at Forbantia, two and a half miles to the north, it doesn't appear that he then visited Igusa at all). In another passage in *Ulysses Found* he writes: "I spent several weeks off here one summer, exploring the islands and sailing between them"; but doesn't dilate beyond that on his acquaintance with them. Perhaps, then, Mr Bradford wasn't long enough on Igusa to explore it closely, and may so be excused a few mistaken observations. It is not a "seven-mile-long island"; from tip to tip its length is about five and a half miles. It isn't, alas, "quite rich in trees"; there's hardly a tree left on the whole island other than fruit. The slopes of the mountain do not "still shelter their goats, relatively few today for the land is intensely cultivated"; no goats graze on the slopes of the mountain – there's no longer either grazing or cultivation on its slopes. It isn't the south wind that "still whirls the water up the buff-coloured" rocks but the *south-east*, the "scirocco", a very different wind; the south blows seldom and never for long – the two prevailing winds are the north-westerly and the south-easterly and from these directions come the big and prolonged gales.[149] Not one of Igusa's fishing-boats has "the oculus painted on their bows"; if Mr

[148] Hodder & Stoughton, 1963; Sphere Books, 1967. [Author's footnote]

[149] Norman Douglas, a stickler for precision, presumably agreed to *South Wind* because no novel could survive called clumsily *South-East Wind*. But the merciless scirocco, which was Douglas's south wind, blows, hot or cold, from the south-east. The gentle south wind, when there is any, laps rather than blows [Author's footnote].

Bradford was looking for a direct line to antiquity, he might have noted the "beaked ships" – all the larger fishing-boats have that pronounced classical profile.

In support of his belief that Odysseus' landfall was at Cala Grande, Mr Bradford declares, with the authority of a seaman, that the flotilla, coming up from Africa on a south wind (or a south-east), couldn't have reached the bay on the north coast of Igusa (where the present *porto* is), because with this wind they couldn't have doubled back round the north of the island, assuming they'd been carried past its western point, Cala Grande (where Mr Bradford wants them to have beached). But I, who am no seaman, do know the tricks of our winds; and it's just one of those tricks that could have brought Odysseus safely into Igusa bay. The south-easter, the scirocco, will almost predictably, after beating from across Marsala for two or three days, turn suddenly about and come roaring back from its opposite, the northwest – or a northwest gale will do the same thing, abruptly doubling back from the south-east. The two winds play a kind of volley-game between them, back and forth, back and forth. Now if luck so had it, just as Odysseus' ships were being carried north west past Cala Grande, that a scirocco at that moment switched round to north-west, they could have been brought straight down into the northern bay and the amiable conditions described in *Odyssey* IX.

I reject Cala Grande's claim to be the Odyssean landing-place for two reasons. Firstly I can't see how any vessel, driving up on a southerly wind with visibility almost entirely shut off by night and a thick mist, could have performed the navigational antics necessary for getting round the southern point of Gala Grande at a sharp right angle – in order to beach on some sand instead of being smashed on the rocky point where the lighthouse now stands. But my second reason seems conclusive by itself. A good ten miles away from Sicily, you couldn't see smoke there and hear voices and the bleating of sheep with the huge mass of the bare brown mountain in between.

The morning after they'd beached, Odysseus and his men went off shooting goats and then, writes Mr Bradford, "they sat down afterwards to feast on this fresh meat and washed it down with the good wine of Ismarus" – and the *Odyssey* story itself goes on: "... the ships had not yet run dry. . . . There was still some in the holds. ... There we sat, and as we looked across at the neighbouring land of the Cyclops, we could see not only the smoke from their fires but hear their voices and the bleating of their sheep...." There is the conclusive argument: from Cala Grande they couldn't have looked across the neighbouring land of Sicily – a thousand feet of mountain stands between, and the Sicilian coast, invisible from there, is ten or more miles distant. I don't think Cala Grande will do at all as the place where they sat eating and drinking beside their boats and looked over at Sicily.

But farther east even than the main bay on the north coast, where the *paese* is today on the eastern side of the mountain, there's another haven which would have nicely fitted the craft of Odysseus' day – the Cala San Nicòla, it's known as now, and it was used as a harbour by Phoenicians and Romans in turn during the Punic wars. The neighbouring rocks, too, bear the imprint of a very early tunny fishery – earlier perhaps than the Punic wars. If they beached their ships here – and this haven has a fine sweep of sand protected by an arc of rocky reef – they could, by climbing a few yards above the beach, have looked across that at the land of the Cyclops; and, given the right atmosphere clarity, have seen the smoke from any fires near the coast. As for hearing voices, I don't know; at times here, in summer, the air is so rare and fine that men carry on conversations at a distance of a quarter of mile and can make themselves understood at a half. Over the water, I have listened to fishermen conversing a mile out to sea, and at night one can hear the engines of big ships thumping twenty miles away. There can be only one objection to Cala San Nicòla: the narrowness of the entrance through the reef into this tiny harbourage – these ships, coming down on the north-west wind, would have needed a lot of luck, or the help of Athene, to get them through this needle's eye. But who can say, in this convulsive region, what the entrance may've been like nearly three thousand years ago? Whether or not, if ever a Odysseus came that way, the bright-eyed goddess piloted his ships safely through the narrow opening to the anchorage of San Nicòla, this is the bay the author of the *Odyssey*, or his topographical adviser, must have picked after a thorough survey of the island. Nowhere else fulfils as well the requirements of the story or fits as nearly the description in *Odyssey* IX.

Crusty old Samuel Butler, wittiest debunker of the Victorian hypocrisies he was brought up to and author of *The Way of All Flesh* and *Erewhon,* was so conscientious analyst of the *Odyssey* that he paid several visits to the islands and hills and caves of western Sicily to collate topography and text together, which is more than most Homeric scholars have done. In *The Authoress of the Odyssey,*[150] that absorbing, impressive and yet droll attempt to attempt to show that the story must have been written by a woman of Sicily, he gives a number of reasons for agreeing with the "considerable weight of authority, ancient, medieval, and modern" which "carries us to the island of Egusa, anciently called Aegusa or Goat Island, as the one on which Ulysses and his men hunted the goats".

[150] First published 1897; reissued 1967 by University of Chicago Press. Any reader of the *Odyssey* who knows this part of Sicily will be fascinated and almost persuaded by Butler's pungent arguments [Author's footnote].

Appendix V: Favignana's dialect

Like the preceding, this was included in one of the partial drafts of Sicilian Vespers *written in 1969, Davidson's final intentions for it are unknown, and it has been relegated here as being valuable but esoteric.*

The island's language differs little from that of Sicily's western province of Trapani with some small differences: in southern Italy one village dialect is often "foreign" to a neighbour a few kilometres away. Below are a few examples of how history has compiled the vocabulary of Egusa; but first Trapani - here's a striking illustration of the obstinacy with which antique vernacularisms will live on in the middle of a world which them. The name Tràpani has the stress on the first syllable because it descends from the Carthaginian Drepana, the Greek Drepanon, the Latin Drepanum - all signifying, tradition says, the sickle or scimitar which is the shape of the slim curving promontary on which the old town sits. Now, in the dialectal speech of the born-and-bred Trapanese, the name of his city is to this day pronounced *D*rapani, with an emphatic initial "D" - although Italy generally, and even Egusa only twelve miles away, calls it by the name it's borne at least from the middle ages - Trapani. But to the true Drapanese his city is Drapani.

On Egusa:

For *io*, the first person singular, in Italian pronounced in two firmly separated syllables, they say a quick, sheer *yo* - straight from the Spanish.

For the "v" in *vino*, they use "w", a "weeno" - straight from the Greek.

For *lavoro*, work, and the infinitive *lavorare*, they say *travaio, travaiare* - obviously French. This is the colloquial word for "work" or "labour" - and has nothing to do with the Italian verb *travagliare* which means "suffer", "have a hard time or a rough passage" but is unrelated to "labour" in the sense of a job of work.

For *quello*, "that one," "him," "that" as distinct from "this", they say *idro* (or *idra* feminine) obviously descended, through *idem*, from Latin.

For *dove*?, "where?", "whither?", they say *unè* (oonay) a relic, I suspect, from the Catalan tongue.

For *ecco*!, *allora*!, in the sense of "well, then!", "that's right!", "there you are then!" "just what I said!", they say *unga* (oongah) – a characteristically Sicilian amputation of the Italian *dunque*, "so", "well then" – dunque = dunca = 'unca, = unga.

For *vaso di fiori*, flower-pot (the ordinary earthenware pots that stand on every windowsill and balcony, one at least holding basil) they say *grasta* – a word straight from the Greek and taken from Sicilian by Boccaccio for the Pot of Basil.

For occasions when a special courtesy is required towards one of her husband's friends whom she doesn't know well enough to address by his first name alone, a woman will sometimes prefix "Si" – Si Mariano, Si Ciccio, and so on, signifying "Mister" Mariano, "Mister" Ciccio. A suggestion comes easily that this is an abbreviation of "Signor" – but where in all Italy has one ever heard of such an abbreviation? Surely, this again is a legacy from Saracen times. "Si", at the present day, is a Moorish honorific used for addressing formally any gentleman of standing – Si Abderhaman, you say, Si Dris – and of course always Si Mohammed to anybody bearing the Prophet's name, an urchin shoeblack as well.

For the reservoir and its tackle of endless buckets worked by a donkey which every farmer uses for watering his lands, they say *gebbia* – a word as purely Arabic as the mechanism it describes.

For a simple negative in answer to a question, they seldom say *no* or *non*. A slow upward tilt of the head, so that the chin lifts to the level of the ears and the eyes half close, like a doll being laid on its back, is negative enough and needs no uttered "*No*". (Mr Luigi Barzini[151] mistakenly says this Sicilian gesture means "I don't know" – it doesn't: it means "No", just that) – This is a pure Greek negative, today still used wherever there are Greeks, in Cyprus, Smyrna or Athens. During

[151] *The Italians* [Author's footnote]

> five or six centuries Sicily learned to speak the Greek of antiquity, and through some three centuries that of Byzantium – when was this pan-hellenic negative of the lifting chin acquired? Often, on Egusa, you will hear a man accompany this Greek indication of "No" with a gentle "ts" made with his tongue against his front teeth – the sound the scolding nursemaid used to make. This tongue-click comes from the Saracens – it's the usual disclaimer still today made all over North Africa. Thus on Egusa we say "No" in both Greek and Arabic, without uttering a word.

That handful of examples gives an idea of the cheerful eclecticism with which, over two or three thousand years, the Sicilian speech has taken what it wanted from the confusion of tongues that have fed it. There must be, in the large vocabulary of this rich and expressive language, if only one could find them, some words or roots from the idioms of near pre-history: the old Sicel and Sican and Elymian – of the Punic, almost certainly there are traces in the Trapani and Marsala districts.

By the fifth century A.D., after some seven hundred years of Roman rule or influence, low Latin had seeped through the foundations of Sicily's speech and that Latin is the basis of it today. But this book isn't for the student of the Sicilian language; and nobody else will be interested in the curious whims of its pronunciation and its consonantal quirks – the change, for instance, of "ll" to "dd", as in "beddo" for "bello"; or the preference for the hard "g" in "figghiu" (son) or "mogghiu" (wife) instead of the soft "gl" of "figlio", "moglie". But it's only ignorance that makes some writers speak, as some writers do, of the "harsh consonants" of Sicily. The consonants aren't harsh – they're lazy: Sicilian is a lazy language. It's probably easier to say "'iamare" for "chiamare" (call), or "'ioco" for "gioco", game. With no guttural harshnesses like the Teutonic and Semitic, Sicilian is a melodious language (when spoken gently, which rarely it is); and Dante himself, and Petrarch too, honoured it as the prime source of Tuscan poetry, of which the literary school of Frederick Hohenstaufen at Palermo was the acknowledged precursor. Double consonants like "dd" and "gg" look harsh when transliterated on to paper; in Sicilian speech they're mild and elastic. (Sicily still today possesses, based upon Palermo, a flourishing coterie of poets writing in the Sicilian dialect, often movingly or wittily – a prominent islander of Egusa is among them. There's a flourishing fortnightly review devoted to dialect writing, prose and verse.)

If Sicilian is a dialect, not a language, it's a dialect, I suppose, of late Latin, not of Italian; yet there's enough incomprehensibility today between it and Italian, in pronunciation and vocabulary though less in structure, for it to be labelled a language in its own right – they're as different from each other as Portuguese from Spanish. But whatever its status in the parliament of tongues – and we've seen that it has an honourable place in the ancestry of literary Tuscan – there are people who, inclined to denigrate the character of Sicilians, denigrate too their language as a kind of barbarous patois.

Mr Denis Mack Smith, in his most valuable *A History of Sicily*[152] so short, alas, that he has to gallop all the way to complete the course in the time allowed – obviously disapproves of Sicilians although he finds them a fascinating people to study; but like them or admire them he rather donnishly cannot. At one point Mr Mack Smith reproaches the Sicilian dialect with echoing some deficiency or futility in the Sicilian character. Discussing this people's reputed incapacity for taking thought for the morrow, he remarks: "Perhaps this unreadiness to think ahead was reflected in the absence from the Sicilian dialect of a future tense." One might as well say that English has no future tense, which has to compound itself with an auxiliary. The Sicilian future follows exactly the simplest English form, and is exactly as effective: "I go to London next week," "I am moving house in August." Using the present tense and an adverb of time, Sicilian compounds a faultless future: "lo facciamo domain" – "we do it tomorrow" ("we *shall* do it tomorrow"). There is the form of the Sicilian future tense: what could be more purposeful, more ready to think ahead?

What could be more charming, asked Norman Douglas, than a thoroughly defective verb?

---

[152] Chatto & Windus Ltd., 2 vols., 1968. [Author's footnote]

Index

Printed in Great Britain
by Amazon

15643335R00233